EDITING GRAMMAR FOR STYLE AND CORRECTNESS

24 frag

Fragments
a Attaching fragments
b Turning into sentences
c Stylistic uses
d Trouble-Shooting Checklist

25 fs/cs

Fused Sentences and Comma Splices
a Forming two sentences
b Joining with comma, coordinating conjunction
c Joining with semicolon
d Joining with colon
e Joining with semicolon, conjunctive adverb
f Subordinating

26 agr

Subject-Verb Agreement
a Separation by words
b Predicate nominative
c Subject following verb
d Plural verb, compound subject
e *Or, either … or,* etc.
f Indefinite pronouns
g *Who, that, which*
h Collective nouns
i Plural noun, singular meaning
j Plural title, words as words

27 agr/ref

Pronoun Agreement and Reference
a Singular antecedent
b Specific antecedent
c Indefinite pronoun antecedents
d Compound antecedents with *and*
e Compound antecedents with *or*
f Collective nouns
g Relative pronouns
h *Self* pronouns

28 case

Case
a Nominative case
b Objective case, direct object
c Objective case, subject
d Pronoun as appositive
e Elliptical expressions
f Possessive case, gerund
g *Who, whom*

29 vb form

Verb Forms
a Basic verb forms
Common Irregular Verbs
b Auxiliary verbs
c *Sit/set, lie/lay, rise/raise*

30 tense

Verb Tenses
a Basic verb tenses
b Consistency of tenses
c Present tense, special uses
d Past tense
e Perfect tense

31 voice

Voice
a Active voice
b Passive voice

32 mood

Mood
a Subjunctive mood, *if* clauses
b Subjunctive mood, *that* clauses

33 adj/adv

Adjectives and Adverbs
a Differences between them
b Use of adverbs
c Adjective, subject complement
d Adjective, object complement
e Comparative and superlative

34 nonst

Editing to Correct Nonstandard English
a Necessary verbs
b Plural nouns
c Plural verbs
d Possessives
e Personal pronouns
f Double negatives
g Articles
h Forms of *be*
i Forms of *do*
j Forms of *have*
k Irregular verbs
l Regular verbs
m Prepositions
n Spelling, capitalization, accents

PUNCTUATION

35 ⊙ ? !

Period
and
a Pe
b Pe
c Q
d Ex

36

Commas
a With coordinating conjunction
b Between items in a series
c Between coordinate adjectives
d Introductory phrases, clauses
e With nonrestrictive units
f With titles, degrees, dates
g With interruptions
h With elements out of order
i For contrast or emphasis
j With interjections, short questions, *yes, no*
k With quotations, dialogue
l For omissions

37 no ∧

Unnecessary Commas
a Between subject and verb, verb and object
b Between dependent, compound elements
c With restrictive modifiers
d Before first word, after last word in a series
e Before adverbial clauses
f Between unequal adjectives
g Before opening parenthesis
h With other punctuation

38 ;

Semicolons
a Between independent clauses, no coordinating conjunction
b Between independent clauses, with conjunctive adverb, transitional phrase
c With coordinate clauses that contain internal punctuation
d Between items in a series with internal punctuation
e Misuse

39 :

Colons
a Introduce series, quotation
b In salutations, time, ratios
c Misuse

40 ∨ ∨

Apostrophes and Quotation Marks
a Apostrophes for possession
b Apostrophes for contractions
c ...hes for plurals of ... letters, words as ...
... apostrophes
... ...tations
... marks for
... marks for titles
... ...rks
h Quotation marks and other punctuation
i Misuse of quotation marks

(Continued on next page)

41 — ( ) [ ] …

Dashes, Parentheses, Brackets, and Ellipses
a Dashes for summary, amplification, explanation
b Dashes for interruption, change of thought
c Dashes for a list that contains commas
d Parentheses for additional information
e Parentheses for numbered lists within sentences
f Parentheses for in-text citations
g Parentheses and other punctuation
h Brackets
i Ellipses

MECHANICS

42 ital

Underlining for Italics
a Titles of major works
b Names of specific ships, aircraft, vehicles
c Words, phrases as subject of discussion
d Uncommonly used foreign words
e Genuses and species
f Emphasis, sparingly used

43 ab

Abbreviations and Acronyms
a Titles before and after names
b Organizations, technical terminology
c Dates and numbers
d Parenthetical matter, addresses, documentation

44 num

Numbers
a One- or two-word numbers
b Specific places, figures

45 cap

Capital Letters
a Words that begin sentences
b In direct quotation

c Poetry
d Pronoun *I*, interjection *O*
e Abbreviations and acronyms
f Proper nouns, derivations
g Titles of books, articles
h Genuses, geological periods, stars, planets

46 hyph

Hyphenation
a Compound words
b Prefixes and suffixes
c At end of line

47 sp

Spelling
a Identify troublesome words
b Proofreading
c Homophones
d Prefixes and suffixes
e Use of *ie*, *ei*
f Plural forms
g Troublesome words
h Misspelling for a purpose

ACADEMIC WRITING

48 log

Logic
a Structure
b Induction, deduction
c Essay organization
d Definition of key terms
e Addressing opposing arguments
f Common fallacies

49 essay exam

Writing an Essay Examination Answer
a Planning
b Addressing the point
c Understanding the terminology
Sample exam on literature

50 res

Writing the Research Paper
a Choosing, narrowing topic
b Preliminary thesis sentence

c Working bibliography
d Research resources
e Thoughtful note-taking
f Plagiarism
g Planning, writing first draft
h Integrating quotations
i MLA style of documentation
j List of works cited
k Formatting of final version
l Sample MLA research paper

51 res/cur

Writing Research Papers across the Curriculum
a APA style of documentation
b Note style of documentation
c Documentation of other disciplines
d Requirements of the discipline
e Sample APA research paper

BUSINESS AND TECHNICAL WRITING

52 bus

Business Correspondence
a Memos
b Business letters

53 résumé

Résumés and Job Application Letters
a Résumés
b Job application letters

54 bus rep

Business and Technical Reports
a Language and tone
b Format and organization

gl

Usage Glossary

A WRITER'S HANDBOOK
STYLE AND GRAMMAR

JAMES D. LESTER

Austin Peay State University

Harcourt Brace Jovanovich, Publishers

San Diego   New York   Chicago   Austin   Washington, D.C.

London   Sydney   Tokyo   Toronto

Cover: © Emily Mason, *Upon a Jib*, 1989. Oil on canvas,
            54″ × 52″, Grace Borgenicht Gallery.

ISBN: 0-15-597648-6

Library of Congress Catalog Card Number: 90-83122

Printed in the United States of America

Preface

The term *style* has various meanings in writing. We speak of one writer's flowery prose and of another's clipped, staccato sentences. This reference to a writer's characteristic manner of creative expression is perhaps the most common definition of *style*, but the term has another, simpler meaning. *Style* also refers to the manner in which a writer constructs a composition — the clear, functional, effective way he or she creates a sentence, puts it together with other sentences to form a cohesive paragraph, and combines the paragraphs to frame an original, compelling work. It is this second definition of style that *A Writer's Handbook* addresses.

The goal of this book is to blend the science and the art of writing. More than a book of rules, it encourages students to revise and edit their grammar, punctuation, and mechanics for style as well as for correctness. Thus, this handbook gives students not only the ways to punctuate a compound sentence but also the reasons to write one. It explains not only that a complex sentence consists of a main clause and one or more dependent clauses but also what subordination is and the reasons for using it.

A Writer's Handbook begins with the traditional first essay. Part 1 is devoted to the composition process and features a sample student essay in its stages of development. Parts 2, 3, and 4 then examine the rhetorical and grammatical variations in paragraphs, sentences, and usage. Part 5 presents basic grammar, and part 6 shows how to edit grammar for style as well as for correctness. Parts 7 and 8 address matters of punctuation, mechanics, and spelling. Part 9 focuses in detail on the research paper and other forms of academic writing across the disciplines, and part 10 concludes the text with a discussion of business and technical writing.

A Writer's Handbook emphasizes the importance of the revision process, as is evident in the numerous examples throughout. In particular, handwritten revisions demonstrate how students can rework paragraphs and sentences to strengthen the focus and to improve the effectiveness of their writing.

To help students understand and remember important points, this book summarizes complex or lengthy material in review boxes placed at the end of the passages or sections. Copious and varied exercises throughout the book reinforce and solidify the students' comprehension.

A Writer's Handbook recognizes that many errors of word choice are the result of careless thinking. For example, chapters 17 and 27 address the issues of biased language in their discussion of usage and pronoun agreement. But rather than confining its discussion of biased language to sexism, the text broadens the topic to insist that students must not allow sexist, ageist, racial, or any other bias to enter their writing. Writers must, above all, respect their audience.

One of the book's most notable features is chapter 34, which explores in depth an area not often addressed adequately in handbooks: editing to correct nonstandard English. As further evidence of its comprehensive view of language, *A Writer's Handbook* addresses fourteen specific problems of students from broad racial and ethnic backgrounds as well as from non-English speaking backgrounds. In contrast, most college handbooks provide examples of only Black English as nonstandard.

This handbook is also designed to be an easy reference tool. The head tabs allow readers to locate specific sections directly, and the endpapers give readers quick reference to key sections. The front endpapers provide an abbreviated table of contents, and the back endpapers feature samples of common errors to help students identify writing problems. Revision and proofreading symbols complete the back endpapers.

Instructional aids to accompany *A Writer's Handbook* include an Instructor's Manual that features classroom discussion topics and answers to the exercises in the text, a Workbook, diagnostic tests (in printed and software form), and an Instructor's Revision Chart. Various software packages include a Grade Calculation Template for the instructor and PC-Write Lite for the student.

Acknowledgments

Acknowledgments begin with accolades to my wife, Martha, who fosters a style of life that invigorates my research and inspires my writing. Amanda Clark contributed significantly to the first draft, and Tom Hinton and my son, Jim Lester, provided critical commentary on several portions of the text. I also wish to thank several students who provided longer samples of written compositions: Lisa Barnett, Aimee Claire Beaudoin, Ryan Brewer, Glenda Harris, Lori Martin, Carol Mathis, Melissa Rogers, and Marla Walker.

I express my gratitude to the following reviewers for their thoughtful advice during development of the manuscript: Dale Barnes, Louisiana State University, Baton Rouge; Barbara Brumfield, Louisiana State University, Alexandria; Albert C. DeCiccio, Merrimack College; Barbara Dicey, George C. Wallace Community College; and Norman Stafford, Arkansas State University, Jonesboro.

Recognition must also go to the staff of Harcourt Brace Jovanovich. Bill McLane, now executive editor, guided this project from its inception with inspiration tempered by discipline. Sarah Helyar Smith, manuscript editor, was magnificent in editing the manuscript and pulling together all the loose ends. Michael Kleist, production editor, handled all the proof; Don Fujimoto, designer, created the handsome internal and external designs; Mary Kay Yearin, production manager, kept the composition and printing on schedule; and Sandra M. Steiner, marketing manager, organized the package.

JAMES D. LESTER

Contents

PART 1   PLANNING AND WRITING

1   Planning an Essay   3

    a Select a subject.   4
    b Write with a purpose.   5
    c Consider your audience.   8
    d Define your writing project.   11
    e Generate ideas on your subject by doing prewriting exercises.   12
    f Narrow the subject to a specific topic.   20
    g Focus your topic with a thesis sentence.   21
    h Use your thesis sentence to suggest a structure for the essay.   24
    i Create an outline.   26

2   Drafting the Essay   31

    a Concentrate on main ideas.   31
    b Write a fully developed introduction.   32
    c Write a body that fully explores the issues.   34
    d Conclude effectively.   36

3   Revising, Editing, and Proofreading   42

    a Revise for coherence.   42
       Revision checklist   43
    b Edit for tone, point of view, and general mechanics.   46
       Editing checklist   52
    c Proofread with care.   56
    d Use peer review to help you revise your paper.   56

PART 2   PARAGRAPHS

4   Paragraph Unity   67

    a Develop one key idea and focus it with a topic sentence.   67
    b Place the topic sentence for best effect.   69
    c Eliminate irrelevant details.   70

5   Writing Coherent Paragraphs   73

    a Choose an organizing principle.   74
    b Use parallel structures to enhance paragraph cohesion.   81

CONTENTS

c   Use clear transitions.   82
d   Repeat key words and phrases.   84

6   Developing Paragraphs   86

a   Write fully developed paragraphs.   86
b   Narrate a story or a series of events.   88
c   Describe to illustrate your thesis.   89
d   Use examples to clarify a concept and to stimulate interest.   90
e   Define your terminology.   91
f   Describe a process.   92
g   Discuss cause and effect.   92
h   Classify or analyze.   93
i   Compare and contrast items of equal importance.   95
j   Combine paragraph patterns.   97

7   Improving Paragraph Style   102

a   Write in a clear style.   103
b   The purpose determines style.   106
c   The audience determines style.   108
d   Use rhetorical schemes to enhance paragraph style.   110

PART 3   SENTENCES

8   Sentence Coordination   123

a   Use coordination to form compound sentences.   123
b   Use parallel constructions to strengthen coordinate ideas.   125
c   Repeat words for clarity in coordinate constructions.   127

9   Sentence Subordination   130

a   Subordinate less important ideas.   130
b   Use the subordinating conjunctions.   131
c   Use subordination to revise short, choppy sentences.   132
d   Subordinate one or more clauses of long compound sentences.   133
e   Reduce clauses to modifying words and phrases.   134
f   Avoid inverted subordination.   137
g   Eliminate excessive subordination.   138

10   Improving Sentence Style: Emphasis   142

a   Use emphatic placement.   142
b   Use strong, active verbs.   150
c   Avoid nominalizations.   153

11 Improving Sentence Style: Variety 156

a Use both loose and periodic sentences. 156
b Use different types of phrases and clauses. 159
c Write sentences of differing structures. 164
d Write sentences that express different methods of development. 167

12 Correcting Misplaced Parts and Dangling Modifiers 170

a Eliminate dangling modifiers. 170
b Place modifiers where their meaning is clear. 172
c Do not interrupt the flow of the sentence with modifiers. 175

13 Grammatical Completeness 179

a Add verbs, prepositions, and other words to complete compound structures. 179
b Add the word *that* to prevent the misreading of subordinate clauses. 181
c Add words that are necessary to complete comparisons. 181
d Use Intensifiers only with complete phrasing. 182
e Add the articles for grammatical completeness. 183

14 Correcting Mixed Constructions 185

a Edit sentences for correct grammatical constructions. 185
b Avoid using *is when*, *is where*, and *is because*. 186
c Correct illogical connections. 187

15 Correcting Shifts 189

a Make verbs consistent in tense, voice, and mood. 189
b Avoid shifts in person. 192
c Be consistent in number. 193
d Avoid shifts between direct and indirect discourse. 193
e Avoid shifts between formal and informal language. 194

PART 4 WORDS AND LANGUAGE

16 Appropriate Language 199

a Match the level of formality to your subject and audience. 199
b Use jargon sparingly. 202
c Use slang and colloquialisms only for special effects. 202
d Avoid pretentious and bombastic language. 203
e Use new and invented words carefully. 205

CONTENTS

17 Using the Exact Word 208

a Use the dictionary to find the correct form of a word. 208
b Use a dictionary and a thesaurus to discover appropriate synonyms. 211
c Use the word with the correct meaning. 213
d Understand connotations and denotations. 215
e Use concrete and specific words. 217
f Avoid sexist or biased language. 220

18 Concise Language 224

a Avoid long generalizations, and edit and cut unnecessary wording. 224
b Use positive contructions for clarity. 231

19 Figurative Language 233

a Use both metaphor and simile. 233
b Use figurative language to sway opinion, view life, and surprise the reader. 234
c Create fresh similes and metaphors. 235
d Do not mix metaphors or make strained comparisons. 237

PART 5 BASIC GRAMMAR

20 The Parts of Speech 243

a Nouns 244
b Pronouns 246
c Verbs 249
d Adjectives 250
e Adverbs 251
f Prepositions 252
g Conjunctions 254
h Interjections 256

21 The Parts of the Sentence 258

a Subject 259
b Predicate 260
c Direct objects, retained objects, indirect objects, and object complements 262
d Predicate nouns and predicate adjectives 263
e Sentence constructions 264
f Sentence patterns 266

22 Phrases 268

a Use a variety of phrases. 268
b Prepositional phrases 269

c   Verbal phrases   270
d   Absolute phrases   273
e   Appositive phrases   273

23   Clauses   274

PART 6   EDITING GRAMMAR FOR STYLE AND CORRECTNESS

24   Fragments   279

a   Attach fragments to sentences.   280
b   Turn fragments into sentences.   281
c   Use some fragments for stylistic purposes.   282
d   Edit fragments with a trouble-shooting checklist.   282

25   Fused Sentences and Comma Splices   286

a   Form two sentences.   286
b   Use a comma with a coordinating conjunction.   287
c   Use a semicolon.   288
d   Use a colon.   288
e   Use a semicolon and a conjunctive adverb.   288
f   Use a subordinating conjunction to make one clause subordinate.   289

26   Subject-Verb Agreement   292

a   Make the verb agree with the subject even when words and phrases separate them.   292
b   Make the verb agree with the subject, not with a predicate nominative.   293
c   Make the verb agree with a subject following the verb.   293
d   Use plural verbs for most compound subjects joined by *and*.   294
e   When a compound subject is joined by *or, nor, either . . . or, neither . . . nor, not . . . but*, make the verb agree with the nearer part of the subject.   294
f   Use a singular verb with most indefinite pronouns.   295
g   *Who, that*, or *which* require verbs that agree with the antecedent.   295
h   Use a singular verb with a collective noun unless a plural meaning is clearly intended.   296
i   Use a singular verb with nouns having a plural form but singular meaning.   296
j   Use singular verbs with titles of works and words used as words.   297

CONTENTS

27 Pronoun Agreement and Reference 299

a Use a singular pronoun to refer to a singular antecedent. 299
b Make pronouns refer to a specific antecedent. 300
c Use a singular pronoun to refer to most indefinite pronoun antecedents. 302
d Use a plural pronoun to refer to compound antecedents joined by *and*. 302
e With compound antecedents joined by *or, nor, either . . . or, neither . . . nor, not only . . . but also*, use a pronoun that agrees with the nearer antecedent. 303
f Consider collective nouns as singular unless you intentionally refer to members, not the group as a whole. 303
g Use the relative pronouns appropriately. 303
h Use *self* pronouns only with clearly stated antecedents. 304

28 Case 307

a Use the nominative case of pronouns for subjects and predicate nominatives. 308
b Use the objective case of a pronoun used as a direct object, an indirect object, or an object of a preposition. 309
c Use the objective case of a pronoun for both the subject and the object of an infinitive. 309
d Use the same case for a pronoun used as an appositive as the word it renames. 310
e After *than* or *as* in elliptical expressions, use a pronoun that agrees with the unexpressed words. 311
f Use the possessive case with gerunds. 311
g Use *who (whoever)* and *whom (whomever)* correctly. 312

29 Verb Forms 314

a Understand the basic verb forms. 314
b Understand the function of auxiliary verbs. 317
c Do not confuse *sit* and *set*, *lie* and *lay*, *rise* and *raise*. 318

30 Verb Tense 320

a Know the basic verb tenses. 320
b Keep tenses consistent. 322
c Edit for special uses of the present tense. 322
d Use the past tense appropriately. 323
e Use the perfect tenses appropriately. 324
f Use verbs in the correct tense. 324

31 Voice 326

a Edit the active voice to emphasize the subject. 326
b Use the passive voice only to emphasize the receiver and occasionally to add sentence variety. 327

32 Mood   329

   a Use the subjunctive mood in *if* clauses that express conditions contrary to fact.   330
   b Use the subjunctive mood in *that* clauses following words such as *ask, request, desire, insist, recommend, wish*.   330

33 Adjectives and Adverbs   332

   a Understand the differences between adjectives and adverbs.   332
   b Use adverbs to modify verbs, adjectives, and other adverbs.   334
   c Use an adjective as a subject complement.   334
   d Use an adjective as an object complement.   335
   e Use comparative and superlative forms of adjectives and adverbs appropriately.   335

34 Editing to Correct Nonstandard English   338

   a Include all necessary verbs.   338
   b Add *-s* to form plurals of most nouns.   339
   c Use *-s* or *-es* endings for verbs in the present tense that have a third-person singular subject.   340
   d Use *'s* to form most possessives.   341
   e Use personal and demonstrative pronouns carefully.   342
   f Avoid double negatives.   343
   g Use the articles *a, an, and the* correctly.   343
   h Use the correct person, number, and tense for the verb *be*.   345
   i Use the correct person, number, and tense for the verb *do*.   346
   j Use the correct person, number, and tense for the verb *have*.   348
   k Select the correct form of irregular verbs.   349
   l Add *-ed* when needed to form the past and past participle of regular verbs.   350
   m Use prepositions correctly.   352
   n Check spelling, capitalization, and use of accents.   353

PART 7   PUNCTUATION

35 Periods, Question Marks, and Exclamation Points   357

   a Use a period to close statements.   357
   b Use a period after most abbreviations.   358
   c End direct questions with a question mark.   358
   d Use exclamation points only to show strong exclamatory emphasis.   359

36 Commas 346

a Use a comma before a coordinating conjunction (*and, but, for, nor, or, so, yet*) that connects independent clauses. 360
b Use commas between items in a series of three or more words or word groups. 361
c Use commas between coordinate adjectives. 361
d Use a comma to set off introductory phrases and clauses. 363
e Set off nonrestrictive units with commas. 364
f Use commas with titles, degrees, dates, and places. 366
g Use commas to separate units that interrupt the natural flow of the sentence. 367
h Use commas to set off sentence elements that are out of normal order. 368
i Use commas to show contrast or emphasis. 369
j Use commas to set off interjections, short questions, and the words *yes* and *no*. 369
k Use commas with direct address and interrupted quotations or dialogue. 369
l Use commas to mark omissions. 369

37 Unnecessary Commas 371

a Do not use a comma to separate the subject from the verb or the verb from its object or its complement. 371
b Do not use a comma between compound elements unless they are independent clauses. 372
c Do not use commas with restrictive modifiers. 373
d Do not use a comma before the first word or after the last word in a series. 373
e Do not use a comma before adverbial clauses that end sentences. 374
f Do not use a comma between adjectives that cannot be separated with the word *and*. 375
g Do not use a comma before an opening parenthesis. 375
h Do not use a comma before or after a period, question mark, exclamation point, or a dash. 375

38 Semicolons 377

a Use a semicolon between independent clauses not joined by a coordinating conjunction (*and, but, for, or, nor, so, yet*). 377
b Use a semicolon between independent clauses joined by a conjunctive adverb or a transitional phrase. 379
c Use a semicolon with a coordinating conjunction only if one or both independent clauses contain internal punctuation. 378
d Use a semicolon between items in a series when one or more items contain internal punctuation. 378
e Do not use a semicolon to connect a subordinate clause with an independent clause. 379

39 Colons 381

a Use a colon after an independent clause to introduce a series, a quotation, an appositive, a definition, or an amplification. 381
b Use a colon in salutations, in numbers to show time, and in ratios. 383
c Do not use a colon after a linking verb, preposition, or relative pronoun. 383

40 Apostrophes and Quotation Marks 385

a Use an apostrophe to create possessive nouns. 385
b Use the apostrophe to form contractions or show omissions. 386
c To prevent misreading, use the apostrophe to form plurals of letters used as letters and words used as words. 387
d Do not misuse the apostrophe. 387
e Use quotation marks around direct quotations in your text. 388
f Use quotation marks to show dialogue and unspoken thoughts. 389
g Use quotation marks around the titles of short works. 389
h Use quotation marks correctly with other punctuation marks. 390
i When you use words in a special or ironic sense, do not use quotation marks. 392

41 Dashes, Parentheses, Brackets, and Ellipses 393

a Use dashes to set off a summary, restatement, amplification, or explanation. 393
b Use dashes for an interruption or an abrupt change of thought. 394
c Use dashes with a list that contains commas. 394
d Use parentheses for additional information or digressions. 394
e Use double parentheses for numbered or lettered lists within sentences. 395
f Use parentheses for in-text citations. 395
g Use parentheses correctly with other punctuation marks. 395
h Use brackets appropriately. 396
i Use ellipses appropriately. 397

PART 8 MECHANICS

42 Underlining for Italics 401

a Underline (italicize) titles of major publications and other works. 401
b Underline (italicize) the names of specific ships, aircraft, and other vehicles, not the name of the type of vehicle. 403

CONTENTS

c Underline (italicize) words, phrases, letters, and numerals that serve as the subject of discussion. 403

d Underline (italicize) unusual foreign words used in English sentences. 403

e Underline (italicize) names of genuses and species. 404

f Underline (italicize) for emphasis sparingly and only for good reason. 404

43 Abbreviations and Acronyms 406

a Abbreviate titles before and after full proper names. 406

b Use acronyms and abbreviations for organizations and corporations as well as for geographic and technical terminology. 407

c Abbreviate dates and numbers in your text. 408

d Use abbreviations in parenthetical matter, addresses, and documentation. 408

44 Numbers 410

a Spell out numbers that you can write in one or two words; use figures for other numbers. 410

b Use figures in your text for specific places and exact figures. 411

45 Capital Letters 413

a Capitalize words that begin sentences. 413

b Capitalize the first word of a direct quotation if it begins a complete sentence or is an exclamation. 414

c Capitalize poetry exactly as it appears in the original. 414

d Capitalize proper nouns and words derived from them. 414

e Capitalize titles of books, articles, and works of art. 417

f Capitalize the pronoun *I* and the interjection *O*. 418

g Capitalize abbreviations and acronyms formed from proper nouns. 418

h Capitalize the names of genuses (but not species), geological periods, stars and planets. 418

46 Hyphenation 420

a Form compound words effectively. 420

b Use hyphens with prefixes and suffixes only in special cases. 421

c Follow conventions for end-of-line hyphenation. 422

47 Spelling 424

a Write word lists and practice speaking troublesome words. 424

b Proofread for spelling errors. 425

  c Distinguish between words that sound alike, and spell them correctly. 426
     Homophones 426
  d Understand and apply the rules for adding prefixes and suffixes to a root word. 430
  e Use *ei* and *ie* correctly. 432
  f Spell plurals correctly. 432
  g Improve your spelling skills by focusing on your troublesome words. 434
     Troublesome words 434
  h Misspell only for a purpose. 436

PART 9 ACADEMIC WRITING

48 Logic 441

  a Learn to structure arguments. 442
  b Use inductive and deductive arguments. 444
  c Use argument structure to organize an essay. 446
  d Carefully define key terms. 448
  e Recognize and address opposing arguments. 449
  f Avoid common fallacies. 449

49 Writing an Essay Examination Answer 456

  a Plan your answer. 456
  b Address the point of the question. 458

50 Writing the Research Paper 460

  a Choose a subject and narrow it to a workable topic. 460
  b Draft a preliminary thesis sentence. 463
  c Use all resources available to you for research. 463
  d Prepare a set of working bibliography cards. 471
  e Take notes thoughtfully. 474
  f Avoid plagiarism in your notes and text. 480
  g Plan and write the paper. 482
  h Integrate quotations carefully. 484
  i Use the MLA style of documentation for language and literature courses. 488
  j Create a list of works cited. 493
  k Format and proofread the final version of the paper. 499
  l Sample research paper in MLA style 499

51 Writing Research Papers across the Curriculum 512

  a Use the APA system for most papers in business, social sciences, and education. 512

CONTENTS

b Use the note system for papers in the humanities other than languages and literature. 516
c Use the appropriate styles of other disciplines. 517
d Organize your paper according to the requirements of the discipline. 519
e Sample paper in APA style 521

PART 10 **BUSINESS AND TECHNICAL WRITING**

52 Business Correspondence 532

a Write succinct memos. 532
b Write professional business letters. 533

53 Résumés and Job Application Letters 539

a Design a well-aimed résumé. 539
b Write persuasive letters of application. 541

54 Business and Technical Reports 543

a Use objective language and a neutral tone. 543
b Follow a standard format and organization. 544

Usage Glossary 548

Planning and Writing

1
Planning an Essay
2
Drafting the Essay
3
Revising, Editing, and Proofreading

CHAPTER
1
Planning an Essay

A well-written essay does not spring fully formed from a writer's pen. The essay takes considerable forethought and consideration, and it takes time. Yet writing an essay is stimulating, inspiring, energizing, and always challenging.

Successful writers usually begin with a vague idea of what they want to write about, and through a thoughtful process they begin to shape the essay. They use their idea to decide what they wish the purpose of the essay to be and whom they will direct their writing to. They then explore the general subject, determining what and how much they know about it and what aspects of it interest them, and they consult other persons and books to glean more information. Once they are familiar with the subject, they narrow the focus to a specific topic. Now they are ready to formulate a thesis sentence — a single statement that summarizes what they wish to say — and to use that sentence as a focal point on which to build their essay.

Although the entire process at first may seem overwhelming, do not be disheartened. All writers face similar challenges: finding, developing, and organizing an idea; understanding what they are trying to say and expressing that effectively; anticipating the reader's needs and getting the message across; and finally, of course — what all writers hope for — making their point clearly, correctly, and with style and personality.

Be willing to explore your ideas on paper, and do not try to think of everything at once. Complete one step at a time as you develop the whole essay. Do not worry about small mistakes at first; just get the ideas down on paper. You will correct the errors later before submitting a polished essay.

1a   Select a subject.

If you are given the opportunity to choose your own subject for an essay, try to select one that you know well or feel strongly about. Start first with a broad or general subject of interest. If the subject is a common one, think of a novel approach or search for ways to combine ideas that are not often associated with each other.

When asked to write an essay on a subject of her own choosing, one student, for example, jotted down a few ideas:

> working and going to college
> the working woman
> stereotypes of the working woman

This student unconsciously worked her way toward a topic that would reflect her strong feelings about the public image of women in the workplace.

Another student made these notes in search of a topic:

> my need for financial aid
> my right to privacy
> the government's regulations and management of the
>   individual

He was working his way toward a manageable topic, which he titled "Self versus the System."

If at first you cannot find an idea that sparks your interest, you may want to draw upon general subjects that have a track record for producing good papers:

health	government
love and family	crime and justice
sports	death
hobbies	work and a career
science	college education
art and literature	advertising
nature	gender and role models
society	communications

Then make one of these more specific by considering your own knowledge and interests. You might narrow "college education" to *television classrooms, SAT exams, honors programs*, or *keeping science books up-to-date*. You might narrow "gender and role models" to *teenagers in college, on being a jock, coed competition,* or *women in advertising.* (See section **1f.**)

You might also combine two or more subjects, as with *dating violence* (gender and crime), *announcing the death of the rain forest* (nature and communications), or *physique for jogging* (sports and health or sports and genetics). These combinations, in fact, often bring new insights to readers who have not considered such relationships. (See also **1e.**)

1b Write with a purpose.

Your **purpose** is the reason *why* you are writing. You may be writing to express a personal opinion, to explain a complex subject, or to argue a point of view. The same subject matter can serve different purposes. For instance, a story about running out of gas one evening on a back road could entertain readers with the humorous absurdity of being stranded all night on a deserted country road or it could inform them about the hazards of being ill-prepared for emergencies on a long trip. The purpose of the first approach is to amuse, and the purpose of the second is to teach.

Once you have selected a subject, ask yourself what you want to do with it. For example, "What should I do with my knowledge about the Brazilian rain forest?" Your answer to the question will help you clarify your purpose, which will probably be one of the following:

1. Express personal experiences and feelings

    After the field trip to Brazil, I understand only too well the term "rain forest."

2. Explain a complex subject

    I want my readers to understand the relationship between rain forests and changing climatic conditions.

3. Persuade

    I want my readers to join environmental organizations dedicated to preserving the rain forest.

You can have as your purpose any or all of these, but be aware that each purpose affects the way you address the reader, the way you generate and focus your ideas, and the way you organize the entire essay. (See also section **1d.**)

Write to express yourself.

Expressive writing grows out of your experiences and thoughts. It takes the form of an opinion paper, an autobiographical reminiscence, or a personal, introspective essay. It invites the reader into your private life, and you use personal experiences to explore universal values.

An expressive essay must make a point; it should not merely narrate a directionless episode. For example, using the general subject of love and family (as suggested in section **1a**), one student writer affirmed the value of family love by reflecting on the atmosphere of Thanksgiving dinner at her grandmother's table. Another recalled childhood swimming excursions at a stream to condemn its contaminated condition today. Still another shared travel experiences by comparing poverty in his home town with that in a Peruvian village.

The following paragraph illustrates expressive writing:

> I started into the kitchen but stopped short of the door. Mom and Dad were standing by the sink with their arms around each other. At first, I thought something must be wrong, but then I realized that they were kissing each other, a serious kiss, like lovers. A strange feeling rushed over me. Astonishment. I had never thought of Mom and Dad as lovers, yet here they were, kissing like two lovesick teenagers on a Saturday night date.
>
> —J. A. KOCH, student

The purpose of this expressive paragraph is to share the writer's personal attitude about the universal experience of love and family.

Write to explain.

Explanatory writing (also called *expository writing*) appears daily in newspapers, magazines, general interest books, reports, and textbooks. It makes a topic understandable, and it contributes to the world's knowledge: biology textbooks explain osmosis; astronomy articles analyze the big bang theory; news articles describe the latest space launch. In business, annual reports explain financial strength, just as the secretary's minutes inform an organization's members. Even a recipe for soup has an explanatory purpose.

In effect, explanatory writing focuses on the topic, not on the emotions of the writer. Writers should avoid using the first person ("I") when explaining because readers want and expect facts, not opinion. The following paragraph illustrates an explanatory purpose:

Children view their parents, in many cases, as asexual human beings. The mother and father may sleep together, but the children seldom think of them as participating in sexual activity. In like manner, parents often view their children as asexual beings. Parents negligently think of 9-year-old Susan and 11-year-old Jeff as little children, yet the children may have sex drives as strong as, if not stronger than, those of their parents.

—JESSE WALLACE, student

The writer's purpose is clear in this paragraph: to explain that children and parents view erroneously the other's sexuality. The writer may or may not need research to continue this explanation.

Write to persuade your readers.

Persuasive writing takes one side of a controversial issue and defends it with convincing evidence. In addition, it anticipates readers' reactions and tries to win them to the writer's side. Advertisements, law briefs, and editorials are traditional forms of persuasive writing. Forms of persuasive writing in course work might be an essay arguing for the cleanup of a polluted local stream or, using an earlier example, arguing for preservation of the rain forest in Brazil.

In general, persuasive writing is in the third person ("he," "she," "it") to emphasize the issues, as shown below:

Parents today, more than ever before, need to guard their children from peddlers of pornography who sneak into the home through electronics, not just the print media. Recordings especially contain suggestive and explicitly sexual lyrics, but television's soap operas and even sitcoms flaunt all sorts of sexual relationships and abusive behaviors.

—SANDY LYNN LYLE, student

This writer wants to win over her readers, to convince them to her way of thinking, and to motivate them to action. (See chapter **48**.)

Purposes often overlap.

Persuasive writing often explains a topic, and personal expression can be persuasive. In the following example, expressive and persuasive purposes overlap.

My children are exposed to media pornography, and I detest it. Television, recordings, magazines, and even newspapers are

now glutted by subtle and suggestive overtones as well as explicit sexual descriptions. I cannot cope with such massive as-
saults against the innocent minds in my home. Every year it
increases; even worse, nobody seems capable of stopping it.

— REBECCA ARMSTRONG, student

IN REVIEW

The *purpose* of your writing should be to *express* personal
feelings and experiences that have a universal value, to *explain* issues and processes, and/or to *persuade* readers to support your position.

EXERCISE 1.1   Choose one subject below and write a sentence
that shows (1) an expressive purpose, (2) an explanatory purpose,
and (3) a persuasive purpose.

birdwatching	sunbathing
body building	water purity
acid rain	the national debt
aggressive females	macho males
CIA activities	campus safety

EXAMPLE: Deer hunting
Expressive: I grew up on a farm where deer were pests and
highly destructive to our crops.
Explanatory: Conservation laws both protect the deer population and control its growth.
Persuasive: Farmers must be allowed unlimited deer hunting on
their own property.

1c   Consider your audience.

As you are deciding the purpose of your essay, you need to consider who your reader is going to be. Writing addresses an **audience**:
a memo addresses the members of a department, an inventory report addresses a supervisor, an essay on Appomattox addresses a
history instructor. These readers and others share common characteristics, and knowing them can direct your writing to your audience's expectations and interests.

A general audience

The most common and yet most elusive audience is the **general audience**, a group of readers with diverse interests, backgrounds, and educations. Most general-interest magazines address this audience with an informal style and familiar vocabulary. Writing for general audiences should

1. show personality;
2. have a clear, direct, and readable message;
3. have content worthy of their time;
4. show respect for their general knowledge; and
5. satisfy their desire for new, innovative ideas.

The following definition addresses a general audience:

> Scoliosis is an abnormal sideways curve of the spine. The adult vertebral column has four natural curves. A congenital defect, injury, disease, or chronic bad posture may result in the formation of one or more abnormal curves. If bad posture alone is responsible, the curve can usually be corrected by appropriate exercises professionally prescribed and directed. Such exercises are of greatest benefit during childhood, when the bones are still growing at a relatively rapid rate.
>
> If incorrect posture in childhood is maintained for some time, a postural deformity (one that can be corrected voluntarily) may become gradually transformed into a structural deformity (one that cannot be corrected voluntarily). Surgical correction may then be required.
> — EDWARD R. BRACE, *A Popular Guide to Medical Language*

These paragraphs are clear, introduce the reader to factual data, and avoid technical language in favor of words that the average reader can understand.

A specialized audience

Newsstands feature special-interest magazines on computers, automobiles, home decorating, rock music, sports, and so on. Each one explores complex topics and uses terminology of the field for a select audience. College writing also often addresses **specialized audiences** — for example, an essay exam for a physics professor or a case study for a psychology class. Specialized audiences have the same expectations as general audiences and more. Writing for specialized audiences should

1. show a comprehensive, detailed knowledge of the subject;
2. use the specialized vocabulary of the subject, such as "moraine," "syncline," and "igneous" for a geology report; and
3. display a formal and rigorous treatment of the subject, as in an analysis of a poem or in a research paper (see chapter **16**).

Note this example written for medical professionals:

> Scoliosis is an appreciable lateral deviation in the normally straight vertical line of the spine. (Compare kyphosis and lordosis.) There are 13 different forms. *Brissaud's*, also called *sciatic* scoliosis, is a list of the lumbar part of the spine away from the affected side in sciatica. *Cicatricial* is due to a cicatricial contraction following caries or necrosis. *Coxitic* scoliosis occurs in the lumbar region and is caused by hip disease. *Empyematic* is caused by empyema. *Habit* scoliosis is due to improper posture. *Inflammatory* scoliosis is due to vertebral disease, and *ischiatic* scoliosis is due to hip disease. *Myopathic* is paralytic scoliosis. *Ocular* or *opthalmic* scoliosis is attributed to tilting of the head on account of astigmatism or muscle imbalance. *Osteopathic* is caused by disease of the vertebrae. *Paralytic* scoliosis, also called *myopathic* scoliosis, is due to muscle paralysis. *Rachitic* is spinal curvature due to rickets, and *rheumatic* scoliosis is due to rheumatism of the dorsal muscles. *Static* scoliosis is due to a difference in the length of the legs.
>
> — *Dorland's Illustrated Medical Dictionary*

IN REVIEW

When writing for a general audience, use nontechnical language and provide explanations of special terms. When writing for a specialized audience, use technical language and expect the readers to have a detailed understanding of the topic.

EXERCISE 1.2   Name the probable audience for each statement below:

1. This software requires a computer with hard drive or two floppy drives and at least 640 RAM.
2. When I approached the age of 16, I overreacted by dating too many guys, staying out too late, and straying too far from home.
3. Sweet Dream hybrid canteloupe, a vigorous plant, is resistant to fusarium wilt and responds well to methoxychlor.
4. You should not work just for the money; a job should also complement your lifestyle.
5. Collecting baseball cards has moved beyond a childhood hobby to become a business for entrepreneurs.

1d   Define your writing project.

For guidance through the early stages of creating an essay, some writers summarize in a single sentence what they have decided about their essay, explaining their *purpose* for writing about a particular *subject* for a specific *audience*:

> I am going to explain   [purpose]   to novice photographers [audience]   how to use natural lighting   [subject].

Such a statement defines the writing: the essay will be an explanation of lighting for beginning photographers.

To use the technique, write a note at the top of a sheet describing the subject. Next jot down your goal for the essay. What do you expect your readers to learn from it? Then identify your audience as clearly as possible.

SUBJECT: Hypothermia.

PURPOSE: To explain it as a warning to others.

AUDIENCE: People who spend a lot of time outdoors.

Finally, formulate a complete description:

> I want to explain to hikers, campers, and people who enjoy the outdoors how hypothermia occurs and how dangerous it can be.

This writer has now clearly identified the writing project by deciding *what* it will be about, *why* it will be written, and *whom* it will be written for.

1e Generate ideas on your subject by doing prewriting exercises.

Now that you have made the primary decisions about the essay, how do you begin to develop it? You need to think about all that you want to say and the ways you could say it. This step is called **prewriting**, which encompasses a wide range of exercises intended to stimulate thought about your subject.

One way to generate ideas is simply to start writing. The physical act of writing challenges the mind and, like practice in any sport, improves technique. Making lists, clustering topics, free-writing, keeping a journal — such forms of writing develop confidence and skill and get pencil to paper.

Other ways to generate ideas are to think and read about the subject. Asking questions about the subject, brainstorming with fellow students, and reading articles and books help you classify the issues and broaden your understanding of the subject.

Even if your instructor assigns a subject to write about — say, the results of a geology field trip or a review of a history book — you must generate ideas that will help you define the scope of the essay. Several methods will prove helpful.

List words and phrases.

Many writers generate ideas with a list. *Listing* allows the writer to explore a general subject in detail. It helps the writer discover ideas and issues, make connections and see relationships, and build a vocabulary on the subject. The technique is simple and can be accomplished quickly in any setting. It requires you to jot down every word or phrase that you associate with a topic, no matter how offbeat it may seem or where it might lead you. Later you can select the best and discard the others. For example, one writer started with the subject "the problems of waste disposal" and produced this list in about one minute:

> contamination
> destruction of the environment
> irresponsibility
> new inventions defy erosion
> burning destroys ozone layer
> recycling is the best answer

This writer has generated a few ideas that might ultimately lead to an essay on the topic.

Ask basic questions about your topic.

A list of questions will generate ideas, even if you cannot answer each one right away. The "journalist's questions" (Who? What? When? Where? Why? and How?) are good for exploring a subject.

> *Who* is dumping toxic wastes?
> *What* is a toxin?
> *How* does toxic poisoning occur?

These are basic, informative questions that you must answer for your readers. Next, ask analytical questions and formulate answers:

> Can I *define* toxin?
> What *causes* toxic poisoning?
> What are its *effects*?
> What are the stages in the *process* of toxic poisoning?
> Can something like rat poison be *compared* to toxic poisoning?
> Are there different *types* of toxins?

(See chapter **6** for a discussion of *definition, cause and effect, process analysis, comparison*, and *classification*.) With every question and its answer you build the foundation of your essay.

Organize ideas by clustering.

Although it looks like a hodgepodge of circles, **clustering** actually generates a map of connected thoughts. Some writers develop their papers directly from a clustered chart rather than from a separate outline (see section **1i**).

Begin clustering by writing your subject in the center of a sheet of paper (or on a blackboard) and draw a circle around it.

(waste disposal)

Next, jot down related ideas, circle them, and draw connecting lines to the main subject.

(minimum space)   *(atmosphere)*

(waste disposal)

(burying)   *(recycling)*

Now branch out by connecting new ideas to one or more of the satellite circles. Since everything cannot connect logically to the main subject, you will begin to discover minor, supporting ideas and facts.

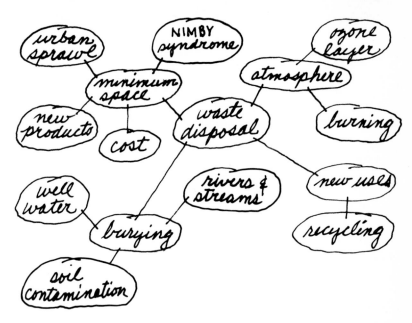

If you run out of ideas, ask probing questions about the subject. Write down your one- or two-word answer, circle it, and connect it to an appropriate circle on the diagram. When you have completed the cluster, you will find that you have established a hierarchy among the ideas. You can use the cluster as a visual aid when structuring the essay.

Try exploratory free-writing.

Free-writing is similar to list-making, except that instead of spontaneously creating a list, the writer creates a freewheeling, nonstop paragraph on a single topic. For five or ten minutes the writer records whatever comes to mind without worrying about style, spelling, grammar, or neatness. Free-writing gets basic ideas on paper; then, as in listing or clustering, the writer must look back over the material to discover ideas, concerns, and relationships. The germ of an essay, perhaps even an organizational formula, may be hidden within the slapdash scurry of free-written notes.

To begin free-writing, jot your subject or idea at the top of a page and use it as your starting point, writing anything that comes to mind, as in the following example:

Family relationships

People seem to be more concerned about themselves than others. No one willing to take time to try to understand others. If you don't meet them, they don't want to meet you, simply push it off as dislike when they haven't even really tried. Influence of peers pulls and forms opinions of someone you've never met. How do you decide what to believe? Take it on yourself to find out what you really believe about someone. Relationships aren't important in our world anymore—self! self! self! emphasized everywhere. So much divorce. People not willing to give time to try to make a marriage work. Both parties have got to try / in friendships too / to have a friend, you've got to be a friend. No one has time for listening to others but they expect others to listen to them. Deeper relationships. People should at least attempt to interact more. Can be so boring without relationships, good or bad, at least you'll have contact with others. Important to try to make it work. Nobody wants to try anymore. Instant coffee—instant relationships—no time to brew and the flavor isn't rich. Parents should try to relate to kids just as kids should try to relate to parents. Empathy. Try to understand the situation and discuss it thoroughly. Takes more than we're willing to give.

This writer should now look for key ideas, or perhaps one sentence—"Nobody wants to try anymore"—and expand the thinking with additional free-writing. She could also cluster the various ideas to identify her main ideas and subtopics.

Keep a journal.

A journal is a record of your thoughts and the significant events in your life. It allows you to reflect upon and make sense of your experiences and observations and to record ideas in private before they are forgotten. It becomes a storehouse of your knowledge on a wide range of topics, a catalog of miscellaneous thoughts and ideas for essays and stories.

To begin a journal, simply keep a notebook handy, and if something interests you, write it down. For example, one writer made this entry:

2-7-89

President Reagan has turned the White House over to George Bush. The transition from one U. S. president to another just happens in America without great upheaval. We expect a president to bow out gracefully, and he does. Amazing. He quietly moves out of the White House, forsakes his role as commander-in-chief, and moves back to California. Yet rulers in other countries all around the globe for centuries have clutched egotistically to their supreme command. Now what will happen if we someday have a president who refuses to relinquish the White House and its powers? What's more, suppose he has the support of the Pentagon?

This writer describes not only an event of the day but also how he feels about it. The entry might serve as inspiration for a complete essay on presidential exits from the White House.

Brainstorm.

Brainstorming is an oral, sharing form of listing, clustering, and free-writing. It is a free exchange among a small group of classmates or co-workers of ideas, topics, and related issues. At first the goal is to formulate subjects of mutual concern. As discussion continues, the group explores fundamental issues and specific details.

Brainstorming usually leads to specific facts and ideas for everyone. You learn to formulate ideas and express them publicly, you are exposed to and stimulated by the ideas and opinions of others, and you indirectly discover your essay's purpose and identify your audience.

To brainstorm, form a small group, decide on a general subject of interest to all, and toss out ideas. Or take turns and openly discuss each person's subject. Everyone should participate to create ideas for others to build on. Designate one person as recorder and then share the notes, or keep your own notes.

NOTE: An alternative to brainstorming with a group is a one-to-one *interview*, especially if you can find a knowledgeable person who will share ideas with you. Again, you learn by listening and recording notes.

Read about your subject.

Reading is probably the most fruitful method of gaining knowledge about a subject. It opens doors to a full spectrum of issues and thereby helps generate ideas for writing. Initial reading on a subject is exploratory, yet most writers keep notes and refer to them later during composition.

When you read an article in *Omni, Time,* or *Psychology Today*, you can discover a general subject, learn what others have said about it, and confront its fundamental issues. You will learn how professional writers approach their topics, structure their essays, and use terminology of the field effectively.

As you read, write notes and summaries. List key words and phrases. Record a pertinent, well-phrased sentence that you might wish to quote in your essay. Question the ideas of the author. Select one idea and do your own free-writing about it. Some of your best writing will develop from careful and thoughtful reading.

NOTE: If you make notes from a source — if you copy something directly or summarize the main ideas — write down the full bibliographical information: author, title, publication date, place, publisher, and specific page numbers. Later, if you use the source in your paper, you will have the information you need to cite the source accurately and completely (see chapter **49**).

IN REVIEW

Generate ideas for writing by making lists, asking questions and answering them, clustering topics, free-writing, keeping a journal, brainstorming with classmates or co-workers, and reading articles and books.

EXERCISE 1.3   Use the following exercises to discover and explore a subject.

1. Write a list of ten words or phrases for one of the following subjects or for a subject of your own choosing:

    just say no to drugs
    individual rights versus social conformity
    the role of worms (or spiders) in nature
    the argument against zoos
    political news coverage
    foreign imports
    state-sponsored lotteries
    walking, jogging, or running

2. In your journal or on a separate sheet of paper, free-write on a subject for five minutes. If you need a subject, select one from the list above.

3. Practice clustering with rock music as the central idea. These items may remind you of related subjects:

youth cults	hidden messages	racial themes
satanic influences	in songs	groupies
drugs	concerts	Christian rock
messages	sexual themes	age differences

4. Brainstorm with two of your classmates for 30 minutes about your subject and theirs (10 minutes for each subject). Make

notes during the discussion and, if applicable, use them in your next essay.

5. As a preliminary exercise to drafting your paper, write answers in *full* sentences to the following questions about your subject:

   Who?   What?   When?   Where?   Why?   How?

6. As a basis for a first draft, explore your subject by writing a sentence in response to each of the following:

   a. Define the subject.
   b. Compare it with something familiar to your readers.
   c. Describe it.
   d. Give three examples of it.
   e. Illustrate it with a story or an anecdote or relate an event about it.
   f. Explain why it affects you and your reader.

7. List books or articles that you have read or might read for ideas on the subject.

1f   Narrow the subject to a specific topic.

At first, writers investigate and consider every possible aspect of a subject (see sections **1a** and **1e**). Once they have done some prewriting exercises and have become familiar with the subject, however, they must focus on one specific issue. They must narrow their subject to have a workable idea that they can develop fully in a few pages and thereby avoid broad generalizations on wide-ranging issues.

For instance, "Abraham Lincoln" is too far-reaching, but "Lincoln's Emancipation Proclamation" is more specific. Yet even that topic appears broad and unmanageable, so further narrowing might produce this idea: "The Emancipation Proclamation did not forbid slavery in border states loyal to Lincoln and the North." Now the topic is controllable and workable.

Listed below are other subject areas narrowed to effective topics by student writers:

GENERAL SUBJECT: *Nuclear disarmament*
TOPICS: 1. How community activist groups can influence political policies

2. How *glasnost* affects the arms race
3. Elementary school children's views on nuclear war

GENERAL SUBJECT: *Parent-child relations*
TOPICS: 1. The tragedy of child abuse in one family
2. How I met adolescence and lived to tell the story
3. How businesses adapt to child-care needs

GENERAL SUBJECT: *Preserving the environment*
TOPICS: 1. Must we kill sea lions to save salmon?
2. Preserving natural habitats in an office park: winners, losers, and trade-offs
3. Innovative garbage disposal systems

1g Focus your topic with a thesis sentence.

The **thesis sentence** is the key point of a composition. In a single declarative statement, it expresses a writer's convictions about a topic and controls everything in the essay. The thesis sentence does *not* merely tell what the paper is about; it expresses a position: "I learned to enjoy competition, not withdraw from it." Reports as well as essays need a thesis to control factual evidence and evaluate the results of an investigation. Even a letter of recommendation has a thesis: "I recommend Samuel Levy for a position as sales representative with your firm."

Here are thesis sentences that produced good student essays, all developed from narrowed topics:

SUBJECT: The War between the States
NARROWED TOPIC: Lincoln's emancipation of the slaves
THESIS: Economic issues in general—not merely emancipation—triggered the War between the States.

SUBJECT: Preserving the environment
NARROWED TOPIC: Preserving natural habitats in an office park
THESIS: Natural streams and man-made ponds or lakes add beauty to any business complex.

SUBJECT: Politics
NARROWED TOPIC: The sources of political strength
THESIS: Political power starts at the grass-roots level.

SUBJECT: Day-care centers
NARROWED TOPIC: company-funded day-care centers
THESIS: Although many working parents and their children
     benefit from company-funded day-care centers, such ben-
     efits may discriminate against nonparents.

Once the prewriting exercises, such as free-writing and clustering, have helped you identify and narrow your topic, you can begin to develop the thesis sentence. It may begin as an implied, unstated thesis until you can enunciate it clearly. Explanation and persuasion require an expressed thesis. Expressive writing, such as the personal narrative, may have a thesis that remains just below the surface, being implied to the reader by events of the autobiography.

The following examples show the writer progressing toward a clearly enunciated thesis for her essay on the problem of waste disposal:

FIRST DRAFT: This paper is about the problem of waste
     disposal.

This sentence merely announces a general topic.

SECOND DRAFT: The increasing population means a con-
     stant growth in waste and a decreasing amount of disposal
     areas.

This revised sentence explains the problem but suggests no direction for the paper to take.

THIRD DRAFT: Mountains of trash face both Americans and
     Russians, the rich and the poor, the people of the cities
     and those on the farms, so all members of this world com-
     munity must initiate new, innovative methods of disposal.

This last thesis sentence, by giving a clear indication of the path the paper will follow, will guide the writer's note-taking, outlining, and drafting of the essay and will ultimately provide the focal point for the reader.

Follow four steps in framing a thesis sentence:

1. Name your specific topic (for example, the meaning of the term *macho*).
2. Write a preliminary thesis sentence about the topic (for example, "attempting to be macho can get a person killed").
3. Analyze the preliminary thesis statement you formulated in step 2 to determine the purpose of your thesis. It should not express the obvious, such as "The effort to appear macho gets some young Chicano men into serious trouble." Avoid such truisms. Argue instead the damage such behavior might cause:

   > Gaining a macho reputation is usually a slow and dangerous journey toward death for a Chicano youth.

   Or refute a prevailing opinion:

   > Although masculine aggression is defended by some experts as a natural release of emotions, it cannot excuse the brutality of date rape.

   Or defend an idea:

   > James Dickey's *Deliverance* is a retelling of Joseph Conrad's *The Heart of Darkness*.

4. Review your thesis sentence to be certain that it limits the scope of your writing, summarizes your main point, and controls development of the essay (see section **1h** and chapter **6**). Be willing to change your thesis if evidence or additional considerations alter your position. Do not bind yourself to a thesis that prevents you from exploring other possibilities suggested by further thinking, reading, and note-taking. Here are two more examples.

   > The fact that Republican presidential candidates have won the Southern states does not mean the Democrats have lost the solid South; it just means the South wants a conservative candidate for president.

   The thesis sentence names the subject, narrows it to Southern politics, argues for a position, and points forward to the essay's examination of Southern conservative thought.

   > The minimum wage is just that, minimum; it ought to be $5.00 an hour.

This thesis sentence names the subject, narrows the focus to the amount of the wage, argues for a position, and suggests that an analysis of economic realities will follow.

IN REVIEW

Every manuscript needs an expressed or implied thesis. As the focal point for your ideas, it guides your note-taking, outlining, and drafting. It also guides your reader to an assertion that will be supported in the finished paper.

1h   Use your thesis sentence to suggest a structure for the essay.

The form of your essay, not just the content, must support your thesis sentence (see section **1g**). In fact, a good thesis will help you determine the internal structure and the strategy of the essay (see also chapter **6**). Note this example:

> THESIS: Birth order affects the development and personality of children.

This writer's thesis sentence implies that the essay will examine the consequences of being born first or second or last. The paper will study family relationships. It may be necessary for the writer to develop a clear image of the audience: "I want to address grade school teachers" or "I want to address parents of two or more children."

> THESIS: Too many people file divorce papers without considering other alternatives, such as counseling by a minister or psychologist.

Very likely, this paper will first provide a convincing argument against a hasty divorce, then suggest several alternatives that couples have to resolve their conflicts. The writer can define alternatives and compare them.

> THESIS: Oppressed people deal with their oppression by adjusting to it, fighting it with violence, or resisting it with nonviolence.

This thesis sentence classifies three ways of dealing with oppression, and the essay must describe each in detail and suggest possible consequences that will follow each choice.

> THESIS: Leasing land for farming makes better sense today than buying the property.

This writer will need to compare and contrast leasing and buying to establish the leasing as superior. The writer will address farmers, land owners, lending officers, and others.

Finally, the thesis sentence will also determine other ways to arrange the essay, such as a time sequence, a step-by-step chronology, or a general-to-specific order. Allow your purpose and thesis to help you form an outline (see section 1i) and direct your first draft (see section 2a).

EXERCISE 1.4 Label each of the following sentences as Good (a thesis sentence with potential) or Poor (a sentence or phrase that does not give the writer or reader a clear direction).

1. Many students attending college receive scholarship money and special grants.
2. Student grants, fellowships, and scholarships should be tax-free.
3. Many college students work full-time while they are enrolled full-time.
4. Most people spend two-fifths of the week working for the government.
5. Full-time students who also work should receive tax relief.
6. The term *free ride* in reference to scholarship athletes is a misnomer.
7. The term *scholar-athlete* is a misnomer.
8. Scholarship athletes receive benefits beyond a tuition grant.

EXERCISE 1.5 Narrow these to specific topics and write a thesis sentence for each.

1. Divorced mothers
2. Nuclear disarmament
3. Gender and its influences on social order
4. Effects on children when parents divorce
5. Foreign investments in the United States
6. Signals to and from outer space

1i   Create an outline.

Just as construction workers need a blueprint to build a house, writers need a design that systematically specifies the location of various details, both major and minor, to write an essay. Some well-disciplined writers can follow a mental plan, but most writers need an **outline**, a written plan that directs them from one stage to the next, thereby assuring a complete, consistent, and logical paper. A short paper may call for only a few key words in a scratch outline to bring order, but a long essay or a research paper may require carefully drawn subdivisions in a formal outline.

A scratch outline

A **scratch outline** is merely a quick list of major issues that the paper needs to explore. A cluster of ideas (see section **1e**) may serve this purpose. Writers use this simple kind of outline for letters, essay exams, short reports, and some themes, but not usually for research papers.

One writer started with a major point for a paper on suntanning and added specific points under it:

> The dangers of getting a tan
> > the tanning process by natural sun or tanning bed
> > ultraviolet exposure
> > protection by sunscreens

This writer can begin drafting the essay directly from this list or, if time permits, can add subdivisions, perhaps mentioning several consequences or the types of sunscreens.

Sometimes ideas fall into natural categories, as in this next scratch outline:

> A problem for everybody
> > Mountains of trash in America, Japan, Russia, etc.
> > An issue for the rich and poor, socialist and capitalist
> An increasing volume
> > The shrinking amount of space
> > The increase in artificial products
> Traditional methods of disposal
> > Burning
> > Burying

New solutions for disposal
    Public awareness and action
    Recycling

This writer established three categories that form an organizational plan to explore the worldwide waste disposal problem. (See chapters **2** and **3** for the drafts of the essay produced from this outline.)

A formal outline

For long or complex writing assignments, a **formal outline** provides a detailed structure with clear headings and multiple subdivisions. Whether it uses topics or complete sentences, it follows specific guidelines.

1. It uses the standard system of roman numerals, letters, and arabic numerals.

  I. First major heading
    A. Subheadings of first degree
      1. Subheadings of second degree
      2.
        a. Subheadings of third degree
        b.
          (1) Subheadings of fourth degree
          (2)
            (a) Subheadings of fifth degree
            (b)
    B.
      1.
      2.
        a.
        b.
          (1)
          (2)
            (a)
            (b)
  II. Second major heading

2. It requires parallel headings on each level:

  A. Universal problem
  B. Increasing volume

C. Traditional methods of disposal
D. New solutions for disposal

3. It uses two or more subdivisions for each category. If you divide a subject, logic suggests that you must have at least two parts. If you find yourself listing only one subdivision, omit it or incorporate it into the previous level of generality:

    I. Shopping malls serve as social centers
       A. Many types of people gather at malls
          1. Teenagers meet friends and sweethearts
          2. Exercisers walk the empty hallways
          3. Older people socialize and watch people

4. Headings appear in a logical, sequential order (from teenagers to exercisers to older people).
5. Subdivisions must feature smaller, logical parts of a larger category.

Formal outlines appear in one of two forms: the topic outline or the sentence outline. In a *topic outline* every heading is a noun phrase (friends at the mall), gerund phrase (meeting friends at the mall), or an infinitive phrase (to meet friends at the mall). Using only one type helps assure balanced and parallel ideas.

II. Shopping malls as social centers
    A. Teenagers
       1. Meeting friends
       2. Meeting sweethearts
    B. Exercisers
       1. Walking in the morning
       2. Jogging in the parking lot
    C. Friends and relatives
       1. Running into acquaintances
       2. Meeting by appointment
    D. Senior citizens
       1. Watching the crowd
       2. Talking with friends

The topic outline quickly and precisely names your main issues and shows items of equal importance, but its brevity can hide structural problems.

A *sentence outline* requires full sentences for each item. The complete thoughts of a sentence outline can reveal any organizational problems that a topic outline might hide.

II. Shopping malls serve as social centers for many people.
  A. Teenagers visit them for several social purposes.
    1. The mall offers teenagers video arcades, restaurants, and other gathering places.
    2. Sweethearts can meet at malls, away from the scrutiny of parents.

An additional advantage of a sentence outline is that the headings can become topic sentences for your paragraphs (see chapter **4**).

IN REVIEW

> Create an outline to identify your major topics, to discover your supporting subtopics, and to bring an overall order to your essay.

EXERCISE 1.6   Organize the list below into a scratch outline for the topic "the role of the cities in the conservation of natural resources." Eliminate irrelevant items and add other necessary supporting items.

greenbelts and parks	water
industrial waste	public garbage
dump sites	burning of trash
automobile emissions	urban planning
city codes	new housing developments

EXERCISE 1.7   Revise the following topic outline so that items of the same level appear together in parallel form. Make sure that each level has at least two subdivisions. In addition, revise the order of items to give the outline a logical, progressive development.

  I. Finding diets that are safe and sane
 II. Exercising
   A. Walking
   B. Running at least three miles a day
   C. Swim for your health
   D. Other exercise is good too

III. Counting calories
  A. A safe level and ones that are not
IV. Using drugs, herbs, stimulants, etc.
  V. Balancing the body's needs
  A. Fats and carbohydrates
  B. Proteins are good for the body
  C. Minerals and vitamins
VI. Dieting as a lifestyle
  A. The beautiful people as necessarily skinny
  B. Designers who focus on small sizes
  C. Facilities (chairs, aisles, check points) that seem tiny

EXERCISE 1.8 In preparation for writing your own essay, work these exercises.

  1. List your general subject (section **1a**).
  2. Identify your purpose and audience by defining your writing project (sections **1b, 1c, 1d**).
  3. Generate ideas by listing, asking and answering questions, clustering, free-writing, entering ideas into a journal, brainstorming with peers, or reading (section **1e**).
  4. Write your narrowed topic (section **1f**).
  5. Write your thesis sentence (sections **1g, 1h**).
  6. Develop a scratch outline (section **1i**).

CHAPTER
2
Drafting the Essay

2a Concentrate on main ideas.

A rough draft is a first attempt at composing the entire essay. Using your thesis statement and your outline as guides, your goals are to organize your notes into a whole, to begin to develop each of your main ideas, and to be certain that your evidence supports your purpose and your thesis sentence. If you feel your paragraphs are sketchy and undeveloped and your phrasing seems awkward, don't worry; you can make the necessary revisions and corrections in later drafts.

To begin the draft, organize your essay into three parts: the introduction, the body, and the conclusion. The **introduction** invites the reader into the paper, establishes the important issues, and advances the thesis (see section **2b**). The thesis sentence in most papers will appear in the introduction. The **body** of the paper traces the sections and subsections of the outline, making clear their relevance to the thesis (see section **2c**). The **conclusion** summarizes the argument and affirms the thesis (see section **2d**).

Some writers find it easier to draft the body of the essay first and then to progress to the introduction and conclusion. Proceed in any manner that works best for you.

Similarly, write your title now or develop it later (see section **3a**).

2b   Write a fully developed introduction.

The introduction catches your readers' attention and invites them to listen to what you have to say. In addition, it names your topic and suggests your specific approach. Identifying your topic and stating or implying your thesis can be accomplished within two or three sentences. Attracting your readers is sometimes more difficult, yet crucial. Several techniques for inviting readers into the essay are shown below. The technique you choose will depend upon your purpose (**1b**) and your audience (**1c**).

> Explain and define special terminology.
> Explain the timeliness of the topic.
> Offer background information or historical facts.
> Include interesting biographical facts about people.
> Open with an anecdote or descriptive scene.
> Provide enlightening quotations from others.
> Take exception to a well-known idea.
> Challenge an assumption.
> Raise a question.
> Present statistics, figures, or other data.
> Compare briefly past events with those of the present.
> Contrast favorable features with negative ones.
> Compare an obscure subject to something familiar. (See
>   analogy, section **6i**.)

The opening is also your opportunity to establish for readers a tone and a voice—that is, humorous, critical, angry, reflective, concerned, and so on (see section **3b**).

Lead to the thesis.

One of the most widely used and effective introductions is a paragraph that begins with a short scenario or idea that leads to the thesis statement (shown here in italics).

> You know the couch potato: the flabby muscles and a generous waistline; one hand on the remote control and the other in a bag of chips. Medical research now has confirmed the aptness of this depiction. *Long hours in front of the tube and obesity,* it turns out, *go together like Monday Night Football and beer nuts.*
> —ELIZABETH STARK, "Couch Potato Physique"

This opening invites the reader to observe a familiar scene. It uses concrete examples ("flabby muscles," "bag of chips") and confirms the metaphor that is commonly observed. The final sentence, the thesis, links the cause and effect: the couch potato exists in a vegetative state.

Elaborate on the thesis statement.

In some introductions an early sentence or two establishes the thesis, and the rest of the paragraph elaborates on it, pointing the way the essay will continue.

> *Whether we know it or not, we have been called to arms.* Forty-four years after Hiroshima and Nagasaki, the world is at war again. It is a fight to save the earth and the future of our species. And the enemy is us.
> —ALSTON CHASE, "Welcome to World War III"

> *The continuing efforts to impose unrealistic academic standards on college athletes deserve only scorn.* They are premised on an elitist notion that a university's mission excludes all but purely cerebral endeavors. They are a vestige of bygone days when universities were seen as ivory towers isolated and protected from the ugly influences and values of the working classes. It's time to discard these notions.
> Regardless of an athlete's academic aptitude or motivation, if he wants a chance to play professional basketball or football, he must go to college. Virtually every young man out of high school needs additional physical development and training before he can hope to play at the professional level. The only preprofessional programs are at colleges.
> —GARY R. ROBERTS, "Rules for Athletes Are Elitist"

Open with an anecdote.

Writers use the anecdote, a short narration of an interesting event, to catch the attention of readers and to point to the thesis that follows immediately. Such openings are effective because they make a general idea specific or personalize a common experience. (Note that introductions can be longer than one paragraph.)

> In medical school the paradigm patient is known as "the 70-kilogram man." He's the physiological average, the everyman, and something of a joke among the students. They learn how

much his heart weighs and what his minimum urine output should be. In the course of their studies they watch him suffer through allergies, diarrhea, appendicitis, and prostate problems, among other ailments. Make no mistake though: The 70-kilogram man is all man; he is never afflicted with endometriosis or any other "female" disorder. He's a versatile fellow, but there are limits.

The 70-kilogram man is, in fact, a manifestation of how traditional medicine conducts its business. The studies on disease that affect both sexes have typically used male subjects exclusively, with the results generalized — as if males were the generic humans. *Partly, perhaps, as a consequence, women's physical symptoms have often been dismissed by their doctors as imaginary or psychosomatic.*
— PERRI KLASS AND LILA WALLIS, "Macho Medicine"

The anecdote attracts the reader's attention to the thesis of doctors not taking women's symptoms seriously.

2c   Write a body that fully explores the issues.

The body defends the thesis, developing the major ideas with several paragraphs of specific detail to show how subissues bear on the thesis. The body must accomplish two primary tasks.

1. It should classify and explore the major issues and subtopics.
2. It should supply facts, examples, comparisons, and other details of support.

The outline can provide guidance because it enumerates the primary divisions and subdivisions (see section 1i). One writer classified three issues about waste disposal:

the increasing world population
the increase in synthetic products
the use of recycling rather than burning or burying

In general, follow your outline, but remember that a first draft is a time of discovery, so let ideas flow freely to expose new, invigorating thoughts. If you need methods for developing the body, choose from the following list (see also chapter **6**):

Define technical, unusual, or obscure terminology.

Give a history of the subject.

Offer reasons and explanations.

Compare and contrast two or more items.

Offer supporting quotations or paraphrases from outside sources.

Trace a time sequence or explore a process.

Explore positive and negative factors.

Provide a set of questions and answers.

Provide illustrative descriptions.

Forecast consequences.

Use negation to tell what something is *not*.

Provide a brief biographical sketch of the main character's career.

Challenge prevailing myths and prove them false.

Delve into the unknown.

Present the prevailing opinion on a subject and refute it.

Abstract conjecture is often appropriate for the introduction and the conclusion, but not for the body. The body needs an abundance of facts. Consider one writer's imprecise development with another's explicit wording:

VAGUE AND UNDEVELOPED: German troops attacked Poland in the autumn of 1939. Britain and France then declared war on Germany, but the support came too late. The Germans quickly overran Poland.

PRECISE AND WELL DEVELOPED: German troops attacked Poland on September 1, 1939. Britain and France then honored their alliances with Poland by declaring war on Nazi Germany. However, German troops used *blitzkrieg* techniques to send Panzer divisions rumbling onto the boulevards of Warsaw before the British and French troops could move into defensive positions. The quick victory lured Hitler's regime to an arrogant disdain for the allied forces.

The second version has a thoroughness that provides readers with specific facts. To accomplish this in your own rough draft, draw the details from your own experiences, your reading and research, your clustering and freewriting notes, and your brainstorming ideas.

Finally, allow your thesis to dictate how you build the body of the paper (see section **1h**). You may need to explain the subject with definition, examples, comparison and contrast, and process analysis; or, for a persuasive essay, you may need cause-and-effect analysis, expert testimony, and carefully reasoned answers (see chapter **6** for an explanation of these and other methods of development).

2d   Conclude effectively.

A well-crafted ending leaves a reader with a sense of satisfaction and finality. It synthesizes the main issues. That is, it does more than summarize or repeat the thesis: it affirms your theory or judgment, expresses your concern, offers your solution, or gives a call to action. It must leave the reader with something to contemplate and remember:

> We must all learn to speak out with a public voice. The struggle for individuality in contemporary society may ultimately become a battle for the opportunity to be heard. All people should be able to express their views about all things, even if their positions are not popular. By listening to other people, we gain knowledge. By speaking out, we frame our own ideas and thereby identify our own social standards. After all, America is built on the compromises of diverse groups brought together by effective communication.
>
> — SHEILA ORLACH, student

This ending makes a final, emphatic call to action that the author wants readers to think about.

Sometimes the best way to end a rough draft is simply to stop. If you have effectively built to a climax, there may be nothing more to say until you survey and evaluate the whole. At some point, however, you will need to express your final thoughts so your readers will have a satisfying sense of closure. Here are some useful techniques for writing your conclusion:

Restate your thesis and then point beyond it.
Establish guidelines and directives for your readers.
Defend your theory on the basis of a quick reference to your evidence.

Quote or paraphrase an expert on the subject.

Compare briefly the past with the present to affirm contemporary ideas.

Offer a solution to a problem.

Discuss the meaning of test results.

Summarize the evidence and interpret it.

Explain the significance of your findings.

Suggest additional investigation that is needed.

Rank one issue over another and justify the ranking.

A good conclusion for an essay often reaches a judgment about personal experiences, as demonstrated below:

> When the war finally ended, my uncle came home a confused man with a distorted view of the world. He has never really overcome the horrifying nightmare of war, but his numbed senses have enabled him to disregard some of his most devastating memories. He chooses to isolate himself from society in an attempt to escape the possibility of more heartache, but deep within his soul, I am sure he longs to put his trust in someone. A Greek philosopher once stated, "Trust, like the soul, never returns once it is gone." So I have learned a great deal from my uncle including many values that each individual should embrace. Remote men like my uncle require a deep understanding for what they have so miraculously survived. In a sense, they are still paying for our liberty.
>
> — MARLA WALKER, student

This writer uses personal experience to express a universal concept that touches the lives of all readers.

In the case of truly complex issues, you might intentionally leave the reader with unanswered questions, as in this conclusion to an essay about acid rain:

> What does all this mean for human health? Most environmental-health scientists believe the pollutants we breathe in are more likely to harm us than those that rain down upon us. But even considering acidity alone, what *are* the effects of acid rain on human skin and hair? How low a pH level and what periods of exposure are likely to be damaging? At what point does it make sense to start taking personal precautions? The questions are too new for dermatologists to have any ready answers. At this point, I think it would be foolish to panic at being caught in the rain. Just the same, if I were to wake up exuberant one rainy

morning and feel an irresistible urge to do a long drawn-out singin'-in-the-rain number, à la Gene Kelly, in the driving downpour, I think I'd feel easier doing it with an umbrella.

— ALBERT ROSENFELD, "Forecast: Poisonous Rain"

Rosenfeld admits that answers to his questions do not exist, at least not yet, so he offers his own tongue-in-cheek response.

The best conclusions avoid any sort of apology, do not suddenly introduce new ideas, and do not offer rambling afterthoughts. Conclusions are succinct and to the point. They do not require *thus, in conclusion*, or *finally* in the last paragraph. The conclusion needs no fancy artwork or the words "The End."

IN REVIEW

Concentrate on your main ideas during the first draft in order to build these three central parts:

1. An **introduction** that advances your thesis and that uses proven techniques to invite readers into your discussion of a narrowed topic
2. A **body** that classifies and explores with full factual data the major issues of the topic
3. A **conclusion** that affirms your judgment, expresses your concern, offers your solution, or gives a call to action

---

EXERCISE 2.1

1. Find an essay or an article whose beginning invites you to read further. Write an introduction of your own to imitate the strategy and structure of the model.
2. Read four or five essays in magazines such as *Atlantic, Harper's, Esquire*, or *New Yorker* or an essay anthology. Write down the title of each essay and the main strategy or method the authors used for the introductions and for the conclusions. Base your analyses on the strategies in **2b** and **2d**.

EXERCISE 2.2

1. Write two different opening paragraphs to your paper, using the different strategies discussed or listed in **2b**.

2. Write a rough draft of your paper's body. Discover ideas for the body by reviewing the information in **2c**. Remember to classify each major issue and examine each issue fully in one or more paragraphs.
3. Write two different conclusions to your paper, using the different strategies discussed or listed in **2d**.

Sample Paper: A First Draft

The following paper shows the rough draft that Carol Mathis wrote about the global problem of waste disposal. It contains obvious errors, but it begins the project and has potential. After a peer review, she revised and edited the draft and produced a finished version (see section **3d**).

Man-Made Mountains

They walk solemnly and silently across the man-made mountains of trash. This scene foreshadows the umpromising future of pollution, contamination, and destruction for the world. This immense problem does not distinguish between communists, socialists, or capitalists; rather, it includes all people regardless of social, political, or economic status. The problem of waste disposal stares directly into the face of mankind which diverts its attention from the evil eye. Several factors thoroughly reveal the intensity and enormity of the waste disposal porblem and faciltate the search for a solution. As the world population increases the waste increases as well; thus the problem is not a new one. While the vast earth of yesterday provided an ample amount of space for everyone and everything, the vast earth of today provides a minimum amount of space for the earth's inhabitants, not including their wastes. The irresponsibility and disregard for the environment emerged with the

The introduction leads to the thesis with a description that states the significance of the problem.

The thesis sentence appears at what should be the end of the first paragraph. It establishes the explanatory and persuasive nature of the essay.

What should begin the body of the essay develops three primary issues. This part of the paragraph addresses the problem of increasing populations and shrinking space.

introduction of artificial objects, not within the past decade or century. With each new age, paper, glass, plastic, styrofoam and other inventions promise to make people's lives more convenient and enjoyable. In reality, many of these "wonderful", "innovative" items expedite the decay and deteriration of the world.

Typographical errors will be corrected later.

For several years many people disposed of their wastes by burning it or dumping it far away from their property because the waste was an unsightly plague to human eyes. Eventually specialists and environmentalists declared that the mass burning of trash added to air pollution. Within the last few years people scrutinized and denounced both means of waste dicposal. These means of waste disposal results in several disturbing consequences. Burning trash pollutes the air and burying trash pollutes the lasnd and water. Carbon monoxides from factories and trash incinerators deplete the ozone layer. The depletion of the ozone layer has its consequences too. It allows dangerous ultraviolet rays to penetrate the atmosphere and reach the earth. Also, the landfills contaminate the soil and water with hazardous poisons. The depletion of the ozone creates a future problem and the contamination of soil and water also creates a problem for the environment because without clean air, soil, and water the earth's inhabitants cannot have sanitary food and water.

This paragraph examines traditional methods of disposal: burning and burying.

Fortunately, the problem is not irrevocable or _____ if the people of the world become involved. People must inform others who are unaware of the severity of the problem. People must voice

This paragraph suggests a solution for disposal: active participation by the public in recycling programs.

their concerns to important leaders in
government. People must become active in
environmental action groups. Thus, the
first thing needed to fight waste pollution is human action. When there is
enough human participation, the best possible solution, the recycling of reusable
items can begin to help the situation.
The recyling of these items eliminates
much of the waste in landfills, therefore, less space is needed and less pollution occurs.

Over the years mankind destroys its
environment which ensures its survival.
By careless, negligent disposal of
wastes, mankind kills its own world. The
use of recyling stations is an extremely
small price to pay for mankind to save
the endangered environment. Taking the
time today to recycle wastes ensures that
there is a tomorrow.

The conclusion shifts from explanation to persuasion to reaffirm the thesis.

Instructor's Remarks

The opening is effective, but your thesis could be more precise and less metaphoric—that is, personifying waste disposal, which "stares," may not be as effective as a straightforward statement. The introduction is affirmed effectively by your concluding paragraph. The first paragraph encompasses too much, though. Identify the topic sentences and watch your organization. The body touches on three vital issues, but your language is stuck on set phrases and pet words. Open your vocabulary. I notice excessive use of the verb *be* in the last half of the essay.

3

Revising, Editing, and Proofreading

Once you have your basic argument down on paper, in the form of the first draft, you can begin to improve your essay by revising and editing it. **Revising** looks at the larger aspects of your paper, verifying the structure and strengthening the focus and the details of the paragraphs. When you are content with the framework of your essay, you can concentrate on *how* you discuss your topic and make your point. **Editing** examines the individual sentences, analyzing sentence sense and word choice and correcting grammar, spelling, and punctuation. For most writers, this two-step process usually involves more than one draft. When you are satisfied with your paper and you type the final version, your ultimate improvement is to proofread it. **Proofreading** checks the final manuscript for any typographical errors.

3a Revise for coherence.

The goal of revising is to make sure your argument is coherent, that it is presented in a logical, reasonable sequence. (See chapter **48**.) You may need to reconstruct the conclusion to match the thesis — or vice versa — and to rearrange the content of some paragraphs for relevance. If you feel your argument is weak in some areas of the body, you may need to bolster it with greater or more specific detail. In extreme cases, if you are honest with yourself, you may need to rewrite the essay completely.

How do you go about revising the drafts? Ask yourself a few questions, such as the following:

1. Does the draft fulfill your intentions?
2. Does it address an identifiable audience?
3. Is the thesis clearly evident?
4. Is the thesis systematically supported by each paragraph?

Also, check each draft against your preliminary outline. Better yet, prepare a new outline of what you have written and compare it with your original plan. After considering the paper as a whole, examine closely the content of the four major parts: the title, the introduction, the body, and the conclusion.

Write a descriptive title.

The title of an essay, unlike one for fiction or for poetry, declares precisely the subject of the paper. It can be a word, a phrase, or, on rare occasions, a complete sentence.

As you revise the drafts of your paper, revise your title as well. Evaluate the title by asking yourself the following question: Does the title attract readers and inform them of the specific topic? If you are not satisfied with the answer, try to think of an innovative way to catch your readers' attention and to announce the topic without restating the thesis sentence. The examples below show the revision process some essay titles underwent:

> NO CLEAR FOCUS: Feeling Blue
> TOO GENERAL: Stress and Its Effects
> SPECIFIC: Depression among College Students
>
> NO CLEAR FOCUS: Television and Religion
> TOO GENERAL: Television Evangelists
> SPECIFIC: Electronic Salvation for Couch Potatoes

Re-examine the introduction.

As you evaluate the paragraph you have drafted for the introduction, ask yourself the following questions:

Revision Checklist: The Introduction

1. Is the subject clearly identified?
2. Is the focus narrowed to one central issue?

3. Does the introduction provide any necessary background information to make the topic relevant for the audience?
4. Is the reader invited into the essay with a brief anecdote, a description, or an example or two?
5. Is a consistent, appropriate point of view established?

If your introduction does not accomplish these goals, review section **2b**. If it generally accomplishes the goals but seems vague and lackluster, try to revise it to be more precise and to show your personality (see section **3b**).

Review and develop the body for unity.

Systematically revise the body of your paper to achieve a logical sequence of key ideas, to give evidence that supports your key ideas, and to guide the reader from one point to another with strong transitions.

First, read the **topic sentence**—the primary, guiding sentence—of each paragraph (see sections **4a–4c**). Does each topic sentence support your thesis and introduce a key idea? Does each paragraph grow logically from the material that preceded it? (Review section **1h** for information on structuring the body of the essay to support the thesis.)

Second, determine the sequence of your major ideas. Do they proceed from the least to the most important? Do they build to a climax? If not, reorder them so the essay moves clearly toward your conclusion.

Third, examine paragraph content. Do details support the topic sentence of each paragraph? Is there enough evidence? Have you provided sufficient examples? Are there gaps in the logic of any paragraph? Should some short paragraphs be combined? Should some longer ones be divided? Have you emphasized main ideas by placing them at the opening or closing of the paragraph? (For additional discussion of paragraphs, see chapters **4–7**.)

Fourth, provide transitional words and phrases that move the reader smoothly from one idea to another. *Later, meanwhile, consequently,* and *in contrast* are examples of transitional words and phrases (see section **8a**).

Finally, respond to any objections a reader might reasonably raise. Address the tough issues; refute the points you can; grant others. Your reader should not think, "Yes, but you overlook one fact" (see chapter **48**).

Revision Checklist: The Body

1. Does each paragraph have a topic sentence to control it and support the thesis?
2. Is the sequence of ideas effective?
3. Are the paragraphs fully developed?
4. Do strong transitions guide the reader from thought to thought?

Conclude with a final, emphatic point.

As you reread the draft of your conclusion, ask yourself the following questions:

Revision Checklist: The Conclusion

1. Does the conclusion say everything necessary to be convincing?
2. Has it reached a judgment, endorsed an issue, answered a question, or in some other way completed the argument?
3. Does it merely summarize the main points of the essay, or does it connect evidence in the body to the thesis?
4. Does the closing relate to the thesis without repeating what has already been said?
5. Have all apologies, afterthoughts, or minor new points been deleted from it?
6. Does it arrive at the ending without unnecessary labels, such as "in conclusion"?

If you are not satisfied with your answers to these questions, review section **2d** for ways to improve your conclusion.

EXERCISE 3.1

1. Rate as Good or Poor the following titles. How might you revise the poor ones to make them effective?

   Clothing
   Wearing a Tuxedo
   Clothing Varies in Different Parts of the World
   Clothes Change a Person's Appearance
   Blue Jeans
   My Favorite Dress
   Clothes Do More Than Cover the Body

Dressing for Power
Improper Dress for Proper Occasions
Sending Signals by Over-Dressing or Under-Dressing

2. Look at the tables of contents of some general interest magazines such as the *Atlantic Monthly* or *Harper's* or the Sunday *New York Times Magazine*. Are the titles of articles descriptive? Write down five titles that intrigue you and see if they accurately forecast the article. Discuss the titles in class. Can your classmates tell from the titles what the articles are about?

EXERCISE 3.2

1. Write a title for the rough draft that you wrote for exercise 2.2.
2. Revise the first draft of the paper you developed for exercise 2.2. In particular, evaluate your introduction, body, and conclusion. Add more information and details, if necessary. Consider moving ideas, paragraphs, and information around, especially in the body, so the progression of key ideas is logical.

3b   Edit for tone, point of view, and general mechanics.

Editing addresses smaller details than revision, but it has equal importance: it concentrates on sentences, words, grammar, mechanics, punctuation, and spelling. (See parts **5–8** and the revision symbols on the back endpapers.)

Edit for an appropriate tone.

Tone is the attitude your writing conveys to the reader about your subject. Your paper's tone may be humorous, angry, reflective, puzzled, unhappy, critical — in short, any attitude you can support. Edit words, phrases, and sentence structure to convey tone.

> HUMOROUS AND LIGHT: Crashing Daytona Beach in shorts or cutoffs, soaking up a few rays, and enduring a severe case of titillation, the average college student suffers gloriously through spring break.

SERIOUS: The migration of college students to the Florida beaches every spring may release suppressed emotions, but it also activates an overflow of indiscreet, irresponsible, and even bizarre behavior.

Be consistent. If you start seriously, then end seriously. A flippant phrase in a serious context will startle your reader and may cause him or her to lose confidence in your writing.

It's wise to be calm, courteous, and considerate of everyone in the office when you begin a new job. *If you mouth off, you could be canned.* Therefore, listen more than you talk, work more than you *goof off,* and meet every deadline.

The italicized slang phrases do not fit the subject matter or the formal tone of the paragraph.

If you are being humorous, use words that exaggerate and echo your meaning:

Buzz. Zap! Listen to the summer sounds of the great mosquito war.

Match your tone to the formality of your topic. Avoid the light-hearted approach if you are serious about a serious subject, such as the spread of malaria by a new strain of mosquitoes:

Malaria is caused by protozoans, parasites that live in part within female *Anopheles* mosquitoes and then live in part within red blood cells of human beings.

As you can see, formal, long words in a nontechnical paper sound pompous:

Many students who select a professional curriculum leading toward law school matriculation will major in a political science program.

The word *pre-law* can replace the ten-word clause and restore a matter-of-fact tone:

Many pre-law students major in political science.

Edit for an appropriate and consistent point of view.

Point of view in writing refers to the use of first person (*I* or *we*), second person (*you*), and third person (*he, she, it, they*). Choose and *maintain* one of these viewpoints for your paper, depending on your purpose. (See also sections **1b** and **1c**.)

> INCONSISTENT: *Some executives* use subliminal advertising routinely to reach *your* psyche and to touch *your* libido. *I* saw one perfume ad recently in which a woman and three men were all nude. To *me*, that's not even subliminal!

The passage above shifts from "they" to "I," to "you" without reason. Edit for consistency.

> CONSISTENT: Some executives use subliminal advertising routinely to reach the psyche of the audience and to titillate. From sophisticated perfume ads to common grocery store displays, the advertisers sell greed, sex, ego, death wishes, and — along the way — a product.

This edited version keeps its third-person focus on the advertising executives.

First person

Use the first person (*I* and *we*) for expressive writing — personal narration, reflections, position papers, editorials, and letters (see section **1b**):

> As *I* recall, my discovery that hard work pays dividends occurred when *I* passed second grade after a serious six-week probationary period.

However, avoid first person in serious academic writing so your work focuses on the subject, not on yourself.

> INAPPROPRIATE: When *I* looked in the library for information about children between the ages of two and four, *I* found that two-year-olds did not know the difference between right and wrong but three- and four-year-olds did.

Editing to remove "I looked" and "I found" places focus on the primary topic, the children, not on the interviewer.

> BETTER: Evidence shows that two-year-olds cannot tell the difference between right and wrong but that three- and four-year-olds can.

(See also chapter **31**.)

Second person

Use the second person (*you*) in informative writing, especially in how-to instructions:

> First, *you* must dig a hole about twice as large as the root ball of the tree.

Use *you* to address a specialized audience (see section **1c**):

> For *your* first lesson in scuba diving *you* need not bring any equipment.

In general writing, when you are not giving directions, do not address the reader with *you*:

> POOR: Scuba diving is one of the most interesting sports *you* can learn. When *you* take the first dive under water, *you'll* discover a strange and colorful world unlike anything *you* will see on land.

Edit to feature scuba diving, not to address the readers.

> BETTER: Scuba diving is a fascinating sport. Under the water, *divers* see a strange and colorful world unlike anything that exists on land.

Similarly, edit to avoid an accusatory tone.

> MISLEADING: When *you* take cocaine *you* endanger *your* life. The "rush" can interrupt the life-sustaining electrical impulses from *your* brain to *your* heart.

This passage implies that the reader does or will take cocaine. The edited version implies that the reader seeks information.

BETTER: Cocaine users endanger *their* lives. A cocaine rush can interrupt the life-sustaining electrical impulses that the brain sends to the heart.

Third Person

Use the third person (*he, she, it,* or *they*) for most explanatory writing to emphasize the subject.

Competitive bodybuilding gains in popularity every year. It threatens to surpass weightlifting in number of participants.

Avoid the overly formal use of *one* or *one's.*

PRETENTIOUS: *One's* general health can be improved by body-building, and it makes *one* more conscious of *one's* physical appearance.

BETTER: Bodybuilding improves the health of all participants and makes *them* conscious of *their* physical appearance.

For an additional example of third-person point of view, see the paragraph on advertising that began this discussion (page 48).

Edit every sentence.

As you read the sentences for consistency of both tone and viewpoint, be aware also of voice, tense, and grammar. Be willing to change or delete entire sentences that do not develop your ideas, that fail to support your thesis statement, or that repeat information.

Edit for strong active verbs to avoid excessive use of "to be" verbs (*is, am, are, was, were*). (See chapter **31**.)

It was a stormy day when we were driving *hampered our drive* to Mount St. Olympus.

Maintain a consistent tense unless you have good reason to switch (see chapter **30**):

After about an hour the rain *became* mixed with snow, so I *drove* cautiously along the twisting mountain road. Jeff *awoke* with a start when I *slid* on gravel at the road's edge.

Make sure the subject and the verb agree in number in each of your sentences (see also chapter **26**):

> The committee composed of eight members agree~~s~~ by this reso-
> lution to fund Grant 56.

Watch for these common grammatical traps, as well as for any others that may be especially troublesome for you:

> Misplaced and dangling modifiers (chapter **12**)
> Incorrect pronoun reference and case (chapter **27**)
> Unintended sentence fragments (chapter **24**)
> Fused sentences and comma splices (chapter **25**)
> Short, choppy sentences (chapter **8**)
> Shifts in tone, voice, and mood (chapter **15**)

Edit every word.

When you are satisfied with the content of the sentences, look closely at the individual words.

Avoid the use of slang words, vulgar words, and jargon (see sections **16b** and **16c**).

> Purists dislike the ~~new digitized~~ colorization *of* ~~process being ap-~~
>
> ~~plied to~~ old black-and-white movies for television.

Consult a dictionary and a thesaurus to make sure you know a word's meaning as well as its possible connotations (see sections **17c** and **17d**).

Eliminate redundant phrases and deadwood (see chapter **18**):

> He ~~is a person who~~ . . .
>
> ~~The reason why this is so is~~ because . . .
> *Since*
> ~~In light of the fact that~~ . . .
>
> ~~In~~ today's ~~modern society~~ . . .

Avoid overused, imprecise words such as *thing, time, matter, to do.*

> ~~The thing that matters most is to~~ do it right the first time.

Avoid words that stereotype or derogate any person on the basis of sex, race, nationality, creed, age, or handicap (see section **17f**).

Finally, look at each figure of speech to be sure that it is appropriate and fresh, not strained or mixed (see chapter **19**).

Editing Checklist

1. Does the writing have an appropriate tone for the subject and the target audience?
2. Does it maintain a consistent point of view?
3. Is every sentence relevant, accurate, and grammatically correct?
4. Does every word make a precise contribution to the essay?

A sample of student editing

[1] *In the legal system,* Probation ~~in the courts means~~ *refers to* a conditional testing period for a convict ~~who gets to live as a civilian outside~~ *released from* prison. [2] ~~What's more,~~ *But* ~~probation also applies to new jobs because~~ *everybody goes through probationary periods.* Employees *in new jobs* go through conditional periods when managers examine ~~your~~ *their* characters, abilit~~y~~*ies*, and ~~your~~ qualifications~~ to do a good job.~~. [3] *Even* college students ~~get~~ *are* put on probation when ~~you flunk out of~~ *they fail* too many classes.

As shown above, editing often becomes a matter of personal choice. Other writers might have edited the paragraph differently. Here are comments about these changes by the student writer. (The list numbers correspond to the sentence numbers.)

1. The phrase "In the legal system" seems more precise than "in the courts." The correction "released from" replaces a wordy and informal ("gets to") clause.

2. The new sentence introduces examples. The second-person "your" was changed to third-person "their" because this paragraph is explanatory, not a set of directions. The meaning of "qualifications" eliminates any need for "to do a good job."

3. "Fail" replaces the slang "flunk out" to maintain a formal tone.

EXERCISE 3.3

1. Edit the following paragraph for consistency of a serious tone.

Any basketball player can hotdog on the hardwood. The reactions of the coaching staff, however, differ from case to case. Sometimes coaches will chastise and bench a player who perpetually plays to the audience, yet they allow other ego-centered performers to play an entire game. The difference is manifest in production: the player who cans at least 30 points every game can play the fool now and then, but the marginal performers must keep their acts clean.

2. Edit the following paragraph to establish a consistent point of view. Revise it three times: once to put it in the first person, once to give directions in second person, and once to focus on the subject with the third person.

I remember the October evenings when my sister and I made several jack-o'-lanterns to place in our front yard for Halloween. A jack-o'-lantern, of course, is a pumpkin. You first cut it open, scrape out the gooey contents, and cut out the eyes, nose, and mouth. At night you must insert a lighted candle inside the pumpkin so that a scary, glowing face will greet all visitors. The jack-o'-lantern is a mythic tradition; its original purpose, now lost in antiquity, presumably was to light the way through darkness for lost souls. Sis and I didn't know about all the implications, but we knew that our front porch needed a jack-o'-lantern each and every year.

3. Edit every sentence and word of the following paragraph. Change passive constructions to the active voice, combine short sentences, correct discriminatory language, delete unrelated sentences, and cut redundant phrases and deadwood.

A writing notebook should be written in with several written entries every week or otherwise it is wasted and rather useless. Most professionals keep a journal. My aunt used to write in a personal diary every evening. I don't know what happened to that diary; I'd sure love to read it to see what she thought about me. Anyhow, a serious writer will record his ideas and observations so that later, at an appropriate time and place sometime in the future, he can consult this valuable resource of personal thoughts.

4. Edit the following paragraph for grammatical errors. Correct errors in subject-verb agreement, dangling modifiers, pronoun use and reference, word usage, and comma splices.

I just learned that my roommate of last year has AIDS. I know what your thinking, do I have it to. No, I don't think so, but I worry that I might develop the symptoms, which, I understand, appears first as weight loss. To hopefully alleviate the fears of my friends and relatives, a blood test is scheduled for next week. When we will all be assured that I am not carrying the abhorrent germs.

5. Rephrase these sentences to remove the pretentious use of *one* and *one's*.

One's general safety on campus after dark can be secured by one's walking always with one's roommate or friends.

When one reports to the plant supervisor, one quickly learns the meaning of verbal abuse.

6. Revise the following paragraph to change the point of view from the second person to the third person. Do not, however, replace "you" with "one" or "it."

Early American Indians knew that corn could crossbreed, but they thought if you planted two different kinds their roots would mingle to produce a third kind. It was not until 1724 that Judge Paul Dudley of Massachusetts saw that if you plant two different kinds of corn on opposite sides of a river you will get hybrid corn, but if you separate the corn with a high fence, still letting the roots grow together, you will not. Dudley realized that you have to allow open air for corn to crossbreed, but he did not know that you need to use pollen from the male corn tassels to fertilize the female corn silks.

3c Proofread with care.

Mechanical and grammatical errors in an essay suggest carelessness that can seriously weaken your credibility, so proofread your final paper carefully. Reading it aloud is a good way to spot errors. If necessary, make corrections neatly in ink. (Marring a page with a few handwritten corrections is better than leaving damaging errors in your text.)

Check especially for typographical errors, whether you typed the paper or had somebody else type it. Look particularly for errors in spelling and punctuation.

If you have used source materials in your paper, read any quotation against the source for possible transcription errors, and be sure that you have accurately cited the source. (See chapter **50**.)

3d Use peer review to help you revise your paper.

Most professional writers submit their manuscripts — both fiction and nonfiction — to friends, peers, and editors as part of the revision process. Most business executives distribute important reports to associates for review. You too should learn to rely on the opinions of other people. Ask associates, friends, or classmates to read one of your drafts.

You can expect honest, critical evaluation, especially if you help reviewers target their criticism. Give them a few specific questions to consider:

Questions to Ask of Your Reviewers

1. Is the paper's main idea expressed clearly?
2. Does it address an audience? Who is it?
3. Has the paper reached a conclusion? Is it clear and effective?
4. Does it take risks and say new things, or does the content appear safe, conventional, or even dull?
5. Do *you* care about what the paper says?
6. Is the thesis defended and supported?
7. Does the paper need to cite authorities on this topic?
8. Does the essay contain enough examples?
9. Is anything omitted that you think is necessary?
10. Did you enjoy reading the essay?
11. Is the writing style clear and crisp or is it wordy and trite?
12. Are the voice, attitude, and tone appropriate to the content?

Sample peer review

The following is a peer review by Jack Throckmorton of Carol Mathis's rough draft (see pages 39–41) of "Man-Made Mountains." See Mathis's revisions below in response to the review.

Peer Review by *Jack Throckmorton* for a paper by *Carol Mathis*

	poor	good
I enjoyed reading the essay.	1 2 3 4	(5)

Comment: *Yes, you awaken the reader to the seriousness of waste and crowded city dumps.*

The thesis is clearly expressed.	1 2 3	(4) 5

Comment: *I identify it as waste disposal's evil eye and mankind's disregard. A good thesis*

The title is specific.	1 2 3	(4) 5

Comment: *The title is good but not precise.*

The essay addresses an identifiable audience.   1 2 3 ④ 5

Comment: *Everybody is guilty: teenagers with fast-food wrappers, homeowners with stuffed garbage cans, businesses with huge dumpsters, and industries with barrels of contaminants.*

The opening invites the reader into the essay and   1 2 ③ 4 5
clearly focuses the subject.

Comment: *Nice touch about "man-made mountains." The first paragraph is long, though, and needs more focus.*

Each paragraph contributes new, fully developed   1 2 3 ④ 5
ideas.

Comment: *You go from the problem to the old methods and then to the new recycling idea - seems good to me.*

The conclusion reaches a judgment, endorses an   1 2 3 4 ⑤
issue, and does more than summarize.

Comment: *The pitch about the edge of crisis is appropriate - shake 'em and shock 'em.*

Additional tips for revising the essay: *I'd like to see more information, more specifics, such as the problems of disposable diapers, Exxon's oil spillage in Alaska, McDonald's styrofoam containers, and so forth - details and name brands.*

A revision in progress

Here is Mathis's next draft, which she revised and edited from the remarks on the peer review and the instructor's comments (page 41).

Scanning the desolate landscape, mourning the numerous losses, and hoping for a miraculous solution,

Man-Made Mountains

They walk solemnly and silently across the man-made mountains ~~of trash.~~ This *discouraging* scene foreshadows the u*n*promising future of pollution, contamination, and destruction for the *environment,* ~~world.~~ *and these unhappy actors represent the next generation of americans, Soviets and Japanese* This immense problem does not distinguish between communists, socialists, or capitalists; rather, it ~~includes~~ *encompasses all inhabitants of the earth,* ~~all people~~ regardless of *growing* social, political, or economic status. The problem of waste disposal stares directly into the face of *this* mankind which diverts its attention from the evil eye. Several factors *when studied and examined,* thoroughly reveal the intensity and enormity of the waste disposal problem and facilitate the search for a solution. *but* As the world population increases, the waste increases as well; ~~thus~~ the problem is not a new one. While the vast earth of yesterday provided an ample amount of space for *humans, animals, plant life, and trash, the shrinking* ~~everyone and everything, the vast~~ earth of today provides a minimum amount of space for the earth's inhabitants, not including their wastes. The irresponsibility and disregard for the environment *did not* emerged *it emerged* with the introduction of artificial objects *— synthetic items designed to improve life.* ~~not within the~~ past decade or *even the past* century; With each new age *the remarkable inventions (such as* paper, glass, plastic, styrofoam ~~and other inventions~~ promise to make people's lives more convenient and enjoyable. In reality, many of these "wonderful" "innovative" items expedite the *degradation* ~~decay~~ and deterioration of the world. *in one of two ways:*

For several years many people disposed of their wastes *The majority burned their trash* by burning it or *by* dumping it ~~far away from their property~~

because dumping it left a continuous unsavory sight. But
~~because the waste was an unsightly plague to human eyes.~~
Eventually specialists and environmentalists declared that
the mass burning of trash added to air pollution. Within the
have
last few years people scrutinized and denounced both means of
s
waste di~~s~~posal. These means of *the* waste disposal result~~s~~ *of* in
several disturbing consequences. *Many scientists believe that the* Burning *the* trash pollutes the
the *of*
air, and burying trash pollutes the la~~s~~nd and water. ~~Carbon~~ *excessive*
in the atmosphere *chlorofluorocarbons*
~~monoxides~~ from factories and trash incinerators deplete the
in turn,
ozone layer. The depletion of the ozone layer, ~~has its~~
through *ic layers* *moreover*
~~consequences too.~~ ~~It~~ allows dangerous ultraviolet rays to
penetrate the atmosphere and reach the earth. ~~Also,~~ the *dangerous*
presence of
landfills contaminate the soil and water with hazardous
While *more*
poisons. The depletion of the ozone creates a future problem.
for the environment, *an immediate*
and the contamination of soil and water ~~also~~ creates a
problem for the environment because without clean ~~air,~~ soil,
and water, the earth's inhabitants cannot have sanitary food
and water, *which are vital for human survival.*
irreversible
Fortunately, the problem is not irrevocable or ~~A~~
inhabitants *concerned and take action.*
if the ~~people~~ of the world become ~~involved.~~ People must
inform others who are unaware of the severity of the
influential
problem. People must voice their concerns to ~~important~~
leaders in government. People must become active in
element necessary
environmental action groups. Thus, the first ~~thing needed~~
concern and involvement. Next,
to fight waste pollution is human ~~action.~~ When there is
involvement
enough human ~~participation~~, the best possible solution, the
such as aluminum, glass, plastic, and paper —
recycling of reusable items can begin to ~~help the situation.~~
The recyling of these items eliminates much of the waste
necessary
in landfills, therefore, less space is ~~needed~~ and less
and contamination, moreover, the recycling of paper saves thousands
pollution occurs.
of trees each year. time, the one thing that ensures its survival —
Over ~~the years~~ mankind destroys its environment, ~~which~~
~~ensures its survival.~~ By careless, negligent disposal of

its   ~~murders~~   *and commits suicide in the process.*
∧wastes, mankind ~~kills~~ its own world∧ The use of recyˇling

stations is an extremely small price to pay ~~for mankind~~

to save the endangered environment. Taking the time today

to recycle ~~wastes~~ *may* ensure*s* that there is a tomorrow.

The final version: Student essay

Below is Carol Mathis's final version of her essay, which she re-
fined from her second draft, above.

Man-Made Mountains

Scanning the desolate landscape, mourning the numerous

losses, and hoping for a miraculous solution, they walk

solemnly and silently across the man-made mountains. This

discouraging scene foreshadows the unpromising future

of pollution, contamination, and destruction for the

environment, and these unhappy actors represent the next

generation of Americans, Soviets, and Japanese. This immense

problem does not distinguish between communists, socialists,

or capitalists; rather, it encompasses all inhabitants of the

earth, regardless of social, political, or economic status.

The growing dilemma of waste disposal stares directly into

the face of humankind, which diverts its attention from

the problem.

The waste disposal problem is not a new one, but as the

world population increases, the waste increases as well, and

the problem intensifies. While the vast earth of yesterday

provided an ample amount of space for humans, animals, plant

life, and trash, the shrinking earth of today provides a

minimum amount of space for the earth's inhabitants, not

including their wastes. The irresponsibility and disregard

for the environment did not emerge within the past decade or

even the past century; it emerged with the introduction of
artificial objects--synthetic items designed to improve
life and make it easier. With each new age, the remarkable
inventions (such as paper, glass, plastic, and styrofoam)
promise to make people's lives more convenient and more
enjoyable. In reality, many of these "wonderful,"
"innovative" items expedite the degradation and
deterioration of the world.

For several years many people disposed of their waste
in one of two ways: by burning it or dumping it. The
majority burned their trash because dumping left a
continuous, unsavory sight. But eventually specialists and
environmentalists pointed out that the mass burning of trash
added to air pollution. Within the last few years, people
have scrutinized and denounced both means of waste disposal
because of disturbing consequences to the environment. The
burning of trash pollutes the air, and the burying of trash
pollutes the land and water. Many scientists believe that
the excessive chlorofluorocarbons and other waste products
pumped into the atmosphere from factories and trash
incinerators deplete the ozone layer. The depletion of the
ozone layer, in turn, allows dangerous ultraviolet rays to
penetrate through the atmospheric layers and reach the
earth. Moreover, the seepage and runoff from landfills
contaminate the soil and water with severe toxins. While the
depletion of the ozone creates a future problem for the
earth's inhabitants, the contamination of soil and water
creates an immediate problem. Without clean soil and water,
the earth's inhabitants cannot survive.

Fortunately, this problem is not irrevocable or
irreversible if the inhabitants of the world become concerned

and take action. People must inform others who are unaware
of the severity of the problem. People must voice their
concerns to influential leaders in government. People must
become active in environmental action groups. Thus, the
first element necessary to fight waste pollution is human
concern and involvement. Next, when there is enough human
involvement, the best possible solution--the recycling of
reusable items such as aluminum, glass, plastic, and
paper--can begin to help. Recycling these items eliminates
much of the waste in landfills; therefore, less space is
necessary and less pollution and contamination occur.
Moreover, the recycling of paper saves literally thousands
of trees a year. We need the trees because they filter
many toxins from the air and help keep vital topsoils
from eroding.

Over time the world's population has threatened the
one thing that ensures its survival: its environment. By
careless, negligent disposal of its wastes, humankind murders
its own world and commits suicide in the process. Recycling
waste products is an extremely small price to pay to save the
endangered environment. Taking the time today to recycle may
ensure that there is a tomorrow.

Instructor's Remarks

Good work, Carol. Your essay shows effective explanation of a
crucial problem and is persuasive. The body is solid, though I
would prefer more specific detail in every case. For example,
who are you referring to when you say "people"? Give some
examples. The language level is effective, but be careful: using
larger words drawn from a thesaurus is not the same as using
accurate, forceful words.

Paragraphs

4
Paragraph Unity
5
Writing Coherent Paragraphs
6
Developing Paragraphs
7
Improving Paragraph Style

CHAPTER

4

Paragraph Unity

4a Develop one key idea and focus it with a topic sentence.

A unified paragraph focuses on one key idea and develops it with details, examples, and comparisons. That key idea is stated in the **topic sentence**, which provides direction to its paragraph just as a thesis sentence provides direction to the entire essay. This next paragraph is unified because every sentence supports and builds from the topic sentence, which is highlighted in italics.

> *Everyone must have had at least one personal experience with a computer error by this time.* Bank balances are suddenly reported to have jumped from 379 dollars into the millions, appeals for charitable contributions are mailed over and over to people with crazy-sounding names at your address, utility companies write that they're turning everything off—that sort of thing. If you manage to get in touch with someone and complain, you then get instantaneously typed guilty letters from the same computer, saying, "Our computer was in error, and an adjustment is being made in your account."
> —LEWIS THOMAS, "Why Can't Computers Be More Like Us?"

The topic sentence has three functions. First, it stimulates the writer to create detailed sentences of evidence and support. Note how the next topic sentence invites a listing of specific settings and dark images.

Hawthorne uses gloomy settings and dark images to reflect his general mood. One character, a minister, wears a "black" veil that frightens his congregation. Goodman Brown goes into the forest at "night." Robin, in "My Kinsman, Major Molineux," walks a street of nightmares. Hester Prynne in *The Scarlet Letter* comes out of a dark jail to face her tormentors. Hawthorne's characters repeatedly journey in darkness toward unfortunate events.

—PATTY JOHNSON, student

In contrast, an unfocused topic sentence might lead to a wandering, unorganized paragraph. For example, if the topic sentence were "Hawthorne's settings reflect his attitudes about New England," all of Hawthorne's settings—gloomy, bright, indoors, outdoors—would need development, creating a bulky and awkward paragraph.

Second, a good topic sentence relates one paragraph with another. Note below how topic sentences explore separate issues of a central theme.

One way to save money is to make home repairs yourself. Fixing a leaking faucet yourself can save $30 to $55 for the service call and another $35 or so for the actual repair. Painting your own home can save as much as $1500. Checking the circuit breakers before calling the electrician will save about $50 in some cases.

Of course, some do-it-yourself habits can cause problems, even disaster. One of my neighbors bragged about saving money by doing odd jobs around the house himself. He even put pennies behind his fuses to save money. Last April, after years of pennies-behind-the-fuses, my thrifty neighbor smelled smoke and discovered that his fuse box had exploded. He spent over $800 to repair the damage.

—JENNY WILLIAMS, student

The topic sentence of the first paragraph makes a positive assertion; the topic sentence of the second paragraph establishes a contrast with the first.

Third, a good topic sentence relates the individual paragraph to the essay as a whole. It connects the paragraph to the essay's overall thesis sentence (see section **1g**). On this point you might wish to review the model essay in chapter **3**.

4b   Place the topic sentence for best effect.

The most common location for a topic sentence is at the beginning of a paragraph, as shown in all the examples in section **4a**. However, you can place it elsewhere for a purpose.

Since the topic sentence of your introductory paragraph is often your thesis sentence, it may appear at the *end* of the opening paragraph. In the next passage, which opens an essay on scientific scares, author Ellen Kunes builds toward her thesis sentence and her topic sentence.

> Scientifically speaking, 1989 has been a pretty rough year for my three-year-old godchild, Christine Mary. It hasn't been a bed of roses for me, either. That's because both of us have been warned that we are putting ourselves at an increased risk for cancer — me because I swallow a daily estrogen-laden contraceptive pill, and Chris because her all-time favorite snack is a tall, cool glass of apple juice. *We are the hostages of scientific scares — just two of 246 million in this country whose food and water and air and sex lives are subject to the perpetual squint-eyed scrutiny of a pack of study-loving sawbones.*
>
> — ELLEN KUNES, "Suckers for Science"

The introduction must act as an invitation, so the writer may not wish to announce a specific thesis too quickly. (See section **2b** on writing effective introductions.)

The closing paragraph or paragraphs, in many cases, may open with a topic sentence that recalls the thesis to remind readers of the essay's central issue. The paragraph can then progress to the final assertions. In the closing passage of their essay on the failure of bystanders to respond to emergencies, the writers first recall the thesis sentence that opened the essay and then they elaborate upon it.

> *Thus, the stereotype of the unconcerned depersonalized* homo urbanis, *blandly watching the misfortunes of others, proves inaccurate.* Instead, we find a bystander to an emergency is an anguished individual in genuine doubt, concerned to do the right thing but compelled to make complex decisions under pressure of stress and fear. His reactions are shaped by the actions of others — and all too frequently by their inaction.

And we are that bystander. Caught up by the apparent indifference of others, we may pass by an emergency without helping or even realizing that help is needed. Aware of the influence of those around us, however, we can resist it. We can choose to see distress and step forward to relieve it.

—JOHN M. DARLEY and BIBB LATANE,
"When Will People Help?"

The writers above restate the central issue, examine the implications, and state their convictions. See also the closing of the essay in chapter **3**.

The paragraphs of the essay's body should place their topic sentences in the most effective spot. After a transitional sentence, it might come second. In a long paragraph you might lead toward it in the middle and then expand upon it with further details.

One of my neighbors bragged about saving money by doing odd jobs around the house himself. He even put pennies behind his fuses to save money. Last April, after years of pennies-behind-the-fuses, my thrifty neighbor smelled smoke and discovered that his fuse box had exploded. The repairs cost over $800. *Obviously, home repairs can save money, but only if done properly.* Home repair requires three activities, all equally important: purchasing the correct equipment and supplies, using the proper tools, and knowing how to make the repairs.

The topic sentence is not buried because opening sentences point toward it and the closing sentence expands upon it.

4c   Eliminate irrelevant details.

Sometimes writers shift from the main idea in the middle of a paragraph and break the unity with irrelevant statements. The following writer, about halfway through, destroys the unity of a discussion about children.

Young children are highly susceptible to all influenza viruses. Their systems have not yet built an immunity to any viruses, so each one that comes along successfully attacks the new body. Old people have the problem but for different reasons. While most susceptible to many strains of influenza, children mix socially in kindergarten and grammar school classes. In that environment they pass around viruses rapidly, carrying diseases that may affect a large segment of a town's population. It is not uncommon for schools to suspend classes for a few days in order to stop an influenza epidemic.

The one digressive sentence, which begins "Old people," should be deleted to preserve the unity of the paragraph.

IN REVIEW

Stick to one point in each paragraph, use a topic sentence to focus the reader's attention on the paragraph's key idea, and place the topic sentence where it will be most effective.

EXERCISE 4.1   Find and underline the topic sentence in each of the following paragraphs. Also strike through any sentence that does not expand and develop its topic sentence.

1. The constitution of Canada is in part unwritten (like the one of Great Britain) and in part written (like the one of the United States). The unwritten constitution includes general usage and customs, ordinary laws, and some judicial decisions. The written constitution is called *The British North America Act*. It does not control all of North America, of course. As you probably know, Mexico has its own constitution. It is called a North America Act because in 1867 the British North America colonies wished to unite to form the Dominion of Canada.

2. Helen Keller was blind. She was deaf. Yet she learned to speak and to write so well that she earned a college degree at Radcliffe. As an advocate for the blind and deaf-blind, she gave lectures, wrote books and articles, appeared before legislative bodies, and traveled the world. Although she died in 1968, she remains today a notable example of a person who conquered not one but two physical handicaps.

3. Herman Melville wrote *Moby Dick* because he had a story to tell. The story evolved from his own adventures as a crew member on a whaling vessel. It was called the *Acushnet*. It sailed the South Pacific for 18 months before he jumped ship in the Marquesas Islands. *Moby Dick* blends adventure with mundane explanation of the whaling trade. On one level it

describes in great detail utilitarian matters, such as entire chapters on the sperm whale's head and the right whale's head. On the other level it narrates the obsession of Captain Ahab to hunt down and capture the elusive white whale that, years before, had taken a leg from the captain.

EXERCISE 4.2   Identify the topic sentences below that specify single, well-focused topics. Revise the others to make their topics more specific.

1. Movies are popular in my hometown.
2. In some ways, a movie resembles a stage play.
3. As an art form, movies have a brief history in comparison with music, poetry, or painting.
4. Movies both reflect and create social conditions.
5. Television stations air hours and hours of movies.
6. Although the first movie stars were not identified by name on the screen, the American public quickly identified its favorites.
7. Charlie Chaplin starred in several early movies.

EXERCISE 4.3   Underline the topic sentences in one section of a textbook and also in a magazine article. Be prepared to discuss these questions orally or in writing:

1. Do all the paragraphs have clear topic sentences? How often do they appear in the middle or at the end of the paragraphs?
2. Do the topic sentences in textbooks differ from those in magazine articles? How?
3. Can you use the topic sentences in your textbooks as an outline or guide to the content of a chapter?

Writing Coherent Paragraphs

Coherence means that sentences hold together in a reasonable sequence. In comparison, *unity* (chapter **4**) means that all sentences focus on one key idea. A coherent paragraph bonds sentences into a whole because each sentence builds and grows upon those that precede it. Writers accomplish coherence by building a series of examples, by consistently comparing and contrasting, by tracing a sequence of events, or by constructing a network of related ideas. This next paragraph on how to eat an ice cream cone is coherent.

> Grasp the cone with the right hand firmly but gently between thumb and at least one but not more than three fingers, two-thirds of the way up the cone. Then dart swiftly away to an open area, away from the jostling crowd at the stand. Now take up the classic ice-cream-cone-eating stance: feet from one to two feet apart, body bent forward from the waist at a twenty-five-degree angle, right elbow well up, right forearm horizontal, at a level with your collarbone and about twelve inches from it. But don't start eating yet! Check first to see what emergency repairs may be necessary. Sometimes a sugar cone will be so crushed or broken or cracked that all one can do is gulp at the thing like a savage, getting what he can of it and letting the rest drop to the ground, and then evacuating the area of catastrophe as quickly as possible.
>
> — L. RUST HILLS, "How to Eat an Ice-Cream Cone"

The paragraph accomplishes four tasks necessary for coherence:

1. It has a clear, chronological progression of ideas to develop the general thesis (see section **5a**).

2. It uses parallel structures, such as the phrases beginning with "getting," "letting," and "evacuating" (see section **5b**).
3. It provides transitional markers, such as *then*, *now*, and *first* (see section **5c**).
4. It repeats key words *cone* and *eat* (see section **5d**).

5a Choose an organizing principle.

In a coherent paragraph each sentence proceeds logically and systematically to the next. The sentences sustain a clear sequence of ideas that are controlled by a single organizing principle—the topic sentence. For example, events occur from first to last (chronological order), illustrative detail is described from near to far (spatial order), and evidence builds from least to most important (climactic order). In other instances, sentences methodically shift from general information to specific examples, or they move from detailed, precise evidence to a general concluding sentence. They ask a series of questions and then answer them or establish a series of negative ideas answered by positive ones. The systematic arrangement keeps the paragraph and the reader on track.

Chronological order

Chronological order is the arrangement of material in the order that events happen or happened. Writers use it for narration, instructions, explanation of a process, and explanations where steps follow one after another. Coherence is lost in a recipe, for example, if instructions are given in a random order.

The next example narrates the order of events when a gerbil is dropped into the cage of a captive rattlesnake. The description alternates between the movements of the snake and the gerbil, but the reader can follow each action as it happens.

> The gerbil began to walk around the bottom of the big glass jar. Zebra, whose body was arranged in a loose coil, gave no sign that he was aware of the gerbil's presence. Under a leaf, over a rock, sniffing, the gerbil stepped up onto Zebra's back. Still Zebra did not move. Zebra had been known to refuse a meal, and perhaps that would happen now. The gerbil walked along the snake's back, stepped down, and continued along the boundary of the base of the jar, still exploring. Another leaf, another stone, the strike came when the gerbil was perhaps eight inches

from Zebra's head. The strike was so fast, the strike and the recovery, that it could not really be followed by the eye. Zebra lanced across the distance, hit the gerbil in the heart, and, all in the same instant, was back where he had started, same loose coil, head resting just where it had been resting before. The gerbil took three steps forward and fell dead, so dead it did not even quiver, tail out straight behind.

— JOHN MCPHEE, "Travels in Georgia"

The paragraph shows events as they happened — one step at a time and one strike at the end.

Spatial order

Spatial order is a form of description that moves the reader's eye progressively across a space. The passage above, for instance, shows the gerbil moving from leaf to rock to the snake's back and along the base of the jar.

Most writers use a single scene — a large jar holding a rattlesnake, a small workshop crowded with tools, a valley in the mountains. Then they move from one place to the next place within the scene, just as chronology moves from one action to the next within a fixed amount of time.

As the writer, you direct the attention of the reader from top to bottom, from left to right, from near to far, and so forth. However, do not move haphazardly from detail to detail. Begin at one clear point, such as the doorway to a room or a long-distance view toward a mountain, and proceed to the next focal point, then to the one beyond that, and so on.

The following paragraph, describing a solarium, effectively directs the reader's view.

The solarium was crowded with potted palms and ominous plants with broad leaves yellowed and browned at the edges. The air was heavy and moist. The flagstone floor was alternately slick and sticky underfoot. In the center there was a small unpainted iron fountain, its four-foot basin shaped like an open flower fluted at the edges. A hidden electric pump endlessly circulated five gallons of water through the center column, silently pushing it to spill into three progressively larger fluted receptacles. There were four small goldfish and some pennies in the bottom basin. Six dark green wicker chairs faced the fountain, with small circular tables between each pair.

— GEORGE V. HIGGENS, *Wonderful Years*

The passage coheres because the writing progresses spatially toward the center of the solarium, the fountain, and the chairs and tables that surround it, as if the writer were walking up to the fountain, looking at it, and then noticing the furniture.

Climactic order

Descriptions of events, issues, or items should be arranged by their relative importance to build to a climax. In this next example, the order in which the writer lists kinds of book owners reveals who *really* owns books.

> There are three kinds of book owners. The first has all the standard sets and best-sellers — unread, untouched. (This deluded individual owns woodpulp and ink, not books.) The second has a great many books — a few of them read through, most of them dipped into, but all of them as clean and shiny as the day they were bought. (This person would probably like to make books his own, but is restrained by a false respect for their physical appearance.) The third has a few books or many — every one of them dog-eared and dilapidated, shaken and loosened by continual use, marked and scribbled in from front to back. (This man owns books.)
>
> — MORTIMER ADLER, "How to Mark a Book"

Adler's passage progresses in climactic order from the book owner who never reads, to one who only briefly dips into books, and finally to the one who truly owns and uses books.

This next example shows the climax of a series of events. Helen Keller, who was both blind and deaf, writes how she discovered the meaning of the word *water*.

> We walked down the path to the well-house, attracted by the fragrance of the honeysuckle with which it was covered. Some one was drawing water and my teacher placed my hand under the spout. As the cool stream gushed over one hand she spelled into the other the word *water* first slowly, then rapidly. I stood still, my whole attention fixed upon the motions of her fingers. Suddenly I felt a misty consciousness as of something forgotten — a thrill of returning thought; and somehow the mystery of language was revealed to me. I knew then that "w-a-t-e-r" meant that wonderful cool something that was flowing over my

hand. That living word awakened my soul, gave it light, hope, joy, set it free! There were barriers still, it is true, but barriers that could in time be swept away.

       — HELEN KELLER, *The Story of My Life*

General-to-specific order

The most common paragraph is one that opens with a topic sentence, the controlling idea for what comes next, which may be illustrations, examples, definitions, comparisons, and other specific information. The following paragraph makes a general observation about Manhattan island and follows it with specific imagery.

For Manhattan really is an island, even now, separated from the mainland still by a channel just wide enough for the Circle Line boats to continue their pleasure circuits, and it is this condition of enclave that gives the place its sting. Like the bear [in its Central Park cage], its citizens are heightened, one way or another, by their confinement. If they are unhappier than most populaces, they are merrier too. If they are trapped in some ways, they are brilliantly liberated in others. Sometimes their endless pacing to and fro is sad to see, but when the weather is right and the sap is rising, then it assumes an exhilarating rhythm, and the people of Manhattan seem to dance along their avenue, round and round the city squares, in and out the sepulchral subway.

       — JAN MORRIS, "Manhattan: The Islanders"

Specific-to-general order

Some paragraphs build from specific details and examples to a general statement at the end. This type of paragraph usually has the topic sentence near or at the end of the paragraph.

Chinese restaurants in America were once places one went just to eat. Now one goes to dine. There are now waiters in black tie, cloths on the tables and space between those tables, art on the walls and decoratively carved vegetables on the plate — elegance has become routine in Chinese restaurants. What's more, in Chinese restaurants the ingredients are fresh (have you ever found frozen broccoli in a Chinese kitchen?), and the cooking almost never sinks below decent. By its nature Chinese food is cooked to order, except perhaps on buffets. And it is usually moderately priced. In other words, if you're among unfamiliar restaurants and looking for good value, Chinese restaurants now are routinely better than ever.

— PHYLLIS RICHMAN, "Hunan Dynasty"

General to specific and back to the general again

In some cases a paragraph opens with a topic sentence, has the support of specific details, and ends with another idea generated by the evidence. In the following paragraph Robin Lakoff introduces the special language used by women, follows with specific examples, and then moves to a generalization about men and their language:

"Women's language" shows up in all levels of English. For example, women are encouraged and allowed to make far more precise discriminations in naming colors than men do. Words like *mauve, beige, ecru, aquamarine, lavender,* and so on, are unremarkable in a woman's active vocabulary, but largely absent from that of most men. I know of no evidence suggesting that women actually *see* a wider range of colors than men do. It is simply that fine discriminations of this sort are relevant to women's vocabularies, but not to men's; to men, who control most of the interesting affairs of the world, such distinctions are trivial — irrelevant.

— ROBIN LAKOFF, "You Are What You Say,"

Question-and-answer order

Paragraphs sometimes move back and forth from negative to positive statements, from questions to answers, or from a variation of these two. The alternation between question and answer provides momentum to the paragraph, moving the reader quickly from one issue to another. In the following example, the writer uses the question-answer order to examine oppression.

Can oppressed people remain docile forever? No, the desire for freedom eventually displays itself, usually in the form of rebellion. Must emancipation result in angry confrontation, increased violence, and total anarchy, even war? No, in some cases the voices of a few dissidents and civil disobedience by the masses has changed laws, governments, and brought visible and invisible barriers crashing to the ground. Such was the case with

Mahatma Gandhi in India, Martin Luther King in America, Lech Walensa in Poland, and populist movements in other East European countries.

— HOMER ALEXANDER, student

IN REVIEW

Choose an organizing principle that serves the needs of your subject: *climactic order* for dramatic emphasis, *spatial order* for description, *chronological order* for events, *general-to-specific order* for explanation of a general idea, *specific-to-general order* to provide evidence before making an assertion, *question-and-answer order* to highlight a point, or variations of these basic orders.

EXERCISE 5.1 Underline the words in the following passage that establish chronological order.

My experience with your lawnmower has been a disappointment. First, I bought the lawnmower with confidence that your name guaranteed quality. Yet the mower has been in your repair shop more days than in my garage. Second, I bought a maintenance contract under the belief that your people could repair any malfunctioning parts of the lawnmower. Yet nobody can fix it to last for more than two mowings.

— ARLO ARRINGTON, student

EXERCISE 5.2 Underline the words in the following paragraph that establish a spatial order.

The color-beauty about Shadow Lake during the Indian summer is much richer than one could hope to find in so young and so glacial a wilderness. Almost every leaf is tinted then, and the goldenrods are in bloom; but most of the color is given by the ripe grasses, willows, and aspens. At the foot of the lake you stand in a trembling aspen grove, every leaf painted like a butterfly, and away to right and left round the shores sweeps a curving ribbon of meadow, red and brown dotted with pale yellow, shading off here and there into hazy purple. The walls, too, are dashed with bits of bright color that gleam out on the neutral granite gray. But neither the walls, nor the margin meadow, nor yet the gay, fluttering grove in which you stand, nor the lake itself, flashing with spangles, can long hold your attention; for at the head of the lake there is a gorgeous mass of orange-yellow, belonging to the main aspen belt of the basin, which seems the very fountain whence all the color below it had flowed, and here your eye is filled and fixed. This glorious mass is about thirty feet high, and extends across the basin nearly from wall to wall. Rich bosses of willow flame in front of it, and from the base of these the brown meadow comes forward to the water's edge, the whole being relieved against the unyielding green of the coniferae, while thick sungold is poured over all.

—JOHN MUIR, "Shadow Lake"

EXERCISE 5.3 Rearrange the following sentences into climactic order, putting the least important sentence first and progressively moving to the most important.

There, right there behind the bookshelf I find my long-lost sociology paper, the one I never submitted to the professor and, consequently, the one that changed an A to a C. The dreadful day has arrived. My roommate proceeds to dump all trash and abandoned wall decorations into the hall, which soon becomes impassable. Why does graduation day also require a moving day? I snatch the UT pennant from his hand just before it too reaches the dump heap. I place three overdue library books next to the door.

EXERCISE 5.4 First, write a paragraph in spatial order describing a room or other place. Second, rewrite the paragraph to show action within a time frame. The following paragraphs are examples of the two forms.

SPATIAL: The bright lights of the arena glistened from the hardwood floor with a brilliance that was almost blinding. The crowd ringed the playing court, waving banners as the cheerleaders jumped and clapped to the rhythm of the band. High above the baskets at the far end the red lights of the scoreboard patiently showed a line of zeros, waiting for the game to start.

CHRONOLOGICAL: As I entered the arena with the team, the bright lights glistening from the hardwood floor momentarily blinded me. Then, as the band saluted our entrance, I was almost deafened by the tremendous roar of the crowd. In just a few minutes the scoreboard would begin its countdown toward loss and victory.

EXERCISE 5.5 The following ideas for a paragraph appear in random order. Classify and arrange them in general-to-specific order.

taxes on cigarettes
income taxes
federal taxes on individuals
payroll taxes
taxes on commodities
taxes on gasoline
social security taxes

5b Use parallel structures to enhance paragraph cohesion.

Paragraphs with matching structures in phrases, clauses, and sentences will establish a rhythm that helps the reader move effortlessly from one sentence to the next. In this next example, three phrases in parallel form all modify the opening image of the Ferris wheel. Later, a parallel series closes the paragraph.

> The double giant Ferris wheel circled, *its rotating lights sparkling against the dark sky, its swaying benches rolling with the riders, its revolving wheels bicycling across the Nashville skyline.* It served as the midway calling card, for every carnival, whether erected at a huge state fair or a small county outing, must feature a brightly lit, eye-catching ride, one that *frightens the children, dazzles the youthful,* and *tempts the elderly.*
>
> — TOMMY SULLIVAN, student

The parallelism, indicated by italics, awakens the reader to the coherence of ideas. The next passage presents parallel sentence structures.

> To go into the hospital is to surrender your rights as an adult. It comes as a great shock. You have been deprived of your status as a person and become something like a parcel, to be handled as the hospital authorities think best. You are treated with infinite care, but the care, no matter how tender or scrupulous, is

still impersonal. You have become a thing, to be weighed, to be tested, to be X-rayed, to be slit open, sewn up again, venously fed with a saline drip, nursed. *You* do what *they* tell you, or, rather, you passively suffer what they in their wisdom do to you. Nurse knows best, and God help you if you argue.

— WALTER ALLEN, "The Pleasures of Illness"

This writer uses parallel clauses (*"You have been deprived," "you are treated," "you have become"*) and phrases (*"to be weighed," "to be tested," "to be X-rayed"*) to focus consistently on what happens to the patient.

5c   Use clear transitions.

Transitional words or phrases signal changes and show the relationship of one idea to the next. They join ideas. A paragraph without transitional pointers is as hard to follow as an unmarked trail. Note how the highlighted words and phrases in the following paragraph help readers find the way:

Of course, we all get lucky sometimes. *But* there is something to be learned about the structure of chance that may improve your percentage. *In the past*, the role of sudden flashes of insight in the process of discovery has perhaps been overemphasized. Much has *also* been said about the need for plodding, methodical work before and after these creative flashes. *But* I would like to present the case for chance. *What is chance?* Dictionaries define chance as something fortuitous that happens unpredictably and without discernible human intention. *True*, chance is capricious, *but* we needn't conclude that it is immune from human intervention. *Indeed*, chance plays several distinct roles when humans react creatively with one another and with their environment. *Of these*, only one is "pure blind luck."

— JAMES AUSTIN, "How to Make Your Luck Work for You"

The various transitions are not meaningless filler. They bind ideas together ("also," "indeed," "of these," "true"), they show contrast ("but"), and they introduce new points ("In the past," "What is chance?").

You can orient your reader occasionally with phrases such as *during the last years of his life, from a social and cultural point of view*, or *in some parts of the state*. The following list of transitional words and phrases also shows some ways to help your reader follow your meaning.

1. To introduce an example:

   for example, to illustrate, one kind of, for instance, specifically, let me name a few

2. To signal a time change:

   meanwhile, soon, after a short time, after, before, the next day, when, immediately, shortly, thereafter, finally, at the end of the day, one year later

3. To move to a new place:

   above, below, nearby, on the next counter, in the hallway, opposite, to your right, close, just beyond the wall

4. To add information:

   first, second, next, in addition, and, also, besides this one, furthermore, additionally

5. To show contrast:

   however, notwithstanding, on the contrary, nevertheless, but, yet, although, even though, still, on the other hand

6. To compare:

   in like manner, in the same way, also, likewise, similarly, in comparison, to place the two side by side

7. To show cause or effect:

   for this reason, consequently, as a consequence, as a result, therefore, so, thus, in effect

8. To conclude:

   in conclusion, in short, therefore, to sum up, accordingly, in closing

EXERCISE 5.6   Underline the transitional words and phrases in the following paragraph. Then change each one to a different but correct transition. Be prepared to discuss how the different transitions affect meaning.

On the morning of the first day at college, I met my future wife. She was standing in line near me to pay tuition fees. At first, she ignored my chit-chat about weather, the long waiting in line, the cost of fees. So I became desperate. "I think I'm falling in love," I murmured. Finally, she replied, "That's nice." Undaunted, I forged ahead. "It's you. I'm falling in love with you." She turned, looked me in the eye, and said, "Don't ever say that unless you really mean it." Months later, almost a year later, I said it with meaning by giving her an engagement ring.

—CALEB ALLEN, student

EXERCISE 5.7   Add transitional words or phrases to make the following paragraphs more coherent.

Use different tints, hues, and colors to create depth and interest in landscape painting. Lay a background of soft, muted colors. Build a middle portion with layers of progressively rich colors. Splash bright, bold colors across the foregrounds.

Dribbling quickly downcourt, I saw that we had two on one. I passed to Booker on the left wing. He drove straight toward the defender. He flipped the ball over his shoulder to me. I slam-dunked the winning basket.

Caffeine is a drug found in many products, especially coffee and soft drinks. The drug stimulates the central nervous system. It frequently causes nervousness and insomnia. Infrequently it causes confusion. It can cause irritability. The caffeine effect is increased in those women who use oral contraceptives.

5d   Repeat key words and phrases.

Keep your principal ideas before the reader by repeating key words and by renaming them with pronouns (such as *it, she, their,* see section **20b**). Mistakenly, some writers avoid using the same word more than once in a paragraph, believing they should strive for variety. Look again at the paragraph on *chance* on page 82. Austin uses the word *chance* six times. If your paper is about dogs, it will be more coherent if you repeat *dog* several times rather than use *canine, hound, mongrel,* and then *pooch.*

I bought my grandmother a dog. That may seem insignificant, but casual reading suggests that a dog makes a valuable companion for old people. Indeed, statistically, elderly people with dogs as pets live longer than others. Grandmother complained about this intrusion into her life, but I noticed her eyes sparkling as she petted and talked with her new dog.

— JELLETA JOHNSON, student

Repetition of the key word *junk* below maintains a coherence that keeps readers focused on the main point.

No one ever sings the praises of junk. Junk falls into several categories: the junk you read, the junk you eat, the junk you see, and the junk you create. I like all kinds. Junk keeps us humble. Junk reminds us to plant our high-stepping feet on the dirty old ground.

— SUZANNE BRITT, "Junk"

Be careful, however, of excessive repetition. Too frequent use of a key word can distract a reader and lessen the strength of the argument. Thus, every writer must carefully calculate the intended effect and use word repetition, pronoun usage, and synonyms judiciously.

IN REVIEW

Enhance paragraph coherence by the use of *parallel structures* to show similar ideas in a similar form, *transitions* to join one idea with another, and *repetition of key words* to keep the reader's eye focused on your principal idea.

EXERCISE 5.8 The writer of the following passage has searched diligently for synonyms and closely related words. Revise it with effective repetition of key words.

Some writers compose a first draft and assume they have written a finished paper. But creating an essay requires authoring more than one report. The best composers pen two, three, even four versions of a work.

EXERCISE 5.9 The writer of the following paragraph has carelessly repeated the same word time and again without using pronouns. Revise it to make it more coherent.

A triometer is a valuable weather instrument. The triometer gives an accurate reading of barometric pressure. The triometer also provides a thermometer that measures degrees in Fahrenheit. Finally, a triometer measures the percentage of relative humidity.

CHAPTER

6

Developing Paragraphs

Purpose, point of view, thesis sentence, and an outline — all these guidelines give essays a sense of direction and an organizational plan. They also guide the writer to methods of paragraph development. For example, one writer wished to defend a downtown shopping district against the intrusion of a suburban mall. With that purpose in mind, the writer set out to *describe* the features of the downtown area against those of a typical mall, to *narrate* short anecdotes about shopping experiences, and to *classify* the various services to consumers at each place. In addition, part of the essay explored the *causes* that led to mall development, and another part considered the *effects* of a mall on the vitality of old downtown districts.

6a Write fully developed paragraphs.

Too many short paragraphs in academic writing indicate that the writer has not considered the main points fully, has not developed each point with necessary details, and has not grouped related points together. Short paragraphs are useful for dramatic emphasis, for transition from one paragraph to the next, and for dialogue. But for the bulk of the essay, each topic sentence should be supported as fully as possible.

Consider the following:

> Remove a pair of horns from the head of a dead buffalo and place them alongside a good pair of Texas longhorns. The buf-

falo's horns look rather puny. They just do not compare with longhorns in size, length, and over-all beauty.

This short paragraph makes a point but does not support it with proof or examples. It is not only short but also dry and unconvincing. Now consider the original, which expands the comparison.

> Remove a pair of horns from the head of a dead buffalo and place them alongside a good pair of Texas longhorns. The buffalo's horns look rather puny. They just do not compare with longhorns in size, length, and over-all beauty. But place a good mounted head of a large buffalo bull beside a mounted longhorn's head — even if the longhorns are five or six feet from tip to tip — and the sheer bigness of the buffalo's dark shaggy head puts the monarch of the plains into immediate competition with the longhorn for honors. This may be one reason why so many mounted buffalo heads, instead of just horns, hung in saloons and other joints in the West, and even in the East, during the second half of the 1800s. Of course, the buffalo was considered wild game by the sportsmen of the day. The longhorn was not.
> — DAVID A. DARY, *The Buffalo Book*

Dary shows that the buffalo's head is at least equal to the longhorn's in size and grandeur, which may be why it was a popular trophy. The details in the paragraph describe carefully the differences between a longhorn's head and a buffalo's head, showing us the power of the buffalo.

If you have difficulty expanding upon the topic sentence, try some of the methods suggested here:

Ways to develop skimpy paragraphs
   1. Combine two or more paragraphs, especially if the points seem closely related.
   2. Point out and explain an exception to your main idea.
   3. Add examples and details that relate directly to your point. In particular, cite evidence, statistics, proof, or other data. Quote or paraphrase the words of an authority on the subject. Relate an anecdote that illustrates your subject. Trace the history of a subject.

These methods will provide structure to the paragraph, giving it shape, body, and substance. In addition to structuring the essay, you must also consider strategies of development that best meet your needs, as discussed in sections **6b** through **6i**. Rather than provide a general hodge-podge of information, you should guide your content by using narration, description, example, definition, process, cause and effect, classification or analysis, comparison and contrast, or a combination of these. Each method focuses your material to make the writing easier for you and the reading purposeful and intelligible for the reader.

6b   Narrate a story or a series of events.

Narration provides a more convincing and interesting example than a simple statement or summary. Used to explain a point or defend a thesis, a narration may take the form of an illustrative case study, a real-life example, or a series of significant events.

In the example below, writer Stan Luxenberg chose to use narration to explain why McDonald's expanded its product line.

> Louis Groen, the McDonald's franchisee in Cincinnati, had begun to grow desperate. In the early 1960s he was challenging the Big Boy chain that dominated his area, and it appeared he was losing. Groen could struggle along during most of the week but on Fridays his sales vanished. In heavily Catholic Cincinnati customers turned faithfully to the Big Boys on Fridays because they served fish sandwiches. To the franchisee the choice was clear: He would have to add fish or close the store. When Groen approached Ray Kroc with the idea, the chairman of the young hamburger chain was mortified. McDonald's was dedicated to selling only one product. "I don't care if the Pope himself comes to Cincinnati," he told the franchisee. "He can eat hamburgers like everybody else."
>
> The franchisee presented his case to other executives of the company, who proved more sympathetic. They prevailed on the stubborn chairman to try fish. . . . By 1965 so many franchisees requested the sandwich that the company made it a permanent menu item in stores around the country.
>
> —STAN LUXENBERG, "New and Improved"

This narration is clearly more interesting and more informative than a simple statement such as "McDonald's added fish sandwiches to satisfy franchisees in heavily Catholic cities."

Narrate only those events that develop your point and defend your thesis sentence, but you need not tell a story from beginning to end. You can start in the middle, flash back to a time in the past to show background, or jump forward to a time beyond the events to show outcome. But like spatial ordering, make sure the sequence is logical so readers can follow it easily.

In addition, use just one episode or one key figure to control the action in a narration. The reader will become confused if you shift focus from one character to another or from one setting to another in a single paragraph. In the passage above, the writer keeps focused on Groen and his desire to serve a fish sandwich.

6c Describe to illustrate your thesis.

Description makes vivid and memorable a special person, place, or experience that relates directly to the thesis of the essay. Descriptive details add convincing reality because they appeal to the reader's senses — sight, hearing, taste, smell, touch. Notice the difference between these two sentences, one descriptive and one not.

> Wrinkled old Nadine, wispy gray hair curling around her crocheted cap, trudged wearily up the worn hillside path.

> The old woman walked up the hill.

Many writers open an essay with a description that sets the scene for the entire piece. The next paragraph describes the river as darkness approaches. It establishes a setting for the subject — night rafting — as explained in the final, topic sentence.

> Two miles below Rome Ferry, I anchored for the night; listened to the soft, whirring sounds of nature and the distinguishable sounds of night life — night herons, a distant owl, a whippoorwill behind the trees — the sounds heard by raftsmen and riverfolk on a quiet night; watched the river, appearing in the darkness as shiny black satin in contrast to the dull black shadows that marked the banks; then watched the light of a rising, sharp-edged moon transform the surface into a polished silver strip. In the moonlight, on a good stage of water, a raftsman could run all night.
>
> — JACK KNOX, *Riverman*

This description of the river sets the stage for rafting by the light of the moon. The next paragraph provides a sweeping, panoramic view of the Great Lakes.

> There is a fifth coast of North America, one that lies not at the edge like the other four, not along the Atlantic or the Pacific or the Caribbean or the ice-swept, lonely Arctic, but at the center, along the mid-continental line. It is a spectacular coast, where surf rolls in from beyond the horizon to break upon broad sand beaches at the base of great dunes or crash against tall cliffs and bold, rocky headlands. It is a valuable coast, cradling a fistful of great port cities and dozens of smaller ones along its more-than-10,000 mile length. But it is also a *freshwater* coast, the coast of those five enormous, closely connected bodies of water we call the Great Lakes, and because of this it has been belittled, abused, misunderstood — and now may be about to die.
>
> — WILLIAM ASHWORTH, *The Late, Great Lakes:*
> *An Environmental History*

The description of a "spectacular coast" contrasts vividly with the image of dying lakes. The rest of Ashworth's book explores how the Great Lakes have been abused and how that has brought them to the brink of death. The opening description, then, prepares the reader for the topic sentence at the end of the paragraph that serves, in turn, as the thesis sentence for the entire book.

Like narration, description needs a frame of reference. In Ashworth's description above, the coast is the primary focus. But a description does not need to be all-inclusive. A few details, focused on your frame of reference, will show what you think is important.

6d   Use examples to clarify a concept and to stimulate interest.

An **example** points to a single item that represents a concept or an event: "The Spanish Inquisition is an example of religious terrorism, and the rack is an example of one of its instruments of terror." But good examples do more than list; they clarify abstractions, arouse interest, and specify the writer's meaning. A paragraph can feature one extended example or many short ones, depending on the subject matter.

Order examples for a purpose. You can use examples to build from minor to major ideas, to progress from past to present — or vice versa — and to create a specific impression. The following passage starts with a simple example and ends with an elaborate one.

Bloopers are the lowlife of verbal errors, but spoonerisms are a different fettle of kitsch. In the early 1900s the Rev. William Archibald Spooner caused a stir at New College, Oxford, with his famous spoonerisms, most of which were either deliberate or apocryphal. But a real one — his giving out a hymn in chapel as "Kinquering Kongs Their Title Take" — is said to have brought down the house of worship, and to have kicked off the genre. After that, spoonerisms got quite elaborate. Spooner once reportedly chided a student: "You have hissed all my mystery lectures. In fact, you have tasted the whole worm, and must leave by the first town drain."

—ROGER ROSENBLATT, *OOPS! How's That Again?*

The examples in this passage clarify the term *spoonerism* more clearly and concretely than the simple definition, "transposing the sounds of some words."

6e   Define your terminology.

A **definition** clarifies the meaning of a term, phrase, concept, or the nature of something. A good definition does two important things: it names the class to which the defined term belongs, and it differentiates the term from other members of its class to show its uniqueness. For example, a *human being* (term) is a *mammal* (class) that walks upright, lives in social groups, and thinks, speaks, and writes (differentia). The listed characteristics differentiate human beings from other mammals, but only one characteristic — the ability to write — sets human begins apart from *all* other mammals. A writer could use a definition like this as part of a discussion about the very human act of writing or about brain development in different animals.

The next paragraph defines a term and elaborates upon it with a series of examples.

Probation is a period of testing and trial to ascertain a person's suitability for a particular role. It takes various forms, but it appears everywhere in society. In the legal system probation is a conditional testing period for a convict who lives as a civilian outside the prison. Probation on the job means an employee must go through a conditional period during which supervisors judge the employee's character, ability, and qualifications. In college probation means that a student has temporary academic status for a low grade-point average and faces possible dismissal.

— JENNIFER WHITE, student

This writer defines *probation* as a testing period for people. She then extends it across the breadth of social behavior. When you define a term in this fashion, provide enough examples to clarify the concept.

6f Describe a process.

A **process** paragraph describes a series of actions to direct or inform the reader. Writers use the how-to directions to describe the process for reaching a desired end ("Become a Millionaire in Seven Easy Steps"). They use the informative process to explain nature ("From Froth to Frog: The Development of an Amphibian") or to trace the history or development of something ("The Changing Image of Children in Comic Strips"). Here is a how-to example:

> Everyone should know how to use the Heimlich maneuver. If you are confronted by somebody who is choking on a piece of food, stand behind the person and wrap your arms around his or her waist. Ball your hands into a fist just beneath the rib cage. Jerk inward and upward, hard, once, twice, even a third time if necessary. The rush of air forced up through the air passages will usually dislodge the obstruction.
>
> — THOMAS WASHER, student

Make sure when you explain a process that you include every necessary step or stage. Proceed in logical order, and guide your readers with transitional markers such as "first," "next," "then," "finally," and so forth. (See section **5c**.) Compare the following two instructions:

MISLEADING: After typing the document, remove the diskette from its slot when you have used the SAVE command.

CLEAR: After typing the document, use the SAVE command before you remove the diskette from the slot.

6g Discuss cause and effect.

Writers frequently trace **causes and effects** to explain why, to study outcomes, and to predict consequences. In other words, they answer the questions, "Why did this happen?" and "What can we now expect?" They may explore the causes and effects of scientific phenomena ("why stars fall"), historical events ("why the Vietnam War remains a bitter memory for Americans"), and social issues ("why Michael Jackson is popular").

The writer of this next passage states an effect in the topic sentence and provides the causes in the body of the paragraph.

> The U-2 spy episode in 1960 caused Cold War tensions to remain high. President Eisenhower and Soviet Premier Khrushchev had planned a conference for May 1960. However, a few days before the conference, the Soviets shot down an American U-2 spy plane. The pilot, Francis Powers, confessed to spying, and Eisenhower admitted that U-2 planes had been flying over the USSR for four years. When the summit conference began on May 15, Khrushchev demanded that Eisenhower apologize for sending planes over the Soviet Union. When Eisenhower refused, Khrushchev left the conference, which ended quickly the next day. Khrushchev's anger dashed the hopes for a thaw in American-Soviet relations.
>
> —OSCAR LAIRD, student

The next example suggests a hypothetical cause—nuclear war— and forecasts probable effects.

> Many biologists, considering the nuclear winter that these calculations describe, believe they carry somber implications for life on Earth. Many species of plants and animals would become extinct. Vast numbers of surviving humans would starve to death. The delicate ecological relations that bind together organisms on Earth in a fabric of mutual dependency would be torn, perhaps irreparably. There is little question that our global civilization would be destroyed. The human population would be reduced to prehistoric levels, or less. Life for any survivors would be extremely hard. And there seems to be a real possibility of the extinction of the human species.
>
> —CARL SAGAN, "The Nuclear Winter"

Sagan relentlessly hammers home the dire effects of a nuclear war.

6h   Classify or analyze.

Classification divides; **analysis** examines. Classification requires a plural subject—things, ideas, and events such as trees, economic theories, or swimming strokes. Analysis requires a single subject—

one thing, idea, or event such as a cigarette, grief, or a performance of *Medea*. Do not confuse the two.

To classify means to group one broad subject into manageable categories according to one principle. One writer, for example, classified three types of retail stores at suburban malls according to the principle of *function*: anchors (the large department stores), in-line tenants (the smaller stores along the concourse), and kiosks (the small, temporary structures set up in the middle of the concourse). Later, the writer classifed according to the principle of *customer base*: national, regional, and local.

To analyze means to divide one thing into its components and to examine each part in turn. Taken as a whole, anything can be analyzed by a systematic separation of the subject into distinct parts. Yet analysis has one additional function: it explores underlying principles, reasons, and historical or scientific factors. Thus the writer on suburban malls included an analysis of the *kiosk*, not merely to describe or define it but to explore its role in the management scheme of the mall and its relationship to other tenants.

The next two paragraphs show how one essay first classifies three "languages" of sex and then analyzes one of them, the nonverbal language.

> There are at least three "languages" of sex to which an individual becomes exposed: the technical and scientific vocabulary; the vernacular or "street" words; and the various forms of nonverbal communication. This latter category might also include "private languages" or words and signs that people who have an established relationship use in ways that have a special sexual meaning to them but not to others.
>
> Because sensual feelings begin in infancy, the first language of sex is nonverbal; it includes the physical pleasure a child feels through touch, warmth, closeness to the mother, and fulfillment of his physical needs. Soon the infant or young child becomes aware that parts of his body are sources of particular satisfaction. When the young child fondles his genitals, the only word the adult can find to describe the action comes from his adult experience—*masturbation*. For the adult this word may well carry a whole host of judgmental connotations, all of which he may impart to the child before the child can associate words with his actions. Thus, even before he knows the word "masturbation" or has any idea of the terms "good" and "bad," the child learns to associate his sensual pleasure with aftermaths of anger, distress, or punishment.
>
> — FRED V. HEIN, *Living*

Categories should be mutually exclusive and logical. For example, do not classify automobiles simultaneously as sports cars, station wagons, sedans, expensive cars, and fuel-injected cars. This list actually contains three categories: style, price range, and mechanical design. Use an outline to help you classify categories or parts.

6i   Compare and contrast items of equal importance.

Writers **compare** one item with another to show their similarities ("A computer is like the human brain" or "All wars have similar characteristics"). They **contrast** two or more related items to show their differences ("Even though many battles in both World War II and the Vietnam War were fought on the ground, the wars differed in several ways").

Whether you are comparing or contrasting items, do so systematically. Select parallel elements and discuss them one at a time. The following passage first compares the process of human thinking with the narrow boundaries of computer logic and then contrasts them.

> Large computers have some essential attributes of an intelligent brain: they have large memories, and they have gates whose connections can be modified by experience. However, the thinking of these computers tends to be narrow. The richness of human thought depends to a considerable degree on the enormous number of wires, or nerve fibers, coming into each gate in the human brain. A gate in a computer has two, or three, or at most four wires entering on one side, and one wire coming out the other side. In the brain of an animal, the gates may have thousands of wires entering one side, instead of two or three. In the human brain, a gate may have as many as 100,000 wires entering. Each wire comes from another gate or nerve cell. This means that every gate in the human brain is connected to as many as 100,000 other gates in other parts of the brain. During the process of thinking innumerable gates open and close throughout the brain. When one of these gates "decides" to open, the decision is the result of a complicated assessment involving inputs from thousands of other gates. This circumstance explains much of the difference between human thinking and computer thinking.
>
> — ROBERT JASTROW, "Brains and Computers"

Jastrow makes an **analogy**, which explains an unfamiliar or complicated subject by relating it to something well known and easily understood (see chapter **19**). Analogy adds richness to the writing by suggesting images and ideas beyond the ordinary. Here is another example using analogy to describe television and radio signals, showing readers a picture they can comprehend. The description ultimately enables the writer to compare and contrast the two forms of signals.

> A television station sends its transmission signals on a straight, level line. If you imagine throwing a rock into a pond to cause ripples in the water, you have an image of television transmission that flows outward across the surface. In contrast, radio signals bounce up and down from earth to clouds or earth to the stratosphere like a bouncing ball. Accordingly, television signals are cut short by a mountain, but radio signals can bounce over a mountain and travel across the country.
>
> — HARRY ZIMMERMAN, student

Comparisons are not limited to two single items. Writers may choose to compare numerous items with one major topic. For example, you might discuss caffeine as a drug by comparing its effects to cocaine, amphetamines, marijuana, nicotine, and alcohol. This passage demonstrates the technique:

> The best known of the maple trees, the sugar maple is also the most versatile of the maples, valued for its lovely shade and beautiful foliage, the lumber it provides for furniture, and the sap it provides for maple syrup. Also known as *rock maple* and *hard maple*, it grows from Newfoundland down through Georgia, across to Texas, and up to the Great Lakes. It has gray bark and dark green leaves which turn yellow, orange, and red in the autumn. Two cousins to the sugar maple have greater value as wood for furniture: the *bird's-eye maple* of Michigan, which has a spotted design; and the *figured maple*, which has twisted fibers and a wavy grain. For ornamental purposes, the *silver maple* is often chosen over the sugar maple because it grows rapidly; however, its wood is light and brittle. Like the sugar maple, the *red maple* has ornamental value, but it is primarily a lumber tree.
>
> — ANGELICA GREEN, student

The passage above develops a central subject, the sugar maple, and then compares it to its cousins.

A contrast usually focuses on the characteristics of first one subject and then the other. In the next passage author Bruce Catton contrasts General Robert E. Lee, an aristocrat of the South, with General Ulysses S. Grant, the son of a western tanner. He discusses first Lee's background and outlook, then Grant's. His final short paragraph summarizes the differences between the two men.

> The Virginia aristocrat, inevitably, saw himself in relation to his own region. He lived in a static society which could endure almost anything except change. Instinctively, his first loyalty would go to the locality in which that society existed. He would fight to the limit of endurance to defend it, because in defending it he was defending everything that gave his own life its deepest meaning.
>
> The Westerner, on the other hand, would fight with an equal tenacity for the broader concept of society. He fought so because everything he lived by was tied to growth, expansion, and a constantly widening horizon. What he lived by would survive or fall with the nation itself. He could not possibly stand by unmoved in the face of an attempt to destroy the Union. He would combat it with everything he had, because he could only see it as an effort to cut the ground out from under his feet.
>
> So Grant and Lee were in complete contrast, representing two diametrically opposed elements in American life.
>
> — BRUCE CATTON, "Grant and Lee: A Study in Contrasts"

Catton's discussion of Grant and Lee extends itself to a contrast of the political philosophies of the two sides in the conflict, the Union and the Confederacy.

6j Combine paragraph patterns.

At times writers choose to use more than one pattern of development to support a topic sentence. For example, a paragraph exploring the effects of divorce on children might *describe* a child's trauma, give an *example*, and then examine why divorce *causes* problems for children.

The subject matter and your purpose will suggest which paragraph patterns best serve your needs. The writer of the next paragraph combines various methods to persuade his readers that certain teaching methods were ineffective:

At school they tried to teach me how to write an   narration
essay and how to draw a large brass pot full of zinnias. I grieve to say that they failed in both these
laudable aims. I am not sure why I could never draw   effect
a brass pot full of zinnias, but I know why my school-
masters could not teach me to write an essay. The   cause
first reason was that they gave us rather unattractive
models to study and emulate: Charles Lamb, who is   example
a great deal too quaint and old-fashioned for modern youngsters; Robert Louis Stevenson, whose
style is often affected and artificial; and E. F. Ben-
son, whose essays *From a College Window* are mild
and flaccid and middle-aged and uninspiring. The   cause
other reason was that they never explained to us
what an essay was, and what purpose we were attempting to achieve when we wrote one.

          —GILBERT HIGHET, "How to Write an Essay"

This writer uses *narration* to lead into his topic sentence, which gives
an *effect*. He follows with *causes* (reasons), gives *examples*, and ends
with one additional *cause*.

IN REVIEW

An essay usually requires various methods of paragraph development: *narration* to trace significant events, *description* to
sketch a scene with visual images, *example* to clarify abstractions with specific illustrations, *definition* to differentiate and
distinguish words and ideas, *process* to provide step-by-step
instructions or to trace historical and social movements,
cause and effect to explain reasons why something occurs or
to study known effects, *classification or analysis* to identify
categories and to examine one or more in depth, and *comparison and contrast* to debate the merits of two subjects.

EXERCISE 6.1   Write paragraphs modeled after each of the eight
methods explained in this chapter. Choose from this list of basic
patterns and suggested topics:

A. *Narration:* an anecdote to illustrate academic frustration,
blood ties of a family, a grueling sporting event, a job search,
routine home repairs

B. *Description:* a person who profoundly touched your life, types of clothes that reveal personalities, your mother's kitchen on Sunday morning, the sounds of a football or baseball game, main street of your home town

C. *Example:* the advantages of good health, the essentials of an effective diet, the lessons of history, the values of folklore and local legends, variations in the architecture of campus buildings

D. *Definition:* discriminatory language, sexual harassment, racism, religious conviction, electronic evangelism, the shifting notions of moral responsibility, the straight-A student, the effective instructor

E. *Process:* handling an automobile breakdown on an interstate highway, protecting yourself when alone at night, joining a political campaign, performing CPR, separating from a sweetheart with a minimum of heartache

F. *Cause and effect:* effects of nuclear power plants, social effects of the AIDS epidemic, effects of credit card shopping, the causes of continually escalating costs, the causes and effects of sexual promiscuity, alcoholism, the causes and effects of moral integrity

G. *Classification:* types of diets, exercise programs, amateur sports, eaters, bosses, baldness, hands, noses, gossips, nerds, or jocks

H. *Analysis:* a gripping novel, the perfect weekend, the human hand, acrylic paint, one kind of automobile

I. *Comparison and contrast:* television soaps or sitcoms, professors, supervisors, writers, movies and plays, human and animal parents, the forms of discipline for children.

EXERCISE 6.2 Write a paragraph in which you combine several patterns of development to support a topic sentence. Develop your own topic or use one of the following:

A. *Define* electronic evangelism, self-motivation, inspiration, or academic apathy with use of example, comparison, and cause and effect.

B. Show a *process* — dieting, body building, hitting a backhand — with use of description, classification, comparison, and example.

C. *Explain* why one person's hero is another's villain with use of description, a narrative anecdote, example, and comparison and contrast.

EXERCISE 6.3 The following paragraphs are skimpy and need to be developed. First, choose one paragraph and spend a few minutes jotting down ideas and writing notes on ways to develop it. For example, can you add a narrative episode, a comparison, an example? Second, rewrite the paragraph. If you do not like these topics, create your own skimpy paragraph, then use some patterns of development to expand it.

A. Confident people have a different air about them. They aren't cocky or anything like that, they just seem sure of themselves and of their ability to get a job done, and they do.

B. Body language reveals many people's moods, whether they intend to divulge the information or not. The angle of the head, the position of the arms, the pursing of the lips — all communicate something to attentive observers.

C. Kissing may be a passionate response to those we love, but it is also an art. Some people merely use the kiss as a fast lane to other things. But a few people know how to kiss, and they do it better than others.

EXERCISE 6.4 The following passage uses an analogy to clarify an idea. First, identify the analogy. Second, write your own paragraph that uses an analogy for a purpose.

But I'm not here to trumpet the wonders of my contraption. I want to try to explain what it's like to write with a word processor. The nearest thing to it is an experience you may have had as a kid: building sand castles. Sand castles are best built on perilous oceanfronts, not on safe lakefronts. To erect a sand castle under the threat of the waves gives you a delectable sense of defying devastation. A similar foreboding of doom hovers over the writer who uses a word processor. What if there's a power failure and your work is wiped away? At least every half-hour, superstitiously, I tell the computer to save what I've written; and often I make a copy of it.

And yet despite this fear, to see your castle of words start to rise fills you with an odd sense of freedom and playfulness. The experience is like whomping together some piles of wet sand that you want to develop into towers. First you just stack up that sand any old sloppy way, just to indicate roughly the shape of your superstructure. You get the piles to stand up straight, then you pat them smooth, then you take your shovel and tool them to a finely detailed finish. That is much like what you do in producing an essay on a word processor. You gather your material into a rough preliminary shape, then you work on smoothing it. You can jot down ideas, arrange them into an outline, then gradually tool them into a finished form. The whole process completes itself before your eyes.

—X. J. KENNEDY, "Writing with a DECmate II:
Building Sand Castles"

CHAPTER
7
Improving Paragraph Style

The term *style* has two meanings. One refers to the idiosyncrasies of expression by which we recognize certain writers—for instance, Hemingway's clipped sentences with frequent compounding, Martin Luther King's repetition of key phrases, and John Updike's rich description. In these cases, style reveals the individuality of the writer. The other meaning refers to the clear expression of ideas. A writer's first consideration should be sound reasoning in precise prose, as explained by some noted stylists:

> The beginner should approach style warily, realizing that it is himself he is approaching, no other; and he should begin by turning resolutely away from all devices that are popularly believed to indicate style—all mannerisms, tricks, adornment. The approach to style is by way of plainness, simplicity, orderliness, sincerity.
>
> —WILLIAM STRUNK, JR., AND E. B. WHITE,
> *The Elements of Style*

However, these writers do not advocate short, unadorned simple sentences that will make a dull paragraph. Listen to another authority on style:

> The ability to write clear, crisp sentences that never go beyond twenty words is a considerable achievement. You'll never confuse your reader with sprawl, wordiness, or muddy abstractions. But if you never write a sentence longer than twenty words, you'll be like a pianist who uses only the middle octave: You can play the tune, but not with much richness or variation.
>
> —JOSEPH WILLIAMS, *Style: Ten Lessons in Clarity and Grace*

For you, as for all writers, *style* grows out of your choices from a wide spectrum of words, sounds, sentence types, sentence length, repetition, and methods of paragraph development. Style is not merely eccentric adornment; it is your distinctive voice and proof of your personality in a world filled with general dullness, worn clichés, and bureaucratic jargon. It is this second meaning that we are concerned with.

7a   Write in a clear style.

The first step toward effective style is to strip your writing of all excessive wording. Replace *be* verbs and passive verbs with verbs that describe action (see chapter **31**). Eliminate the colloquial, conversational style; street language does not belong in serious writing except in reproducing dialogue (see section **7d**). One student sought clarity of expression in three successive drafts. She first wrote this draft, and the instructor's corrections and comments follow:

Children of alcoholic parents (are ~ *passive voice*

affected) just as much as the alcoholic

parent. I know there is a lot of mental

abuse because my father was an alcoholic.

I can remember thinking, why does he have
misplaced modifier ~ *redundant*
to drink (over and over) (in my mind.) I
~ *this what?*
would keep thinking (this.) Maybe I wanted

too much out of him, but I only wanted

him to be my father instead of a drunk. I

need to overcome the abuse of my father's

alcoholism.

INSTRUCTOR'S NOTE: Your personal voice overwhelms the message. Your topic has universal appeal ("alcoholics affect others adversely"), so develop that idea and tone down the personal element, using perhaps one example of his behavior.

The instructor's note addresses a common problem. The writer has used a personal, narrative style for a discourse on alcoholism. The instructor asks the writer to seek a lucid style that features alcoholism as the subject and uses personal experience as support.

However, the student misinterpreted the message, searched out new words in a thesaurus, and wrote this second draft:

Children of alcoholic parents (are *passive voice* affected) in comparable ways to the alco-

holic. One who has domiciled with an al-

coholic will have experienced mental

abuse, a psychological trauma that af- *phrasing is clouded*

fects a child's mind, and even physical

abuse, a domestic tragedy in the form of

punishment and sexual familiarity with a

child's body.

INSTRUCTOR'S NOTE: Now you have removed your own voice entirely and deadened the paragraph with abstractions and generalizations. Go back to explain the basic subject and then highlight it with one of your experiences. I did not mean for you to abandon entirely your personal voice.

Just as people do not enjoy listening to a person speak in an inflated, pseudo-intellectual tone, they do not enjoy reading something with a lofty, pretentious tone. The writer's voice becomes lost in the grandiose structure and terminology. The writer's voice sets the stage for the entire essay, and if the reader cannot hear the writer's voice clearly throughout the essay, the reader will stop listening. Here is the writer's third draft:

> Alcoholism affects every member of a family, not merely the one person afflicted with the disease. An alcoholic father, alcoholic mother, or alcoholic child inflicts mental abuse, and often physical abuse, on every other family member. I know because I have an alcoholic father. When drunk, he says, "Why in the hell did God give me a child so damn ugly and fat?" When drunk, an alcoholic is cruel.
>
> —GLENDA HARRIS, student

The paragraph is now clear. It progresses logically from one idea to the next, it features the writer's voice appropriately, and it displays certain stylistic elements, especially repetition of key words and word clusters (see section **7d**).

EXERCISE 7.1 Rewrite the following paragraph to make it clear and precise. Eliminate wordiness and seek precision.

> The majority of research articles on suicidal adolescents in magazines and books in the library is, it seems to me, although I'm new to the subject, caught up in studying those adolescents who are in a transitional phase of life between childhood and adulthood, which is often, as you probably know quite well, a situation aggravated by parents who separate or divorce one another for some reason or another that is not relevant here.

EXERCISE 7.2 Choose one topic below and write a paragraph in a quiet, restrained tone that describes the topic with clarity and grace.

> one wing of a nursing home for the elderly
> the courtroom manner of a district judge
> the water of a local stream
> a study area of the library

7b   The purpose determines style.

As writers work to make their style clear, they must also consider once again the purpose and audience of their essays (see sections **1b** and **1c**). An essay's purpose and audience directly determine what words the writer will choose and how he or she will express them. For example, the manner of writing for an autobiography differs greatly from that for a rousing campaign speech or for a recipe for key lime pie.

As discussed in section **1b**, an essay's purpose can be to express an idea or describe an experience, to explain a concept or a procedure, or to persuade the reader to the writer's point of view.

Style and the expressive purpose

Expressive writing chronicles the writer's experiences and beliefs and so uses the first person, "I," throughout the paragraph (and usually throughout the whole essay). In effect, the writer invites the reader into his or her private world for a brief visit. Examples and thoughts explain a writer's point of view in an informal, relaxed voice. Here is an example:

> We call them Twinkies. You've seen them on television acting the news, modeling and fracturing the news while you wonder whether they've read the news—or if they've blow-dried their brains, too. I make my living as a reporter and sometimes-anchorwoman on network television and, like almost everyone in my business, I've an overdeveloped ego and a case of galloping ambition. Some of my colleagues want to be The Anchorman on the Mount. Others see themselves as the Ace Reporter. Because of *60 Minutes*, there's a whole herd of them determined to be The Grand Inquisitor, and because of the way ratings affect our jobs, a heady number want only to be The Friendliest Anchor on the Block. At least one wants to be Jesus. Me, I just didn't want to be thought of as a Twinkie.
> — LINDA ELLERBEE, *"And So It Goes": Adventures in Television*

Ellerbee's autobiographical style demonstrates the standards for expressive writing: self-centered, anecdotal, fortified with personal opinion, and narrated in the first person.

Style and the explanatory purpose

In contrast to expressive writing, **explanatory** writing must maintain a clear focus on the subject matter, not on personal opinion or bias toward one side or another. The writing, while remaining vigorous, must give a lucid explanation of the subject, usually in third person ("it," "he," "she," "they") and only rarely in first person ("I" or "we"). Explanation demands careful classification and definition, detailed clarification of process, a precise use of examples and comparisons. Essay exam answers, themes, reports, research papers — all such explanatory essays pursue a sequence of ideas expressed clearly and with economy. Note the style of the following explanation of the tides.

> The tides present a striking paradox, and the essence of it is this: the force that sets them in motion is cosmic, lying wholly outside the earth and presumably acting impartially on all parts of the globe, but the nature of the tide at any particular place is a local matter, with astonishing differences occurring within a very short geographic distance. When we spend a long summer holiday at the seashore we may become aware that the tide in our cove behaves very differently from that at a friend's place twenty miles up the coast, and is strikingly different from what we may have known in some other locality. If we are summering on Nantucket Island our boating and swimming will be little disturbed by the tides, for the range between high water and low is only about a foot or two. But if we choose to vacation near the upper part of the Bay of Fundy, we must accommodate ourselves to a rise and fall of 40 to 50 feet, although both places are included within the same body of water — the Gulf of Maine. Or if we spend our holiday on Chesapeake Bay we may find that the time of high water each day varies by as much as 12 hours in different places on the shores of the same bay.
> — RACHEL CARSON, *The Sea around Us*

Carson's style is straightforward and clear. She keeps herself in the background, but she invites the reader into the essay with the editorial *we*. She is clear and logical, bases her statements upon factual evidence, and supplies a clear sequence of ideas and examples to support her topic sentence, which opens the paragraph.

Style and the persuasive purpose

Persuasive writing must convince the audience (see section **7c**) by defending one aspect of a complex issue (see also chapter **48**). Persuasion must explore in detail each side of an issue. Consequently, it focuses on the subject and its relevance to the readers. Persuasive writing depends heavily upon comparison and contrast and on the exploration of causes and effects. The following example argues the merits of affirmative action:

> If our goal is educational and economic equity and parity —
> and it is — then we need affirmative action to catch up. We are
> behind as a result of discrimination and denial of opportunity.
> There is one white attorney for every 680 whites, but only one
> black attorney for every 4,000 blacks; one white physician for
> every 649 whites, but only one black physician for every 5,000
> blacks; and one white dentist for every 1,900 whites, but only
> one black dentist for every 8,400 blacks. Less than 1 percent of
> all engineers — or of all practicing chemists — is black. Cruel and
> uncompassionate injustice created gaps like these. We need cre-
> ative justice and compassion to help us close them.
> —JESSE JACKSON, "Why Blacks Need Affirmative Action"

Jackson's style is assertive and aggressive to match his persuasive purpose. It addresses the reader with a serious voice, gives cause-and-effect analysis, and uses parallel parts to explore the two sides of the issue.

IN REVIEW

Use first-person singular ("I") with personal narration and with some anecdotes for explanatory writing; use third person ("he", "she", "it" or "they") with factual evidence for explanatory writing; and use the first-person plural ("we"), if necessary, to draw the audience into the give-and-take of persuasive writing.

EXERCISE 7.3   Choose one of the following topics and write three short paragraphs: (1) express your feelings on the topic, (2) explain the topic, and (3) argue pro and con issues of the topic.

    ghosts and ghost stories
    fear of heights
    credit cards
    Christmas gifts

7c   The audience determines style.

A writer's style changes with the audience and with his or her approach to the audience. News stories address inquisitive readers, how-to essays address do-it-yourself readers, essay examinations address the instructor, and personal letters address friends and relatives. The writer might approach some readers with a serious tone but use a humorous style for others. At times the writer might use satire to shock the reader and, at other times, seek a quiet style to delight the reader with a play on words. (See section **1c**.)

In the next paragraphs, one student writer demonstrates for a general audience his ability to shift from a quiet, descriptive paragraph, to a serious explanatory paragraph, and then to satiric attack on swindlers who prey upon his grandmother and others.

> My grandmother is a gentle soul. She has a serene disposition that has soothed my skinned knees with healing herbs of various smells and colors, dispelled my hurt feelings with hot chocolate, and sustained my self-image with her unbounded love. My grandmother is generous. She devotes her time and talents to her church, to her family, and to a large circle of friends. My grandmother is vulnerable. She lives alone, she has money, and she trusts everybody.

This opening paragraph features a three-part development to reflect the dignity, generosity, and vulnerability of his grandmother. By using concrete details, the writer enables the audience to discover his subject's personality. This style embellishes an idea with both clarity and grace by its use of several elements: figurative language (see chapter **19**); alliteration, which repeats initial consonant sounds; rhythmic cadence; and parallelism. (See section **7d**.)

Warren's essay continues, but his next paragraph shifts to a serious, explanatory style:

> Well-meaning Americans, most of them religiously devout people like my grandmother, will lose millions of dollars this year in investment swindles. The faithful will be duped by their own sense of charity and dedication to their church. They will be conned by financial planners who claim to represent the church or an affiliated organ of the church, but who actually practice only greed and avarice in its worst form—fraud. The victims, like my grandmother, often think that an investment will earn them a profit and also advance the work of the church. Instead, they lose everything invested—$8,000 in the case of my grandmother.

The style of this second paragraph is straightforward—factual information with a cause-and-effect analysis. The writer is earnest, sincere, and authoritative. The paragraph does not dwell on the obvious, pad with irrelevancies, or offer clichés and stale ideas. In general, it features a restrained, unimpassioned language in a coherent sequence of rational sentences. The audience learns how swindlers use the church as a cover for illegal activities.

Warren's next paragraph shifts to a satiric style that attacks the tactics of the swindlers.

> Christians beware! Investment schemes, both legal and illegal, entice the rich and the poor, the wise and the ignorant, the agnostic and the religious. Grandmothers beware! Evangelical prophets in church vestibules and on national television networks entice the faithful to investment schemes using "born again" money (your money borne into their hands) for investments in coins, real estate, oil wells, and stocks and bonds—all the investments having been inspired, of course, from above. They brand doubtful Christians as unbelievers. "Let us *prey*" is their motto.
>
> —GREGG WARREN, student

With sardonic wit and a bitter tongue, the writer educates his audience by exposing get-rich-quick schemes that prey on church members who invest unwisely with pseudo-religious promoters.

7d   Use rhetorical schemes to enhance paragraph style.

Clear, crisp sentences are vital to every piece of writing, yet writing also needs variation and richness. Some techniques, used appropriately, enhance meaning and improve communication. Chapter **19**, for example, explains the value of figurative language. This section explains a few other methods that may serve your special needs.

Alliteration

Alliteration repeats a consonant sound at the beginning of several words.

> *B*oldness at the *b*argaining table soon *b*rought the negotiations to a new level. The union team, although *b*ound by preestablished *g*uidelines, *g*ave *g*round. The management team *p*ressed for a *p*ossible settlement by midnight.

The alliteration of the *b*, *g*, and *p* sounds provides a phonetic theme that ties meaning together. Of course, too much alliteration will call attention to itself and detract from the meaning. In general, repeat one sound no more than four times.

Rhythm and cadence

During reading, the rise and fall of the spoken voice is unconsciously echoed; that is, readers sense the **rhythm** of the sentences. Good prose writers as well as poets achieve **cadence** by controlling the flow of metrical accents and establishing various sound patterns. Note the pleasant rhythms of the following passage.

> A single knoll rises out of the plain in Oklahoma, north and west of the Wichita range. For my people, the Kiowas, it is an old landmark, and they gave it the name Rainy Mountain. The hardest weather in the world is there. Winter brings blizzards, hot tornadic winds arise in the spring, and in the summer the prairie is an anvil's edge. The grass turns brittle and brown, and it cracks beneath your feet. There are green belts along the rivers and creeks, linear groves of hickory and pecan, willow and witch hazel. At a distance in July or August the steaming foliage seems almost to writhe in fire. Great green and yellow grasshoppers are everywhere in the tall grass, popping up like corn to sting the flesh, and tortoises crawl about on the earth, going nowhere in the plenty of time. Loneliness is an aspect of the land.
> — N. SCOTT MOMADAY, "My Kiowa Grandmother"

The writer's rhythmic voice enhances his message because the cadence of the passage reflects the symmetry of the scene being described. Each of the sentences moves rhythmically toward a strong ending. The writer also uses alliteration to reinforce meaning ("great green . . . grasshoppers . . . in the tall grass") and uses figurative language ("popping up like corn").

Repetition

Repetition provides another type of rhythm to reinforce ideas expressed in key words and phrases (see also chapter **8**). Many familiar sayings use repetition: *Nothing ventured, nothing gained. I came, I saw, I conquered. An eye for an eye and a tooth for a tooth.* This next paragraph repeats *we will* several times to draw the audience into active involvement.

The nonviolent resisters can summarize their message in the following simple terms. *We will take direct action* against injustice without waiting for other agencies to act. *We will not obey unjust laws* or submit to unjust practices. *We will do this* peacefully, openly, cheerfully because our aim is to persuade. *We adopt* the means of nonviolence because our end is a community at peace with itself. *We will try to persuade with our words,* but if our words fail, *we will try to persuade with our acts.* *We will* always be willing to talk and seek fair compromise, but *we are ready* to suffer when necessary and even risk our lives to become witnesses to the truth as we see it.

— MARTIN LUTHER KING, JR., *Where Do We Go From Here: Chaos or Community?* (emphasis added)

The next passage repeats form as well as specific words.

And so, my fellow Americans: ask not what your country can do for you — ask what you can do for your country.

My fellow citizens of the world: ask not what America will do for you, but what together we can do for the freedom of man.

— JOHN F. KENNEDY, Presidential inaugural address

Kennedy's contrasting ideas, quickly repeated, strongly state his desires and force the listeners to choose.

The following example repeats form — a set of rhetorical questions — to define and explain as well as to explore an issue.

Should a small group of people, the members of the electoral college, make the final decision about the presidential election? Should they have the power to name a president who did not win a majority of the popular vote?

Sometimes writers repeat a sentence in order to stress its magnitude. The next paragraph opens and closes with the same sentence, and the four sentences in between support the topic sentence with a strong parallel structure.

There in the mist, enormous, majestic, silent, and terrible, stood the Great Wall of China. *Solitarily,* with the indifference of nature herself, it crept up the mountain side and slipped down to the depth of the valley. *Menacingly,* the grim watch towers, stark and foursquare, at due intervals stood at their posts. *Ruthlessly,* for it was built at the cost of a million lives and each one of those great grey stones has been stained with the bloody tears of the captive and the outcast, it forged its dark way through a sea of rugged mountains. *Fearlessly*, it went on its endless journey, league upon league to the furthermost regions of Asia, in utter solitude, mysterious like the great empire it guarded. There in the mist, enormous, majestic, silent, and terrible, stood the Great Wall of China.

— W. SOMERSET MAUGHAM, *On a Chinese Screen*
(emphasis added)

The repetition of the topic sentence is not necessary, of course, but it represents one aspect of Maugham's style, which repeats important ideas to reinforce them.

NOTE: Use such repetition only if your content warrants it and the length of the paragraph can sustain it.

The structured series

Writers sometimes pay careful attention to the length and structure of the units within a series. The individual units gain emphasis, provide rhythm and repetition, and contribute to the meaning of the passage. In the following paragraph the writer compares and contrasts winter with summer and uses a series of verb phrases to deliver action and liveliness to the scene.

> Winter and summer, then, were two hostile lives, and bred two separate natures. Winter was always the effort to live; summer was tropical license. Whether the children rolled in the grass, or waded in the brook, or swam in the salt ocean, or sailed in the bay, or fished for smelts in the creeks, or netted minnows in the salt-marshes, or took to the pine-woods and the granite quarries, or chased muskrats and hunted snapping-turtles in the swamps, or mushrooms or nuts on the autumn hills, summer and country were always sensual living, while winter was always compulsory learning. Summer was the multiplicity of nature; winter was school.
>
> — HENRY ADAMS, *The Education of Henry Adams*

The symmetry of the writing keeps the reader focused on specific activities that made life stirring and stimulating for this writer.

Dialogue

Use **dialogue** to let others speak for themselves and thereby bring additional voices into your essay. The actual words of a person add emphasis and a sense of reality and immediacy to a paragraph.

Dialogue features the conversation of two or more people. In the next passage, which opens an antismoking essay, the dialogue exposes the personality of each character.

> She lit a cigarette, inhaled deeply, and blew the smoke across the table. "Care for a cigarette?" she inquired, hoping to strike up a conversation.
>
> "No. Make that NO, as in never," Ted responded.
>
> "Whew, aren't you the touchy one."
>
> "Cigarettes are killing people every day, and here you are — killing yourself and inviting me to join you," Ted said.
>
> She stood and turned to walk away, but she looked back, "I don't need your moral pompousness in my life." With that she left the snack bar, the cigarette propped between her delicate fingers.
>
> I overheard that conversation last week as I sat with Ted and several friends at a table in the snack bar. At first I was angry with Ted for being rude to somebody who only wanted to be friendly. Today, after having researched the subject of smoking, I endorse Ted's position wholeheartedly.
>
> — GEORGIA ANN STOCKBRIDGE, student

This brief anecdote uses dialogue to enliven the antismoking message. See also chapter **40** on punctuating quotations and sections **50e** and **50f** on handling direct quotation.

Special word forms

If your subject, audience, and skill with writing offer you the opportunity, you might wish to add variety to your essay with new words or unusual spellings, as did one student with this opening to an essay on farm life in Kentucky:

> Zap! Pow! ZZZapp!
>
> The old tractor bawled in protest as I cranked the motor. Nothing. I twisted its tail again.
>
> Pow! Pow! ZaZumm!
>
> "Ah, that's better, you old bag of nuts and bolts," I said. "Let's go to work."
>
> — RANDALL PERRY, student

CAUTION: Experimental writing demands a fundamental knowledge of basic grammar, punctuation, and spelling rules. Do not write such prose to escape the use of conventional form. First prove your ability to handle standard English and then begin experimenting.

EXERCISE 7.4

A. Identify the alliteration in each passage below.

Studies serve for delight, for ornament, and for ability. Their chief use for delight is in privateness and retiring; for ornaments, is in discourse; and for ability, is in the judgment and disposition of business.
— FRANCIS BACON, "Of Studies"

The iron tires of the spring wagon rolled silently along the twin wheel tracks worn into the grass: parallel trails wandering northward and away to their vanishing point on the treeless folds of the benchland. Behind, the rudimentary road dipped and disappeared in the river valley.
— CHET HUNTLEY, "The Generous Years"

B. Write a paragraph of your own that features alliteration.

EXERCISE 7.5

A. Explainly briefly how the rhythm and symmetry of the following passage supports the ideas being expressed by Kennedy.

Now the trumpet summons us again — not as a call to bear arms, though arms we need; not as a call to battle, though embattled we are; but a call to bear the burden of a long twilight struggle, year in and year out, "rejoicing in hope, patient in tribulation," a struggle against the common enemies of man: tyranny, poverty, disease and war itself.
— JOHN F. KENNEDY, Presidential inaugural address

B. Write your own paragraph that duplicates the style of Kennedy's passage.

EXERCISE 7.6

A. Explain briefly the role played by repetition in the following passage. Specifically, how does the repetition enhance the message?

The worst part of war is not death and destruction but just soldiering; the worst part of soldiering is not danger but nostalgia; and the worst part of a soldier's nostalgia is the lack of intimacy, the lack of privacy, and the deprivation of the rights of self-determination and ownership.

— ROBERT HENRIQUES, *The Voice of the Trumpet*

B. Write a paragraph of your own that duplicates the style of Henriques.

EXERCISE 7.7

A. The following paragraph opens an essay on oranges — their arrival at Christmas time, the way they were packed, how they smelled, and especially how they tasted during the dark winters of North Dakota. Explain briefly the role dialogue plays in the paragraph. Specifically, how does the dialogue enhance the message?

Oh, those oranges arriving in the midst of the North Dakota winters of the forties — the mere color of them, carried through the door in a net bag or a crate from out of the white winter landscape. Their appearance was enough to set my brother and me to thinking that it might be about time to develop an illness, which was the surest way of receiving a steady supply of them.

"Mom, we think we're getting a cold."

"*We*? You mean, you two want an orange?"

This was difficult for us to answer or dispute; the matter seemed moved beyond our mere wanting.

"If you want an orange," she would say, "why don't you ask for one?"

"We want an orange."

"'We' again. '*We want an orange*.'"

"May we have an orange, please."

"That's the way you know I like you to ask for one. Now, why don't each of you ask for one in that same way, but separately?"

"Mom . . ." and so on. There was no depth of degradation that we wouldn't descend to in order to get one.

— LARRY WOIWODE, "Wanting an Orange"

B. Choose a topic for an essay, and by duplicating the technique of Woiwode's passage develop your own opening that uses dialogue.

EXERCISE 7.8

A. The following passage features a special syntax with unusual spelling. Explain briefly the role played by this technique. Specifically, how does the unusual word usage enhance the message?

As the weight of the wagon eased on their collars, the team of grays, sensing unhitching and feed, blew out their nostrils and swung into an easy, mile-consuming trot, manes flying in the March wind. The muffled thud of the hooves, the occasional creak of the wagon, the jangle of the tug chains and bridle snaps were high-spirited rhythmic beats augmenting the melody . . . the melody of grass . . . the song of the immense and boundless land.

Sha-a-a-a-e-e-e-sha-o-o-o-m-m-m-m.

It rose out of the land, filled it sky to sky; waves of sound, rolling, rolling, building and diminishing. Toward the source of the wind, to the west, the grass sang in shrill sibilance . . . the reed and flute sections. The violins and horns were on the lee side, and their voices were picked up by the wind and carried over the endless sea of grass.

Sha-a-a-a-e-e-e-sha-o-o-o-m-m-m-m.

Wind and grass in assonant conversation. The grass . . . the incredible grass!

—CHET HUNTLEY, *The Generous Years*

B. Using the above passage as a model, write a passage of your own on a different subject and, like Huntley, use an unusual spelling of a word or words in a syntax that distinguishes the word from the remainder of the passage.

EXERCISE 7.9 Imitation is an effective way to develop an awareness of style. First, select one paragraph from the four reprinted below. Second, copy the paragraph word for word. Third, rewrite the paragraph using a different subject while using the same form and style of the original.

A. The sun lay on the grass and warmed it, and in the shade under the grass the insects moved, ants and ant lions to set traps for them, grasshoppers to jump into the air and flick their yellow wings for a second, sow bugs like little armadillos, plodding restlessly on many tender feet. And over the grass at the roadside a land turtle crawled, turning aside for nothing, dragging his high-domed shell over the grass. His hard legs and yellow-nailed feet threshed slowly through the grass, not really walking, but boosting and dragging his shell along. The barley beards slid off his shell, and the clover burrs fell on him and rolled to the ground. His horny beak was partly open, and his fierce, humorous eyes, under brows like fingernails, stared straight ahead. He came over the grass leaving a beaten trail behind him, and the hill, which was the highway embankment, reared up ahead of him. For a moment he stopped, his head

held high. He blinked and looked up and down. At last he
started to climb the embankment. Front clawed feet reached
forward but did not touch. The hind feet kicked his shell along,
and it scraped on the grass, and on the gravel.

       —JOHN STEINBECK, *The Grapes of Wrath*

B.   Pity the poor bore. He stands among us as a creature formi-
dable and familiar yet in essence unknowable. We can read the
ten infallible signs whereby he may be recognized and of the
seven tested methods whereby he may be rebuffed. Valuable
monographs exist upon his dress and diet; the study of his mat-
ing habits and migrational routes is well past the speculative
stage; and statistical studies abound. One out of three hundred
and twelve Americans is a bore, for instance, and a healthy male
adult bore consumes *each year* one and a half times his own
weight in other people's patience. But in all this vast literature
(and this is not to disparage the scientists who have selflessly
carried forward their research, nor the generous philanthropic
foundations that endowed their gleaming laboratories) one
grave defect persists: the bore is always described externally, in
a tone of distance and distaste. Hence the central question —
what makes a few people bores when the rest of us are so fascinating — remains cloaked in mystery. Yet bores, unlike Red Indians, were not here to greet the Pilgrims. They do not, like
rabid bats, come up from Mexico. No: the shameful truth, suppressed by both the public press and the spokesmen of our federal government, is that bores are created *out of our own number*.

       —JOHN UPDIKE, "Confessions of a Wild Bore"

C.   Pinball is a metaphor for life, pitting man's skill, nerve, persistence, and luck against the perverse machinery of human existence. The playfield is rich with rewards: targets that bring
huge scores, bright lights, chiming bells, free balls, and extra
games. But it is replete with perils, too: culs-de-sac, traps, gut-
ters, and gobble holes down which the ball may disappear
forever.

       —J. ANTONY LUKAS, "Pinball"

D.   He thought his happiness was complete when, as he mean-
dered aimlessly along, suddenly he stood by the edge of a full-
fed river. Never in his life had he seen a river before — this sleek,
sinuous full-bodied animal, chasing and chuckling, gripping
things with a gurgle and leaving them with a laugh, to fling itself
on fresh playmates that shook themselves free, and were caught
and held again. All was a-shake and a-shiver — glints and gleams
and sparkles, rustle and swirl, chatter and bubble. The Mole was

bewitched, entranced, fascinated. By the side of the river he trotted as one trots, when very small, by the side of a man who holds one spellbound by exciting stories; and when tired at last, he sat on the bank, while the river still chattered on to him, a babbling procession of the best stories in the world, sent from the heart of the earth to be told at last to the insatiable sea.

— KENNETH GRAHAME, *The Wind in the Willows*

Sentences

8
Sentence Coordination
9
Sentence Subordination
10
Improving Sentence Style: Emphasis
11
Improving Sentence Style: Variety
12
Correcting Misplaced Parts and Dangling Modifiers
13
Grammatical Completeness
14
Correcting Mixed Constructions
15
Correcting Shifts

8

Sentence Coordination

When writers construct a paragraph, they relate the statements to the topic sentence and to one another. They use parallelism and transitional devices to link the ideas and to create the structure of the paragraph. Similarly, when writers construct a sentence, they arrange the words, phrases, and clauses to show the hierarchy of the sentence parts and to make the statement clear, forceful, and effective.

Two methods that show how ideas relate to one another in a single sentence are coordination and subordination. *Coordination* joins ideas of equal importance, and *subordination* establishes the dominant and supporting ideas. This chapter addresses coordination in sentences, and chapter **9** addresses subordination in sentences.

8a Use coordination to form compound sentences.

A compound sentence is made of main clauses (see chapter **23**) joined in specific ways to show the relationship between the coordinate ideas. Meaning and purpose dictate how writers choose ideas to coordinate and connect them. Here are the ways to join clauses of equal weight.

Comma and a coordinating conjunction

Use a comma and one of the **coordinating conjunctions** (see section **20g**), which are

and, but, or, nor, for, so, yet.

For example,

> Let joy light the way to a brave new world, **and** let love laugh away darkness and despair.

> The president envisions a new program of social reform, **but** he does not comprehend its staggering expense.

When overused, this form causes the singsong monotony of run-on sentences:

> Mark Twain wrote *Huckleberry Finn*, and he based it on his own childhood in Hannibal, Missouri, so the novel has an autobiographical base, but it has a fictional plot.

See chapters **9** and **25** for ways to correct run-on sentences, as shown by this revision:

> Mark Twain based *Huckleberry Finn* on his childhood in Hannibal, Missouri, to give the plot an autobiographical base.

Semicolon and a conjunctive adverb

Use a semicolon and one of the conjunctive adverbs, which are adverbs that connect (see sections **20e** and **20g** and chapter **33**). The commonly used conjunctive adverbs are listed here:

also	however	next
anyhow	incidentally	nonetheless
anyway	indeed	otherwise
besides	instead	similarly
consequently	likewise	still
finally	meanwhile	then
furthermore	moreover	therefore
hence	nevertheless	thus

These connective words signal a stronger separation than the coordinating conjunctions, which is why a semicolon separates the clauses and a comma usually follows the conjunctive adverb.

> In his autobiography Mark Twain recalls his friendly companionship with the slaves on his uncle's farm; **consequently**, he championed the causes of emancipation in his adult life.

> The team must win this next tournament game; **otherwise**, it must pack up and go home tomorrow.

Semicolon without a conjunction

Use a semicolon without a conjunction. The semicolon establishes a close relationship between what would otherwise be two separate sentences. The second statement often parallels the first.

> Aerospace engineers design and develop aircraft and spaceships; metallurgical engineers develop and test the metals used in aerospace design.

Semicolon and a coordinate conjunction

Use a semicolon with a coordinate conjunction to separate main clauses that have internal commas.

> The embolism, now blocking several vessels, threatens the heart itself; **so** the doctor has scheduled an operation.

Colon without a conjunction

Use a colon without a conjunction to signal amplification. The second clause must explain or expand upon the first.

> Aerospace engineers design and develop aircraft and spaceships: they have provided such diverse products as long-range bombers, helicopters, the space shuttle, and satellites.

8b Use parallel constructions to strengthen coordinate ideas.

Duplicating the form of two or more word groups reinforces important ideas and meets the reader's need for order and symmetry. (See section **5b**.) Many of the most quotable quotations feature parallelism.

> I came, I saw, I conquered.
>
> —JULIUS CAESAR

To achieve this effect, balance nouns with nouns, verbs with verbs in the same tense, prepositional phrases with prepositional phrases, clauses with clauses, and so on (see chapter **20** for definitions of the parts of speech).

> *What you need* and *what I want* differ like coal oil and quicksilver.   [parallel noun clauses]

Walking on water and *raising the dead* are miracles; *falling in love* is mortal.   [parallel noun phrases]

Your tax funds will be used *to purchase new buses, to retire existing debt,* and *to eliminate most maintenance.*   [parallel infinitive phrases]

Good breeding consists in concealing *how much we think of ourselves* and *how little we think of the other person.*
— MARK TWAIN   [parallel noun clauses]

Some people not only *do the right things* but also *enjoy the right things.*   [parallel verb phrases]

Parallel clauses and sentences can be powerful:

I am in earnest — I will not equivocate — I will not excuse — I will not retreat a single inch — and I will be heard!
— W. L. GARRISON, salutory address of *The Liberator*

The repetition of balanced clauses, separated by dashes, adds climactic force to each of Garrison's assertions.

It was the best of times, it was the worst of times, it was the age of wisdom, it was the age of foolishness, it was the epoch of belief, it was the epoch of incredulity, it was the season of Light, it was the season of Darkness, it was the spring of hope, it was the winter of despair, we had everything before us, we had nothing before us, we were all going direct to Heaven, we were all going direct the other way.
— CHARLES DICKENS, *A Tale of Two Cities*

The parallel clauses that open Dickens's classic establish the conflicting forces that he wished to explore in his novel. Note that Dickens chose to punctuate with commas to establish these relationships, although punctuation conventions usually would call for semicolons or periods (see chapters **35** and **38**).

Also use parallelism with the **correlative conjunctions** (see section **20g**), which are *both . . . and, either . . . or, neither . . . nor, not . . . but, not only . . . but also,* and *whether . . . or.*

Either we attend the lectures *or we fail* the course.

Not one person protested during the performance, *but more* than 200 people later requested a refund.

Whether you love me *or you merely play* at love reflects on your maturity.

8c Repeat words for clarity in coordinate constructions.

To coordinate sentence elements, writers must often repeat articles (*a, an, the*), prepositions (*by, for, in,* etc.), the infinitive *to*, and auxiliary verbs. (See chapter **20**.)

> Don Juan was known *as a* lover of women and *as a* swordsman of skill.

Repetition of the preposition and the article prevents misreading.

> We wrote a proposal asking that the agency fund *both the* collection and interpretation of data *and the* development of a working plan to correct the problem.

Repetition of the coordinate conjunction and the article makes clear the two units to be funded.

In general, repeat introductory relative pronouns (see section **20b**), such as *who, which*, and *that*.

> Some say *that* Zen training makes us the totality of life and *that* it makes us self-reliant.

The second *that* introduces the second half of a compound noun clause (see section **23**).

> She is an excellent student *who* seems to study in every spare minute, *but who* actually takes time to tutor illiterate adults on weekends.

The *but who* makes clear the two contrasting phrases.

In some sentences where coordinate parts are clear, you can omit the connecting words and the infinitive *to*, as shown in this next sentence.

> The special club activities for Saturday are *to conduct* the car wash in the morning, *decorate* the meeting hall in the afternoon, and *sponsor* the dance in the evening.

The reader will not misunderstand the coordination of *decorate* and *sponsor* with *conduct*.

> **IN REVIEW**
>
> Use coordination to join ideas of equal importance, and use parallelism to strengthen the relationship of coordinate ideas.

EXERCISE 8.1   Identify the coordinate construction in each of the following sentences and explain briefly how the structure contributes to the meaning of the sentence.

1. Francis Scott Key wrote the text for "The Star-Spangled Banner," but he borrowed the music from "To Anacreon in Heaven," an English drinking song.
2. Key watched with anxiety the bombing of Fort McHenry in Baltimore harbor throughout the night; he saw with elation that "our flag was still there" on the following morning.
3. An attorney by profession, Key served as district attorney for the District of Columbia; a poet by avocation, he penned enough poetry to fill a book, *Poems of the Late Francis S. Key, Esq.*
4. Key considered becoming a clergyman, so religious themes appear in many of his poems.
5. "The Star-Spangled Banner" may not remain the national anthem; the new anthem may be "America the Beautiful."

EXERCISE 8.2   Combine and rewrite the following sets of sentences to create coordinate constructions.

1. "America the Beautiful" is one of the favorite patriotic hymns of the American people. "The Star-Spangled Banner" is the national anthem.
2. Francis Scott Key wrote "The Star-Spangled Banner" during the War of 1812. It was named the national anthem by Congress in 1931.
3. In Great Britain membership in an order of knighthood entitles the holder to be called *sir*. When women are given the corresponding rank, they are called *dame*.

4. Several pioneer forts in Kansas still attract visitors. Fort Larned protected travelers on the Sante Fe Trail. Fort Riley was a cavalry center where General George A. Custer once served as commander.

5. Americans must learn to recycle most of their waste. If we don't, communities will face never-ending debates over disposal sites.

CHAPTER

9

Sentence Subordination

Not all ideas are equal in weight, so writers express important thoughts in main clauses and put lesser ideas in subordinate clauses and phrases. Only when ideas have equal value do writers use compound sentences (see chapter **8**).

9a Subordinate less important ideas.

Consider two sentences of equal weight, one a positive statement and the other a negative statement:

The network of connections among power companies assures a steady supply of electricity to homes, businesses, and industry. Blackouts can spread quickly throughout the entire system.

How do these contradictory ideas relate? The writer's purpose for the paragraph or the essay determines which statement should be subordinated. To emphasize a *positive* purpose, the writer can subordinate the negative idea:

Although blackouts can spread quickly throughout the entire system, the network of connections among power companies assures a steady supply of electricity to homes, businesses, and industry.

To emphasize a *negative* purpose, the writer should subordinate the positive idea:

> Although the network of connections among power companies assures a steady supply of electricity to homes, businesses, and industry, blackouts can spread quickly throughout the entire system.

In both examples, notice how use of the subordinate conjunction *although* reduces the importance of the first clause and emphasizes the main clause.

9b   Use the subordinating conjunctions.

The **subordinating conjunction** connects two or more clauses in a sentence, usually introducing the subordinate one. Some common subordinating conjunctions are listed below:

after	even though	than	where
although	how	though	wherever
as far as	if	till	whether
as soon as	now that	unless	while
as if	once	until	
because	since	when	
before	so that	whenever	

Subordinating conjunctions serve two functions. They can introduce **adverb clauses** (see chapter **23**), which modify verbs and sometimes adverbs, nouns, and adjectives.

> *When* the meeting began, we suspended the reading of the minutes.

Or they can introduce **adjective clauses** (see chapter **23**), which modify nouns or pronouns.

> The exact time *when* death occurred cannot be determined without an autopsy.

Relative pronouns (see section **20b**) can also be subordinating conjunctions:

that	which	whoever	whomever
what	who	whom	whose

The police officer *who* saved the boy's life has four children of his own.
The reward, *which* now totals $2,000, remains in a trust fund.
The reward *that* Rachel Thompson won totaled $4,200.

Using these subordinating conjunctions enables writers to build **complex sentences**, which feature one main clause and at least one subordinate clause (see section **23c**). Here is a complex sentence that contains three subordinate clauses in addition to the main clause (which is highlighted in boldface):

At the next campaign stop in New Hampshire, *where* his career seemed suspended yet *where* he needed desperately to win, **George Bush turned into a scrappy campaigner** *who* stepped out of President Reagan's shadow to assume his own identity.

Notice how the subordination helps build a far stronger image than a string of simple sentences might produce.

9c Use subordination to revise short, choppy sentences.

Except in rare circumstances, writers do not want to produce a "grade school primer" effect (see chapters **10** and **11**). A simple way to eliminate short, choppy sentences is to subordinate some of them, even if the ideas are originally equal and coordinate:

CHOPPY: It was raining. The day was gloomy. We had nothing to do. We sat moodily by the fire.

SUBORDINATED: Because it was a rainy, gloomy day and we had nothing to do, we sat moodily by the fire.

The writer's primary idea, "we sat moodily by the fire" is now supported by the secondary, subordinate ideas: "Because it was a rainy, gloomy day and we had nothing to do." The writer thereby reduces four clauses to a complex sentence of one main clause and one sub-ordinate clause.

Here is another passage that subordination will improve:

> CHOPPY: The time arrived for a decision. Ned Smith made the motion to adjourn. Dot Watson insisted on a vote before adjournment. The chair called a five-minute recess for caucus meetings.

This writer has been lazy; a moment's reflection could produce a revision that subordinates most ideas and emphasizes the chair's decision:

> REVISED: When Dot Watson challenged Ned Smith's motion to adjourn and called for a vote, the chair called a five-minute recess for caucus meetings.

9d Subordinate one or more clauses of long compound sentences.

Too many compound clauses strung together can give a singsong effect and distract the reader from the point at hand. Writers can avoid this problem by subordinating some of the structures. The singsong example below can be tightened by subordinating the phrases or by using either a subordinating conjunction or a relative pronoun with a dependent clause.

> SINGSONG: No one can tell how long the oil resources of the United States will last, and the endurance of the reserves will depend on imports of foreign oil, and the imports will depend on foreign relations and the world economy.

> SUBORDINATED PHRASES: No one can tell how long the oil resources of the United States will last *because of foreign imports, diplomatic relations, and the world economy.*

> SUBORDINATE CONJUNCTION: No one can tell how long the oil resources of the United States will last *because* foreign imports affect domestic oil fields and diplomatic relations affect the world economy.

RELATIVE PRONOUN: Few analysts will attempt to predict the future of American oil resources, *which* are affected by imports, diplomatic relations, and the world economy.

9e   Reduce clauses to modifying words and phrases.

Writers often tighten their work by expressing secondary ideas in adjectives, adverbs, and modifying phrases rather than in clauses (see chapters **20**, **22**, and **23**). The following example changes three sentences into a single simple sentence by combining the images that the adjectives provide and using an introductory *participial phrase* (see section **22c**) to modify the main clause.

CHOPPY: The blooming daffodils were a sign of spring. They were planted in a terra-cotta pot. They added a touch of color to the front porch.

TIGHTENED: Blooming in the terra-cotta pot on the front porch, the colorful daffodils cheerfully signaled spring.

The next revision changes a compound sentence into a simple sentence.

COMPOUND: In the late 1980s, Mikhail Gorbachev was disturbed by the failure of the Soviet economy, so he instituted a series of reforms that reshaped the Warsaw Pact nations and thawed relations with the West.

SIMPLE: In the late 1980s, Mikhail Gorbachev, disturbed by the failure of the Soviet economy, instituted a series of reforms to reshape the Warsaw Pact nations and to thaw relations with the West.

Another effective method to tighten writing is to reduce a sentence or a clause to an **appositive**, which is a word or phrase that labels or explains the main idea and is set off by commas (see section **22e**).

WORDY: The new business building is to be named Carpenter Hall, and it will receive initial funding in 1990.

REVISED: The new business building, Carpenter Hall, will receive initial funding in 1990.

Notice how the revision eliminates the passive verb "is to be named" (see chapter **31**) and focuses the reader's attention on the 1990 funding.

Subordinate other ideas with adjective phrases (recall section **9b**).

WORDY: The industrial waste continued to ooze into the stream. It was putrid in the morning sun, and it was sour with untreated contaminates.

TIGHTENED: The industrial waste continued to ooze into the stream, putrid in the morning sun and sour with untreated contaminates.

What otherwise might appear as a run-on compound structure now becomes two adjective phrases to modify the main clause. Here is another example:

CHOPPY: They skated onto the arena ice. They were confident of their program. And they felt good about their ability to execute all the intricate moves.

TIGHTENED: They skated onto the arena ice, confident of their program and in their ability to execute all the intricate moves.

This version uses one adjective phrase to replace two complete sentences. The sentence is precise, and its rhythm is more pleasing to the ear than the original.

IN REVIEW

Put secondary ideas in phrases and in subordinate clauses to feature the main idea, which might get lost in a series of choppy sentences or unnecessary compound sentences.

EXERCISE 9.1 Combine the following choppy sentences by subordinating. For example:

> CHOPPY: Irrigation makes desert farming possible. Some water is pumped from underground supplies. Some water is diverted from rivers. Irrigated farms are common in the western United States and in Canada, Israel, and Russia.

> REVISED: Irrigation, using water pumped from underground supplies or diverted from rivers, makes desert farming possible in the western United States and in Canada, Israel, and Russia.

1. Most African farmers live in villages. They farm very small plots of land. They raise only enough food for their families. Some typical crops are peanuts, yams, and grains.
2. Japan has many small farms. Japan's farms are the most modern in Asia.
3. Chinese farmers have few modern machines. China depends on the large population to supply labor.
4. Farmers in central Asia are mostly nomads. They roam the countryside with their animals. They have domesticated goats, sheep, and cattle.
5. Many small farms in the United States are being sold. When crop prices are low, small farmers cannot earn enough money to pay their debts. Large agribusinesses now own much of the farmland.

EXERCISE 9.2 Revise the following compound sentences by subordinating minor ideas.

1. The student planning committee met at 2:00 in the conference room, and Professor Hatcher explained her preliminary ideas for the organization of the Astronomy Club.
2. Your computer seems to have a problem, and we do not have the necessary parts to repair it.
3. People like to work because it gives them the opportunity to use a skill that they have learned, or they can use their hands to build something, or they can contribute a talent to the world, and they can get paid for it.
4. "Equal pay for equal work" was a slogan for working women more than a decade ago, and women are still trying to make the slogan become a reality.

5. This versatile garden hat keeps you cool while you work outside, for the wide brim protects you from sunburn, and the mesh lets air circulate. It also is very lightweight.

9f   Avoid inverted subordination.

Writers sometimes put their main idea in a subordinate clause or phrase, which results in *inverted* or upside-down subordination. The writer knows the important element; the reader learns it only by interpreting. For instance, the next sentence appeared in an essay about people who cannot stop smoking.

> INVERTED: Cigarettes, which many people cannot stop smoking, cause cancer and heart disease.

The writer's main idea is subordinated; the sentence needs to be revised.

> REVISED: Even though cigarettes cause cancer and heart disease, many people cannot stop smoking them.

The key to revision is to determine which idea is primary and then to place it in the main clause. Writers can correct inverted subordination in several ways.

Tighten the sentence into one main clause.

> INVERTED: He has a habit of talking excessively about himself, which means that he probably feels insecure.   [most important idea is that he feels insecure]

> REVISED: He reveals his insecurity by talking excessively about himself.

Make the subordinate clause the main clause.

> INVERTED: I had just deposited the day's receipts in the all-night teller when a stranger grabbed me and demanded all my cash.   [most important idea is the robbery]

> REVISED: Just after I had deposited the day's receipts in the all-night teller, a stranger grabbed me and demanded all my cash.

Reduce a minor idea to a phrase.

> INVERTED: His new position is executive assistant to the president, which will allow him to utilize his talents for fundraising.   [the main idea is the talent for fundraising]

> REVISED: His new position, executive assistant to the president, will allow him to utilize his talents for fundraising.

EXERCISE 9.3   In each set of sentences below, find the major idea and then change the major idea into a main clause and the minor idea into a subordinate clause or phrase.

1. *Collage* comes from the French term *coller*, which means "to paste." It is a picture or design made by gluing pieces of material onto a board or canvas.
2. A collective farm is a government-owned farm. Communist countries use collective farms to maintain control over farm workers.
3. Sushi and sashimi are trendy foods. They contain raw fish.
4. *Gardyloo* was a warning cry in Scotland when slops were emptied from a window. It may have come from the French *garde à l'eau*, which means "look out for the water."
5. Entrepreneurs must know how to anticipate and take on responsible tasks. Books giving career advice say that they can create their own new businesses.

9g   Eliminate excessive subordination.

A sentence sprawls when it has too many subordinate ideas. Like a compound sentence overloaded with a series of independent clauses, a sprawling sentence tries to pack many subordinate ideas around a main clause. Readers get lost in the maze and cannot keep the relationships of parts clearly in mind. Often a sprawling sentence is simply too long.

> SPRAWLING: Most people, savvy business types especially, use clothing to gain an edge over someone they hope to do business with because a dark dress or suit with subdued accessories evokes power and sends the message that one is controlled and cool under fire.

The main idea, "people dress for power," gets lost in minor details and excessive subordination. In the revision, the writer emphasizes key ideas to control the sprawl:

> REVISED: Business people often dress for power by wearing dark dresses or suits with subdued accessories, thereby suggesting control and composure.

The key idea is now in the opening main clause, and two phrases contain the supporting ideas. The following techniques will help control sprawl.

To avoid sprawl, break a long sentence into multiple shorter ones.

Cut one long sentence into two or three sentences, adding transitional words, if necessary.

> SPRAWLING: Designers cannot justify ugly and drab furniture in offices and yet standard, uniform gray or brown designs appear time and again in private as well as public work areas, which means purchasing agents or their superiors are either insensitive to office design or they remain completely indifferent.

> TIGHTENED: Designers cannot justify ugly and drab furniture in offices. Nevertheless, standard, uniform gray or brown designs appear time and again in private as well as public work areas. It means purchasing agents or their superiors are either insensitive to office design or they remain completely indifferent.

Editing that isolates each main idea into its own sentence reduces sprawl and increases clarity.

Split a long string of relative clauses.

Multiple clauses that begin with *which, who,* or *that* can confuse the reader and distract him or her from the main point.

> CONFUSING: Television news seldom offers its viewers the human point of view, which means it carefully avoids the

voice of one person who might cut through the bureaucratic haze which fogs and distorts an honest evaluation of
events.

BETTER: Television news seldom offers its viewers the human
point of view. It carefully avoids the voice of one person
who might cut through the bureaucratic haze.

Editing that removes the "which" clauses creates two clear sentences
and avoids sentence sprawl.

> **IN REVIEW**
>
> Sprawling sentences are too long and overloaded with mis-
> cellaneous and unnecessary tidbits of information, so revise
> them.

EXERCISE 9.4   Revise the following sentences to eliminate excessive subordination. Break up the sentences so all the ideas are stated
clearly in main clauses or in subordinate clauses and phrases.

1. A school system is only as good as the support it receives from
the parents, so parents, who are concerned about their child's
future, must emphasize to the child the importance of education and let the child know that they will take an interest in
homework, school programs, and teacher conferences.
2. Industrial designers have long been aware that attractive and
colorful furniture in offices actually increases morale and effi-
ciency, in contrast to drab gray and brown designs that are
used so often it must mean that purchasing agents or their su-
periors are insensitive to the importance of office design or
think that dark colors are more serious and practical.
3. On their first day in the canyon, adventurers who ride burros
down the trails may concentrate on the swaying rhythm of
their animals, and worry about steep descents, but a few may
contemplate the grandeur of the walls around them, marvel-
ing that seas once flowed there, even before the mountains
rose and then dissolved into sand and mud.
4. Now a piece of furniture that can be ordered from many catalogs, the Adirondack chair, built of rough pine, but remarka-
bly comfortable because of the broad boards used in its seat

and back and handy because its wide arms can hold a book or a drink, was commonly found on cabin and hotel porches in the eastern mountain resort area, hence its name.

5. Taught that they must always be objective, newspaper reporters reveal nothing about themselves in their stories, which makes them different from most writers, whose words betray, if you will, their opinions and thus their personalities, which gives their writing a personal style.

Writers communicate their thoughts more effectively when they emphasize the main point of each sentence. They achieve the emphasis by placing the key words carefully; by using strong, active words; and by avoiding abstract language.

10a   Use emphatic placement.

Where ideas appear in a sentence is as important as *what* ideas appear in a sentence. Read the following example.

> In skating over thin ice, our safety is in our speed.
> — RALPH WALDO EMERSON

Emerson saves his key word, "speed," for the end of the sentence to stress it. In contrast, "To be safe, skate fast over thin ice" does not have the same impact. Here are some suggestions about how placement can help emphasize an idea. (See also section **11a** for the discussion of the *loose sentence*, which emphasizes an idea early in the sentence, and the *periodic sentence*, which makes the end of the sentence emphatic.)

The end of a sentence

The end of a sentence is the most emphatic position.

> UNEMPHATIC: Some people who wish to protect home and family purchase a gun, but a handgun may get the owner's children killed if they find it in a dresser drawer.

Without regard to the striking content, this writer has merely listed phrases. Note this revision:

> EMPHATIC: A homeowner who possesses a gun may wish to protect home and family, but a child who finds it may die.

In the next example, the key idea, the Arthurian romance, is buried in the middle of the sentence. Editing moves the important point to the end of the sentence where it receives more notice.

> UNEMPHATIC: The enduring popularity of the Arthurian romance shows that these tales speak to each succeeding generation.
> EMPHATIC: Each succeeding generation reinforces the enduring popularity of Arthurian romance.

The beginning of a sentence

The beginning of a sentence is also a strategic position to emphasize a point. Here are more examples where revision improves sentence emphasis.

> UNEMPHATIC: Our earth has what I consider to be a serious ecological problem of acid rain.
> EMPHATIC: Acid rain is a serious ecological problem.

> UNEMPHATIC: Evidence for the belief in witchcraft can be found throughout history.
> EMPHATIC: History provides plenty of evidence for the belief in witchcraft.

Punctuation

By controlling the flow of the sentence with punctuation, you can emphasize words and phrases. For example, an interrupting phrase late in the sentence, set off by dashes or commas, puts emphasis on the last word.

> Marketers plan promotions for known effects on consumers: popularity, preference, and — most important — purchase.

Commas can enclose parenthetical expressions and appositives to emphasize an idea.

> The field trip with the engineering group became a travesty, an absurd comedy of errors.

See part **7** for more information on using punctuation to highlight specific ideas.

Inverted word order

Reverse normal word order to emphasize your object and sometimes your verb.

> The opening allegro I disliked, but the sonata overall was grand.

Use this device rarely because surprise is part of its effect.

Repetition

Repeating a key word adds emphasis.

> Most of the time I don't have any fun. The rest of the time I don't have any fun at all.
>
> — WOODY ALLEN

Allen's repetition contributes emphasis to his ironic statement.

> Under a government which imprisons any unjustly, the true place for a just man is also a prison.
>
> — HENRY DAVID THOREAU

Thoreau gains emphasis with the repetition of derivatives of words: *imprisons–prison* and *unjustly–justly.*

> Never let a fool kiss you or a kiss fool you.
>
> — JOEY ADAMS

Adams achieves emphasis by reversing the noun-verb sequence of *fool* and *kiss.*

Alliteration

Using similar initial sounds is called **alliteration,** which provides uniformity that emphasizes key words. The technique ties meaning together with its string of similar sounds.

Worry, pain, time, and six children wore wrinkle after wrinkle into my weary forehead.
— WANDA THOMPSON, student

Let us have faith that right makes might; and in that faith let us to the end, dare to do our duty as we understand it.
— ABRAHAM LINCOLN

The first sentence repeats the *w* sound; the second, the *d* sound.

Metaphor and simile

A metaphor or simile provides emphasis by comparing a subject (the *tenor*) with an object, person, or event (the *vehicle*) to establish a dramatic and unexpected figure of speech. A **metaphor**, such as the one that follows, implies the comparison:

One hundred years later, the life of the Negro is still sadly crippled by the manacles of segregation and the chains of discrimination.
— MARTIN LUTHER KING, JR.

King used metaphor to say that blacks (the tenor) were still encumbered like a prisoner on a chain gang (the vehicle). Comparisons like this one, made from unrelated fields of experience, give stylistic emphasis unavailable in literal comparison (such as *the life of the Negro is still like the life of slaves*).

Another figure of speech, the **simile**, uses *like, as, looks like, seems to be* and other such words to express the comparison openly:

Laws are like cobwebs, which may catch small flies, but let wasps and hornets break through.
— JONATHAN SWIFT

The laws (the tenor) are said to be like cobwebs (the vehicle) to show how laws catch the weak and defenseless but allow the powerful criminals to escape the legal webs. (See chapter **19** for details about writing figurative language.)

Expletives

In general, limit the use of expletives. **Expletives**, or anticipatory subjects such as *there, what,* and *it,* delay the important idea of the sentence. They usually make weak beginnings.

UNEMPHATIC: There is another theory that explains the extinction of dinosaurs.

EMPHATIC: Another theory explains the extinction of dinosaurs.

UNEMPHATIC: What we need are people of courage and vision.

EMPHATIC: We need people of courage and vision.

However, if used carefully and sparingly, expletives can help build suspense and emphasis for sentence endings:

What was decided at the meeting remains secret to this day.

Building to a climax

Write a series of words, phrases, or clauses from shortest to longest or from least important to most important. (See section **5a**.) Keep the elements parallel to strengthen the series (see chapter **8**). Stylistically, the last item in a series has the emphatic position. Here is climactic order with a series of words.

The philosopher Thomas Hobbes said that life in a state of nature is solitary, poor, nasty, brutish, and short.

Its position at the end emphasizes the word *short*, which is an ironic misfit; its meaning builds quickly upon the misery of the first four conditions. Next, note the order of a series of four noun clauses.

The women, the fish market, the piled hoop of nets, and the sprawl of boats drawn up on shore all came together in a pictorial composition.

Each succeeding phrase is longer than the previous one, culminating in the sprawl of boats that apparently dominates the foreground of the painting. If you reverse the order, the emphasis will shift to the market and the women.

A series of compound verbs can also build to a climax, as they do in the "swirling" finale of this next example.

The sonata started briskly with the opening allegro, slowed with the adagio, danced through the third movement, and swirled into grandeur with the finale.

Even clauses can build to a climax.

> The experiment began with speculation, it continued with laboratory experiments, and it culminated with the discovery of a new, effective medication.

Reverse the order of the clauses above and the effect is anticlimactic.

IN REVIEW

Use emphatic wording to reduce wordiness, to reinforce your best thoughts, and—most important of all—to put your most important points where readers will notice them.

EXERCISE 10.1   Remove the unnecessary expletives in the following sentences.

1. There were only four people who volunteered to work on Christmas Day.
2. What was needed to manage the store was fourteen people.
3. It was decided by the local supervisor to close the store for Christmas day.
4. What happened then was that the supervisor was reprimanded by the district manager who said it was mandatory that the store be open on Christmas day.
5. There were many disgruntled employees who reported for work that day.

EXERCISE 10.2   Rewrite five of the following sentences to emphasize what you think are the most important ideas. Consider the word's grammatical function, its position in the sentence, and word order. You may wish to omit extraneous ideas or divide sentences. Be prepared to defend your revisions.

1. "No bigger than a snowflake" was a phrase once used to describe the fourth president of the United States, James Madison, who was a small and ordinary man.
2. Behind his unprepossessing looks, however, there was a brilliant political mind that bears the most responsibility for the Constitution of the United States, a document that has stood the test of time, even though it was the result of compromise between different political factions.

3. By the mid-1780s, after the Revolutionary War, the young United States was in disarray, with Congress not meeting regularly, with Virginians accusing New Englanders of attempting to divide the country into separate confederations, and even without a permanent capital, Congress meeting in different cities such as Philadelphia, Princeton, Annapolis, and New York City.

4. Current political thinking, based on the ideas of a French political philosopher, Baron de Montesquieu, maintained that a republican government could not exist in a large territory because if people lost direct control over their representatives they would be tyrannized by long-distance corrupt governors.

5. Madison disagreed, thinking that what the country needed was a strong central government, instead of powerful independent states.

6. After a small preliminary meeting in fall of 1786 with representatives from only five (of the thirteen) states, 55 men from twelve states (not Rhode Island) met in the spring of 1787 to draft a new constitution for a strong national government.

7. Many on the constitutional committee were prominent citizens, including George Washington, James Madison, Alexander Hamilton, and Benjamin Franklin; Thomas Jefferson and John Adams were in Europe, and, because he said he "smelled a rat," Patrick Henry stayed home in Virginia.

8. Because Madison understood that whoever sets the agenda controls the meeting, he persuaded the governor of Virginia, Edmund Randolph, to present Madison's ideas under the guise of the "Virginia Plan."

9. Madison called the slave trade a great evil and said that "a dismemberment of the union would be worse"—so slavery was not forbidden by the constitution.

10. To protect the rights of the people against too much federal government control, the Anti-Federalists, as critics of the constitution were called, persuaded the convention to adopt a bill of rights, which are the first ten amendments.

EXERCISE 10.3   Copy each of the following sentences to get a feel for structure and style. Then compose your own sentence in a similar structure.

> MODEL: If a thing is worth doing, it's worth doing well.   [repetition of key words]

IMITATION: If killing baby seals is a sport, then it is a sport worth killing.

1. I can find nothing, nothing, absolutely nothing to keep me in this town.   [immediate repetition of a word]
2. What I saw in you was hope, hope for a future, for a chance at success, for a touch of happiness.   [repetition at the beginning of each unit in a series]
3. To the marriage ceremony staggered the groom.   [inverted sentence order]
4. Some men love you, some lie to you, and some simply leave you.   [balanced phrases with repeated words and alliteration]
5. In a white fury she stabbed him with her cutting words.   [figurative sentence]

EXERCISE 10.4   Describe the methods of emphasis that the writers use in the following quotations.

MODEL: Never in the field of human conflict was so much owed by so many to so few.
— WINSTON CHURCHILL

DESCRIPTION: Churchill uses repetition ("so much," "so many," "so few") to show both emphasis and contrast.

1. Her skin was a rich black that would have peeled like a plum if snagged, but then no one would have thought of getting close enough to Mrs. Flowers to ruffle her dress, let alone snag her skin.
— MAYA ANGELOU, "A Lesson in Living"

2. I say to you today, my friends, that in spite of the difficulties and frustrations of the moment I still have a dream. It is a dream deeply rooted in the American dream.
— MARTIN LUTHER KING, JR.

3. Power tends to corrupt and absolute power corrupts absolutely.
— LORD ACTON

4. Money is like muck, not good except it be spread.
— FRANCIS BACON

5. It is the best of all trades, to make songs, and the second best to sing them.
— HILAIRE BELLOC

6. Are they not criminals, books that have wasted our time and sympathy; are they not the most insidious enemies of society, corruptors, defilers, the writers of false books, faked books, books that fill the air with decay and disease?
   — VIRGINIA WOOLF, "How Should One Read a Book?"

7. Nothing is ever enough when what you are looking for isn't what you really want.
   — ARIANNA S. HUFFINGTON, "The Fourth Instinct"

8. We must indeed all hang together, or, most assuredly, we shall all hang separately.
   — BENJAMIN FRANKLIN

9. This man I thought had been a Lord among wits; but, I find, he is only a wit among Lords.
   — SAMUEL JOHNSON

10. If you're going to write, don't pretend to write down. It's going to be the best you can do, and it's the fact that it's the best you can do that kills you.
    — DOROTHY PARKER

10b   Use strong, active verbs.

Overuse of the verbs *be* and *have* (*is, are, was, were; have, has, had*) results in dull prose with frequent lapses into the passive voice:

> Eye contact *is* one facial expression that *is* probably the most common form of nonverbal communication. By the eyes alone one can tell if the other person *is* listening to what *is* being said. Eye contact *is* a good indicator of how a person feels about the other. The eyes *have* always *been* used extensively to show interest in someone of the opposite sex.   [63 words]

To edit forms of *be* and *have* from such writing, identify the important action and make it the verb. Decide who or what performed the action and let that be the subject. Make the receiver of the action the direct object. Using the passage above as an example, the noun *expression* can become the verb *expresses*, and the noun *indicator* can become the verb *indicates*:

> The face *expresses* most nonverbal communication. Eye contact, for example, *indicates* how one person feels about another. The eyes *receive* signals to learn if someone *is* listening attentively,

and they also *send* signals of love, hate, and even disinterest. [39 words]

As this example shows, active verbs make the writing emphatic and interesting, whereas passive verbs blur and sometimes hide the actors (the subjects), add unnecessary words, and weaken the sentence (see chapter **31**). In the **active voice**, the subject acts on the direct object; it says who or what delivers the action. In the **passive voice**, the subject is acted upon.

PASSIVE: The field goal was kicked successfully.

ACTIVE: Ted Zubrinski successfully kicked the field goal.

Surely the writer should give the actor, Ted Zubrinski, credit for scoring the field goal.

PASSIVE: This program has been performed by the band in almost every Christmas parade for the last six years.

ACTIVE: The band usually performs this program in the Christmas parade.

PASSIVE: Finally after many years the Roman Empire was brought to an end, and a new period of European history was started about A.D. 400. It was called the Middle Ages.

ACTIVE: The Roman Empire ended, and a new period of European history—the Middle Ages—started about A.D. 400.

Changing the passive voice to an active voice makes the writing concise and emphasizes the primary ideas. (See section **31b** for the few occasions in which the passive voice is appropriate.)

EXERCISE 10.5 Revise the following sentences by replacing the forms of the verb *be* and *have* with strong, action verbs, as shown below. Add modifying words and recast the sentences if you wish, but do not change the basic meaning.

ORIGINAL: This program was started in 1986 to serve military dependents who were in need of employment.

REVISED: The Army created this program in 1986 to serve dependents who needed employment.

1. This dress rehearsal will be the final test for the entire crew, actors as well as technicians.
2. The boxer is a medium-sized dog of a breed that was developed in Germany and that is known for "boxing" with its front paws.
3. The chemistry laboratory has been closed for three days because of the high radiation levels.
4. Bicycling is an exercise that is good for the whole body because it is a muscle builder and a heart and lung strengthener.
5. Paul Theroux is a travel writer who has been a passenger on trains through Asia, South America, and Europe.
6. How and where actors are listed in movie advertisements is a matter that is negotiated between the actors' agents and the studios.
7. Although each player who was involved in the fight has been questioned by the coaching staff, there has been no official announcement about disciplinary action.

EXERCISE 10.6   Underline the passive constructions and circle the forms of the verbs *be* and *have* in the following paragraph. Then rewrite the paragraph using the active voice and strong verbs.

Customers' needs must be satisfied by a product, or it will not be purchased. Many companies were started with the development of a product that was an inspiration in anticipation of what people would buy, but later those same companies have been failures with some of their ideas and products. For example, the low-cost, mass-produced automobile that was invented by Henry Ford caused the opening up of new automobile markets. But the refusal of Ford to offer choices in colors and styles meant that General Motors was able to gain more of the market. Today well-made products, from computers to cake pans, are sent to the marketplace by both large and small companies, but many have not been bought. Market research into the satisfaction of the buyers' psychological and practical needs is a necessity to be competitive in the current situation of the market.

EXERCISE 10.7   Revise the following sentences in the active voice, as shown below.

> ORIGINAL: All foreign governments around the globe are examined daily by the CIA.

> REVISED: The CIA examines daily all foreign governments around the globe.

1. The performance by the guest pianist is scheduled for May 15.
2. The decision to delay the vote for one week has been endorsed unanimously by the committee.
3. Discussion and analysis of the problem of role playing in human relationships were provided by Dr. Smothers.
4. Soon the discovery will be made by young people that they will inherit a gigantic national debt if economic policies are not changed.
5. The following information must be provided before the application can be processed: name, birthdate, social security number, and citizenship.
6. To calculate the time taken by the liquid to leach through the ground layers, the same formula used by Pratt and Chung has been adapted in this study.
7. It was evident by noticeable failing of eyesight and stiffness in his joints that age was telling on our faithful dog, Jackson.
8. Because the final safety check was not performed, the plane was allowed to take off with malfunctioning radar, but the error was discovered soon and a safe landing was achieved.
9. A realistic and current design that is typical of many automobile bodies was selected by the president.
10. An experimental study has been made by psychiatrists of the growth patterns of children from birth through adolescence.

10c   Avoid nominalizations.

Nominalizations change an action to an abstraction. That is, the writer changes a strong verb into a vague noun, which makes the sentence difficult to understand. Nominalizations cause wordy constructions that hide both the actor and the action. This next sentence uses two nominalizations.

> *Formation* and *implementation* of athletic policy is the job of the athletic director.

Compare the revised version, which identifies the actor and converts the nominalizations to active, emphatic words.

> The athletic director *forms* and *implements* athletic policy.

Adjectives also become nominalized when a writer changes a strong adjective into a vague noun, as shown by this next sentence.

> The *brightness* of the lights caused several drivers to swerve off the road.

Compare the revised version, which converts the nominalization to an adjective.

> The *bright* lights caused several drivers to swerve off the road.

The following verbs and adjectives often fall victim to nominalization (note that many nominalizations end in *-tion* and *-ness*):

Verb	*Nominalization*
act	action
implement	implementation
determine	determination
discover	discovery
investigate	investigation
prepare	preparation
exaggerate	exaggeration

Adjective	*Nominalization*
happy	happiness
sad	sadness
curious	curiosity
bright	brightness

EXERCISE 10.8   Change the nominalizations in the following sentences to verbs and adjectives. Rewrite the sentences to name actors if necessary.

1. The *discussion* about the rule by the referees continued for several minutes.
2. An *agreement* was reached by the referees to stop play for five minutes.

3. The *drawing* of the blueprints was done carelessly by two assistant architects.
4. Seat belt laws for the *prevention* of highway deaths now exist in most states.
5. The *use* of a high-quality brush by the homeowner will aid in the *timeliness* of painting the house.

CHAPTER

11

Improving Sentence Style: Variety

Imagine an essay that consists entirely of short, simple sentences or of long, compound or complex sentences. The result would not be a pleasure to read; it would not show any creativity, rhythm, or sense of style, and it would not highlight the essay's purpose. We have seen that one method to improve sentence style is to write sentences in ways that emphasize their key points (chapter **10**), but what good is a strongly crafted sentence if it is written in a manner that is identical to the rest of the sentences in the paragraph or the entire essay? The sentence would become lost in the monotony. Writers need to vary sentence structures in an essay to keep readers' interest active, to maintain an appealing rhythm, and to make sure that the truly important points stand out.

Sentences in an essay should display a range of forms and functions. Changing sentence lengths is one method to achieve variety, but four additional techniques are equally important. The essay should also contain (1) both loose and periodic sentences, (2) different types of phrases and clauses, (3) sentences written in different grammatical forms, and (4) sentences that express different methods of development.

11a Use both loose and periodic sentences.

In most sentences, words follow the pattern of subject-verb-object, with modifying phrases frequently trailing after.

```
                    direct
    subject   verb  object            modifying phrases
```
Oysters change sex one or more times during their lifetimes.

This traditional pattern, known as a **loose sentence**, enables a writer to express a key idea and follow it with details.

However, as we saw in section **10a**, delaying the main idea until later in the sentence can be highly effective.

Although some people merely think about changing their sex, consider this: the oyster does it several times during a lifetime.

Known as a **periodic sentence**, this pattern suspends the punch—the main clause—until the end.

The two sentence structures, loose and periodic, re-create two ways we think. The first is a natural flow of thoughts as they come; the second is a premeditated delay for suspense, forcing a reader's anticipation. Here are more examples of loose and periodic sentences.

Several professors sternly graded my piano recital, at which I played Beethoven's *Sonata Number 8 in C Minor* and Gershwin's *Rhapsody in Blue*.

The loose sentence above contains the writer's key concern, professors grading the recital, early in the sentence.

Igniting somewhere near the boiler room and racing through the building's century-old ductwork, feeding all the while on valuable books and documents, flames destroyed the Woodson Library.

The periodic sentence above saves the key idea, the destruction of the library, until the end.

NOTE: Do not overuse periodic sentences; too many give your writing the rhythm of crescendo after crescendo, with no lull.

The following paragraph mixes loose and periodic sentences.

The walls of the pavilion shed were scribbled all   loose over with dirty drawings and words and detailed

slanders on the prettier girls. After hours, when the
supervisors were gone, if you were tall enough you   periodic
could grab hold of a crossbeam and get on top of the
shed, where there was an intimate wedge of space
under the slanting roof; here no adult ever both-   loose
ered to scrub away the pencilings, and the wood
fairly breathed of the forbidden. The very silence of
the pavilion, after the day-long click of checkers and   periodic
pokabok of ping-pong, was like a love-choked hush.

           —JOHN UPDIKE, "The Playground"

In the final sentence Updike carefully delays his predicate, which
contains his primary metaphor: the silent sanctuary of the pavilion
shed "was like a love-choked hush."

One student writer positioned a periodic sentence with a loose
one for this effect:

Covered with dark river mud, small-boned and frail   periodic
looking, with soulful moans and pitiful whimpers,
the baby calf cried out for its mother. The cow at-   loose
tacked the fence to reach her calf, breaking through
at a weak, rotted cedar post.

           —TOMMY POSTMAN

EXERCISE 11.1   Revise each of the following groups of short sentences first into a *loose* sentence, in which ideas string along after the
main clause, and then into a *periodic* sentence, which builds to a
climax.

1. Advertising serves the entire community. It promotes increased sales of consumer products. It stimulates manufacturing and trade. It supports public service projects.
2. An allergy is the body's reaction to certain external substances. Some causes of allergies are house dust, mold spores,
   pollen, and the hair of house pets.
3. Ancient cultures continue to affect us. The ancient Hebrews
   gave us the Bible, the ten commandments, and the belief in
   one God. Ancient Egypt contributed paper and a calendar
   to the world. Greece bequeathed music, drama, and
   architecture.
4. A human even at a slow walk can easily outrun a turtle, but
   human hands cannot easily break through the turtle's shell.

Similarly, a cheetah can easily chase down a porcupine only to find the catch rather sticky. The laws of compensation in the animal kingdom provide unusual, sometimes humorous, circumstances.

5. The beauty of the bubbling creek called to me. Especially delightful were the reflections of sun and sky sparkling above the dark shadowy figures of the circling trout.

11b   Use different types of phrases and clauses.

Writers often have a favorite sentence structure — that structure is part of their style — but during editing they look for ways to expand their work that accent and highlight the key points. They create variety in their sentences with different types of phrases and subordinate clauses that expand and focus the main ideas.

Adverb clause

An **adverb clause** (see chapter **23**) modifies the verb of the main clause. It can appear in any part of the sentence, but to highlight the main clause it is most effective at the beginning of the sentence.

> *After he had passed the midterm exam* and *even after he had finished the research paper*, Jerome abruptly withdrew from the course.

This periodic sentence uses the adverb clause to prepare the reader for the main idea, Jerome's sudden withdrawal.

Relative clause

A **relative clause** is an adjective clause — that is, it modifies a noun and begins with a relative pronoun, such as *who, whoever, that,* or *which* (see section **20b** and chapter **23**).

> My father brought home a German bride, Ingrid, *who became my dearest friend* and *who became, except for natural childbirth, my mother*.

In this loose sentence, the relative clauses follow the main clause to explain two things about the writer's relationship with Ingrid.

Noun phrase

Noun phrases (see chapter **22**) are word clusters that function as nouns: *the chief with the weathered face, a beautiful log house*. The noun phrase often appears as an appositive phrase (see section **22e**), which follows and renames another noun:

> The raw-boned Indian, *a Sioux warrior*, stood profiled on the bluff.

Sometimes a noun phrase, set off by commas, adds variety to sentence structure.

> The raw-boned Indian warrior stood profiled on the bluff, *the wind in his face, the sky behind him*.

The noun phrases add to the imagery of the scene.

Verbal phrase

Participles, gerunds, and infinitives (see section **22c**) are the verbals.

> *Thinking of the battle*, the raw-boned Indian warrior stood profiled on the bluff ready *to defend his people*.

The participial phrase introduces the subject and the infinitive phrase tells why he was there. The **verbal phrases** expand upon the main clause, adding information for the reader and variety to the sentence structure.

> Basically the family has fulfilled three social functions—*to provide a basic labor force, to transmit property,* and *to educate and train children* not only into an accepted social pattern but also in the work skills upon which their future subsistence would depend.
>   —J. H. PLUMB

In this loose sentence, the infinitive phrases follow the main clause to form a list that expands and explains the social functions of the family.

Adjective phrase

Adjective phrases (see chapter **22**) modify the subject of the main clause. They often take the form of prepositional phrases, infinitive phrases, and participial phrases.

Consider the beer can. It was beautiful—*as beautiful as the clothes-pin, as inevitable as the wine bottle, as dignified and reassuring as the fire hydrant.*

—JOHN UPDIKE

This loose sentence has trailing phrases to develop visual imagery for the beer can, renamed by the pronoun *it* and modified by the adjectives *beautiful* and *inevitable* and the participles *dignified* and *reassuring*.

Police often face destiny *in the form of a teenager with a Saturday night special in a nervous, quivering hand.*

This loose sentence uses prepositional phrases to modify and expand the meaning of *destiny*.

To show courage in the face of insurmountable odds and yet to protect the dog soldiers from annihilation—the tasks of leadership burdened the aged chief.

This periodic sentence features introductory infinitive phrases that modify the subject *tasks*.

Absolute phrase

The **absolute phrase** (see section **22d**) is unconnected grammatically to the rest of the sentence and usually consists of a noun or pronoun with a participle.

The convict looked down on his accusers, *his head cocked to one side, a smirk drawing up the corner of his lips, his eyes challenging the courage of them all.*

In this loose sentence the absolute phrases follow the main clause to embellish the visual impact of *how* the convict looked.

Prepositional phrase

Prepositional phrases consist of a preposition and its object plus any modifiers (see sections **20f** and **22b**).

She chewed her gum *in time to the music.*

Here two short phrases in the loose sentence follow the main clause to describe vividly the verb *chewed*.

Adverb phrase

Like the adverb clause, the **adverb phrase** (see section **20d** and chapter **22**) modifies a verb, adjective, or another adverb, and it answers the questions *how, how much, when*, or *where*.

> The mice huddled *in one corner in a disorganized cluster of stupor and listlessness.*

In this loose sentence the prepositional phrases modify the verb *huddled*.

IN REVIEW

Create variety in your sentences and form the loose and periodic sentences by expanding the main clause with modifying units, either clauses or phrases that usually precede the main clause or follow it.

EXERCISE 11.2 Write one sentence for each word group below. Expand the main clause (shown on the left) with modifying elements (shown on the right). Create both loose and periodic sentences.

EXAMPLE: The dog barked   at midnight
just below my window
in sporadic, unpredictable
bursts.

The dog barked in sporadic, unpredictable bursts just below my window at midnight.
OR
Just below my window, in sporadic, unpredictable bursts at midnight, the dog barked.

1. The marshal faced the angry vigilantes

his eyes calm
hands resting on pearl-handled revolvers
badge glittering with rays of authority

2. Very few players perform
only for fun the of the
game

not the swift running back
not the All American
lineman
not even the quarterback

3. The snow silently covered
the city

after weathermen had
predicted partly cloudy
skies
after most people had
curled warmly into sleep

EXERCISE 11.3 Rewrite the following sentences so each begins with a word, phrase, or clause other than the subject. You may change words from one part of speech to another, combine sentences, or make other changes as well.

> EXAMPLE: The river stretched lazily, unwinding eastward into the sunrise.
>
> OR
>
> Unwinding eastward, the river stretched lazily into the sunrise.
>
> OR
>
> Stretching lazily, the river unwound into the sunrise.

1. Harry Houdini was a famous magician who specialized in spectacular escapes from handcuffs, straitjackets, locked chests, and jail cells.
2. He challenged the police force wherever he went to keep him locked up, then used his escape as publicity for his show.
3. He embarrassed smug police officers from San Francisco to London by the ease with which he slipped from their most sophisticated manacles.
4. The police in Germany vowed to end their humiliation and get revenge because they feared that Houdini's exploits would encourage criminals to attempt escapes.
5. Houdini claimed that he could escape from any kind of restraint.
6. Inspector Werner Graff maintained that Houdini had escaped from only simple restraints and had used trickery, so he should be prosecuted for fraud.

7. Houdini sued Inspector Graff and the police for libel, a brave and confident act for an American Jew who had embarrassed the German police.
8. The police brought to the trial a specially made pair of handcuffs that, once closed, could not be reopened, even with its own key, in an attempt to embarrass Houdini.
9. Houdini tossed the cuffs on the judge's bench four minutes after he had been locked into them.
10. The police were forced to publish an apology and pay the costs of the trial by a judge who ruled in Houdini's favor.

11c   Write sentences of differing structures.

In order to maintain the reader's interest, essays and individual paragraphs need a mixture of the four sentence types (simple, compound, complex, and compound-complex) (see section **21a**). A careful blend of structures establishes a rhythm that is pleasing to the reader's ear and a cadence that helps the reader focus on the main points of the essay.

Recall that **simple sentences** contain only a main clause, so place them in emphatic positions to make a quick, definitive point, especially at the beginning or end of paragraphs and as transitional bridges from one idea to another. **Compound sentences** contain two or more main clauses joined usually by a coordinating conjunction, so use them to place two significant ideas side by side for comparison or contrast (see chapter **8**). **Complex sentences** contain a main clause and at least one subordinate clause, so use them to highlight your best idea in the main clause and suppress minor thoughts into subordinate clauses (see chapter **9**). **Compound-complex sentences** contain two or more main clauses supported by at least one subordinate clause, so use them to feature two significant ideas in the main clauses and to subordinate minor ideas.

main clause

A little learning is a dangerous thing.

—ALEXANDER POPE   [simple]

```
                                    coordinating
              main clause           conjunction
       ┌─────────────────────────┐  ┌──┐
```
A little learning is a dangerous thing, but
```
       main clause
┌──────────────────────────────┐
```
a lot of ignorance is just as bad.

—BOB EDWARDS   [compound]

```
                      main clause
       ┌───────────────────────────────────────┐
```
A little learning is not a dangerous thing to one
```
            subordinate clause
┌────────────────────────────────┐
```
who does not mistake it for a great deal.

—WILLIAM ALLEN WHITE   [complex]

```
              main clause              subordinate clause
       ┌─────────────────────────┐  ┌───────────────────┐
```
Never learn to do anything: if you don't learn,
```
                    main clause
┌───────────────────────────────────────────┐
```
you'll always find someone else to do it for you.

—MARK TWAIN   [compound-complex]

Form serves meaning and purpose, so all four types of sentences should appear at appropriate places in writing. The best writers orchestrate these forms within paragraphs. The passage below, for example, demonstrates this variety. Only five sentences long, it nevertheless uses three forms: simple, complex, and compound-complex sentences. Sentence length ranges from nine to thirty-eight words.

> Our earth has a serious problem of acid rain.   simple
> This problem first came to the attention of scientists in Northern Europe more than twenty years   compound-complex
> ago, and since then they have proven that it adversely affects water, stone, metal, plants, and especially humans (Skjer and Whorton 54). Although   complex
> statistics show that each year sulfur dioxide and nitrogen emissions increase dramatically, many people seem unaware and—worse—uncon-cerned that the international problem escalates in

seriousness. The rain continually becomes more   simple
acidic. As a result, scientists all over the world now   complex
seek a solution that will accommodate the environment and the human population.

— LISA BARNETT, student

This writer maintains a harmony of ideas and a rhythm of syntax by balancing main ideas with interjections of subordinate thoughts. She opens with a simple sentence to establish the subject clearly. She then balances past discoveries with contemporary findings. Next she uses a subordinate clause to introduce a primary concern — the apathy of the public. She returns to a simple sentence to emphasize again the central topic, and a complex sentence closes the paragraph and focuses on the search for a solution.

EXERCISE 11.4   The following paragraph features an abundance of simple sentences. Revise it to achieve variety, emphasis, and rhythm in the sentence structures by forming complex, compound, and compound-complex sentences in addition to the simple sentences.

The Greek physician Hippocrates lived almost 2500 years ago. Some of his ideas retain amazing currency, however. The Hippocratic school of medicine separated medicine from superstition and speculation, for example. It considered medicine a science based on objective observation and critical deductive reasoning. Hippocrates did subscribe to the ancient belief that disease was caused by an imbalance in the four humors. (These humors, or bodily fluids, were blood, phlegm, black bile, and yellow bile.) However, he thought the humors were glandular secretions. Doctors know today that hormonal imbalances can affect our mental and physical health. Hippocrates also believed that medicine should build the patient's strength through appropriate diet and hygiene. Doctors should resort to more drastic treatment only when symptoms make it necessary. In the Hippocratic tradition a goal of medicine today is good health through proper diet, hygiene, and exercise.

EXERCISE 11.5   The following paragraph features an abundance of compound sentences. Edit it to achieve greater variety in sentence forms, to emphasize the main points, and to establish a rhythm.

The belief in life after death is older than recorded history, for it was first handed down by word of mouth. Many people today accept reincarnation as part of their faith, but most people do not accept it. It is, in truth, a type of human evolution; the life of a person evolves through various stages. The butterfly is an excellent analogy, for it lives first as a caterpillar, then as a chrysalis, and finally as a butterfly. A person is like that: a spiritual being inhabits the physical body.

11d   Write sentences that express different methods of development.

An essay needs variety in sentence content just as it needs variety in structure. As discussed in chapter **6**, sentences function differently: some *define* a subject, some *compare* the subject with similar topics, and some provide *examples*. Other sentences *describe, classify,* or explain *causes and effects*. All sentences in an essay or a paragraph do not need to be written in the same method of development. That is, a definition essay may have sentences that compare, classify, illustrate, and so forth.

Each sentence in the narrative paragraph that follows has a function, which is identified in the margin.

The flag of truce, a white flag wilting sadly down against its hickory pole, seemed to bounce slowly up and down with the hesitant rhythm of the retreating army.	narration
It had replaced the American flag, the stars and stripes, that had accompanied General Winchester through the Revolutionary battles and through several Canadian conflicts in 1812.	explanation
The ordeal of surrender now loomed darkly over the army—submission to a hated enemy, surrender of all weapons, and, most degrading of all, imprisonment.	process
In General Winchester's mind this dismal affair contrasted dramatically with the glory of his victorious march into Baltimore in 1777.	contrast
There the sun sparkled on dancing spectators and parading troops; here dreary rain mixed with sleet pelted the bowed heads of his soldiers.	comparison, narration
He mentally catalogued the causes: inefficient supply lines, logistical errors because of inaccurate maps, and no troop reinforcements for more than three months.	cause and effect, classification

In addition to the initial sentences of narration, this writer uses five different methods of development. These and the other methods detailed in chapter **6** provide variety in an essay and help reinforce the essay's purpose.

IN REVIEW

Use sentences that serve your needs: a compound sentence to contrast ideas, a narrative sentence to provide historical perspective, or other types.

EXERCISE 11.6   Name the development function of the following sentences. Choose from this list: description, narration, definition, contrast, process, comparison, example, classification, cause-effect. Review chapter **6**, if necessary.

A. Agronomists crossbreed plants to produce hybrids by using the pollen of one kind of plant to fertilize another kind of plant.

B. Canning has two primary aims: (1) to sterilize food and keep it germ free, and (2) to seal it and keep out micro-organisms.

C. Former President Gerald R. Ford was born in Omaha in 1913, graduated from the University of Michigan in 1935, won election to the House of Representatives in 1948, and succeeded Richard Nixon as president in 1974.

D. The sun slowly sank into an orange mist, ballooned into a wide red fireball, and then sank reluctantly from sight while defiantly shooting streaks of gold into the clouds.

EXERCISE 11.7   Identify the function of each sentence in the following passages.

A.   ¹Up from the hardball diamond, on a plateau bounded on three sides by cornfields, a pavilion contained some tables and a shed for equipment.   ²I spent my summer weekdays there from the age I was so small that the dust stirred by the feet of roof-ball players got into my eyes.   ³Roof ball was the favorite game.   ⁴It was played with a red rubber ball smaller than a basketball.   ⁵The object was to hit it back up on the roof of the pavilion, the whole line of children in succession.

—JOHN UPDIKE, "The Playground"

B.   ¹A few months ago, I accompanied a male colleague from the science museum where I sometimes work to a lunch of the history of science faculty at the University of California.   ²I was the only woman there, and my presence for the most part was obviously and rudely ignored.   ³I was so surprised and hurt by this that I made an extra effort to speak knowledgeably and well.   ⁴At the end of the lunch, one of the professors turned to me in all seriousness and said: "Well, K. C., what do the women think of Carl Sagan?"   ⁵I replied that I had no idea what "the women" thought about anything.   ⁶But now I know what I should have said: I should have told him that his comment was unnecessary, injurious and out of place.

— K. C. COLE, "Women in Science"

C.   ¹Once, in a dry season, I wrote in large letters across two pages of a notebook that innocence ends when one is stripped of the delusion that one likes oneself.   ²Although now, some years later, I marvel that a mind on the outs with itself should have nonetheless made painstaking record of its every tremor, I recall with embarrassing clarity the flavor of those particular ashes.   ³It was a matter of misplaced self-respect.

⁴I had not been elected to Phi Beta Kappa.

— JOAN DIDION, "On Self-Respect"

CHAPTER

12

Correcting Misplaced Parts and Dangling Modifiers

Adjectives, adverbs, prepositions, participles, and phrases are modifiers (see sections **20d–20f** and **22b**). They qualify or limit the meaning of words.

$$\text{His face } \overset{\text{adjective}}{stern} \text{ and his stance } \overset{\text{adjective}}{rigid}, \text{ the coach glared } \overset{\text{adverb}}{angrily}.$$

Three common problems occur with modifiers: **dangling modifiers** do not logically modify anything in the sentence; **misplaced modifiers** seem to describe the wrong word and cause the reader to stop and puzzle over the writer's intent; and some long modifiers, when placed between main sentence elements, break up the flow of ideas.

12a Eliminate dangling modifiers.

A modifier dangles if it does not logically and clearly refer to the noun, pronoun, or verb it is intended to describe.

> DANGLING: *By studying extra hard*, the final exam should be easy.

Logically, an exam cannot study, so the modifying phrase dangles.

> EDITED: By studying extra hard, *I should pass* the final exam.

Editing the main clause by converting it to the active voice names the actor and corrects the problem.

Introductory verbal phrases

Dangling modifiers are usually introductory verbal phrases, as shown above. Here are a couple more examples.

DANGLING: Overburdened with reading and paperwork, organization was the only answer.

EDITED: Overburdened with reading and paperwork, *I realized that organization* was the only answer.

DANGLING: Although worried about the consequences, tuition was raised $65 per semester.

EDITED: Although worried about the consequences, *the Board of Regents raised tuition* $65 per semester.

Ambiguous subjects

Some opening phrases dangle because two subjects compete for the modifying phrase.

AMBIGUOUS: After receiving the grade of 97, the instructor advised me to remember that hard study earns high marks.

Who received the grade: the instructor or the student? The edited version makes clear who the actor is.

EDITED: *After I received* the grade of 97, the instructor advised me to remember that hard study earns high marks.

Dangling modifiers that follow the main clause

Some word clusters that follow the main clause can also dangle.

DANGLING: The committee meeting was tense, pencils poised for serious note-taking.

A committee meeting cannot poise pencils, so here is the revision.

EDITED: The committee *members were tense, their pencils* poised for serious note-taking.

EXERCISE 12.1   Revise the sentences below that contain dangling modifiers.

1. Beginning in Boston and ending in Seattle, only one stoplight interrupts the longest interstate highway in the United States, I-90.
2. To build a bypass of the stoplight and the town of Wallace, Idaho, an entire mountainside would have to be blasted away.
3. To avoid blasting the mountain to carve out a highway, all I-90 traffic travels through this historic mining town instead.
4. Driving from one end of I-90 to the other, history and geography can be discovered by the automobile traveler.
5. Boston is a fine introduction to what is to come along the highway, steeped in history and contained by the sea.
6. After rolling through the green hills of New England and New York, the flat plains of the Midwest appear.
7. Although boring from the car window, closer inspection of the towns reveals unique buildings like the Clock Tower in Rockford, Illinois, and the Corn Palace in Mitchell, South Dakota.
8. When viewing the Rocky Mountains in Montana, it is amazing that early pioneers managed to overcome them.
9. Exhausted after the harrowing drive through the mountain passes, the deserts of eastern Washington are almost a relief.
10. Eventually arriving at another city influenced by an ocean, Seattle is a long way from Boston in miles but not in spirit.

12b Place modifiers where their meaning is clear.

Put adjectives and adjective phrases next to the nouns they modify.

Place the red rose in the vase.

Place the roses, the red not the white, in the cut glass vase.

Adverbs, however, can float about in the sentence freely, but the words they modify should be clear.

Violently, the horse kicked the stall door.

The horse violently kicked the stall door.

Limiting words

Words such as *only, almost, just, even, scarcely, hardly,* and *nearly* limit the meanings of the words they modify. Writers, then, must be careful to place the limiting words where their meaning is clear: in front of the word or words they modify. Notice how the meaning of the sentence below changes when the position of the word *only* changes.

I *only* have eyes for you.

The *only* modifies the verb *have*, and its placement indicates that the speaker has nothing else to give.

I have eyes for *only* you.

In this case, the placement of *only* before *you*, the object of the preposition *for*, indicates that the speaker has eyes for no one else. Compare these examples.

I *just* ate the cashews and the pecans.   [meaning it just happened]
I ate *just* the cashews and the pecans.   [meaning other kinds of nuts were left]

Modifying phrases

Place modifying phrases next to the words they modify.

MISPLACED: During the ceremony, the colonel awarded medals to honored soldiers of gold and bronze.

The soldiers come in gold and bronze? For the sentence to be clear, the modifying phrase should immediately follow the word it describes.

EDITED: During the ceremony, the colonel awarded medals *of gold and bronze* to honored soldiers.

Here is another example.

MISPLACED: Billy Jean King arrived at the tournament where she had won her first professional match with her husband.

Editing shows that she arrived with her husband, not that she had played with him in the match.

> EDITED: Billy Jean King arrived with her husband at the tournament where she had won her first professional match.

Subordinate modifying clauses

> Place subordinate modifying clauses next to the words they modify.

> I will relax only after police arrest the man *who broke into my home and stole everything of value.*

The relative clause identifies clearly which man broke into the home by placing the pronoun *who* after the noun it modifies.

> MISPLACED: Ingmar Bergman's films have been praised by critics, which are famous as studies in guilt and morality.

What are famous: the films or the critics? Moving the actor forward as the subject and placing the relative pronoun *which* after *films*, the noun it modifies, make the meaning clear.

> EDITED: Critics have praised Ingmar Bergman's films, which are famous as studies in guilt and morality.

Squinting modifiers

A **squinting modifier** looks sideways in either direction; that is, it seems to modify both its preceding word and its following word. To make the meaning clear, the writer should move the modifier.

> SQUINTING: The police officer who was
>
> shooting *haphazardly* fell into the open sewer hole.

> IMPROVED: The police officer who was shooting fell haphazardly into the open sewer hole.

> SQUINTING: Pressing the Save key *often* means a sense of security to computer programmers.

> IMPROVED: By pressing the Save key often, computer programmers gain a sense of security.

EXERCISE 12.2 Rewrite the following sentences so all sentences are clear and have well-placed modifiers.

1. Mount Rushmore is a spectacular sculpture of presidents carved in the side of a mountain of South Dakota faces.
2. The site was only chosen because of stipulations by the sculptor, Gutzon Borglum.
3. The nation inherited a work of art of a sculptor of everlasting quality.
4. According to the plan, the sculptor gave birth to the founding of the United States by George Washington, the country's growth by Thomas Jefferson, its preservation by Abraham Lincoln in the Civil War, and its development by Theodore Roosevelt.
5. Borglum added a face of Theodore Roosevelt to the mountain that many considered unproven as president.
6. Using dynamite continually broke away excess stone.
7. Workers used Roosevelt's head to transport supplies that had a cable anchored on top.
8. The men worked on faces hung over the mountainside in leather harness-like seats.
9. Lincoln Borglum promised to finish the work at his father's deathbed.
10. To finish the sculpture completely satisfied Lincoln.

12c Do not interrupt the flow of the sentence with modifiers.

A single-word modifier sometimes fits nicely between a subject and its verb or between the verb and its object or complement:

The candidates *stubbornly* refused to answer the reporters' questions.

The newly announced nominees appeared *unusually* enthusiastic.

The adverbs *stubbornly* and *unusually* do not impede the flow of the sentences. Longer interruptions, however, can disrupt sentence movement and distract the reader.

Extended modifiers

Place extended modifiers before or after the main clause. In the example below, the phrases precede the main clause.

> Tapping his baton restlessly against his leg and openly displaying his impatience, *the conductor glared at me.*

In the next example, one subordinate clause precedes the main clause, and two modifying phrases follow. (See also **11a**.)

> As I fidgeted with my bow, *the conductor glared at me*, tapping his baton against his leg, his eyes unmoving and his lips rigid.

The final example contains a disruptive phrase between the subject and the verb. Editing moves the phrase to the beginning of the sentence, allowing the key idea, the main clause, to stand out.

> DISJOINTED: The candidates, *stubbornly joining forces against their common enemy*, refused to answer the reporters' questions.

> EDITED: Stubbornly joining forces against their common enemy, the candidates refused to answer the reporters' questions.

Verb phrases

In some cases, you can smoothly interrupt the parts of a complete verb with one or two short modifiers:

> The eagle had *not yet* arrived at its eyrie, so we settled in for a long wait.

The adverb phrase *not yet* interrupts the verb *had arrived* but does not cause confusion or misreading. However, longer modifiers should come before or after the complete verb.

> DISJOINTED: The committee had, *before it submitted the document to media services*, revised it twice and proofread it four times.

As edited below, the interrupting phrase is moved to the end.

> EDITED: The committee revised the document twice and proofread it four times *before submitting it to media services.*

Split infinitives

A **split infinitive** contains a modifier between the word *to* and the infinitive verb: to *hurriedly* run. Sometimes splitting the infinitive sounds natural, but you will always be correct if you place the modifier after or before the infinitive.

> SPLIT: When the storm clouds gathered in the west, the spectators prepared to *hurriedly* run to their cars.

> BETTER: When the storm clouds gathered in the west, the spectators prepared to run *hurriedly* to their cars.

Placing *hurriedly* before the infinitive would cause a squinting modifier. The writer of the next example inadvertently splits the infinitive with an entire clause.

> SPLIT: The golden eagle tries to, *if one is available*, build its nest on an isolated mountain crag, whereas the bald eagle prefers tall trees near water for its nest.

> BETTER: The golden eagle tries to build its nest on an isolated mountain crag, *if one is available*, whereas the bald eagle prefers tall trees near water for its nest.

Moving the adverb clause corrects the split infinitive.

IN REVIEW

Repair dangling modifiers and misplaced parts so that sentences flow smoothly with clarity and no jarring interruptions.

EXERCISE 12.3 Correct modifiers that interrupt the flow of the following sentences. If necessary, rewrite the sentences.

1. My survey, based on research for my sociology class, showed that almost as many men as women, surprisingly, use full service at gasoline stations.
2. The coaches, in their efforts to quickly raise funds to build a new indoor track facility, have recently made several gains, such as renewed student interest, a grant from the booster club, and support of the administration.

3. The advertising program must, because it is now several thousand dollars over its budget, unfortunately end tomorrow.
4. The Children's Hospital Benefit, an event that has successfully attracted many celebrities and politicians, has been canceled by the board of directors.
5. The decision to withdraw all funds from the operation, which we opposed from the start anyway and, for that matter, which would deplete the cash surplus, is wholeheartedly endorsed by the computer group.
6. The club treasurer had, without a vote from the members, donated funds to Hackers Unlimited.
7. He planned to slowly and secretly during the year transfer money to his own account.
8. The group would, in keeping with its main interests, prefer to especially spend the money on Friday afternoon leisure seminars.
9. We discovered that, to our sorrow, our bank account had, by our absconding treasurer, been reduced to zero.
10. Even though our account is, through no fault of the members, in the red, we are determined to, to the best of our ability, balance the account.

CHAPTER
13
Grammatical Completeness

Sentences must contain all the words necessary to make sense. During editing, therefore, writers must watch for incomplete sentences and must correct them.

13a Add verbs, prepositions, and other words to complete compound structures.

In compound structures, one device writers sometimes use is to omit a word that is clearly implied, as in the following:

Beauty is truth, truth beauty.

— JOHN KEATS

Keats's sentence is grammatical because the two clauses are clearly parallel in structure. The omitted word, *is*, would merely be a repetition of the *is* in the first clause.

Writing becomes ungrammatical, however, when the compound phrases, clauses, or sentences actually are not parallel, even though they are intended to be. Writers inadvertently may omit words that connect, relate, or repeat. The example below lacks a correct verb in the second clause.

INCOMPLETE: Four automobiles on display at the mall were vandalized, and one pickup truck stolen.

Although the writer may have intended the two clauses to be parallel, the singular noun *truck* in the second clause needs the singular form of the verb *be* instead of the plural form of the first clause.

EDITED: Four automobiles on display at the mall *were* vandalized, and one pickup truck *was* stolen.

The next example is missing a preposition to make the compound structure complete.

INCOMPLETE: A cautious fish is often

excited and then attracted *to* a spinner bait.

The parallel structure is intended to read "excited to and . . . attracted to," but "excited to" is not *idiomatic* — that is, it is not correct usage.

EDITED: A cautious fish is often

excited *by* and then attracted *to* a spinner bait.

The example below suggests a parallelism where none should exist.

INCOMPLETE: Science club boosters are businesspersons *whom we see* regularly at our meeting and travel with us on field trips.

The incongruity in this sentence comes from the implied "businesspersons *whom* travel." The sentence needs two different pronoun forms: the *objective* form ("businesspersons *whom* we see") in the first relative clause and the *nominative* form ("businesspersons *who* travel") in the second relative clause. (See chapter **28**.)

EDITED: Science club boosters are businesspersons *whom we see* regularly at our meetings and *who travel* with us on field trips.

13b Add the word *that* to prevent the misreading of subordinate clauses.

Writers may omit the subordinating conjunction *that* when there is no danger of misreading.

Our fascination with the egg is in the many forms [that] it takes.

However, readers often misread sentences that omit *that*.

INCOMPLETE: He saw Susan needed help.

COMPLETE: He saw *that* Susan needed help.

At first glance readers will read "He saw Susan" and then must adjust to the rest of the sentence. The direct object of the verb *saw* is not just *Susan* but the entire noun clause *that Susan needed help*.

INCOMPLETE: The supervisor soon determined a new french fry cooker would speed up service.

COMPLETE: The supervisor soon determined *that* a new french fry cooker would speed up service.

Similarly, the supervisor did not determine a cooker; he determined *that a new french fry cooker would speed up service*. (For a discussion of the use of *that* in restrictive clauses, see chapter **23**.)

13c Add words that are necessary to complete comparisons.

Comparisons are parallel structures, so writers should make sure to supply all necessary words to make the comparison grammatically complete.

INCOMPLETE: The fighting in Europe during World War II was just as dramatic as the Pacific. [The fighting was as dramatic as an ocean?]

EDITED: The fighting during World War II was just as dramatic *in Europe* as *in the Pacific*.

The sentence should compare fighting *in Europe* with fighting *in the Pacific*. Notice how the edited version also moves "in Europe" to make the comparison clear. Here is another comparison.

> INCOMPLETE: An attack against an entire Pacific island controlled by the enemy was more intimidating than a European city.   [A city was intimidating?]

> EDITED: *An attack against an entire Pacific island* controlled by the enemy was more intimidating than *an assault on a European city.*

The sentence needs to compare *an attack* with *an assault*, two similar actions.

Your readers should understand clearly the two subjects that you wish to compare.

> INCOMPLETE: President Truman won more votes in Missouri.   [He won more votes than whom?]

> EDITED: President Truman won more votes in Missouri *than Thomas Dewey.*

Advertisers may use incomplete comparisons ("Tide gets clothes whiter"), but you should not:

> INCOMPLETE: The supervisor gave Group A more work than the foreman.   [Group A had more work than the foreman?]

> EDITED: The supervisor gave Group A more work than the foreman *gave them.*

13d   Use intensifiers only with complete phrasing.

Occasionally writers use **intensifiers** such as *so, too,* and *such,* to convey strong feeling. If you use an intensifier, make sure to express a complete thought.

> INCOMPLETE: In their dealings with the Indians, the agents were too thoughtless.   [too thoughtless about what?]

The writer has a choice: delete the intensifier *too* or complete the thought.

> EDITED: In their dealings with the Indians, the agents were *too thoughtless about the Indians' religious affinity with the land*.

In the next example, the writer can delete *so much more* or complete the comparison.

> INCOMPLETE: The professor makes *The Scarlet Letter* so much more understandable.   [more understandable than what or whom?]
>
> EDITED: The professor makes *The Scarlet Letter* so much more understandable *than my high school teacher did*.

13e   Add the articles for grammatical completeness.

Edit your writing so the articles (*a, an*, and *the*) specify nouns clearly for your readers:

> INCOMPLETE: Josh Billings was pen name for American humorist, Henry Wheeler Shaw.
>
> EDITED: Josh Billings was *the* pen name for *an* American humorist, Henry Wheeler Shaw.

> INCOMPLETE: A baby may have birth defect as result of damage suffered during birth.
>
> EDITED: A baby may have *a* birth defect as *a* result of damage suffered during birth.

IN REVIEW

Add needed words to complete your compound structures, your comparisons, and all incomplete phrases and clauses.

EXERCISE 13.1 Revise the following sentences so that all structures and comparisons are clear and complete.

1. Jackie Robinson, first black baseball player in the major leagues, was neither afraid nor stopped by the threats he received.
2. His ten-year career with the Brooklyn Dodgers proved that he was as fine than any player, black or white.
3. Robinson was such a talented base stealer. His ability to distract the opposing pitcher was as valuable as stealing bases.
4. After he retired from baseball, he served as executive with a restaurant chain, insurance company, construction firm, chairman of the board of a bank, and the staff of Governor Nelson Rockefeller.
5. Jackie Robinson often said that he cared about being respected more than accepted.

EXERCISE 13.2 Revise the following sentences so that all structures and comparisons are clear and complete.

1. The Wolf Creek Nature Trail passes through deciduous and evergreen woods, bluffs along the creek, a boardwalk through a marsh, and a small meadow.
2. As wide a variety of plants grow along this trail than anywhere else in the park.
3. In the spring, walking through the wildflowers is like a soft carpet of stars.
4. However, some of the trail has such dangers hikers must register with the ranger before starting out.
5. This trail gives a hiker more variety and exercise.

CHAPTER
14

Correcting Mixed Constructions

In a mixed construction, sentence parts do not fit together grammatically or logically. The writer tries to make words serve functions that they cannot serve.

14a   Edit sentences for correct grammatical constructions.

Construction problems usually occur when a writer begins a sentence with one pattern in mind and switches suddenly to another pattern. In the following sentence the writer begins with an introductory adverb clause but then tries to force it into service as the subject of the verb *can damage*.

> FAULTY: *When children are punished without cause* can damage their self-images.

If the sentence is to begin with the adverb clause, the writer must finish with a subject and a verb:

> REVISED: When children are punished without cause, their self-images suffer damage.

If the writer wishes to emphasize the punishment, the revision might change the adverb clause to a gerund phrase, which *can* serve as a subject (see section **22c**).

> REVISED: *Punishing children without cause* can damage their self-images.

In the next example of mixed construction, the writer opens with the subject *man* and identifies which man with a participial phrase but ends the sentence without a verb.

> FAULTY: The man *dropping the flag to signal the start of the race.*

If the writer wishes to focus on the signal to start the race, then the past tense form of *drop* should serve as the verb:

> REVISED: The man *dropped* the flag to signal the start of the race.

However, the writer might wish to show what happened to the man while he is dropping the flag, in which case the writer must add a verb to the end of the sentence.

> REVISED: The man dropping the flag to signal the start of the race *fell from his perch onto the pavement.*

14b Avoid using *is when*, *is where*, and *is because*.

Grammatically, the verb *be* and its forms (*is, am, are, was, were*) require a noun or adjective as complement. *When, where,* and *because* are adverbs.

> FAULTY: The reason the test tube explodes is because we used the wrong chemicals.
>
> REVISED: *The test tube exploded because* we used the wrong chemicals.

FAULTY: An example of school spirit *is when the crowd gives* the home team a standing ovation after an overtime loss.

REVISED: An example of school spirit *is the crowd giving* the home team a standing ovation after an overtime loss.

Notice how the revised sentences, in addition to being grammatically correct, are also tighter and more emphatic.

14c   Correct illogical connections.

Sometimes the subject and the verb may agree grammatically but may not make sense.

FAULTY: The *increase* in instances of sports violence *escalates* every year.

REVISED: The *instances* of sports violence *escalate* every year.
OR
Sports *violence escalates* every year.

The *increase* cannot escalate, but the *instances* or the *sports violence* itself can. In the next example, the point is not that the employees will be lost but that they will lose a portion of their sick leave.

FAULTY: According to the new contract, all hourly *employees* who have accumulated sick leave *will be lost*.

REVISED: According to the new contract, all hourly *employees* *will lose* accumulated sick leave.

IN REVIEW

Examine your sentences to make sure the subjects and verbs are grammatical and make sense together.

EXERCISE 14.1   Untangle the errors of mixed construction in the following sentences.

1. To buy clothing at Saks Fifth Avenue is far more satisfying than the apparel you find at most department stores.

2. The difference in the design of outfits has deteriorated in the past few years.
3. By purchasing a winter wardrobe during February sales helps save money.
4. One example of the purchasing power of consumers is when they crowd around a sale counter and pick it empty.
5. The reason department stores have special sales almost every week is because nobody wants to pay retail prices anymore.

EXERCISE 14.2   Untangle the errors of mixed construction in the following sentences.

1. It is by constant daily writing that perfected the talents of Thomas Hardy.
2. To read the poetry of Thomas Hardy is more exhilarating than his novels.
3. The best parts of Hardy's poetry are when he satirizes the vanity and weakness of his characters.
4. When I read *Return of the Native* seemed easy to understand.
5. By constantly hammering home the vagaries of fate and its devastating effects on his characters caused many readers to label Hardy a pessimist.

15

Correcting Shifts

Writers inadvertently may switch the tense, voice, mood, person, number, or form of discourse within a sentence or a discussion. For instance, they may be writing about an event that occurred a week ago and suddenly start referring to it in the present tense; or they may be describing an emotion using the first person and switch to the second person halfway through the sentence. Such shifts confuse the reader and distract him or her from the main point of the essay.

15a Make verbs consistent in tense, voice, and mood.

Tense

Verb tense tells when actions occur (see chapter **30**), so a sentence should not shift from one tense to another when describing events that happen at the same time.

present tense

SHIFTING: The river *rises* and *falls* at least a foot whenever the

past tense

tugboat *pushed* loaded barges past the pier.

This sentence does not make sense because of the shift from present to past tense. The writer needs to decide which tense applies here and to revise the sentence accordingly.

EDITED: The river *rose* and *fell* at least a foot whenever the tugboat *pushed* the loaded barges past the pier.   [all past tense]

Historical events

In most instances, report historical events in the past tense. Make no unnecessary shifts to the present within sentences or from one sentence to the next.

Eisenhower retired from active duty and ~~sees~~ *saw* an opportunity to

serve as president of Columbia University as a way to demilitar-

ize his image. He frequently *traveled* to Washington for consul-

tations, so he ~~does~~ *did* not devote all his time to the university. Soon

political winds ~~begin~~ *began* blowing, and he *escalated* his unannounced

campaign for the presidency.

This writer mixed a present tense verb with a past tense verb in every sentence. Changing *all* verbs to the past tense provides consistency; it makes the statements accurate and logical for the reader.

Personal narrations

Because personal narration recounts past activities, it should be written in the past tense.

I *came* to the breakfast table famished for some of grand-

mother's great sausage and biscuits. Soon she *arrived* with a plat-

ter that *made* my mouth water. I ~~say~~ *said* a quick prayer to please her,

and then we *ate* with delirious joy.

Literature

Use the present tense in papers about literature and literary criticism.

Fictional events remain outside a normal time frame, so the present tense suggests that they continue to happen for each reader (see section **30c**).

> When Hamlet *continued* to procrastinate, he *angered* the ghost of
>
> his father who *wanted* Claudius to die.

In like manner, do not shift to past tense for the words of a literary critic, whose voice should continue in the present, as in this passage:

> "Ahab's quest dominates the narrative advance of *Moby-Dick*," *says* John Seelye in *The Ironic Diagram*, "but it is Ishmael who
>
> corresponds at the outset to Melville's earlier questers, Tommo
>
> and Taji" (60).

The present-tense *says* describes Seelye's criticism, just as the critic Seelye uses present-tense *dominates, is,* and *corresponds* to describe the fictional events.

Voice

Use either active voice or passive voice in your sentences, but not both in the same sentence. (See chapter **31**.) The subject can either perform the action (active voice) or receive the action (passive voice) throughout the sentence.

> SHIFT: Hawks *perch* high to watch for their prey, and then the rodents and small birds *are attacked* suddenly and silently. [switch from active to passive voice]

> CONSISTENT: Hawks *perch* high to watch for their prey, then suddenly and silently *attack* the rodents and small birds. [active voice only]

Mood

Consistently use the **indicative** mood for factual statements (*the troops marched*), the **imperative** mood for advice and commands (*prepare to march*), and the **subjunctive** mood for wishes and conditions contrary to fact (*I wish I were marching today*). (See chapter **32**.) Shifts in mood within a sentence and from one sentence to the next distract the reader from the point at hand.

> SHIFT: If Jake *were* more aggressive and if he *was* heavier, he could play linebacker.

> CONSISTENT: If Jake *were* more aggressive and if he *were* heavier, he could play linebacker.

The faulty example shifts from the subjunctive *were* to the indicative *was*; editing puts both verbs in the subjunctive mood.

IN REVIEW

Write generally in the past tense for reporting history and recounting personal experiences, but use the present tense to discuss literary works. Write in a consistent voice, active or passive, throughout a sentence; and sustain one mood— indicative for facts, imperative for orders, subjunctive for wishes.

15b Avoid shifts in person.

Within a discussion, writers should consistently use either the first person (*I* or *we*), the second person (*you*), or the third person (*he, she, it*, or *they*). Many writers, for instance, mistakenly shift to the second person *you* even though they may have begun the sentence or the paragraph in the first or the third person.

> SHIFT: *We* struggled to the top of the rocky ridge, and *you* could not believe how beautiful *our* valley looked.   [switch from first person to second person]

> CONSISTENT: *We* struggled to the top of the rocky ridge, and *we* could not believe how beautiful *our* valley looked.   [first person only]

In general, use the *first person* (*I* or *we*) point of view for personal accounts or narrations, the *second person* (*you*) for directions and how-to essays, and the *third person* (*he, she, it*, or *they*) to describe people, animals, or objects and to report general topics.

I'll never forget the first time *I* climbed to the top of a mountain.   [first person, narrative]

You should first sauté the onions. Then slowly add the beef cubes.   [second person, process]

To collect the sugar maple sap, *farmers* first drill one or more holes into each tree and drive a spout into each hole. *They* then hang a bucket under the spout or connect the spout to the plastic tubes of a pipeline system.   [third person, description]

15c   Be consistent in number.

Maintain the singular or the plural number throughout the sentence. Shifts occur most often when writers start a sentence with a singular noun or pronoun (*everyone* or *each contestant*) and change within the sentence to a plural pronoun:

> singular   plural   plural
>
> SHIFT: *Everyone* brought *their* own desig*ns* for the laboratory project.
>
> CONSISTENT: *All participants* brought *their* own desig*ns* for the laboratory project.   [plural only]
> OR
> *Each* brought *his or her* own desig*n* for the laboratory project.   [singular only]

Use singular pronouns to refer to *each, he, she, it*, or *everyone* and to other singular nouns and pronouns; use plural pronouns only to refer to plural antecedents such as *they, several people, all*, and so on.

15d   Avoid shifts between direct and indirect discourse.

Indirect discourse reports or paraphrases what is said: *The dean of students said to fill in all lines of the application.* Direct discourse quotes the exact words of the speaker: *The dean of students said, "Please fill in all the blanks on the application."* Use one or the other consistently in a single sentence.

indirect

SHIFT: The dean of students *said to return* our applications to

direct

room 36, and *you will hear from my office* within three days.

The sentence uses indirect discourse in the first clause and suddenly shifts, without quotation marks, to direct discourse in the second clause. Rewrite in one of two ways:

> CONSISTENT: The dean of students said, "Return your applications to room 36, and you will hear from my office within three days."   [direct only]
> OR
> The dean of students said to return applications to room 36 and to expect a response within three days.   [indirect only]

Similarly, do not shift from indirect questions to direct questions. The *direct question* asks straightaway:

> She asked, "Has Minnesota ever elected a Democratic governor?"

The *indirect question* restates a question in a declarative sentence:

> She wanted to know whether Minnesota has ever elected a Democratic governor.

Note that the direct question contains quotation marks and ends in a question mark and that the indirect question ends in a period.

15e   Avoid shifts between formal and informal language.

Maintain a consistent level of tone and word usage so that an essay written in a conversational style does not shift into a formal, academic style and, in like manner, an essay written in a formal style does not shift into a conversational style.

SHIFT: These theoretical ideas on nuclear disarmament seem rather *far out* in the context of new alignments by the Warsaw Pact nations. [formal to informal shift]

CONSISTENT: These theoretical ideas on nuclear disarmament seem *absurd* in the context of new alignments by the Warsaw Pact nations. [formal only]

EXERCISE 15.1 Rewrite the following sentences to eliminate distracting shifts in tense, voice, mood, person, number, form of discourse, and language level. The type of shift is noted in parentheses following each statement.

1. Since London held the first world's fair in 1851, cities all over the world have jumped on the world's fair bandwagon even though ten years may be needed to plan and build a fair. (voice)
2. Cities hold the fairs because they generated development and attracted business investments. (tense)
3. Citizens like world's fairs because they provide jobs and tourists who spend money are attracted. (voice)
4. A foreign country or a state exhibits at a world's fair to promote their culture and industry. (number)
5. If I were you and I was also rich, I would go to a world's fair at least once. (mood)
6. Most people enjoy world's fairs because you can see fascinating exhibits, go on amusement rides, and eat exotic food. (person)
7. In fact, when George Washington Ferris introduced his "wheel" at the 1898 Chicago Columbian Exhibition, it causes a sensation. (tense)
8. Today we take for granted some futuristic products first introduced at world's fairs, such as cordless telephones and electronic watches, but do not expect to find jet-powered automobiles or disposable clothes. (mood and person)
9. Because some recent fairs did not meet their sponsor's financial expectations, other cities are asking should we risk the cost and disruption for possible failure. (discourse)
10. The Western nations demonstrated the way to successful economic development, even though silly periods of inflation intervene. (language level)

EXERCISE 15.2   Rewrite the following paragraph so it is consistent in use of tense, voice, mood, person, number, and indirect or direct discourse.

The scene is silent. Spectators are tense. Police have cordoned off the entire block, and the bomb squad awaits their signal. The garbage can was watched carefully, silently. You can hear the ticking coming from the garbage can. No other sound is heard. Each police officer wonders if I'm going to leave here alive this time.

"OK, Jeff, the sandbags are in place," says the chief. Jeff looked as if he was wearing a space suit, padded from head to toe. Slowly he goes up to the garbage can, and the lid is lifted. You can see a paper bag in there, and the ticking got louder. Jeff picks up the bag, but didn't open it, because you can set off the trigger that way. Put bombs in water, instead. Bubbles rise, and the paper bag is slowly peeled away. Then, we all laugh in relief. Would you believe all that trouble over — . All is silent again.

PART

4

Words and Language

16
Appropriate Language
17
Using the Exact Word
18
Concise Language
19
Figurative Language

CHAPTER

16

Appropriate Language

After you have edited the sentences in your draft for content, style, and grammar, it is time to consider the individual words. Is each word as clear, precise, and appropriate to the context as it can be?

16a Match the level of formality to your subject and audience.

English ranges from black-tie formal to beachwear casual. Just as deciding what kind of clothes to wear depends on the occasion, so the formality of language depends on the subject, purpose, and audience. Most writing, like dress, is informal, as the types of writing listed below show.

Formal	*Informal*	*Conversational*
legal briefs	college essays	personal letters
technical reports	business	journal entries
scientific articles	correspondence	notes and memos
scholarly papers	magazine articles	dialogue among
	lectures	friends
	sermons	
	newspaper	
	articles	
	television	
	broadcasts	

Every writer needs to be able to move from one level of formality to another; college students, especially, must shift levels week by week.

Use **formal English** in serious academic and technical writing. It is impersonal, uses no contractions, and is generally written in third person about a serious subject. It employs specialized words of the field.

> Physiological time, like local time on a rotating world, also has a circular character. Resetting any clock, internal or external, by one or several full cycles has no observable effect. But resetting a biological clock within a cycle does have physiological consequences, as the phenomenon of jet lag shows.
> —ARTHUR T. WINFREE, *The Timing of Biological Clocks*

This writer's vocabulary ("physiological time," "physiological consequences," "biological clock") reflects his effort to address an intellectual audience on a complex subject.

Use **informal English** for essay examinations, themes, book reports, and so forth. It is usually impersonal with a third-person focus on the subject but with less specialized language than formal English. The less formal tone uses an occasional contraction, as appropriate to the context.

> In the Middle Ages most people in Europe, with the exception of the Turks and Russians, practiced the same religion and found unity within the same church, the Holy Catholic Church. They found security under the direction of the most important force in their lives, the Holy Roman Empire.
> —JOSH LAWING, student

This writer reaches a middle ground; the language is neither specialized nor conversational.

On occasion in personal essays, how-to essays, and feature articles, you may use a very informal, **conversational** language with an abundant use of the first-person *I*, the second-person *you*, contractions, and even an occasional sentence fragment.

> I can't believe I did it. Finally. Yeah, I did it after years of procrastination, delay, and naysaying. What did I do, you ask? I married my childhood sweetheart. No big deal? People do it all the time. But it happened to me twenty years after a junior high school romance.

This writer's conversational style is marked by the word "yeah," the fragment "finally," the personal voice, and the writer's intimate rapport with the reader.

EXERCISE 16.1 Decide if the following passages are formal, informal, or conversational. List examples of words and sentence elements that influenced your decision.

1. As an undergraduate computer science/mathematics major, I virtually never thought about writing. Writing seems as distant a discipline from computer science and mathematics as art or history. Yet, as I grew intellectually, I began to see the relationships that many disciplines have to one another, and in particular the similarities between computer programming and technical writing.

    — LAUREL BOONE HELM

2. And to write greetings, of course we must have ideas. But ideas are no problem, if you are greeting-minded! Wherever you are, they're all around you, in what you see, or hear, or feel, or what other people see and hear and feel. Sometimes in the most unexpected places!

    — JUNE BARR

3. The structure of *Moby Dick* may be seen as a diagrammatic opposition of forces, expressive of Melville's own conflict of belief. Thus Ahab's quest, his onrush toward the Whale, provides a kinetic, linear element — the "story." Counterposed against this movement are the static, discursive cetology chapters, essays in skepticism given unity by Ishmael's insistence on the relativity of perception.

    — JOHN SEELYE, *Melville: The Ironic Diagram*

4. Many scientists have long felt that whales, mammals gone to sea and uniquely adapted to that foreign environment, resemble no living land mammals and therefore should not behave like them. That attitude is shifting.

    — *National Geographic*

5. In *Cat on a Hot Tin Roof*, Williams exposes the deceit that lies at the heart of the Pollitt family and, by implication, the lies that pervade much of American society. While everything about the play is larger than life, and the obsessions with wealth, power, land, alcohol, and sex are gross in the extreme, *Cat on a Hot Tin Roof* achieves its end by distilling these issues into an enthralling family drama, full of vivid characters and hearty humor.

    — FRED ALBERT

16b   Use jargon sparingly.

The term *jargon* refers to words of a particular field that are not used or understood by general readers. It is intended for specialized audiences. For example, television viewers learn some jargon of NASA scientists during a space launch. This next passage uses computer jargon.

> Word Perfect's Merge function allows you to create one "form" document (called a *primary document*) and use it repeatedly with information that is filled in either automatically (from a list of items stored in a *secondary document*) or manually from the keyboard.
>
> — *Advanced Word Perfect: Features and Techniques*

Certain words in this passage — "merge," "primary document," "keyboard" — are appropriate for addressing computer users, not the general reader.

Avoid jargon that has lost its technical meaning or is used out of context:

Let's set ~~the~~ *limits on* ~~parameters for~~ the conference ~~discourse~~ *agenda.*

Parameter, a term from mathematics, means an "arbitrary constant" or a fixed quantity; *discourse* generally means "verbal expression" in speech or writing.

~~The~~ *We need* ~~bottom line of the athletic program is~~ a full stadium every Saturday *to finance the athletic program.*

Bottom line is a term from accounting that means "net income or loss."

16c   Use slang and colloquialisms only for special effects.

Slang consists of words currently popular with specific groups — teenagers, college students, musicians, valley girls, surfers, athletes, and so on. Although colorful and imaginative, slang fades quickly. In the recent past, for instance, these slang words have meant "leave": *skip, blow, shove off, push off, bug out, hotfoot it, split, take off, scram.* None is clearer than *leave.*

Colloquialisms are words more often spoken than written: *guy* for "person," *gyp* for "cheat," *run into* for "meet," *talk into* for "persuade," *sure thing* for "certainty."

Regionalisms are colloquialisms that appear only in specific parts of the country, such as the Southern *y'all* or the Plains states' *rustle up some food*.

Use slang, colloquialisms, and regionalisms to create a special effect, such as humor, dialogue, or a regional flavor. When used appropriately, such words are colorful and memorable:

> Wilbur and Orville Wright were regarded as two wet smacks who ran a bicycle repair shop in Dayton, Ohio, when they arrived at Kitty Hawk for their airplane experiment in 1903.
> —TOM WOLFE, "Land of Wizards"

"Wet smacks" is a regionalism that pictures the Wright brothers as the equivalent of today's "nerds."

However, do not strive for the offbeat if circumstances call for the more formal or standard expression. This next passage shows slang and colloquialisms edited from a rough draft:

> Going into the battle at Little Big Horn, Custer had met ~~pretty good~~ success. He had won victories over several Indian camps and had begun ~~pumping up~~ *promoting* himself as presidential material. The ~~gross~~ *disastrous* miscalculations of Custer were the result, apparently, of his ~~awesome~~ *enormous* ego.

Serious writing has no place for such words as "pretty good," "pumping up," or "awesome."

16d   Avoid pretentious and bombastic language.

Pretentious language is excessively and unnecessarily showy and flowery. **Bombastic** language is similarly overblown, using big words to make the insignificant sound important.

Since the *onset* of my *collegiate education*, I have been *inundated* with a *plethora* of philosophical theories.

This writer uses pretentious language in the mistaken attempt to elevate the level of formality. It is the opposite of slang, which speakers use purposely to lower the formality. The writer above probably meant to say something like this.

Since the beginning of my college education, I have been exposed to numerous philosophical theories.

Pretentious language, unlike formal language, is not direct, precise, or even correct.

The ~~effusive~~ *brilliant* display of fireworks dazzled the audience.

The word *effusive* means "to gush"; the writer perhaps intended to use *effulgent*, which means "radiant splendor." Bigger is not always better, so unless longer, less common words suit your meaning precisely, choose familiar words.

Formal words in an informal context can sound pretentious:

The thrill of our summer hike around Lake Wales was dampened by a ~~blistered epidermis~~ *sunburn* and an unhealthy dose of *poison* ivy ~~dermatitis.~~

Similarly, an informal expression in a formal essay startles the reader:

Poison ivy dermatitis is caused by resins of the plant *rhus toxicodendron.* ~~It itches like the dickens.~~

The colloquial expression, "It itches like the dickens," has no place in this formal writing.

Use current words, not archaic or obsolete terms.

Obsolete or archaic words sound pretentious or flowery in everyday speech or writing. Avoid such words as *beauteous* for "beautiful," *ere* for "before," or *anon* for "soon."

I think   *to read more*
~~Methinks~~ it is time ~~for another draught of~~ Shakespeare.

Replace artificial or archaic words with modern terminology.

Avoid euphemisms.

A **euphemism** is a pleasant-sounding or innocuous term that is indirect and often pretentious. Most readers accept and understand euphemisms that replace offensive words ("go to the bathroom"), words about death ("passed away"), and words of tact or politeness ("your Johnny is an *underachiever*").

Some euphemisms, however, hide unpleasant truths, manipulate the language, or deceive the reader. Is a "misstatement" a deliberate lie or an unintentional slip of the tongue? Such language often hides responsibility. The following list of euphemisms shows pretentious expressions.

Euphemism	*Meaning*
an important announcement	television advertisement
selected out, out placement	fired
preowned automobile	used car
under the influence	drunk
economically disadvantaged	poor
protective reaction strikes	bombings
sanitation engineer	janitor

See also the discussion of conciseness in chapter **18**.

16e   Use new and invented words carefully.

Neologisms are new words or expressions that are not commonly used yet. Advertisers frequently coin new words, especially by blending two common words: "European style" becomes "Eurostyle," for instance. New concepts also introduce new words: "software," "floppy disk," and "motherboard." *Time* magazine, for example, gained a reputation for coining such new words as "celebutant" and "cinemactress."

Occasionally you might add spice to your writing by coining a new word, surprising the reader with a new perspective:

> Just think, we pay tuition to attend this *universylum*. [*university* and *asylum*]

> As secretary of the Student Government Association, I spend half my time dealing with *administrivia*. [*administration* and *trivia*]

The next sentence uses the noun *strobe* as a verb with a play on "struck blind."

> Stepping into the nightclub, I was *strobed* blind by the flashing lights.

If a new word is immediately clear to readers and fresh, use it. But if it sounds like jargon — say, "columning" for "writing a column" — stay with the familiar term. (See also section **17a**.)

> **IN REVIEW**
>
> Avoid unnecessary and misleading jargon, slang, or pretentious language.

EXERCISE 16.2 Rewrite the following sentences to eliminate jargon, colloquialisms, pretentious language, euphemisms, and other inappropriate language.

1. Your scribe and her consort supped yestreen at El Hoot Kwizeen, a new Frenchtaurant.
2. The victuals they served up were mighty tasty.
3. Our three courses were yummy to the max, especially washed down with the fermented nectar of the grape.
4. The only unfortunate incident of the evening occurred when the waitress misstepped over a tined eating implement dropped on the floor.
5. I let out such a holler when hot soup poured down on my cranium.
6. The restaurant is making good on it, though, by sending my outer vestments to the cleaners and by making our meal a nonchargeable item.

7. Legalwise, the restaurant is liable and hopes I will not employ an attorney to seek personal injury remuneration.
8. The sumptuousness of the spread made up for the uncomfortable situation, however.
9. I ingested so much that my abdomen felt as if it might break in the manner of a balloon.
10. The bottom line is that this new restaurant puts on the best feed in the area.

17

Using the
Exact Word

The right word expresses an idea exactly, so finding it is worth the search. Writers expand their vocabularies by reading, listening carefully, and using a good dictionary and thesaurus. You too should search for the right word to produce precise, specific, and colorful writing. (See also section **17e**.)

17a   Use the dictionary to find the correct form of a word.

The dictionary is an indispensable tool for all writers, because it verifies spelling, meaning, and word division (see chapter **50**). In addition, the best writers use it to find the right word. As the figure below demonstrates, a dictionary provides more than one definition; the sample entry defines the noun *circle* in ten ways and the verb *circle* in two transitive forms and one intransitive form.

> **cir·cle** (sûr′kəl) *n.* **1.** A plane curve everywhere equidistant from a given fixed point, the center. **2.** A planar region bounded by a circle. **3.** Something, such as a ring, shaped like a circle. **4.** A circular course, circuit, or orbit. **5.** A curved section or tier of seats in a theater. **6.** A series or process that finishes at its starting point or continuously repeats itself; cycle. **7.** A group of people sharing an interest, activity, or achievement: *a circle of friends; a sewing circle.* **8.** In some European countries, a territorial or administrative division, esp. of a province. **9.** A sphere of influence or interest; domain: *well-known in scientific circles.* **10.** *Logic.* A fallacy in reasoning in which the premise is used to prove the conclusion, and the conclusion used to prove the premise. —*v.* **-cled, -cling, -cles.** —*tr.* **1.** To make or form a circle around; enclose. **2.** To move in a circle around. —*intr.* To move in circles; revolve: *Crows circled overhead.* [ME *cercle* < OFr. < Lat. *circulus,* dim. of *circus,* circle.] —**cir′cler** (-klər) *n.*

The distinctions in word usage can be important, for in one context *circle* means an *orbit* and in another it means a *group of people sharing an activity*. In addition, the dictionary entry gives illustrative examples ("well-known in scientific circles") usage labels ("logic"), inflected forms ("-cled, -cling, -cles"), and other valuable information.

Here are some examples of how precise and concise editing improves writing.

Every skater prepared to ~~rotate around~~ *circle* the rink for the full 20-lap ~~cycle~~ *race*.

The word *circle* is more precise and concise than *rotate around*, and the word *race* describes the event more accurately than *cycle*.

I ~~suspicioned~~ *suspected* him and reported my findings to the supervisor.

Many words, like the noun *suspicion*, change form, so check the dictionary for correct spelling of a word's different forms:

above suspicion: not to be suspected; honorable
on suspicion: on the basis of suspicion
under suspicion: suspected

Do not make up words when a standard form exists: *analysis*, not *analyzation; tutor*, not *tutorer*. Also, avoid adding *-wise* to words indiscriminately:

It was ~~a good~~ *an exciting, action-filled* movie, ~~actionwise~~.

The dictionary identifies errors of homophones—that is, words that sound similar but have different spellings and meanings, such as *bare* and *bear*. Mistaken use of homophones often creates humorous statements.

Rush hour traffic does not ~~phase~~ *faze* a well-trained traffic police officer.

Two-year-olds go through a ~~faze~~ *phase* when all they say is "no."

A *phase* is a stage of development; *faze* is a verb meaning "disconcert."

A good dictionary is worth the investment; these are good, all-purpose dictionaries:

> *The American Heritage Dictionary* (Second college edition, 1985)
> *The Random House College Dictionary* (Revised edition, 1984)
> *Webster's New World Dictionary* (Third college edition, 1988)
> *Webster's Ninth New Collegiate Dictionary* (1984, 1988)
> *Webster's II, New Riverside University Dictionary* (1984)

IN REVIEW

As you edit your writing, use your dictionary often to explore meanings and different uses for any given word.

EXERCISE 17.1   Look up the word *promise* in your dictionary and write sentences using it (1) as a noun and (2) as a verb.

EXERCISE 17.2   Write sentences using each of the following homophones correctly. If possible, use them both in the same sentence.

Example: pour/pore
I was having a hard time staying awake as I *pored* over my books, so I *poured* myself a cup of coffee.

1. effect/affect
2. discrete/discreet
3. principal/principle
4. peddle/pedal
5. roll/role

EXERCISE 17.3   Rewrite the following sentences to use the correct word form.

1. Firstly, you must believe that you can realizationize your dream.
2. Secondly, you must work hardly and keep your eye firmly on your goal.
3. Luckiness plays a roll, but you have to take advantage of it.
4. For example, if you stumble unforeseenly over an opportunity, pick yourself up and grab it, and try to turn it into usefulness.
5. Finally, remember that even if you fail bad, you have learned something experiencewise.

17b   Use a dictionary and a thesaurus to discover appropriate synonyms.

When editing a paper for the appropriateness of certain terms, writers seldom think of just the right words off the top of their heads. They often must consult a dictionary or a thesaurus to guide them or to remind them of the available word choices.

In addition to providing the various definitions of a given word, good dictionaries also list and define **synonyms**, which are words that have meanings similar to the entry. The illustration below lists the synonyms for the dictionary entry *circle* on page 208.

> **Synonyms:** *circle, coterie, set, clique, club, fraternity, society.* These nouns denote a group of associates. *Circle* can describe almost any group having common interests or activities on a scale large or small: *sewing circle; financial circles.* It can also designate the extent of personal relationships: *circle of friends. Coterie* applies to a small, intimate group of congenial persons. *Set* suggests a large, loosely bound group defined either by condition *(younger set)* or preoccupation with fashionable activity *(smart set; jet set). Clique* pertains to an exclusive group, usually social, with activities in which outsiders are denied participation. *Club* can imply exclusiveness but often means only a group devoted to a common interest best pursued in company: *Rotary Club; bridge club. Fraternity* most commonly denotes a Greek letter society of male students. It can also mean a professional group not actually organized: *medical fraternity. Society,* as compared here, is usually a rather large, formally organized group with common interests, often cultural.

In addition to the synonyms for the word *circle* ("coterie," "set," "clique," "club," "fraternity," "society"), this entry also explains the shades of meanings (see section **17d**) so users can pinpoint the exact word they need.

A **thesaurus**, which is a collection of synonyms without dictionary particulars, provides a spectrum of word choices:

> **circle** (vb) 1. surround, environ, encircle, encompass, compass, hem, gird, girdle, ring, enclose, envelop, circumscribe, restrict (see *limit*); 2. revolve, rotate, turn, gyrate, wheel, spin, twirl, whirl, eddy, swirl, pirouette

This list from *Webster's New Dictionary of Synonyms* gives a writer several choices but no definitions, which means the uninformed writer may need to consult a dictionary before using *circumscribe* or *environ.*

Many word processors and word processing programs also feature a thesaurus. The software *Word Perfect*, for example, gives this list for the verb *circle*:

> **circle** (vb) 1. border, enclose, encompass, envelop, surround; 2. circumnavigate, revolve, rotate, turn, wheel

Each synonym has a precise meaning. Be sure you have found the exact word before you use it.

pirouette
The dancer made a ~~circle~~ at three places on the stage.

circumnavigate
It takes bravery and skill to ~~circle~~ the globe in a small boat.

"Pirouette" is correct dance terminology, and "circumnavigate" is the correct nautical word.

Use a thesaurus for these reasons:

1. To find a word to match a level of formality and, thereby, to maintain a consistent tone.

   In the serious world of stand-up comedy, the humorists who
   improvise   *assess*
   succeed can ~~ad-lib~~ as they ~~size up~~ the mood of the audience.

The chosen words suit a serious treatment of comedy; they replace the conversational words "ad-lib" and "size up."

2. To recall a familiar but forgotten word, especially one with a precise shade of meaning.

   She *walked*. She *strolled*. She *sauntered*. She *paced*. She *ambled*. She *strode*. She *marched*.

   The pain was *bad, excruciating, throbbing, stinging*.

3. To replace overworked words, such as *thing, material, do, make, very*.

   effortless
   Finding the dynamite was ~~easy~~, but removing the dynamite caps
   exceptionally
   was ~~very~~ dangerous.

The edited version is now precise; other words available are the adjective *simple* and the adverbs *dreadfully, exceedingly, extremely, terribly.*

4. To discover new words. Because writers think in words, reading a list of words can provoke thinking and creativity.

Do not, however, use the thesaurus simply to provide synonyms for common or frequently used words. Any word you choose should be better for your purpose than one you reject.

EXERCISE 17.4 Look up the adjective *correct* in a dictionary or thesaurus; choose two of the synonyms given and write sentences using the synonyms. If necessary, use your dictionary to determine precise meanings and correct usage of the new words.

EXERCISE 17.5 Look up the noun *power* in a dictionary or thesaurus; choose two of the synonyms given and write sentences using the synonyms. If necessary, use your dictionary to determine precise meanings and correct usage of the new words.

EXERCISE 17.6 Look up the verb *roll* in a dictionary or thesaurus; choose two of the synonyms given and write sentences using the synonyms. If necessary, use your dictionary to determine precise meanings and correct usage of the new words.

17c Use the word with the correct meaning.

Some words appear to mean one thing but actually mean another: for instance, *simplistic* means "oversimplified, ignoring complications," not "simple" or "easy" or "straightforward"; and *enervate* means "to weaken," not "to energize."

Ken's ~~temerity~~ *timidity* kept him from speaking in class.

Temerity means "recklessness," not "timidity."

Be especially careful with words having prefixes or suffixes: *disinterested* means "impartial," not "uninterested"; both *flammable* and *inflammable* materials burn.

Also, some words have more than one meaning in informal and spoken English. For example, *nauseous* traditionally means "causing illness," but many people use it informally to mean "feeling ill."

Janice felt ~~nauseous~~ *nauseated* after seeing the serious traffic accident on her way to class.

213

In like manner, **idioms** cause problems, especially for non-native speakers of a language. Idioms are words and phrases whose meanings are not literal, logical, or subject to uniform grammatical rules. If someone asked you, "Do you agree to me?" you would be puzzled, because "agree with" is the idiomatic expression. To determine the correct expression, check the dictionary. Color highlighting in the sample entry below shows the idioms of the verb *agree*.

> **a·gree** (ə-grē′) *v.* **a·greed, a·gree·ing, a·grees.** —*intr.* **1.** To grant consent; accede: *agreed to accompany us.* **2.** To come into or be in accord; match: *a copy that agrees with the original.* **3.** To be of one opinion: *didn't agree with me.* **4.** To come to an understanding or to terms: *finally agreed on the solution.* **5.** To be suitable or appropriate: *Spicy food does not agree with him.* **6.** *Gram.* To correspond in gender, number, case, or person. —*tr.* To grant or concede: *agreed that we should go.* [ME *agreen* < OFr. *agreer* < VLat. **aggratare* : Lat. *ad-*, to + Lat. *gratus*, pleasing.]

Most idiomatic errors occur when a writer uses the improper preposition after a verb, such as *capable to* rather than *capable of* in the following example.

The machine has a new keyboard that seems capable ~~to save~~ *of saving* valuable time with math problems.

Note these additional idioms:

accuse of stealing, not accuse with
according to reports, not according with
apologize for an error, not apologize about
capable of winning, not capable to win
die of blood poisoning, not die from
different from another, not different than
except for Mary, not excepting for
in search of gold, not in search for
intend to repair, not intend on repairing
plan to finish, not plan on
similar to my ring, not similar with
try to finish, not try and finish

IN REVIEW

Check your dictionary or a thesaurus if you have a question about the exact meaning of a word or about an idiomatic expression.

EXERCISE 17.7 Complete each sentence below with the one word in parentheses that is correct within the context of the sentence. Be prepared to defend your choice.

1. The (insulation, installation) of new lighting in the science laboratory will (rectify, rehabilitate) the contractor's error.
2. The electrical (circuits, cycles) will receive careful (examination, inspection).
3. New circuit breakers will (absorb, cushion, interrupt) electrical shocks to students at their (stations, status).
4. The (erratic, erotic) lighting situation has (disconcerted, disconcepted) the instructor.
5. For a few weeks electrical wiring will (exude, extrude) from the walls, ceiling, and even the floor.

EXERCISE 17.8 Change any unidiomatic expressions in the following sentences to idiomatic ones.

1. Excepting for Tom and Greg, we are in accordance to the new standards.
2. I agree with Dean Jones, but I will not apologize about yesterday's disruption.
3. If you plan on enrolling late, you must agree with the procedures for late registration.
4. Several freshman students in Professor Barnes' biology course were accused with theft of the final exam.
5. Your negative attitude is different than mine.
6. The biology club went in search for marine fossils at Netherland Bend.
7. I almost took someone else's coat because it was similar with mine.
8. If you intend on going ahead with your plan on painting the room black, count me out as your roommate.
9. When I tripped over my own feet as I was getting my diploma, I thought I would die from embarrassment.
10. The cast will try and get through the entire play at rehearsal tonight.

17d Understand connotations and denotations.

Denotation is the dictionary meaning of a word: a *puppy* is a young dog. **Connotation** is the subtle, underlying, emotional quality or implication of a word. For instance, to a child, a puppy connotes warmth, cuteness, and affection; to the parents, it might connote extra work, trouble, and expense. *Home* has connotations of warmth and family life that *house* does not. Writers use the connotative value of words for different reasons.

Words convey favorable and unfavorable connotations: a *bouquet* sells perfume, an *odor* sells deodorant, yet both *bouquet* and *odor* mean "a smell."

> The financial condition of this company is *precarious.*
> *unpredictable.*
> *suspect.*

The word *precarious* suggests that the company may fail at any time; the word *unpredictable* suggests that the company's finances fluctuate up and down; *suspect* suggests that the company's condition is under question.

IN REVIEW

Edit your writing not only for the spelling and literal meaning of a word but also for its positive or negative connotative values.

EXERCISE 17.9   Complete each sentence below with the one word in parentheses that you think most accurately conveys the meaning in the context of the sentence. Be prepared to defend your choice.

1. The young manager was (scheming/planning) to (take advantage of/grab at) any opportunities she found.
2. The most popular store in the neighborhood (traffics in/sells/purveys) records, tapes, and electronic equipment.
3. The bargain hunter was (cajoled/conned/persuaded) into buying a worthless trinket.
4. The (anorexic/skinny/slender) model (gyrated/danced/moved) through her poses as the camera captured each graceful pirouette.
5. Success is often achieved by the most (grasping/persistent/tenacious) person.
6. Our creamy soap will make your skin feel (soft/mild/smooth).
7. The newly poured cement was beginning to (coagulate/harden/petrify).

8. Waiting to see the doctor always makes me (nervous/restive/ uneasy).

9. The diplomats (debated/negotiated/parleyed) a new trade (agreement/compact/contract).

10. A small (brood/bunch/group) of teenagers (gaped/gawked/ ogled) as the famous rock group casually walked by.

EXERCISE 17.10 Prepare to discuss in class how the connotations of the following paired words differ.

responsibility/duty
expensive/costly
famous/notorious
timid/shy
desire/want

17e Use concrete and specific words.

Concrete words refer to things that we see, touch, hear, taste, or smell: *kiss, sunrise, dollar bill, sirloin steak.* Concrete words range from general to specific: *food* is general, *fruit* is specific, and *apple* is even more specific.

Abstract words refer to intangible ideas, attitudes, and qualities: *government service, nice weather, welfare for the underprivileged.* Concrete details make sentences clear and interesting. For instance, the words *food stamps for the homeless* are more concrete and descriptive than *welfare for the underprivileged.*

The buffet table held ~~lots of good things to eat.~~ *cantaloupe slices, sliced ham and cheese, and rye bread.*

Here are a few guidelines for making your writing concrete and specific.

1. Expand and clarify abstract ideas with concrete examples and details.

ABSTRACT: Wheat is the world's most important grain.

CONCRETE: Wheat products feed millions of people through-out the world.

SPECIFIC: Whole wheat flour contains nutrients of the entire kernel — bran, endosperm, and germ. White flour contains only the endosperm, the starchy part, so it does not contain some of the vitamins and minerals that whole wheat flour has.

2. List the key words of your essay, and narrow each one to its most specific and precise meaning.

ABSTRACT: European changes

CONCRETE: East Germany and West Germany

SPECIFIC: The Berlin Wall separated communism's oppression and the West's economic and political freedom.

3. Avoid using abstractions and generalities as the subjects of your sentences. Show the abstraction through the concrete and specific.

GENERAL: Wonder and enchantment are in a sidestreet bookshop in Kansas City.

SPECIFIC: Rare books, especially old dictionaries and encyclopedias, enchant browsers at a sidestreet bookshop in Kansas City.

Some general sentences do have a clear purpose. For instance, the general statement often functions as a topic sentence (see section **4a**). General sentences must be supported by concrete details.

Blue-collar workers have a more regimented workday than office workers and management. For example, an automobile worker arrives for the first shift at 7:00 a.m., punches the time clock, and joins other workers on the assembly line, passing tasks from station to station. Coffee breaks and lunch breaks follow the clock, with little time off for a quick conversation. Conversely, secretaries and clerks may arrive a few minutes late and may spend a few minutes through the day with their colleagues, exchanging gossip or news of the family. Further, the executives in the front office can arrive late and lose no pay, take two hours for lunch, and visit colleagues to discuss the stock market, their weight programs, or civic duties.

Abstract topic sentence

Concrete sentences of support

In this paragraph, concrete, specific language supports the opening generalization.

IN REVIEW

The right word is often a specific name, term, or phrase, not an unsupported, abstract expression.

EXERCISE 17.11   Add a sentence or two to the following abstract statements to show in concrete terms what they mean.

> EXAMPLE: *Exercise helps human beings stay healthy.* Aerobic dancing, bicycling, and swimming increase circulation, which helps develop a strong heart and increased lung capacity. Stretching exercises keep people limber and supple, which helps prevent backaches. Weightlifting builds strength and muscle tone.

1. Beauty is truth, truth beauty.
2. Happiness is not imposed from without. A person is either happy or not.
3. Maturity is more a matter of accepting responsibility than of age.
4. Large cities must learn how to deal with increasing transportation problems.
5. You might think that you either know something or you don't, so that any method of testing your knowledge will give the same result, but that's not necessarily true.

EXERCISE 17.12   Rewrite the following sentences to be as specific as possible.

> EXAMPLE: Most women carry lots of things in their purses.

> SPECIFIC: My wife's pouchy black purse holds her necessities: wallet with her money and credit cards, checkbooks, keys, pens, address book, sunglasses, bright red lipstick, compact, and even used tissues too good to throw away.

1. Last week I met an old friend.
2. My new car is really neat.
3. The cost of textbooks adds significantly to the cost of education.
4. Communing with nature helps relieve stress.
5. Some people begin their day in a special way.
6. Visiting museums teaches us about the world around us.

7. Children's television shows are nothing more than long commercials.
8. The excellent food at the new restaurant down the street whets my appetite.
9. Some habits, legal and illegal, can be dangerous to your health.
10. Foreign countries manufacture many durable goods that we import.

17f   Avoid sexist or biased language.

Words and phrases that stereotype people by sex, race, religion, nationality, age, or handicap limit an essay's effectiveness because they show a writer's thoughtless acceptance of common biases rather than careful thought. Most people today wish to avoid stereotypes, but not everyone recognizes them. (See also section **27a**.)

Inappropriate stereotypes	*Appropriate alternatives*
mailman	mail carrier
fireman	fire fighter
policeman	police officer
foreman	supervisor
delivery boy	runner or messenger
girl Friday	secretary
male nurse	nurse

The best solution, the one that gives writing precision, is exactness: *officer Nancy Hodges*, *nurse Horace Taylor*, and *chairperson Paul Bishop*. Avoid biased language with the following revision techniques.

1. Use *people, persons, human beings, humanity,* or *we* rather than *man* or *mankind* to refer to people in general;

    Although ~~man is a~~ *humans are* social being*s*, territorial jealousy often surfaces.

2. Avoid general expressions that exclude or highlight one sex.

    An urban legend is similar to ~~an old wives' tale.~~ *a fable.*

3. Do not stereotype jobs or roles.

   chairperson
   The ~~chairman~~ of each academic department should submit a
   revised budget.

4. Treat names of persons equally.

   Two people, Jennifer Stephenson and Nelson Bridges, will

   represent the committee; ~~Miss~~ Stephenson is the voting dele-

   gate, and Bridges is the alternate delegate.

5. To avoid the generic pronoun *he*, use plural pronouns (*they,
   their*) or the dual singular pronouns (*he or she, his or her*), alternate the references between discussions (*he, his* for one discussion; *she, her* for the next), or delete the gender pronouns
   altogether. Make sure to adjust the verb to reflect the singular
   or plural pronoun.

   All of the musicians brought *their* favorite disks to the session.   [plural nouns and pronouns]

   Each of the musicians brought *his or her* favorite disk to the
   session.   [dual singular nouns and pronouns; this option is
   awkward when overused]

   Each of the musicians brought *her* favorite disk to the session.   [alternate references; avoid stereotyping the subject]

   Each musician brought *a* favorite disk to the session.   [no
   gender reference]

6. Avoid demeaning or patronizing labels, such as "delivery boy,"
   "lady electrician," "black officer," "dope addict," "drunk as an
   Irishman."

   careless
   The ~~woman~~ driver almost cut me off.

7. Do not use a strained nonsexist term.

   work hour
   The company set new ~~personhour~~ limits for production of
   each component.

> **IN REVIEW**
>
> Edit papers to remove any instance of biased, discrimina-
> tory language, especially the generic use of *he* to denote
> people in general.

EXERCISE 17.13 Correct instances of biased language in the following sentences.

1. Everyone must bring his sales reports to the session on
   Wednesday.
2. Memo to Gene: Send one of the office girls to arrange
   catering for next week's luncheon.
3. The training session ended when firemen and policemen as
   well as several FBI men ordered everyone to evacuate the
   building.
4. Memo to Gene: I have hired Fred Lothridge and Andrea
   Hightower. Send Lothridge to the Birmingham office and
   Miss Hightower to Atlanta.
5. Each member of the sales staff must file their reports on time,
   no exceptions.

EXERCISE 17.14 The following paragraphs include incorrect
words and word forms, confused homophones, unidiomatic expressions, sexist language, and connotations inappropriate to the subject. Rewrite them to solve the problems.

    Seven years after it bursted, Mount St. Helen's was reopened
for hikers and mountain climbers. Since 1980, when the burp-
ing volcano finally stopped regurgitating, only scientists had been
allowed to enter. These men examined the volcano for the analyzation of the dust, the measurings of its vibrations, and the
probity of its fissures. But the once-symmetrical volcano that
blew off its north face in 1980 has been returned to the people—and the people are returning, coming from all through
the world to ogle a smoldering crater.

    Some of the hikers are unprepared, though. No spikes or
pitons are needed, for there are no shear cliffs, but the trail is
filled with dangerousness. Sudden blizzards called "whiteouts"
can trap a man even on a sunny warm day. Ledges of snow hang
out twenty feet over the crater; they can easily break off from a

man's weight. The glare from off the snow can cause painful snowblindness.

It is a hard five-hour climb to the summit, but some men are wearing tennis shoes, not boots. Some don't even wear shirts. They carry no water or change of clothes. But the only requirement from the U.S. Forest Service is that every climber have a permit. It isn't required to protect greenhorn climbers from themselves.

CHAPTER
18
Concise Language

Speakers fill gaps in their thoughts with "um" or "er" and empty phrases such as "you know" and "like." Writers also fill their sentences with useless words. As you revise, delete meaningless and redundant words, unnecessary detail, and indirect wordy phrases.

18a Avoid long generalizations, and edit unnecessary wording.

When writers become preoccupied with ideas and abstractions, they often write in a wordy style, burdening the reader who must hunt for a specific point.

Say only as much as necessary in each sentence. You can assume that your readers share some general knowledge and background information with you. Avoid explaining the obvious:

Over 90 percent of the families in the United States watch tele-

vision, which shows both news and entertainment.

Most readers know what appears on television. Explain briefly, if necessary, but do not overdo it. If you need to define terms or concepts, do so in a manner that does not offend your readers.

Expert skiers crowd the dry, powdery snow of the North American Rockies and the Swiss Alps. Here, Olympic hopefuls speed through a slalom course, zigzagging their way between strategically placed flags.

The description of a slalom course serves the nonskier. The writer assumes that readers know the Rocky Mountains, the Swiss Alps, and the Olympics.

If you are writing an essay addressed to your instructor or classmates, give only enough details to set the context. Do not include the background of every point you make or define every term.

Nathaniel Hawthorne, *in* ~~who was born in 1804 in Salem, Massachusetts (the home of the famous witch trials), wrote~~ *The Scarlet*

~~*Letter* in 1850. A graduate of Bowdoin College, he also wrote~~

~~such classics as *The House of the Seven Gables* and *Twice-Told Tales*.~~

The Scarlet Letter explores the integrity of Hester Prynne in con-

flict with the moral scruples of her religious neighbors and their

amoral minister.

Editing will help you eliminate the needless words, phrases, and even sentences.

Compress clauses to phrases, phrases to words.

Some subordinate clauses (see chapter **23**) beginning with "that" or "who" are wordy:

> WORDY: Two books *that have been recent targets of attempts at censorship* are *Huckleberry Finn* and *The Wizard of Oz*.

Editing, shown below, eliminates the wordy subordinate clause.

> CONCISE: Two recent censorship targets are the books *Huckleberry Finn* and *The Wizard of Oz*.

Reduce adjectival and adverbial prepositional phrases (see chapter **22**) to specific one-word modifiers if possible:

~~In spite of~~ his ~~advancing age,~~ the *aging* pitcher threw fastball after fastball.

The train arrived ~~before its scheduled time.~~ *early.*

As shown above, one or two words can often replace four or five.

Prune deadwood

Deadwood, as the word suggests, is lifeless verbiage — wordy phrases or words that add nothing to your sentence. To cut deadwood, substitute a concise word for the wordy phrase or simply delete the meaningless phrase:

~~The fact that~~ Senator Grayson*'s* supported *of* the agriculture bill ~~was a factor in his popularity~~ *made him popular* with ~~a large number of~~ *many* farmers.

The list below provides some common substitutions.

Wordy	*Concise*
in order to	to
due to the fact that	because
in all probability	probably
in many instances	often
in the process of	doing
on a daily basis	daily
in excess of	more than
in a similar fashion	similarly
during the time that	when
a large number of	many
a small number of	few
in the event that	if
at this point in time	now
is able to	can
the truth is	actually

Eliminate redundant words and repetitive ideas.

Keep your writing concise by avoiding needless repetition.

At 6 p.m. we presented to the ~~newspapers and~~ media ~~last night~~ ~~all~~ the reasons ~~and rationale~~ for ~~deciding to~~ proceed*ing* ~~and plac-~~ ~~ing the matter before the voters as a~~ *with the* referendum.

Newspapers are one of the media; *6 p.m.* is precise without *last night; rationale* means reasons. *Deciding to proceed* is the same as proceeding, and a *referendum* is to place a measure before the voters.

Like deadwood, redundant word pairs waste space:

> *Redundancies*
> each and every
> willing and able
> true and accurate
> first and foremost
> any and all
> basic and fundamental

Each ~~and every~~ eligible person has voted.

Some modifiers mean the same thing as the word modified:

> *Redundancies*
> free gift
> exact same
> mentally imagine
> true facts
> terrible tragedy
> future plans
> past history
> audible sound

This sample is a ~~free~~ gift.

Certain general nouns—*nature, color, size,* and *field,* for example— seem to invite redundancy: yellow *in color,* tall *in height,* large *in size, field of* economics, *area of* manufacturing.

He majored in ~~the field of~~ chemistry ~~in order to study in the~~ *to prepare for* ^ *pharmaceutical school.* ~~profession of pharmacy.~~ ^

Chemistry is a field of study, *pharmacy* is a profession, and the phrase *in order to* is almost always deadwood.

The similarities between President Lincoln and President

Kennedy become most striking at the ends of their lives. ~~Both~~

~~men's assassinations were similar to each other.~~ Not only were

their assassinations similar, but ~~other things made their lives~~ *also both men* ∧

~~similar. Both presidents~~ shunned bodyguards and ~~both~~ were

succeeded by vice presidents named Johnson.

Avoid meaningless intensifiers and qualifiers.

Intensive modifiers — *a lot, really, very, generally, basically, great, fantastic, too, so* — are imprecise. Usually they do nothing more than tell the reader you liked or disliked something:

Star Trek: The Next Generation is a really interesting television show, and I like it a lot.

What made the show interesting, and to whom? How much is "a lot"? The reader needs more precise wording.

Star Trek: The Next Generation, one of my favorite television shows, stimulates the imagination of science fiction fans.

Here is another imprecise sentence:

The mythology course is fantastic.

What makes a "fantastic course"?

The mythology course discusses intriguing myths and some eccentric and entertaining gods and goddesses.

Avoid unnecessary introductory qualifying phrases.

Do not use *in my opinion, it is clear that, it has been shown that,* or *I would say* (or *argue*) *that.* Readers know that your essay gives your opinion and that you wish to make something clear.

The opening makes a poor first impression, but ~~in my opinion it~~

~~is clear that~~ the movie presents an intelligent and interesting

look at marriage.

Avoid "it is" and "there are" constructions.

It is and *there are* often delay the real subject and the action of the verb (see the discussion of expletives in section **10a**).

~~There are many reasons to eat~~ leafy green vegetables, ~~They~~ supply iron, calcium, and vitamins.

~~It is obvious that~~ we must clean up our industrial wastes or drown in them.

It is and *there are* often create passive constructions:

Remove

~~There is~~ deadwood ~~that can be removed~~ from your sentences.

> **IN REVIEW**
>
> Eliminate all unnecessary words and phrases, especially deadwood, redundancies, and meaningless qualifiers.

EXERCISE 18.1 Rewrite the following passage to eliminate wordiness, repetition, and unnecessary details.

The arrival of cable to the world of television has brought many changes to television, both for viewers and for programmers. Cable uses a different technology from television that is transmitted over the airwaves. As its name says, it comes into viewers' homes and television sets on actual cables that are strung on electric and telephone poles. Since viewers must pay to have their homes wired for cable and then pay a fee every month, cable is called "pay TV."

First and foremost, cable television worries the owners of free television stations because now viewers have more choice of what to watch, including movies, films of actual live comedy and entertainment acts, and news and weather reports all day long. That means that not as many people are watching the shows on the free stations, which really cuts into their revenue. Traditional stations make their money by selling advertising time on their shows, and they bill by the number of people watching. The more people watching, the more money they charge.

That's what the ratings companies figure out — the number of people watching a particular program.

Because cable is here to stay, I think that changes in programming on free TV will occur. Already networks are cutting costs and trimming the budgets of their news organizations. Programmers seem less willing to gamble on shows that do not follow a proven formula. But as viewers see better movies or superstar entertainers or lots of live sports events on cable, in my opinion they are going to be more likely to desert the copy-cat, mirror-image look of traditional television.

EXERCISE 18.2   Revise the following sentences to eliminate deadwood, redundancies, and empty phrases. Recast the sentences if necessary.

1. The past history of this fine and upstanding young man would indicate that he will be an employee of an exemplary nature.
2. In order to accomplish the task of getting the sailboat seaworthy and shipshape, each and every one of us has to pitch in and do our share of the work.
3. In the modern world of today's different lifestyles, we have to choose among many ways to live.
4. When I returned back to my office, I discovered an excess of telephone messages that a large number of my clients had left on a daily basis.
5. In the event that you have an emergency illness or accident, it is necessary for you to leave the telephone number and address of your parents or spouse or next of kin.
6. Due to the fact that this car has eight cylinders and 120 horsepower, it is absolutely necessary to give it fuel of high-octane gasoline.
7. The burnoose, a hooded cloak, is a garment worn by members of Arab and Berber nationalities.
8. In the time before Christopher Columbus sailed west to find India, it was considered an actual fact by people that the world was flat in shape.
9. An encyclopedia is a valuable reference work for doing preliminary research, but do not depend on it for in-depth and complete analysis of every aspect of your subject.
10. The pickup truck has become a new status symbol vehicle found parked in the garages of suburban households.

18b   Use positive constructions for clarity.

Needless negatives (constructions such as "not unknown") are wordy and puzzle readers.

The expedition faced a ~~not easy~~ *difficult* climb up the west face to Everest's summit.

Negative constructions may reverse your actual meaning:

I have missed ~~not~~ seeing my favorite soap operas this semester.

"Missed not seeing" means the writer regretted watching.

EXERCISE 18.3   Edit the following sentences to compress phrases and clauses and to eliminate needless negatives.

1. Srivivasa Ramanujan, who was not a rich, educated Indian, became one of the best and greatest and smartest mathematical geniuses who ever lived upon this planet.
2. He gained his entire mathematical education due to the fact of reading and studying in two books that he borrowed in order to read them.
3. What is even more surprising is that his work is not unmeaningful in areas he would not have been familiar with, such as fast algorithms in computer science.
4. At this point in time Ramanujan never earned a college degree, although he tried twice to obtain one.
5. He took a basic and fundamental job in an office as a clerk to support his wife and his mother-in-law, who lived with the couple.
6. Generally, he spent all of his time away from work writing mathematical results, even at mealtimes when his wife fed him in order that he could continue to write while he ate.
7. It has been shown that his managers at work were not unmindful of the fact that he was a genius and a great number of them encouraged him to send his work to mathematicians in England so they could evaluate and judge it.
8. His genius was recognized by the best mathematicians, and the truth is he was invited to study at Trinity College, Cambridge, where he spent five years working.

9. Unfortunately, Ramanujan, who was a vegetarian in his diet and eating habits, was unable to get proper and nutritious food, which a large number of people suspect may have been the cause of a mysterious illness he came down with in 1817.

10. He died and was buried appropriately in 1820 at the very young and tender age of 32, but he left behind him a lot of papers that basically contained as many as 4000 mathematical results.

CHAPTER
19
Figurative Language

19a   Use both metaphor and simile.

Metaphor and simile are the basic tools of **figurative language**, which uses words imaginatively, not literally.

> LITERAL: The eye is an organ of sight.

> FIGURATIVE: Her eyes were windows on the joy of innocence.

Like analogy (see section **6i**), similes and metaphors compare the subject with a particular quality of another subject so the reader can see the subject in an entirely new light.

Both metaphor and simile compare a *tenor* (the subject) with a *vehicle* (a second, dissimilar subject).

tenor   vehicle

Her eyes were windows on the joy of innocence.

A **simile** compares dissimilar things by using *like* or *as*. Use the simile to announce a comparison boldly and clearly.

tenor   vehicle

He had eyes *like* mud, dull and opaque.

tenor   vehicle

The brain is *like* a muscle. When it is in use we feel very good.
—CARL SAGAN, *Broca's Brain*

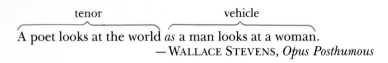

```
       tenor                        vehicle
```

A poet looks at the world *as* a man looks at a woman.
— WALLACE STEVENS, *Opus Posthumous*

A **metaphor** makes an implied comparison of dissimilar things. It does not use *like* or *as*. Use the metaphor for unannounced, subtle comparisons.

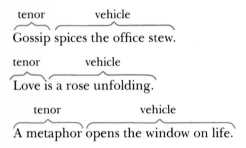

```
  tenor        vehicle
```
Gossip spices the office stew.

```
  tenor        vehicle
```
Love is a rose unfolding.

```
   tenor              vehicle
```
A metaphor opens the window on life.

Metaphors can be as brief as a single word.

ADJECTIVES: his *muddy* eyes, the *raging* river, a *dancing* kite

VERBS: My mind *whirled* in confusion.
The adding machine *raced* through the figures.
The skyline *bristled* with smokestacks.

NOUNS: The *tentacles* of the cable system embrace homes near and far.
Footprints of shame traced his reluctant steps.

19b   Use figurative language to sway opinion, view life, and surprise the reader.

Metaphors and similes create mental images to sway opinion. This next passage argues that weight loss is an outright war between the mind and the body.

Unfortunately for weary veterans of the weight war, there are no shortcuts to slenderness — no secret potions, no magic elixirs. In the absence of easy solutions, and with the possibility that metabolism, setpoint and the yo-yo syndrome are conspiring to battle against us, the prospect of losing weight might not seem too promising. The mind, however, can be a powerful weapon.

—KELLY D. BROWNELL, "When and How to Diet"

In this passage the dieters become veterans of a desperate war in which the *yo-yo syndrome* (itself a metaphor) engages the battle, but the dieters can rely on a powerful weapon, the mind.

A good metaphor can also embody the way a writer sees the world. This next writer takes an unusual view of his prenatal existence with a twin brother.

For Ross and me, competition started the moment the lights winked on in the womb, though it was a competition marked by accommodation. If we weren't two gladiators tied together for a fight to the finish, we were two gymnasts attempting a trapeze act in an upended bottle. (Either way, the management never approved of our struggle for comfort.)

—GREGG LEVOY, "Born Rivals"

This writer's primary metaphors (twin fetuses are like gladiators or like gymnasts competing in a trapeze act) contributes to his thesis: "Whereas others begin life separate and must learn intimacy, Ross and I began life intimate and had to learn separateness."

Figurative language gives you a stylistic edge; you can delight the reader with fresh comparisons, share your special view of the world, and explain a complex idea.

19c   Create fresh similes and metaphors.

Figurative language catches the reader unaware, shakes away the lethargy, and sharpens the attention. Experiment with the following techniques for developing fresh metaphors and similes to illuminate your ideas.

Compare dissimilar things.

His life was *blotched with patches of anger*.
Some Third World people are like *gulls on an oil-soaked beach*.

Compare people and human features to nonhuman ones — animals, vegetables, minerals, furniture, automobiles, and so on.

> The thief *scurried like a spider* into the dark doorway.
> The pickpocket had *fingers as tapered as okra* — and as slippery.
> The sleek young man *stretched out like a chaise lounge.*

CAUTION: Avoid clichés, which are figures grown old by excessive usage: *eyes glittering like diamonds, a cabbage head.*

Develop personifications.

Personification, the opposite of the technique above, gives human characteristics to nonhuman objects.

> The *computer printer's chatter* broke the quiet.
> The *pencil sharpener ground* its teeth.
> Looming above my head was the *giant fist of bureaucracy, clutching* a mass of red tape.

CAUTION: Avoid ridiculous and inflated images such as "The swaying flowers *nodded their heads* and *clapped their leafy hands* in time to the music of the breeze."

Take an old saying or a cliché and twist it into a variation.

Note how this writer handles the cliché "spur of the moment."

> I feel the *spur of the moment thrust* deep into my side. The present is an inexorable rider.
> — HENRY DAVID THOREAU, *Journal*

Make a humorous connection of dissimilar things.

> The harried commuter looked *like Dagwood* in a race for the bus.

Extend a metaphor through several sentences to explain difficult and obscure ideas.

The next passage compares voting to playing a game.

> All voting is a sort of gaming, like checkers or backgammon, with a slight moral tinge to it, a playing with right and wrong,

with moral questions; and betting naturally accompanies it. The character of the voters is not staked. I cast my vote, perchance, as I think right; but I am not vitally concerned that that right should prevail. I am willing to leave it to the majority.
— HENRY DAVID THOREAU, "Civil Disobedience"

Use hyperbole.

Hyperbole is a deliberate exaggeration or overstatement.

The state legislature *raped* the education budget.
My instructor is a *demon of intellectual lust*.

19d Do not mix metaphors or make strained comparisons.

Unfortunately, writers sometimes compare dissimilar things inappropriately. A **mixed metaphor** changes images midway through the comparison, with confusing, often ludicrous results:

The fullback *bolted like a quarter horse* through the line and ~~sailed~~ *galloped*

into the end zone for a touchdown.

When edited, the sentence maintains the comparison of a fullback to a horse.

The next example makes a comparison that is inappropriate to the subject:

The old waterfront hotel was like ~~an abandoned oasis, dried up~~ *a wretched bag lady,* ~~and useless.~~ *drooping and tattered.*

The image of a desert oasis is out of keeping with the waterfront, so the edited version substitutes an image of urban decay.

EXERCISE 19.1   Complete the following phrases with an original metaphor or simile.

1. His smile was _____.
2. The crowd at the rock concert was as crazy as _____.
3. My parents treat me like _____.

4. The glare of the sun in the mountains _____.
5. The dead branches _____.
6. The city at night quietly _____.
7. The sun shone as bright as _____.
8. The moon rose over the desert like _____.
9. His angry speech _____.
10. Sadness is _____.

EXERCISE 19.2 Rewrite the following sentences to eliminate mixed, strained, or inappropriate metaphors or clichés. If you cannot replace a metaphor with a fresh figure of speech, be straightforward.

1. He was as happy as a clam, and his smile gaped as wide as a Halloween mask's.
2. The gargantuan bus lumbered up the street, nibbling passengers at every corner.
3. Michael Jordan, the great basketball guard, runs like a gazelle and leaps like a flea.
4. Drug tests may catch those who are as innocent as newborn babes as well as those who are as guilty as sin.
5. The jackals of Wall Street have robbed the small investors at gunpoint.
6. The trapped flies and insects squirmed like rare jewels in the spider's crystal web.
7. The bee sting on my hip is as red as a beet.
8. As the blushing bride left the bosom of her loving family to join her fiancé in holy matrimony, tears of joy welled up in my eyes.
9. Thunderheads reared up in the west like eggs that would crack at any minute.
10. The flowers, stretching their necks toward the sun, were trying to get a sun tan.

EXERCISE 19.3 Underline all figurative language in the following passages.

> Just weeks ago, the Rhode Tive estuary was an unprepossessing sight, its mouth, mud flats and marshes painted in a drab palette. Except for an osprey wheeling overhead uttering its piping cries, the landscape appeared almost lifeless.
> — BAYARD WEBSTER, "A Tranquil Estuary Reveals the Speed of Its Life Cycle"

She [a moth] burned for two hours without changing, without bending or leaning—only glowing within, like a building fire glimpsed through silhouetted walls, like a hollow saint, like a flame-faced virgin gone to God, while I read by her light, kindled, while Rimbaud in Paris burnt out his brains with a thousand poems, while night pooled wetly at my feet.

—ANNIE DILLARD, "Transfiguration"

EXERCISE 19.4 Use five of the clichés listed below and extend or transform each into a new and rich metaphor.

stopped dead in my tracks
sober as a judge
busy as a bee
happy as a lark
go over like a lead balloon
quiet as a mouse
red as a beet
fresh as a daisy
as American as apple pie
fit as a fiddle
free as a bird
butterflies in the stomach

EXERCISE 19.5 In your journal or notebook, try creating metaphors or similes by comparing the following pairs. If one of them stumps you, make your own pair of images.

1. frosted flakes and money
2. a floppy diskette and romance
3. a soccer ball and human emotions
4. a log cabin and the human figure
5. a calendar and history
6. the growth of grass and maturation
7. the yellow line of a highway and success in life
8. a family pet and despair

EXERCISE 19.6 Bring to class a newspaper column or short essay in which you have marked all the figures of speech. Be sure to include single words used figuratively. Be prepared to discuss the figures of speech.

Basic Grammar

20
The Parts of Speech
21
The Parts of the Sentence
22
Phrases
23
Clauses

The Parts of Speech

Grammar is the system of rules that define a language. It comprises the classes of words, their pronunciations, and their functions and relations in the sentence. The eight classes of words, or **parts of speech**, are nouns, pronouns, verbs, adjectives, adverbs, prepositions, conjunctions, and interjections. While some words can function as only one part of speech, others can serve several roles in a sentence. *And*, for example, serves exclusively as a conjunction, whereas *down* can function as several different parts of speech:

> Shirley fell *down*.   [adverb]
> Shirley slipped and fell on the *down* slope.   [adjective]
> Such problems will never *down* Shirley.   [verb]
> Shirley crawled *down* the hill.   [preposition]
> Shirley gained twelve yards on the first *down*.   [noun]

A dictionary will show these classifications and provide examples. As shown on the following page, *down* functions principally as an adverb, in fourteen different ways. It also serves as an adjective, preposition, transitive verb (requiring an object), intransitive verb, and noun. The writer who understands the distinctions of each part

down¹ (doun) *adv.* **1. a.** From a higher to a lower place or position. **b.** Toward, to, or on the ground, floor, or bottom. **2. a.** Into a lower posture. **b.** In or into a prostrate position. **3.** Toward or in the south or in a southerly direction. **4. a.** Toward or in a center of activity: *going down to the office.* **b.** Away from the present place: *down on the farm.* **5.** To the source: *tracking a rumor down.* **6.** Toward or at a low or lower point on a scale. **7.** To or in a quiescent or subdued state. **8.** To or in a low status, as of subjection or disgrace. **9.** To an extreme degree. **10.** Seriously or vigorously: *get down to work.* **11.** From earlier times or people. **12.** To a reduced or concentrated form: *boiling down maple syrup.* **13.** In writing; on paper: *taking a statement down.* **14.** In partial payment at the time of purchase: *five dollars down.* —*adj.* **1. a.** Moving or directed downward: a down elevator. **b.** In a low position. **c.** At a reduced level. **2. a.** Sick: *he is down with a cold.* **b.** Low in spirit; depressed: *feel down.* **3. a.** In games, trailing an opponent by a specified number of points, goals, or strokes: *down two.* **b.** *Football.* Not in play. Used of the ball. **c.** *Baseball.* Having been put out. **4.** Being the first installment. —*prep.* **1.** In a descending direction along, upon, into, or through. **2.** Along the course of. **3.** Toward the mouth of a river. —*n.* **1.** A downward movement; descent. **2.** *Football.* Any of a series of four plays during which a team must advance at least ten yards to retain possession of the ball. —*v.* **downed, down·ing, downs.** —*tr.* **1.** To bring, put, strike, or throw down. **2.** To swallow hastily; gulp. **3.** *Football.* To put (the ball) out of play by touching it to the ground. —*intr.* To go or come down; descend. —*idioms.* **down and out.** Lacking friends or resources; destitute. **down in the mouth.** Discouraged; sad. **down on.** *Informal.* Hostile or negative toward; out of patience with. [ME *down* < OE *dūne* < *adūne: a-,* from (< *of*) + *dūn,* hill.]

down² (doun) *n.* **1.** Fine, soft, fluffy feathers forming the first plumage of a young bird and underlying the contour feathers in adult birds. **2.** *Bot.* A covering of soft, short fibers, as on some leaves. **3.** A soft, silky, or feathery substance, such as the first growth of human beard. [ME *doun* < ON *dūnn.*]

down³ (doun) *n.* **1.** Often **downs.** An expanse of rolling, grassy upland used for grazing. **2.** Often **Down.** Any of several breeds of sheep having short wool, developed in the downs of England. [ME *doune* < OE *dūn.*]

(margin labels: adverb, adjective, preposition, noun, transitive verb, intransitive verb, idioms, noun, noun)

of speech or who uses the dictionary effectively can express ideas precisely and clearly.

20a   Nouns

Nouns name a person, place, thing, quality, or idea: *Tom, Mars, automobile, beauty, justice.* A writer's style depends in part on his or her choice of nouns, especially the precise use of proper nouns and concrete nouns.

Proper nouns name a particular person, place, or thing: *Samuel Smith, New York, Mississippi River*, so they are always capitalized (see chapter **45**). Use proper nouns whenever possible; they add precision and interest to your writing.

Jack Hestle scored the winning touchdown with two seconds left.

Common nouns name one or all members of a class or group and do not require capitals: *touchdown, seconds, city, river, man, idea, light.* Common nouns can be abstract or concrete. In general, use **concrete nouns** because they name tangible items — things readers can perceive with their senses such as *desk, symphony, lemon, smoke, sunrise.* Use **abstract nouns** less often because they name intangible qualities and ideas: *liberty, justice, sweetness, love, evil, intelligence.*

ABSTRACT: The supervisor's decision is unfair.

CONCRETE: The supervisor's new work schedule will ruin summer vacation plans for most employees.

The concrete nouns of the second sentence give specific information to the reader.

NOTE: Most common nouns change form to show *number* (singular or plural): *visitor–visitors; baby–babies; child–children.* Some, however, have the same form for singular or plural (*scissors, deer*), and a few have a plural form but a singular meaning (*physics*). (See also chapters **26** and **27** on agreement.)

EXERCISE 20.1 Underline the nouns in the following sentences. Identify each as either a proper noun or type of common noun (abstract or concrete).

1. Some growing cities find traffic gridlock one of their most serious problems.
2. Bellevue, Washington, for example, has grown so fast that thousands of cars now try to drive on streets planned for hundreds.

3. Regional transportation authorities rush to construct more roads, bus lanes, and rail systems, but the construction just adds to commuters' woes.
4. Jobs and housing move to the suburbs, leaving new transportation systems outdated before they are completed.
5. Most rush-hour public transportation moves only in the direction of the central city, so inner city residents cannot reach suburban jobs without a car.

20b Pronouns

A **pronoun** acts in the place of a noun, phrase, or clause called its **antecedent**: "After naming Alexander Hamilton once, a writer can refer to *him* to describe *his* actions and what *he* accomplished." The pronouns *him, his,* and *he* substitute for the antecedent, Alexander Hamilton. The pronouns and the antecedent denote the same person.

For stylistic purposes, the pronoun enables a writer

1. to avoid repetition (imagine repeating *"Alexander Hamilton"* time and time again),
2. to intensify words ("The queen *herself* presented the trophy"), and
3. to relate one item to another ("The gun *that* fired the fatal shot has disappeared").

A pronoun may refer to an unknown or unspecified antecedent: "*Someone* lost a wallet," "*Whoever* leaves last must lock the door," or "*Something* is in my eye." Other pronouns function as limiting adjectives, sometimes specifying a particular noun ("*My* birthday is this Saturday") and sometimes substituting for an understood noun ("*Yours* is next month"; "*These* belong to you").

Personal pronouns refer to specific persons or things. They change form to show number.

	Singular	*Plural*
First person	I, me	we, us
possessive	my, mine	our, ours
Second person	you	you
possessive	yours	yours
Third person	he, she, it, him, her	they, them
possessive	his, hers, its	their, theirs

In third person, pronouns change form to show gender (*he, she, it, they*) and to show function in the sentence ("*She* wanted *me* to take *my* videotape to *her* house").

Relative pronouns introduce dependent clauses (see chapters **9** and **23**), and *relate* them to the main clause.

The relative pronouns are as follows:

> who, whoever, whom, whomever, whose [refer mainly to people and occasionally to animals and things]
> that [refers to people, animals, and things]
> which, whichever [refers to animals and things]
> what [means *that which*: "The vat is *what* exploded"]

Relative pronouns may or may not have a specific antecedent.

> The producer announced *who* would star in his next film. [noun clause, no antecedent]
> The actress *who* will star in the film has won three Oscars. [adjective clause; *actress* is the antecedent]

Interrogative pronouns introduce a question: *who, whose, whom, what, which.*

> *Who* spoke at the lecture last evening?
> *What* is the subject of tonight's meeting?

Reflexive and **intensive pronouns** are the "self" pronouns:

myself	herself
yourself	itself
yourselves	ourselves
himself	themselves

(Do not use *hisself* and *theirselves*, which are nonstandard forms.) **Reflexive pronouns** name a receiver of an action that is identical to the one doing the acting: "he submitted *himself* to authorities." **Intensive pronouns** emphasize and distinguish a noun: "he delivered the baby *himself.*" Do not use them in place of personal pronouns.

> My friend and ~~myself~~ *I* saw the new James Bond movie. [The pronoun *I* is part of the subject of the sentence: ". . . I saw . . ."]

Demonstrative pronouns show which nouns perform or receive the action.

> this, these [refer to something close by]
> that, those [refer to something farther away]

The words can be adjectives when they precede a noun ("*This* switch has several functions"), but as demonstrative pronouns they substitute for a noun.

> The new computers are now in place in the laboratory. *Those* on the far wall have hard disks. *These* at stations 2 and 4 have color monitors.

Be sure when you use demonstrative pronouns that the antecedent is clear (see chapter **27**).

Indefinite pronouns stand for a vague or unspecified number of people or things: "*Many* are called but *few* are chosen."

all	both	many	one
another	each	neither	other
any	either	nobody	several
anybody	everybody	no one	some
anyone	everyone	none	somebody
anything	few	nothing	someone
			something

Like the demonstrative pronouns, indefinite pronouns become adjectives when they precede a noun:

> A *few* people left early. [adjective]
> *Few* left early. [indefinite pronoun]

Some indefinite pronouns combine to form **reciprocal pronouns**: "The candidates praised *each other*."

EXERCISE 20.2 Underline the pronouns in the following sentences and label them (personal, relative, interrogative, reflexive, intensive, demonstrative, or indefinite). Draw an arrow to each antecedent, if one exists.

1. Although bloomers were named after Amelia Bloomer, she did not invent them.
2. Elizabeth Smith Miller designed them to have something modest to wear while gardening.

3. At first they consisted of a short dress worn over "Turkish trousers," full pants gathered at the ankles.
4. Suffragists, who liked the freedom of "pantalettes," as they were called, led the trend to wear them.
5. Finally, even Amelia Bloomer herself stopped wearing the "Bloomer costume" because it diverted attention from more important women's issues, which were her main concern.
6. Each new generation of women starts a fashion trend.
7. You might ask, "Who has shocked the nation in recent years?"
8. Gussie Moran shocked officials but not herself by wearing lace-panty undergarments at the staid Wimbledon tennis tournament.
9. "Those are pioneers of the women's movement," said one un-named source.
10. A woman who wishes to be free must sometimes appear bold to everybody else.

20c   Verbs

A **verb** shows either action (process, feeling, movement) or a state of being.

> The hot air balloon *collapsed*.   [action]
> The crowd *loved* the performance.   [action]
> Winter *is* warm in the tropics.   [being]

A verb may appear in several forms:

> we *face* the enemy   [infinitive form]
> he *faced* the enemy   [past tense]
> we *have faced* the enemy   [past participle]
> we *are facing* the enemy   [present participle]

See chapters **29** and **30** for discussion of these forms.

All **regular verbs** have past tense and past participle forms that end in *-ed* or *-d*, such as *walked, talked, barked* (see section **29a**). **Irregular verbs** take irregular forms in the past tense and past participles, such as *write, wrote, written* or *drink, drank, drunk* (see sections **29b** and **29c**).

Linking verbs express a state of being rather than an action.

> John *is* the boss. He *appears* harried.

The most common linking verbs are the irregular forms of *be: am, are, is, was, were, being, been.* Other linking verbs, such as *seem, become, appear, stand, taste, feel, smell, sound, look,* will give your sentences more precision (see sections **21d** and **21f**).

Auxiliary verbs often precede the main verb. The modals *can, will, shall, should, could, would, may, might,* and *must* act only as auxiliaries, not as main verbs: "Mason *should* pay for the damage." Some auxiliary verbs can act as main verbs: *be, am, is, are, were, being, been, do, does, did, have, has, had.*

> The clock *has been reset* twice this week.   [auxiliary]
> She *has* my money.   [main verb]

(See chapter **30**.)

EXERCISE 20.3   Underline all the verbs, including auxiliary verbs, in the following sentences.

1. Computer flight simulation has taught many people to fly, both real pilots and the arm-chair types.
2. Using a computer keyboard, the pilot applied full throttle and taxied down the runway, steering with the rudder to keep a steady course and to avoid zig-zagging.
3. Quickly and repeatedly pressing a key is the equivalent of pulling back on the control yoke of a real aircraft.
4. As the pilot pulls back on the control yoke, the nose of the plane lifts off the ground.
5. Once airborne, the pilot raises the elevators on the wings to maintain climbing speed, but he lowers them when the plane is at flying altitude.
6. The pilot makes turns by using the ailerons to bank the plane and by moving the rudders to *yaw* it, or turn it to the left or right.

20d   Adjectives

Adjectives modify nouns and pronouns. (See also chapter **33**.) Use adjectives in your writing to add colorful and interesting detail to describe, to limit, or to specify.

> *plaid* shirt, *heavy* traffic   [describe]
> *the first* person, *my only* child   [limit]
> *that* apple, *his favorite* uncle   [specify]

> *The three* students walked to *their favorite* pizza parlor.

The **indefinite articles** *a, an* and the **definite article** *the* are also classified as adjectives.

Words, phrases, and clauses can serve as adjectives:

The *graduate* students *in the biology lab* act as proctors.

Predicate adjectives follow linking verbs and limit the meaning of the subject: "The plan seems *incomplete and unusually expensive.*"

Three adjective groups have the same form as pronouns, but they modify a following noun rather than replace a noun.

> **Demonstrative adjectives** (*this, that, these, those*): "*This* plan needs more refinement." (Compare demonstrative pronouns, page 248.)
>
> **Possessive adjectives** (*her, his, your, its, our, their*): "*Your* plan needs more work."
>
> **Indefinite adjectives** (*any, each, every, some*): "*Every* plan submitted today has several flaws." (Compare indefinite pronouns, page 248.)

20e   Adverbs

Adverbs modify verbs (and verbals), adjectives, and other adverbs. (See chapter **33**.) Adverbs show or clarify time, place, manner, and degree; they also affirm or deny.

> **When?**   again, always, early, never, forever, often
> **Where?**   above, below, up, down, here, there, everywhere
> **Why?**   why, therefore, wherefore, then
> **How?**   badly, easily, foolishly, how, not, no, surely
> **To what degree?**   almost, much, more, most, little, less
> **Affirm or deny**   yes, no, maybe, perhaps

Adverbs that modify a *verb* can appear in any position in the sentence: "*Secretly* he laughed. He *secretly* laughed. He laughed *secretly*."

Adverbs that modify *adjectives or other adverbs* must precede the word they modify because they intensify or limit it: "She gave an *extremely* short performance."

Adverbs *derived from adjectives* usually take an *-ly* ending: *peacefully, greatly, marvelously*.

Words, phrases, and clauses can act as adverbs:

```
        adverb                          adverb clause
He always finishes his work when he has a vacation planned.
```

Adverbs sometimes modify an entire clause: "*Unbelievably*, she jumped from the edge of the cliff." Adverbs modify some prepositional phrases: "Your work is *seldom* on time." *No* and *not* are adverbs, even when they appear with a helping verb: "You can*not* understand my position."

EXERCISE 20.4   Underline and label the adjectives (adj.) and adverbs (adv.) in the following sentences. Draw arrows to the words each modifies. (From Wayside Gardens 1988 Fall Catalog.)

             adj.   adj.   adj.

EXAMPLE: When *garden* catalogs arrive in *the mid-winter*
                      adj.

mail, they excite *the* imagination of gardeners, who
  adv.   adj.   adj.

mentally transform *their barren* backyards into
  adj.

flowering vistas.

1. The Star of Gold daylily blooms early, producing masses of dainty golden yellow flowers whose lightly ruffled petals and sepals curl back slightly to create a bell-like flower.
2. The tree peony Renkaku, a Japanese variety, has pure white flowers, gracefully crimped and curved, with a translucent quality like the finest porcelain.
3. Bee balm, irresistible to hummingbirds, bears flower whorls surrounded by colorful bracts above their spicily scented leaves.
4. The artistic beauty and richness of Hosta foliage is unequaled in any other shade-loving plant; moreover, the late-blooming spiked flowers lend a sparkle of light to the shade.
5. The iris Song of Norway is a cool light blue, so light as to appear almost white, with just a touch of the palest blue veining on its lightly ruffled blooms.

20f   Prepositions

Prepositions are words used with a noun or pronoun (and their modifiers, if any) to form a phrase that shows place, position, time, or means: *at college, in the city, on Monday, by the first available taxi.*

object of
prep.   adj.   prep.

The defendents stood *before* a stern judge.

They function as adverbs or adjectives to elaborate upon the nouns and verbs of the sentence:

adjective   adverb

Three members *of the team* left early *for the airport.*

Adjectival prepositional phrases tell *which one* and *what kind of.* Adverbial prepositional phrases tell *when, where, why, how,* and *under what circumstances.*

It is permissible to end a sentence with a preposition: "Chaos in the library is something I have learned to live *with.*"

Prepositions can be single words or phrases:

about	by reason of	onto
above	concerning	out
according to	despite	outside
across	down	over
after	during	past
against	except	rather than
ahead of	for	since
along	from	through
among	in	throughout
around	in addition to	till
as well as	in case of	to
at	in front of	toward
because of	in place of	under
before	in spite of	underneath
behind	inside	until
below	inside of	up
beneath	instead of	upon
beside	into	with
besides	like	with respect to
between	near	with the
beyond	of	exception of
but	off	within
by	on	without

EXERCISE 20.5 Underline each prepositional phrase in the following sentences; then circle the prepositions and label their objects.

1. A group of scientists is exploring ways of using energy produced by the sun.
2. Direct energy from the sun is powerful.
3. Only about 50 percent of the sun's radiation even reaches the surface of the Earth, the rest being absorbed by dust, water vapor, and dry air molecules.
4. Of the radiation that does reach Earth, less than 90 percent can be used for energy, even in the areas with the most usable sunlight, because of darkness, cloud cover, and other factors.
5. The likeliest places to use direct solar energy are those in the Torrid Zone (between the tropics of Cancer and Capricorn) at relatively high altitudes.
6. Condensation of water caused by the sun replenishes the water supply of earth.
7. Almost one-fourth of the power used in America and Europe is water generated, but worldwide only 2 percent is, despite large potential for water power in China, the Soviet Union, and South America.
8. Ironically, in Brazil large areas of the rain forest, which is a vital part of the solar energy cycle, are being flooded to provide hydroelectric power.
9. Wind power is a third form of solar energy, symbolized best perhaps by the windmills seen on farms from the Netherlands to the Great Plains of the United States.
10. Current technology does not exist to harness the wind in the stratosphere.

20g Conjunctions

Conjunctions connect words, phrases, and clauses to show order and to relate two or more ideas. The three classifications of conjunctions are coordinating, correlative, and subordinating.

Coordinating conjunctions (*and, but, or, nor, for, so,* and *yet*) join equal items.

Bob *and* Betty syndicated their talk show.   [joins two words]
We will live in a dorm *or* in an off-campus apartment.   [joins two prepositional phrases]
We left the party early, *but* everyone else stayed late.   [joins two independent clauses]

Do not depend heavily on *and* as your only conjunction. (See section **8a** for stylistic tips about using conjunctions.)

Correlative conjunctions also join items of equal grammatical rank, but they always function as a pair. See section **8b**.

> The best jobs promise *both* financial rewards *and* exciting challenges.

Both . . . and connect equal elements—the "financial rewards" and the "exciting challenges." Other correlative conjunctions are *either . . . or, neither . . . nor, not [only] . . . but [also]*, and *whether . . . or*.

Subordinating conjunctions (such as *although, since, unless, while*) introduce dependent clauses and signal their relationship to the rest of a sentence. Subordinating conjunctions show relationships of cause, time, location, degree, and manner. See section **9b** for a list of common subordinating conjunctions.

> *Unless* the committee acts quickly, the president will disband it.

If the sentence contains a dependent clause, it must also include an independent clause (see chapters **9** and **24**).

      independent clause   dependent clause

> The committee cannot agree, *even though* it meets daily.

A **conjunctive adverb**, used with a semicolon, sometimes serves to join independent clauses:

> The apostles are any of the twelve original disciples of Christ; *however*, the Apostolic Fathers were contemporaries of the apostles.

See sections **8a, 20e,** and **25e** for a discussion of these common conjunctive adverbs: *consequently, finally, furthermore, however, moreover, nevertheless, similarly, then, therefore,* and *thus*.

EXERCISE 20.6   Rewrite the following sentences, changing *and* to a more precise conjunction. If necessary, change punctuation and other words as well. If you think *and* is the best choice, explain your reasons.

1. The tree service will remove the dead treas, *and* the garden will get more sun.
2. Scientists do not understand what triggers migration of birds, *and* they think that birds might have built-in biological clocks.

3. We think violence occurs often in real life, *and* it occurs in so many television shows.
4. Terry Fox ran all the way across Canada, *and* he had only one leg.
5. I will not be able to afford my books, *and* I earn some money.
6. Professor Mills did not lecture on the Civil War, *and* he did not cover it on the test.
7. Behavioral psychologists help people change bad habits, *and* people often cannot change on their own.
8. All the engineers studied the problem, *and* the building still fell down.
9. Baseball and football players walked off their teams on strike, *and* they were tired of not being able to be free agents.
10. Hans will graduate with honors *and* then attend medical school.

20h   Interjections

Interjections show surprise or emotion. They are short outbursts—a sound, a word, a phrase, or even a sentence—that serve no special grammatical function. Therefore, set off interjections from the rest of the sentence by a comma, an exclamation mark, or a period. Most interjections are informal or colloquial, appropriate only in speech and dialogue and in some informal essays.

Oh no, we've lost the game.
Glory be! We won!

EXERCISE 20.7   Label the parts of speech in the following nonsense poem. Identify each one in the manner of the first line:

```
pronoun
        verb  noun  conj.    adj.    noun
      'Twas brillig, and the slithy toves
            Did gyre and gimble in the wabe;
      All mimsy were the borogoves,
            And the mome raths outgrabe.
      "Beware the Jabberwock, my son!
            The jaws that bite, the claws that catch!
      Beware the Jubjub bird, and shun
            The frumious Bandersnatch!"
```

He took his vorpal sword in hand:
    Long time the manxome foe he sought—
So rested he by the Tumtum tree,
    And stood awhile in thought.
And as in uffish thought he stood,
    The Jabberwock, with eyes of flame,
Came whiffling through the tulgey wood,
    And burbled as it came!
One, two! One, two! And through and through
    The vorpal blade went snicker-snack!
He left it dead, and with its head
    He went galumphing back.
"And hast thou slain the Jabberwock?
    Come to my arms, my beamish boy!
O frabjous day! Callooh! Callay!"
    He chortled in his joy.
'Twas brillig, and the slithy toves
    Did gyre and gimble in the wabe;
All mimsy were the borogoves,
    And the mome raths outgrabe.

                      — LEWIS CARROLL, "Jabberwocky"

A sentence is a grammatically self-contained unit of speech that contains a subject (section **21a**) and a predicate (section **21b**). The subject either performs or receives the action of the sentence, and the predicate expresses the action of the sentence.

subject predicate
Fish swim.

Sentences may express an assertion, a question, a command, a wish, or an exclamation.

Michael caught the error.   [assertion]
Do all mammals walk?   [question]
Listen.   [imperative command]
We hope for a peaceful solution to the war on drugs.   [wish]
The homeless know anguish!   [exclamation]

We shall fight in France, we shall fight on the seas and oceans, we shall fight with growing confidence and growing strength in the air, we shall defend our island, whatever the cost may be, we shall fight on the beaches, we shall fight on the landing grounds, we shall fight in the fields and in the streets, we shall fight in the hills; we shall never surrender.
— WINSTON CHURCHILL   [assertion]

NOTE: Imperative sentences have an unstated, implied subject — *you.*

In most sentences, the subject precedes the predicate (see section **21f**).

subject predicate

The *dolphins escorted* the boat to the harbor.

But the purpose of the sentence may invert the order, as in the examples below:

pred. sub. pred.

Are you going to the library tonight?   [question]

predicate   subject

Across the desert *trudged* the weary *caravan*.   [literary mechanism, for emphasis or rhythm]

subject

There are three *ways* to open an account.   [expletive — see section **18a**]

21a   Subject

The **subject** of the sentence acts, is acted upon, or is discussed. The **simple subject** is a *noun* or *pronoun* without its modifiers:

Classes start tomorrow.

The **complete subject** is the simple subject plus any modifiers:

complete subject

Adult education *classes* at the museum start tomorrow.

In most cases, you can find the subject by asking *who* or *what* about the verb: *What* starts? *Classes* start.
   A **compound subject** has two or more simple subjects joined by a coordinating conjunction such as *and, or, but* or a correlative conjunction such as *either . . . or* or *neither . . . nor*. (See section **20g**.)

Neither Ford nor General Motors has dominated the domestic automobile market.

Noun phrases and clauses (see chapters **22** and **23**) also function as subjects:

To live each day fully is my credo.

EXERCISE 21.1   Underline the complete subject of the following sentences.

1. Some early literature in America was devoted to descriptions of life in the colonies.
2. The primary audience for the early writings was the European reader, who was greatly interested in the New World.
3. During the 1600s, religious writings formed the bulk of American writings.
4. There is still great interest in the writings of Jonathan Edwards, Cotton Mather, and John Woolman.
5. Each wrote numerous religious tracts during the 1700s.
6. Naturally, there were a few poets who wrote primarily about religious themes.
7. In the mid-1700s, political literature in the form of pamphlets and poems gained a wide following.
8. One of the most famous political writers was Benjamin Franklin.

21b   Predicate

All sentences have a **predicate**, which tells what the subject is doing, indicates what is being done to the subject, or expresses something about the subject.

The **simple predicate** consists of the *verb* alone (see section **20c**):

Jesus *wept*. The bells *rang*.

The **complete predicate** consists of the verb, which is the grammatical center of the predicate, and any modifiers, objects, and complements (see sections **21c** and **21d**).

complete predicate

The unscrupulous clerk *sold* Ted an overpriced stereo.

A **compound predicate** has two or more verbs joined by a coordinating conjunction, plus adverbial modifiers.

Ted *collects old records* and *plays them in a jazz club*.

A predicate with a *linking verb* consists of the subject complement, a word or word group, that (1) describes the subject with a **predicate adjective** or (2) renames it with a **predicate noun** (see section **21d**).

predicate adjective

This set of blood samples *may be* contaminated.

predicate noun

The Pied Piper of Hamelin *is* a mythical character.

A predicate with a **transitive verb** includes a direct object that names the receiver of the action (see also section **21c**). The transitive verb transfers the action from the subject to the receiver, which is the direct object.

transitive verb

After conquering Peru, Francisco Pizarro *founded* the city of

direct object

Lima.

This sentence has the transitive verb *founded* in active voice, which means the subject (Pizarro) acts and the direct object (Lima) receives the action. Transitive verbs in passive voice reverse the order with the subject receiving the action. Passive voice: *The city of Lima was founded by Francisco Pizarro.* (See chapter **31** for additional discussion of active and passive voice.)

A predicate with an **intransitive verb** cannot take direct or indirect objects (see **21c**), nor can it take predicate nouns or predicate adjectives (see **21d**). It may be followed by an adverb or adverbial word group.

intransitive
verb   adverb

This new concept *disagrees* completely with orthodox teaching.

See chapters **29–32** for additional discussion of verbs.

EXERCISE 21.2   Underline the complete predicate in each sentence below.

1. Some early pioneers traveled west on large flatboats that could carry the entire family and its livestock.
2. Independence, Missouri, served as the staging area for many pioneers.
3. There were often problems at the Cimarron crossings.
4. Pioneers constructed special rafts to ferry wagons and supplies across the Cimarron.
5. Guides were vital for the pioneers.
6. A good guide could save travelers not only precious time but also their very lives.
7. The northern route traveled through Fort Kearny, Fort Laramie, and across the mountain range.
8. Those who chose the southern route passed through Council Grove and Sante Fe.
9. Some pioneers walked the trail.
10. Most pioneers had a wagon, pack animals, and often a cow.

21c   Direct objects, retained objects, indirect objects, and object complements

A **direct object** receives the action expressed by a transitive active verb.

Sarah bought *flowers*.

Identify direct objects by asking *who, whom,* or *what* about the subject and verb: Sarah bought *what*? Sarah bought *flowers*.

A **retained object** occurs in the passive voice (see chapter **31**) of some transitive verbs which "retain" the ability to take an object even though the receiver of the action is the subject.

passive verb   retained object

The speech *was awarded first place* by the judges.

The judges are the actors, the speech received the award, and *first place* is the retained object to tell what was awarded.

The **indirect object** receives the action of the verb indirectly; it tells *to whom* or *for whom* something is done.

indirect object

Sarah *bought* her *mother* flowers.

Indirect objects occur often with the transitive verbs *ask, bring, find, give, pay, promise, send, teach,* and *throw.*

indirect object

The Lipinskis *gave* the *library* their collection of rare books.

An **object complement** is either a noun that renames the direct object or an adjective that describes the direct object.

object complement

The new chemist *calls* a test tube a *vial.*

object complement

The players all *consider* the new offense *inferior* to the old wishbone attack.

The noun *vial* renames; the adjective *inferior* describes.

21d Predicate nouns and predicate adjectives

Predicate nouns and predicate adjectives—also called subject complements—complete a linking verb by renaming or describing the subject. Thus, they form part of the predicate.

A **predicate noun** renames:

predicate noun

Dunwoodie is the *head of the research team.*

A **predicate adjective** describes or modifies:

predicate adjective

Dunwoodie seems totally *humorless.*

EXERCISE 21.3   Label direct and indirect objects, retained objects, object complements, predicate nouns, and predicate adjectives.

1. John La Farge's intense commitment to his art helped him to greatness.
2. He is famous in part for his work with stained glass.
3. He was an American painter known for beautiful murals.
4. After his graduation from college, he took a long European grand tour before returning to the United States to study law.
5. Shortly thereafter, however, he gave up the law for painting.
6. La Farge was awarded honors by his patrons in New York City.
7. Japanese prints influenced his early work of landscapes and flowers and his later stained glass windows.
8. Art critics usually judge each new work superior.
9. His stained glass was judged superior art not only in America but in Europe, Japan, and the South Sea islands.
10. La Farge will probably always seem a maverick in the development of American art.

21e   Sentence constructions

Sentences with one clause (a subject plus a predicate — see chapter **23**) are called **simple sentences**.

We cried.

Simple sentences, however, are not always short. The simple sentence below opens with an introductory participial phrase (section **22c**) and closes with two prepositional phrases (section **22b**).

Standing in the silent stadium long after the game ended, *the coach and his wife cried* about the end of a long, illustrious career.

The next simple sentence has a three-part subject and a two-part predicate.

Television anchors, sportscasters, and *weather reporters write* their own material *and present* it on the air.

Do not let compound units mislead you; the sentence above still has only one subject and one predicate.

Compound sentences have two or more independent clauses joined by a coordinating conjunction or a semicolon. They have no subordinate clauses (see chapters **8, 9,** and **23**).

first independent clause

Some journalists travel all over the world for their stories,

second independent clause

but most spend their time on the telephone.

Complex sentences contain one independent clause and one or more subordinate clauses (see chapter **9**):

subordinate adverb clause

Although television journalism looks glamorous,

independent clause

reporters work long hours behind the cameras.

subordinate adjective clause

The person who wins will receive a $2000 scholarship.

Compound-complex sentences contain at least two independent clauses and at least one subordinate clause:

independent clause

Many television reporters started in radio,

independent clause

but others moved to television from newspapers,

subordinate clause

where the emphasis is on investigation and good writing.

EXERCISE 21.4   Label the following sentences (all written by H. L. Mencken) as simple (S), compound (C), complex (Cx), or compound-complex (C-Cx).

1. There are some politicians who, if their constituents were cannibals, would promise them missionaries for dinner.
2. Time is a great legalizer, even in the field of morals.

3. It is the dull man who is always sure, and the sure man who is always dull.
4. Nothing can come out of an artist that is not in the man.
5. The difference between a moral man and a man of honor is that the latter regrets a discreditable act, even when it has worked and he has not been caught.
6. Conscience is the inner voice that warns us that somebody may be looking.
7. The older I grow the more I distrust the familiar doctrine that age brings wisdom.
8. Injustice is relatively easy to bear; what stings is justice.
9. Of all the escape mechanisms, death is the most efficient.
10. No one ever went broke underestimating the intelligence of the American people.

21f   Sentence patterns

Sentences contain a *subject* (section **21a**) and a *predicate* (section **21b**), and may include *objects* (section **21c**), *subject complements* (section **21d**), or *object complements* (section **21c**). These parts of the sentence can form five basic sentence patterns:

1. Subject-verb.

   I speculated.

2. Subject-verb-object.

   I typed the proposal.

3. Subject-verb-subject complement.

   The proposal was complicated.

4. Subject-verb-indirect object-object.

   I gave the president my proposal.

5. Subject-verb-direct object-object complement.

   The president considered the proposal premature.

Familiarity with these patterns is essential. Knowledgeable writers, of course, add words, phrases, and clauses to these basic patterns.

EXERCISE 21.5 Identify the pattern of these sentences with the appropriate letter, as listed below.

  A. subject-verb
  B. subject-verb-object
  C. subject-verb-subject complement
  D. subject-verb-indirect object-object
  E. subject-verb-direct object-object complement

  1. New York is the Empire State.
  2. It outranks other states in foreign trade.
  3. New York gives America fame and fortune.
  4. New York has land rich in river valleys, forests, mountains, lakes, and scenic attractions.
  5. New York City bustles with commercial activity.

Phrases

A phrase is a group of grammatically related words that may contain a subject or a verb, but not both.

> in the morning
> to cook a pot of chili on an open campfire
> running across the concourse of the airport to catch a flight

A phrase functions as a single part of speech — noun, verb, adjective, or adverb. It differs from a clause, which has a subject and a verb (see chapter **23**).

22a   Use a variety of phrases.

Phrases help build full sentences by providing detail that brings to life a scene, definition, or explanation.

Verb phrases consist of the main verb and any auxiliary verbs: *were going, had been fighting*.

> The committee *may consider* your application today.

Noun phrases consist of a main noun and modifying words: *the canvas tent flapping in the breeze, the first one in line at the lunch counter, Sam the bartender*.

Gerund phrases (section **22c**) and appositive phrases (section **22e**) always serve as nouns, and infinitive phrases (section **22c**) may serve as nouns.

My screaming into the darkness attracted the rescue squad.   [gerund phrase as subject]

Several men tried *to build a fire*.   [infinitive phrase as direct object]

Weather conditions, *subfreezing temperatures and strong winds*, can numb both body and brain.   [appositive phrase to rename subject]

Adjective phrases tell *which one* or *what kind* about a noun that immediately precedes or follows the phrase.

The smile *on Jack's face* faded at the news.   [prepositional phrase]

Smiling for the photographer, the children anticipated the flash of strobe lights.   [participial phrase]

A test *to check radon levels* is advised for most homeowners.   [infinitive phrase]

NOTE: Participial phrases (section **22c**) function always as adjectives. Prepositional phrases (section **22b**) and infinitive phrases (section **22c**) are sometimes adjectives, but not always.

Adverb phrases tell *why, where, when, how, under what conditions,* and *to what degree* to describe a verb, adjective, or another adverb. They do not always appear next to the word they modify.

Work *with extreme caution* when you set the fuse.   [prepositional phrase]

We used dynamite *to demolish the building quickly*.   [infinitive phrase]

The dust of the explosion covering the site, we could not yet determine our success.   [absolute phrase]

The absolute phrase (section **22d**) is always an adverb phrase, but the propositional phrase (section **22b**) and the infinitive phrase (section **22c**) are not always adverbs.

22b   Prepositional phrases

A **prepositional phrase** consists of a preposition (see the list in section **20f**) and its object, and it generally functions as an adjective or adverb. When used as an *adjective* (see section **20d**), the prepositional phrase modifies the noun or pronoun next to it.

The chairman is a person *of honor*.

Consumers admired the new cars *in the dealer's showroom*.

Nonsmokers do not need a legal prescription *for nicotine chewing gum* to relieve symptoms *of anxiety*.

When used as an adverb (see section **20e**), the prepositional phrase tells *how, why, where, when,* and *under what conditions*. It need not appear next to the word it modifies.

> *On Tuesday*, all workers must report at 7:00 a.m.
> All workers must report *on Tuesday* at 7:00 a.m.
> All workers must report at 7:00 a.m. *on Tuesday*.

On rare occasions, prepositional phrases serve as nouns: "Old age for some people means *over the hill*."

EXERCISE 22.1 Underline the prepositional phrases in the following sentences and identify the phrase as adjective or adverb. (Adapted from Steven R. Weisman, "On Language.")

1. The primary language of India is Indian English.
2. For a foreigner, English usage in India serves as a road map to certain subtleties of culture and of politics, since many peculiarities derive from the grammar and from the modes of thought in south Asia.
3. Indian English sometimes reflects a general love of rococo euphemism, of courtesy, or of indirection.
4. Many of our useful English words in the West are drawn from Indian origins, such as *veranda, bungalow, pundit, khaki,* and *mango*.
5. In the Indian language many words are spoken twice for emphasis.

22c Verbal phrases

Verbal phrases, which are groups of words that contain verb forms, function as nouns, adjectives, and adverbs (see also section

22a). The three types of verbals are gerunds, participles, and infinitives. The *gerund phrase* is always a noun; the *participial phrase* is always an adjective; and the *infinitive phrase* may be a noun, adjective, or adverb.

A **gerund phrase** serves primarily as a subject or an object in sentences. The gerund always ends in *-ing*:

> *Watching television* can numb your brain.   [gerund phrase as subject]
> Many people continue *drinking and driving* despite strict laws. [gerund phrase as direct object]

(See also section **28f** regarding the possessive case with gerunds.)

A **participial phrase** functions as an adjective and should appear immediately before or immediately after the word it modifies (see section **12a**).

> *Defeated by his Republican opponent*, the congressman withdrew to his coastal retreat.

Notice that an introductory participial phrase is followed by a comma and then by the word it modifies.

The participle is usually in the present or past tense (see section **30**):

> Some mourners, *overcome by grief*, faint at funeral services.
> Any secret *kept for a week* is usually safe.

The **infinitive phrase** combines *to* with the base form of a verb (*to see, to have, to excite*) and usually takes an object (*to have money*) or an adverb (*to arrive safely*). (The *to* is implied in certain verbs: "He helped me [to] wash the car.")

Infinitive phrases serve as any form of noun, especially as subject, predicate noun, or direct object.

> *To practice patience and forethought* is the mark of a wise person. [infinitive phrase used as subject]
> The scientists tried *to isolate another strain of bacteria*.   [infinitive phrase used as direct object]

In some circumstances the infinitive may take a subject:

> The coach wanted his *players* to learn patience.   [subject of the infinitive]

When used as adverbs, infinitive phrases indicate when, where, why, or how, and they may show conditions and degree.

> She bought a gun *to protect herself and her children.*   [infinitive phrase used as adverb to explain *why*]

When used as adjectives, infinitive phrases usually appear immediately after the noun they modify.

> With a final chance *to win the debate trophy*, we stepped nervously to the stage.

EXERCISE 22.2   Underline the verbal phrases in the sentences below and identify each as a gerund, participial, or infinitive phrase. Further, identify the function of each infinitive phrase as a noun, adverb, or adjective.

1. The Statue of Liberty, commemorating the French and American Revolutions, was originally known as *Liberty Enlightening the World*.
2. The Franco-American Union, organized in 1875, raised the funds to pay for the statue.
3. The French sculptor Frederic-Auguste Bartholdi designed it to look like his mother.
4. Constructing the statue took hundreds of workers almost ten years.
5. Made of copper sheets welded to a frame, the statue stands 152 feet high on a 150-foot pedestal, making it visible for a long distance.
6. The base of the statue, an 11-pointed star, belonged once to a fort built on the site to defend the harbor of New York City.
7. Dedicated in 1886 and refurbished and celebrated in 1986, this symbol of freedom welcomes millions of visitors each year.
8. An elevator runs to the top of the pedestal, but walking up a staircase in the statue's arm is the only way to reach the top of the torch.
9. To visit the Statue of Liberty is a moving experience.
10. Serving as a beacon of hope for millions, the Statue of Liberty is probably the best-known symbol of the United States.

22d Absolute phrases

An **absolute phrase** modifies an entire clause rather than one word and is grammatically unconnected to the clause, so it is set off by commas.

That being the case, I defer to your judgment.

It is formed with a noun and participle and usually contains additional modifiers.

Their child being hurt on the playground, the parents sued the city.
The general paced the room, *voice pitched with passion, eyes darting from one person to another, hands gesturing wildly.*

22e Appositive phrases

Appositive phrases rename or give additional information about a noun:

Roger Bannister, *one of the world's most famous athletes*, was the first to run a sub-four-minute mile.

They appear next to the noun that they modify, and they usually are set off by commas.

My roommate, *a girl from South Dakota*, is the first member of her family to attend college.
This questionnaire, *an examination of political beliefs*, shows bias in its fourth and fifth questions.

EXERCISE 22.3 Underline and label the absolute and appositive phrases in the following sentences.

1. Leaves falling, air smelling of crisp apples, and white clouds billowing against the sky, no other season matches autumn.
2. Crowds poured into the streets to welcome home the victors, the hometown football team.
3. The team having won all its games, Chicago celebrated as never before.
4. Even the stern history professor, his face smiling and eyes shining, dismissed us to join the throng.
5. An unnecessary tragedy, an athlete's neck injury, marred the final days of the winning football season.

CHAPTER

23

Clauses

Clauses, like phrases, are grammatically related word groups. Unlike phrases, however, clauses have both a subject and a predicate. Clauses are either independent or subordinate.

An **independent clause** is a complete sentence:

Birds fly.
Emus are one of the few species of flightless birds.

(See also chapter **8**.)

A **subordinate clause** cannot stand alone as a complete sentence because it contains a subordinating conjunction or a relative pronoun (see chapter **9**). It must connect to an independent clause, serving as a noun, adjective, or adverb:

Although some birds cannot fly, they have the same biological characteristics as other birds.   [adverb clause]

The introductory adverb clause names a condition.

Subordinate conjunctions such as *although, because, since* (section **20g**) and relative pronouns such as *that, which, who, whom* (section **20b**) introduce subordinate clauses and connect them to the main clause:

The man *who came to dinner* stayed forever.   [relative pronoun introduces an adjective clause]
Although he only came for dinner, the man stayed forever.   [subordinate conjunction introduces an adverb clause]

Noun clauses generally appear as subjects or objects of a sentence. They do not modify, but neither can they stand alone.

Why he forgot his appointment is a mystery.   [clause as subject]

The Chicago *Tribune* reported *that Dewey defeated Truman.*   [clause as direct object]

Reserve this book for *whoever is next on the list.*   [clause is the object of a preposition]

Adjective clauses modify nouns and pronouns. They usually immediately follow the word they modify.

The athlete *who distinguishes himself on the field* can also win lucrative endorsement contracts.

Your men installed new lights *that are too bright.*

Honeysuckle, *which attracts hummingbirds*, is orange and trumpet-shaped.

NOTE: Set off nonrestrictive subordinate clauses with commas, but do not set off restrictive modifiers. *That are too bright* identifies which lights, but *which attracts hummingbirds* does not limit the description of honeysuckle. (See section **36e**.)

Adjective clauses usually begin with relative pronouns (*who, whom, whose, which,* or *that*), although they can begin with words such as *when, where,* or *why:*

Days *when we have no chores to do* are as rare as winning lottery tickets.

Adverb clauses tell when, where, why, under what conditions, or to what degree. Usually they modify the verb and may appear anywhere in the sentence. They begin with subordinate conjunctions such as *when, if, unless, where.*

I will starve *unless I get a job.*

Because no distribution network existed, some of the food sent to Ethiopia rotted.

NOTE: An introductory adverb clause, like the one directly above, must be set off with a comma.

EXERCISE 23.1 Identify the subordinate clauses in the following sentences and label them as noun clauses (n.), adjective clauses (adj.), or adverb clauses (adv.).

1. Marie Curie, who discovered radium, was the first person ever to win two Nobel prizes, one in physics and one in chemistry.
2. Scientist and inventor, Curie unlocked the secrets of radioactivity, which led to the beginnings of the atomic age.
3. Curie began her scientific training as a child, when she became an unpaid laboratory assistant for her father, a chemistry professor.
4. She shared her life and her work with her husband, Pierre, a physical chemist, who abandoned his studies of magnetism to assist Marie in her research into radioactivity.
5. When Pierre was killed by a truck after only eleven years of marriage, Marie devoted herself to her research and her scientific writing.
6. One of Marie Curie's accomplishments, with the help of her daughter Irène, was the development of X-ray equipment, which she personally installed in mobile stations near battlefields during World War I.
7. Irène Joliot-Curie and her husband, Frédéric Joliot-Curie, won a Nobel Prize for research that involved bombarding elements with alpha particles.
8. Irène Joliot-Curie was an active Socialist whose anti-Nazi activities during World War II forced her to flee to Switzerland.
9. Marie Curie's support of talented young women extended to Marguerite Perey, a former lab assistant of Curie's who discovered a new radioactive element, francium.
10. Ironically, Marie Curie, her daughter and son-in-law, and Marguerite Perey all died of leukemia or cancer that was caused by radiation exposure.

Editing Grammar for Style and Correctness

24
Fragments

25
Fused Sentences and Comma Splices

26
Subject-Verb Agreement

27
Pronoun Agreement and Reference

28
Case

29
Verb Forms

30
Verb Tense

31
Voice

32
Mood

33
Adjectives and Adverbs

34
Editing to Correct Nonstandard English

C H A P T E R

24

Fragments

A fragment is an incomplete sentence; it is a group of words detached from a main clause.

> In mathematics, universal sets consist of all members being considered at any one time. *Called a* universe *and represented by the letter* U.

The second word group above is punctuated like a sentence, but it is a fragment—a verb phrase without a subject.

Some sentence fragments are phrases, like the one above, and do not have a subject, verb, or both. If the fragment is a clause, it has both subject and predicate but begins with a subordinating conjunction (see chapter **9**).

> The council does make an occasional mistake. *Especially when committee members vote in haste on matters such as yearbook and newspaper funding.*

The italicized clause looks like a sentence because it has a subject (*members*) and a predicate (*vote*) and ends with a period. Yet the word *when*, a subordinate conjunction, makes the entire clause subordinate, which means it needs a main clause for support.

You can occasionally use fragments for stylistic effect (see section **24c**). However, to fix an unintentional or ineffective fragment, attach it to a complete sentence (see section **24a**) or turn it into an independent clause (see section **24b**). Check your drafts for fragment trouble spots (see section **24d**).

EXERCISE 24.1 Mark with an *F* any word group below that is not a complete sentence. Some are correct. Some have an understood *you* as subject.

1. Stand tall, young man.
2. Joining the Marine Corps and making the journey through basic training in South Carolina.
3. Why we have a Marine Corps.
4. A great maritime nation such as the United States must be able to defend itself on land and at sea.
5. The Marine Corps, a fleet of marine forces combined with air and ground units.
6. The motto of the corps is *Semper Fidelis*. Always Faithful.
7. Marines have been the first to fight in almost every major war of the United States.
8. Marine recruits receive eleven weeks of basic training at one of two depots. In Parris Island, South Carolina, or in San Diego, California.

24a Attach fragments to sentences.

Most fragments are merely separated from the main clause. The verbal phrase below, in italics, tells how the members vote; attach it to the main clause.

The committee members often vote in haste. *For example, deny-*

ing funding to the yearbook and the newspaper.

The subordinate clause in the next example, in italics, tells when the council makes mistakes; attach it to the main clause.

The council does make an occasional mistake. *Especially when*

committee members vote in haste on matters such as yearbook and news-

paper funding.

The subordinate clause below, in italics, tells when it will be safe to walk; attach it to the main clause.

> *If, as promised, the administration improves campus security patrols*
>
> *and installs adequate lighting*~Then we can walk safely at night.

24b Turn fragments into sentences.

Sometimes a fragment will not attach easily to a main clause. Turn that fragment into a sentence by deleting the subordinate conjunction.

> We have scheduled the conference for mid-January. ~~So that~~ it
>
> will coincide with equal rights celebrations in honor of Martin
>
> Luther King, Jr.

In the next example, removing the subordinate conjunction *although* makes the second clause independent.

> Some art scholars believe that the glory of Chinese painting
>
> ended around 1800. ~~Although~~ others challenge that opinion,
>
> stressing the bold strokes of modern Chinese artists.

With phrases that are fragments, add a subject, a verb, or both, or change a verbal to a verb. In the example below, adding "are dangerous" (verb and adjective) makes an independent clause.

> Some personal habits can endanger the lives of other people. In
>
> particular, smoking excessively in confined public places and
>
> driving an automobile while under the influence of alcohol or
>
> drugs~ *are dangerous.*

24c Use some fragments for stylistic purposes.

Although fragments generally weaken communication between you and your readers, they occasionally serve a purpose. Carefully used fragments, not unintended ones or mispunctuated clauses and phrases, may help you create useful effects.

Use fragments to create a series of distinct descriptive images.

> The soft harvest moon. The aroma of hay. The swaying of the wagon and the gentle rhythm of the horses. All these, plus the presence of my friends, helped boost my morale and enliven my spirits after a summer of hospital pain.

> Mewling, puking babies. That's the way we all start. Damply clinging to someone's shoulder, burping weakly, clawing our way into life. *All* of us.
> — JEAN SHEPHERD, "The Endless Streetcar Ride"

Use fragments for a careful, emphatic enumeration of items that otherwise would form a series.

> Shakespeare provides a grand vision of political and social intrigue in his tragedies, comedies, and histories. He entices all readers into love for his linguistic genius. Most of all, he offers magnificent characters, larger than life, in play after play. Macbeth. Hamlet. Lear. Falstaff.

Use fragments in dialogue when you wish to echo speech patterns.

> The salesman said, "You will love the way this car handles in town."
> "And on the highway?" I asked.
> "Superb. Absolutely superb," he responded.

24d Edit fragments with a trouble-shooting checklist.

Use this checklist to edit your preliminary drafts.

Fragment Trouble-Shooting Checklist

1. Make sure every sentence contains a subject and verb.

   The meeting *is* being held in a convention hall adjacent to four

   large hotels with convenient access to the hall.

2. Check clauses that start with subordinate conjunctions *(when, although, so that, if, because)* to be certain that they connect with an independent clause.

   I need the college degree, Although several friends seem to

   be moving up the corporate ladder without one.

3. Check any clause that starts with a relative pronoun such as *who, whose, which,* and *that*; insert a subject.

   As a counselor, ~~who~~ *I* must express myself clearly in written

   reports and evaluations.

4. Connect fragmented appositive phrases to the words they re-name or modify.

   Concerned readers can learn about contemporary issues by

   reading regularly a few magazines, For instance, *Psychology*

   Today, Omni, and *New Republic.*

5. Check any phrase or clause that begins with a verbal (see section **22c**) such as *to feel, feeling,* or *felt.*

   Susan Goshen remained seated in the back row of the class-

   room, Feeling suddenly bashful before a group of her peers.

6. Check any clause before and after a semicolon to be sure that it is an independent clause. If it is not, change the semicolon to a comma or rewrite the sentence.

Engineers spend much of their time on the job writing; al-

though their training focused on math and physics.

7. Use fragments only for a purpose.

> UNACCEPTABLE: Running off at the mouth. The student uttered one platitude after another without rhyme or reason.

The opening fragment seems purposeless; readers will see it as an error. Attach it to the main clause.

> ACCEPTABLE: Awesome. A mean machine. A symbol of freedom, the open road, self-gratification. My new Harley-Davidson rested quietly between my legs awaiting the first burst of power and passion.

The opening fragments — adjective and noun phrases — serve a purpose by anticipating the idea of a motorcycle. The writer has assured the reader that the fragments are intentional.

EXERCISE 24.2   Correct any fragment by rewriting it as a complete sentence or by connecting it to a main clause. Mark any correct sentences with a *C*; mark any fragments that you think are acceptable with an *A*.

1. Some evening when you tire of watching *Star Trek* reruns or playing Nintendo again. Slide a how-to tape into the VCR and learn to build your own computer.
2. You can build a PC clone. Using mail order parts.
3. Even if you think "hardware" means hammer and nails. You can build a sophisticated machine with the right equipment.
4. You may not want to, however. Especially when you discover that the parts will cost over $700 and the videotape over $100.
5. You can buy a good computer for under $1,000 today. That even includes the price of a monitor.

6. As a student who has different requirements for a computer, such as word processing, calculating, statistical analysis.

7. Words. Numbers. Graphics. Games. Decide which is most important to you because some computers are better at one task than others, and software for different computers varies.

8. Whatever you decide on, beware of one problem with all computers today. Which is, they are outdated almost as soon as they leave the store. Because technology changes so fast.

9. Join a user's group for your kind of computer. Where you can discuss problems, trade software, and learn new uses for your computer.

10. You can even network with other computers and call up information data banks on your screen. Using a modem, sending and receiving data over telephone lines.

Fused Sentences and Comma Splices

Fused sentences and comma splices occur when the writer incorrectly joins two independent clauses. The **fused sentence** joins two independent clauses without any punctuation:

> FUSED SENTENCE: The actor who allows his ego full reign will become arrogant and obnoxious he will impress only himself and perhaps a few close friends.

Most writers recognize the need for some sort of punctuation after *obnoxious* to separate the first clause from the second. But a comma alone between the independent clauses is not sufficient because it creates a **comma splice**:

> COMMA SPLICE: The actor who allows the ego full reign will become arrogant and obnoxious, he will impress only himself and perhaps a few close friends.

This writer can correct these problems in two ways: (1) make each clause into a separate sentence, or (2) separate the two clauses with something stronger than a comma, such as a semicolon or a comma with coordinating conjunction.

25a Form two sentences.

Two separate sentences will identify ideas that deserve independent attention:

The actor who allows the ego full reign will become arrogant

and obnoxious; he will ultimately impress only himself.

If one sentence is quite long and contains internal punctuation, it should be independent.

European settlers had little right to take land from the native

Americans; the Indians for centuries had lived on it, depended

on it for food and shelter, and respected it.

25b Use a comma with a coordinating conjunction.

The comma and the coordinating conjunction (*and, but, or, nor, for, so, yet*) announce the related independent clause, which may be an addition, a contrast, or an option to the initial clause. This correction enables you to establish a close relationship between independent clauses. (See chapter **8**.)

A drop of water contains millions of water molecules, *and* each one

consists of two hydrogen atoms and one oxygen atom.

The conjunction *and* corrects the comma splice by signaling an additional idea. The next example corrects a comma splice with *but* to reinforce a contrast:

Cannabis is an Asiatic plant that provides hemp to the world

marketplace, *but* it also supplies a more profitable (though illegal)

product: marijuana.

(See also sections **20g** and **36a**.)

25c   Use a semicolon.

Use a semicolon between independent clauses for a stronger effect than a comma with a coordinate conjunction.

> The actor who allows the ego full reign will become arrogant and obnonxious; the actor who remains humble and somewhat embarrassed by success will win friends.

A comma with coordinating conjunction would weaken the force of the dual images created by the sentence. (See Chapter **38**.)

25d   Use a colon.

When the second clause explains or summarizes the first, fasten it to the first with the colon. (See chapter **39**.)

> Developers mass produced suburbia like a product: they standardized it, packaged it, and moved it off the shelf.

25e   Use a semicolon and a conjunctive adverb.

To show exactly how the ideas in the two clauses relate, use a semicolon with conjunctive adverb to repair the comma splice or fused sentence. Some common conjunctive adverbs are *consequently, finally, furthermore, however, moreover, nevertheless, similarly, then, therefore,* and *thus*. (See section **8a** for a list of conjunctive adverbs.)

> Foreign nations eager to buy American hardwood pay high prices for it; *however,* those high prices drive up the cost of new American houses.

(See also section **20g** and chapter **37**.)

25f   Use a subordinating conjunction to make one clause subordinate.

Sometimes two clauses joined improperly should not be a compound sentence at all. If one clause takes precedence over another, you should restructure the minor clause. Make it a subordinate clause to create a complex sentence, or reduce it to a phrase so your main idea dominates the sentence. (See chapter **9**.)

although

∧Almost everyone pays lip service to energy conservation, few

make it a part of their daily lives.

This correction creates an introductory adverb clause and emphasizes the main clause. The next example corrects a comma splice by forming an adjective clause of the less important idea. (See chapter **23**.)

, who

Jorge∧has been interested in mechanical design since childhood,

has

~~he~~ won a blue ribbon at the science fair for his engine design.

EXERCISE 25.1   Identify the fused sentences (FS) and comma splices (CS) below. Then revise the sentences by using one of the methods suggested in this chapter.

1. The history of the Cherokee Indians is fascinating not many people are aware of it.
2. They were a large tribe living in the southeastern United States, by the sixteenth century they had an advanced culture based on agriculture.
3. They were peaceful, they welcomed white settlers, they sided with the British against the French in battles for control of the colonies.
4. In the middle of the eighteenth century tragedy struck, the first blow was a smallpox epidemic that destroyed about half the tribe.
5. White settlers provoked the Cherokees into war in 1760 the badly decimated Cherokees surrendered in 1762.

6. The Cherokees recovered by 1820 they had formed a government like the whites, in 1827 the Cherokee Nation elected a Principal Chief, a Senate, and a House of Representatives.
7. But soon gold was discovered on their lands in North Carolina, whites then wanted their land, a small group of Indians made an illegal treaty agreeing to move west of the Mississippi River.
8. The Cherokee government protested, the United States Supreme Court upheld the Nation's autonomy, a judge in Georgia secured the tribe's removal nevertheless.
9. Thus in 1838 began the long trek through Georgia, Tennessee, and Kentucky, the Trail of Tears, it finally ended in the Indian Territory that is now Oklahoma.
10. The Cherokees rebounded by forming a new Nation, Tahlequah, Oklahoma, was the capital.

EXERCISE 25.2 Correct the following sentences by using the methods suggested in parentheses.

1. The Cherokees were the only Indian tribe to have a written language, it meant they could keep tribal records and publish newspapers. (Use a semicolon.)
2. The written language was developed in the 1820s by a Cherokee named Sequoyah, a silversmith and trader in Georgia, he based it on the sounds of Cherokee syllables. (Form two sentences.)
3. Sequoyah transcribed 85 syllables in the Cherokee language into symbols, he took letters from an English spelling book. (Subordinate one of the clauses.)
4. To fit the Cherokee sounds, he modified, inverted, and invented letters they do not look like English. (Subordinate one of the clauses.)
5. He visited Cherokees in Arkansas in 1822, he taught thousands of Indians to read and write. (Subordinate one of the clauses.)
6. He printed parts of the Bible in Cherokee, in 1828 he began a weekly newspaper. (Use a coordinate conjunction.)
7. Establishing a written language is a remarkable accomplishment by one man, it requires imagination, vision, and persistence. (Subordinate one of the clauses.)

8. Being able to communicate in writing helped unite the Cherokee Nation in Oklahoma, they became leaders among Indian tribes. (Semicolon with conjunctive adverb.)

9. Written tribal records now exist people can trace their Indian ancestors. (Use a comma and coordinating conjunction.)

10. The giant evergreen is named after Sequoyah, he also had a "white" name, George Guess. (Subordinate one of the clauses.)

CHAPTER

26

Subject-Verb Agreement

A verb must agree with its subject in number and person. That is, a singular subject requires a singular verb and a plural subject requires a plural verb. We must say *he plays* but not *they plays* or *Sally was exuberant* but not *six people was exuberant*.

However, errors occur when words separate the subject and verb or when compound nouns and collective nouns cause confusion. This chapter addresses those problems and suggests ways to correct them in your drafts. Also, consult chapter **34**, which examines nonstandard English usage and gives additional methods for correcting agreement errors.

26a Make the verb agree with the subject even when words and phrases separate them.

> The unruly *behavior* of the players at some games *is* being investigated by the coach.

The verb is singular in the example above because the *behavior* is under investigation, not the games.

A singular subject followed by a phrase beginning with *as well as, in addition to, with, together with,* or *including* takes a singular verb:

The last *chapter*, as well as the first three chapters, *is* mandatory reading for the final examination.

The *raccoon*, in addition to some birds and rodents, *adapts* well to urban environments.

26b Make the verb agree with the subject, not with a predicate nominative.

A predicate nominative follows a linking verb and renames the subject (see section **21d**). Make sure the verb agrees with the subject:

          subject   predicate nominative

The various *reactions* of each rat *are* my primary interest.

        subject   predicate nominative

A major *source* of funds *is* the contributions by a few generous friends of the arts.

26c Make the verb agree with a subject following the verb.

Edit carefully any clause beginning with an expletive (*there, here, it*):

There just *happen* to be several *videotapes* of the movie in the front office.

The subject *videotapes* requires a plural form of the verb, *happen*. Below, the subject *youngsters* requires the plural form, *are*.

Fast food companies should be happy that there *are* growing *youngsters* who love junk food.

Better yet, edit out the expletives for more economical, vigorous expression: *The front office has several videotapes of the movie* or *Growing youngsters who love junk food should make all fast food companies happy*.

26d   Use plural verbs for most compound subjects joined by *and*.

Lectern and *pulpit mean* basically the same thing.

However, when a compound subject forms a single idea, use a singular verb.

> The *ebb and flow* of the stock market *is* a fundamental condition of Wall Street.
> The well-known *actor and director* [one person] *teaches* an honor course every spring quarter.

Treat as singular a compound subject introduced by *every, each, no,* or *such a*.

> *Every* room, office, and building *needs* to be locked every night.
> *Such a* man and woman *is* not to be found.

But treat as plural any compound subject *followed* by *each*:

> The man and woman each *represent* different constituencies.

26e   When a compound subject is joined by *or, nor, either . . . or, neither . . . nor, not . . . but*, make the verb agree with the nearer part of the subject.

> Neither the students nor the *professor is* correct.

The verb agrees with *professor*.

> Either you three people or your *supervisor remains* liable for damages.

The verb agrees with *supervisor*.

26f Use a singular verb with most indefinite pronouns.

Pronouns such as *neither, everyone, nobody,* or *everybody* (see section **20b**) are singular even though they do not refer to a specific person or thing:

> *Neither* of your ideas *is* acceptable.
> *Somebody* among all these people *knows* the answer.
> *Each* of the ten islands *contributes* to the nation's economy.

Usage varies with *none, some, part, all,* and *half,* which are words that may be singular or plural according to the noun or pronoun that follows in a prepositional phrase.

> *None* of these model homes *are* finished.
>
> *None* of the construction *is* finished.

Use a plural verb with countable items and a singular verb with compound nouns or items considered as a whole.

> *Half* of the first-grade class *is* absent.
>
> *Half* of the first-grade students *are* ill with influenza.
>
> *Some* of the blood sample *is* still on the slide.
>
> *Some* of the samples *are* in the various microscopes.

26g *Who, that,* and *which* require verbs that agree with the antecedent.

> He portrays *heroes* who *use* brawn rather than brain.

The verb agrees with *heroes,* the plural antecedent of the relative pronoun *who.*

26h Use a singular verb with a collective noun unless a plural meaning is clearly intended.

Words such as *couple, committee, jury, class,* and *family* designate a pair or group as a single unit. Only occasionally will you treat a collective noun as plural.

> The *staff has* filed its monthly statement.
> *Staff members were* questioned in depth by the FBI agent.

In the first sentence *staff* names one element and takes a singular verb; in the second sentence the writer adds *members* to clarify the plural subject.

Use the articles *a* and *the* to signal intent. *The number* is singular, but *a number* is plural.

> *The number* of diagnostic tests *remains* six.
> *A number* of diagnostic tests *remain* on the desk.

Use a singular verb with expressions of weight, time, quantity, and extent that you consider as a unit.

> *Three miles becomes* a long run when temperatures climb to 100 degrees.

26i Use a singular verb with nouns having a plural form but singular meaning.

Words such as *economics, measles, molasses, news,* and *summons* are singular in meaning and so take a singular verb.

> The *pair was* dancing the tango.
> *Genetics is* fascinating and enlightening, especially to expectant parents.

Use a singular verb with *United States* unless you mean individual states:

> The *United States provides* foreign aid to almost every country in the free world.

A few nouns, although singular in meaning, nevertheless require plural verbs: *slacks, scissors, odds.*

> His *odds* of winning *are* 100 to 1.
> Your *trousers are* lost or stolen.

Some nouns with plural form (*headquarters, wages, pains*) can take either a singular or a plural verb. If in doubt, check your dictionary. Nouns ending in *-ics* can take singular or plural verbs.

> *Politics is* dynamic, enriching, and often a dirty business.

However, nouns ending in *-ics* that denote activities and qualities take plural verbs.

> Your *politics have* changed during the current administrative crises.

> These *statistics appear* questionable and unreliable.

26j Use singular verbs with titles of works and words used as words.

> *Letters and Panegyrics* [title of a book] *appears* in both the original words of Pliny the Younger and the translation by Betty Radice.

> *Perversions is* the word used repeatedly by the prosecuting attorney.

EXERCISE 26.1 Underline the subject in each of the following sentences and cross out the incorrect verb in parentheses.

1. The rugged border through the mountain range between the two countries (is, are) being contested.
2. The regular army, as well as armed guerilla forces, (patrols, patrol) frequently along the back roads.
3. Glimpses into the unkown mysteries of life (does, do) sometimes occur.
4. A course in psychology revealed that there (is, are) systematic methods for studying human behavior.
5. Illiterate parents cannot prepare their children to succeed in school, so the cycle of illiteracy and poverty (repeats, repeat) itself.

6. A famous poet once declared that the number of ways to look at a blackbird (is, are) thirteen.
7. Either my calculations or your information (is, are) incorrect.
8. The supplies that you must bring to the first class (includes, include) notepad, pencil, and calculator.
9. Time and tide (waits, wait) for no one.
10. Each man and woman and boy and girl (receives, receive) a small gift with a paid admission ticket.

EXERCISE 26.2   Cross out all incorrect verbs in the following sentences and write in the correct ones. Label any correct sentences with a *C*.

1. The needs of my child is my only concern.
2. None of the colonies send a representative to Parliament.
3. Inspector Maigret is one of those intellectual detectives who solves mysteries with insights, not fistfights.
4. German measles are a disease women in early pregnancy must not catch.
5. Twenty-six miles are the length of a standard marathon.
6. Napoleon's army were starved and frozen on the ill-fated march from Russia.
7. Neither of the candidates debates with the skill of a superb college debater.
8. The Southern Cross is one of those constellations that are visible only in the Southern Hemisphere.
9. It is the only one of those constellations that are recognized by almost everyone.
10. On the table lies the office keys.
11. Professor Mullins insisted that there is any number of ways to approach the problem.
12. All the soldiers of the 18th platoon merits medals for bravery.
13. Sunflower seed, wheat, milo, and millet makes the ideal wild bird feed.
14. Neither of the school's top gymnasts have scored well in competition this year.
15. The jury have found the defendent not guilty.

CHAPTER

27

Pronoun Agreement and Reference

A pronoun (see section **20b**) should agree with its antecedent in number, gender, and person. A pronoun's *antecedent* is the noun that the pronoun refers to.

Sarah Frances Thompson won *her* first swimming trophy at age nine.

The *scientists* conducted *their* research within sterilized cubicles.

Use singular pronouns with singular antecedents and plural pronouns with plural antecedents. Most writers have few problems with definite pronouns (such as *my, she, they*). However, problems develop in other areas, as discussed below.

27a Use a singular pronoun to refer to a singular antecedent.

Historically, writers have used the pronouns *he* or *his* to refer to all members of a class, as in the following examples.

TRADITIONAL: No *doctor* wants *his* patients to suffer needlessly.

If *anyone* plans to drop a class, *he* must first see *his* adviser.

However, *doctors* can be women, and *anyone* can be female, so most writers today avoid the generic *he*. In its place, unfortunately, some writers use plural nouns and pronouns to refer to singular antecedents.

> ERRONEOUS: No *doctor* wants *their* patients to suffer needlessly.
>
> If *anyone* plans to drop a class, *they* must first see *their* adviser.

Their and *they* are both plural but they refer to the singular *doctor* and *anyone*. Such mixing of singular and plural pronouns and antecedents can confuse readers and distract them from the point that the writer wishes to make. Here are several cures for the problem. (See also section **17f**.)

Make both the noun and the pronoun plural.

_{*all*} _{*s*} _{*their*}
ₐA student‸planning to drop a class must first see ~~his~~ advisers.

_{*s*} _{*their*}
A doctor must present ~~his~~ unbiased testimony to the jury.

Edit the sentence so that a pronoun is unnecessary.

The doctor presented ~~his~~ unbiased testimony to the jury.

_{*a*}
Someone parked ~~his~~ car in my private space.

Use *he or she* or *his or her* as a last resort.

If anyone plans to drop a class, *he or she* must first see *his or her* adviser.

But reframe the sentence if possible: *Students who plan to drop a class must first see an adviser.*

27b Make pronouns refer to a specific antecedent.

Writing is often vague when it contains pronouns that do not have a clear antecedent.

In Hawthorne's *The Scarlet Letter* ~~he~~ contrasts the outer strength of Hester Prynne with the inner shallowness of Arthur Dimmesdale.

Hawthorne does the acting, so make *Hawthorne* the subject.

The edited version of the next example corrects the vague pronoun reference by changing *this* to an adjective that modifies the subject *educational background*.

> The speaker has undergraduate degrees in philosophy and bi-
> *educational background*
> ology and an MA in business. *This* is one key to his success.

In the original version of the following example, the pronoun *it* could refer to either the Camaro or the van.

> The Camaro approached the red van. ~~It~~ suddenly veered to the
>
> right and crashed into a construction barrier.

Editing deletes the vague pronoun and makes clear which vehicle is the actor (subject) of the sentence.

Delete any pronoun that has no clear antecedent or function:

> In the Bible ~~it~~ says that God created the world in six days.

> In Faulkner's story "Spotted Horses," ~~it~~ demonstrates the willingness of gullible people to embrace the flim-flam artist.

> Florence Griffith-Joyner, ~~she~~ runs beautifully with powerful, long strides.

Overuse of *it* as an expletive (anticipatory subject) also makes the antecedent unclear:

> *was rainy,*
> ~~It was~~ the first day of vacation ~~when it began to rain,~~ but *it* was a
>
> fun day anyway.

Do not mix the second-person pronoun *you* with antecedents in first or third person. *You* must clearly refer to either one specific reader or everyone in the general audience. (See section **3b**.)

When I arrived at the beach, ~~you wouldn't~~ *I couldn't* believe how huge the waves were.

27c   Use a singular pronoun to refer to most indefinite pronoun antecedents.

Indefinite pronouns do not name or rename specific persons or things. Most are singular: *any, anyone, anybody, each, either, everyone, everybody, everything, neither, none, no one, someone,* and *something*.

Everything has ~~their~~ *its* reasons for existence.

Not *one* of the women believed that ~~they~~ *she* would receive an invitation.

After the fire *somebody* confessed ~~that they were guilty of~~ *to committing the* arson.

Editing the faulty sentences above eliminates the plural pronouns that cannot agree with *everything, not one* (or *no one*), and *somebody*.

Some indefinite pronouns are plural (*both, many, few*) and should be treated as such.

The defectors were found guilty; *both* forfeited *their* citizenship.

27d   Use a plural pronoun to refer to compound antecedents joined by *and*.

Johnny Womble and Professor White published *their* paper in a national psychology journal.

Only if both parts of the compound refer to the same person or a single unit should you use a singular pronoun:

The *college student and manager of a fast-food outlet* juggled *his* schedule to meet the demands of work and academics.

27e With compound antecedents joined by *or, nor, either . . . or, neither . . . nor, not only . . . but also*, use a pronoun that agrees with the nearer antecedent.

Neither the flute player nor the *violinists* had prepared *their* music.

Neither the violinists nor the *flute player* had prepared *his* music.

27f Consider collective nouns as singular unless you intentionally refer to members, not the group as a whole.

Collective nouns name a general group or class: *audience, committee, class, family, group, jury, club, organization*. When you mean a single unit, refer to it with singular pronouns.

The crowd developed ~~their~~ *its* wave cheer for the third time.

The crowd is acting as a unit, so the noun takes a singular pronoun.

The crowd shouted, "Touchdown, touchdown," and clapped ~~its~~ *their* hands.

The fans are clapping their hands individually, not as a unit, so the noun takes a plural pronoun.

27g Use the relative pronouns appropriately.

Use *who, whom,* and *whose* to refer to individual persons.

The *person who* won the state's $10 million lottery three years ago is now broke and in jail.

303

Use *that, which,* and *what* to refer to animals or things.

> Several members of the cast have the *measles, which* some call the red measles and others call rubeola.

> The *diagnosis* is *what* I expected.

In some cases *whose* can replace an awkward *in which* to refer to animals and things.

> *whose*
> We have a computer ~~in which the~~ software is installed on the hard disk.

27h   Use *self* pronouns only with clearly stated antecedents.

Reflexive and intensive pronouns — the *-self* pronouns — must refer to an antecedent.

> *Jackson* solved the problem *himself.*

EXERCISE 27.1   Rewrite the following sentences so the pronouns agree in number with their antecedents. Change verbs to agree with their subjects, if necessary. Avoid using "he or she" and "his or her" with singular indefinite pronouns. Label with a *C* any correct sentences.

1. Either the lead actor or the director does not understand their role in this production.
2. Anyone who has tried to contest their tax assessment knows how frustrating government red tape can be.
3. The Sailing Club reluctantly voted to raise their dues.
4. Every new military recruit quickly discovers that the drill sergeant will work them hard from morning to night.
5. The candidate appealed to the voters by proclaiming that the government had their hands in everyone's pocket.
6. Each applicant must list his educational background and previous work experience.
7. The registrar or the dean's office insists that they receive copies of all class lists.

8. Both candidates acted their worst during the campaign.
9. When the river subsided, no one minded that all their work erecting sandbag barriers was not needed after all.
10. The audience looked around in amazement, then rose and left its seats.
11. Someone has left their keys on the table.
12. Few people know themselves well before they are thirty.
13. Neither the football players nor their coach prepared his game plan until the last minute.
14. As the crew rowed in the distance, their oars waved like a butterfly's wings.
15. All governments agree that each international passenger must show his own passport and visa to the customs officer.

EXERCISE 27.2   Revise the following sentences to make all pronoun references clear. Some sentences may have more than one correct version. Mark with a *C* any sentences that are already correct.

1. As the hawk swooped down on the small bird, it made a sudden lunge to the left.
2. When the moderator introduced the panelists to the audience, they laughed aloud.
3. The mechanic told the sales representative that his car needed a new transmission.
4. Business leaders have told government bureaucrats that they need better educated workers.
5. To teach illiterate adults to read, you need well-trained volunteers.
6. People today need more advanced reading skills to cope with more advanced technology. This is the problem facing educators.
7. The disgruntled employees which were fired for absenteeism have taken their dispute to the grievance committee.
8. Union members belong to all kinds of professions. You might be a teacher, a newspaper reporter, a truck driver, or a police officer.
9. In this week's *Time* magazine they say that the government must examine some medical laboratories for illegal drug manufacturing.
10. Extended-wear contact lenses may harbor germs that cause infection and ultimately loss of sight. This makes some ophthalmologists hesitate to prescribe them.

EXERCISE 27.3 Like exercise 27.2, revise the following sentences to make all pronoun references clear. Mark with a *C* any sentences that are already correct.

1. Chief Justice William O. Douglas helped save many natural areas in the United States as national parks and wildlife areas. That was what he believed about the value of conservation.
2. As for the goals of Greenpeace, it wants to clean up industrial and toxic wastes.
3. As environmental groups now compete with each other for the citizen's dollar, you are not always sure which group to support.
4. It is clear that it takes money and dedication to clean up the world.
5. A barge full of garbage from Islip, New York, was towed around the Atlantic Coast and the Gulf of Mexico trying to unload its cargo. This has become a major problem for large cities in the United States.
6. Although residents do not want garbage landfills in their neighborhoods, they have to be somewhere.
7. Some sanitary districts want to build garbage incinerators, but they are still unproven.
8. Many plastics, from styrofoam fast-food containers to disposable diapers, never disintegrate, and if you burn them, they give off poisonous gas.
9. Some African countries sell land to foreign countries so they can bury their toxic wastes. They help their economy, but they may harm their citizens.
10. Recycling cans, bottles, and newspapers helps the environment, and they can earn money as well.

CHAPTER

28

Case

Pronouns and some nouns change form to show their *grammatical* relationship with other words in the sentence. Case, then, denotes the grammatical function of a word: **nominative case** (also known as subjective case) for subjects and predicate nouns, **objective case** for objects, and **possessive case** for words that show possession.

Nouns and some indefinite pronouns change form only in the possessive case. (See chapter **40**.)

possessive
noun

possessive
indefinite
pronoun

The *manager's* recommendation did not get *everyone's* vote.

Pronouns, however, change case form frequently.

nominative   possessive

I believe that approval of *my* application for

objective

financial aid will enable *me* to enter Harvard this fall.

The following table shows these various case forms. (See section **20b** for a discussion of the types of pronouns.)

Personal Pronouns

Singular	Nominative	Objective	Possessive
First person	I	me	my, mine
Second person	you	you	your, yours
Third person	he, she, it	him, her, it	his, her, hers, its
Plural			
First person	we	us	our, ours
Second person	you	you	your, yours
Third person	they	them	their, theirs

28a Use the nominative case of pronouns for subjects and predicate nominatives.

The use of *I, you, he, she, we,* and *they* is seldom a problem in simple sentences: *they need cash* or *he has the brains of the family.* However, compound word groups sometimes confuse readers because the subject may become blurred. One common mistake is to use the objective pronoun *me* in place of the nominative pronoun *I.*

My brother and ~~me~~ *I* were both guilty of negligence for not watching the stock market daily.

Brother and I is the compound subject of *were guilty*; you would not say "me was guilty."

Statements like "it's me" are often heard in speech. In writing, however, use the nominative case:

The negligent persons were my brother and ~~me~~ *I*, but it was ~~me~~ *I* who lost $52,000.

The pronoun *I* must serve as the predicate nominative; otherwise recast the sentence.

28b   Use the objective case of a pronoun used as a direct object, an indirect object, or an object of a preposition.

Our team beat *them*.   [direct object]
The water swirled around *me*.   [object of preposition]
She gave *him* the surprise of his life.   [indirect object]

Edit carefully to distinguish subjects from objects.
    Edit also for errors with compound objects, which frequently cause problems, especially after *with, among,* and *between.*

The conservative candidates defeated Ted and ~~I~~. *me*

In the sentence above, *Ted and me* is the direct object of *defeated: candidates defeated me,* not *defeated I.*

Jan is going with Mary and ~~I~~ to the theater. *me*

In this sentence *Mary and me* is the object of the preposition *with: with me,* not *with I.*

Just between you and ~~I~~, this department deserves an award. *me*

The phrase *you and me* forms a compound object of the preposition *between,* which requires the objective case.

28c   Use the objective case of a pronoun for both the subject and the object of an infinitive.

The one exception to the rule about using the subjective case for subjects is for the subject of an infinitive. The **infinitive** is the base form of a verb plus *to: to be, to dive, to exhibit* (see section **22c**).

Her mother wanted *her* to be the best dancer in the class.

NOTE: The entire infinitive phrase, *her to be the best dancer in the class,* is the direct object of *wanted.*

Our coach wanted *us to beat them.*

Here the word *us* serves as subject of the infinitive phrase. Both *us* and *them* require the objective case.

28d   Use the same case for a pronoun used as an appositive as the word it renames.

An **appositive** renames a noun or pronoun that precedes it (see section **22e**).

> The two liberal candidates, Ned Jones and ~~me~~, *I* appeared to-gether at the political forums.

The nominative case *Ned Jones and I* renames the subject *candidates*.

> The political forums gave all candidates — especially Ned Jones and ~~I~~ *me* — a chance to advance our platforms.

The objective case *me* agrees with *candidates*, the indirect object of the sentence.

NOTE: When a proper noun renames a pronoun, edit for the correct case.

> When ~~us~~ *we* Johnsons gather, pandemonium reigns.

We serves as the subject of *gather: we gather. Johnsons* is the appositive renaming *we*.

> When all of ~~we~~ *us* Johnsons gather, pandemonium reigns.

Us serves as the object of the preposition *of. Johnsons* is the appositive renaming *us*. The word *all* is the subject of *gather*.

28e After *than* or *as* in elliptical expressions, use a pronoun that agrees with the unexpressed words.

In **elliptical expressions**, constructions in which omitted words are clearly understood, mentally fill in the missing words of the clause to be sure that your choice of pronoun indicates your meaning.

We thought no one wrote as well as ~~her.~~ *she [wrote].*

The public trusted no other president as much as ~~he.~~ *[it trusted] him.*

In the first sentence, *she* must serve as the subject of the understood verb *wrote*. In the second sentence, *him* serves as the understood object of *trusted*.

You can indicate your intent with the pronoun.

He likes Barnes more than I [like Barnes].
He likes Barnes more than [he likes] me.

28f Use the possessive case with gerunds.

The **gerund** is the *-ing* form of the verb used as a noun: "*Swimming* is my favorite sport." (See section **22c**.) In general, use the possessive case of nouns and pronouns that immediately precede a gerund:

I was listening to *Bob's* snoring when the storm broke.
His snoring woke me up.

Do not use the possessive case for a word preceding a participle, which is an adjective that sometimes ends in *-ing* like a gerund: "We watched everybody rushing for the exits" *but* "Everybody's *pushing* and *shoving* caused two injuries."

EXERCISE 28.1 Correct any nouns and pronouns not used in the correct case. Mark any correct sentences with a *C*.

1. Us sailors would rather be on the water than safe in bed.

2. Last night my wife, Betty, my son, Ted, and me went on a moonlight sail.
3. The president asked Stanford Jones and I to chair the committee on writing better business memos.
4. We were proud of him winning the gold medal.
5. Just between you and I, Martin Stevick writes better memos than us.
6. Can she and him find happiness?
7. I think Jane misses the dog even more than me.
8. I object to your attorney's handling of the case.
9. The policeman saw someone's breaking and entering the jewelry store.
10. The Mayan ruins were examined by archeologists, anthropologists, and even us biochemists.

28g   Use *who (whoever)* and *whom (whomever)* correctly.

The distinction between *who* (nominative) and *whom* (objective) has begun to disappear in speech. In writing, however, you should distinguish between *who* and *whom* in all but the most informal writing.

The way you use the pronoun in its own clause determines its case. That is, use *who* and *whoever* for subjects and predicate nouns and *whom* and *whomever* for objects.

> Flannery O'Connor is a writer *who* shows the grotesque in human nature.

Who serves as subject of *shows* and uses the nominative case.

> *Whoever* is hired must be well-qualified.   [But: "I will report to *whomever* the company hires."]

Whomever is the direct object of the noun clause *the company hires whomever*; the entire clause is the object of the preposition *to*.

> The ancient mariner narrated his tale of horror to *whoever* would listen.

Here, *whoever* serves as subject of *would listen*; the entire noun clause *whoever would listen* serves as object of the preposition *to*.

Ignore intervening phrases such as *I think, we know,* and *they said* in determining the subject and verb of a clause.

> Many of the president's advisers, *who* some people say are yes men, do not give him bad news.

The nominative case *who* serves as subject of the clause *who are yes men*, not as an object. The same usage applies with questions that use *who* or *whom*.

> *Whom* do psychologists choose as subjects for their experiments?

The objective case *whom* serves as direct object of the clause *psychologists do choose whom?*

> *Who* do historians say caused the start of World War I?

The nominative case *who* serves as subject of the clause *who caused the start of World War I*.

EXERCISE 28.2 Cross out the incorrect pronoun in each of the following sentences.

1. I do not know (who, whom) should receive the invitations.
2. Send a catalog to (whoever, whomever) requested one.
3. The winner, (who, whom) had many talents, planned to use the money for college.
4. Her roommate, (who, whom) she wanted us to meet, was supposed to return soon.
5. That is the man (who, whom) had his wife murdered.
6. The committee will award medals to (whoever, whomever) finishes among the top three.
7. (Whoever, whomever) wins in the local competition will be eligible to compete in the state finals.
8. She is one of those people (who, whom) seems to succeed at everything she tries.
9. Many of the people (who, whom) feel nostalgic about the freewheeling days of the 1960s are the parents of today's college students.
10. Most physicians carry beepers so they can be reached by (whoever, whomever) needs them.

Verb Forms

29a Understand the basic verb forms.

Verbs are either regular or irregular in form, and they combine with auxiliary, or helping, verbs to show tense, voice, and mood.

Regular verbs form the past tense and the past participle with *-ed* or *-d: danced, rejoiced.* **Irregular verbs** change form in a variety of ways, most frequently by altering the internal vowels.

Infinitive	*Past*	*Past Participle*
run	ran	run
think	thought	thought
see	saw	seen
write	wrote	written

The verb *be*, the most common irregular verb, has nine forms:

Infinitive: You are to *be* the first.
Present tense singular (first person): I *am* dismayed about the news.
Present tense singular (second person): You *are* hot.
Present tense singular (third person): The project *is* doomed.
Present tense plural (all persons): Jobs *are* scarce.
Present participle: It *is being* canceled.
  These projects *are being* canceled.
Past tense singular (first or third person): It *was* a good idea.

Past tense singular (second person) or plural: The projects *were* canceled.

Past participle: The project has *been* canceled.

A list of many troublesome irregular verbs follows. It is not exhaustive, so if you have problems with irregular verbs, make a list of the verbs that trouble you and use a good dictionary.

Common Irregular Verbs

Present	*Past*	*Past Participle*
awaken	awoke *or* awakened	awakened *or* awoken
bear	bore	borne
bet	bet	bet
bite	bit	bit *or* bitten
bleed	bled	bled
blow	blew	blown
burst	burst	burst
choose	chose	chosen
deal	dealt	dealt
dive	dived *or* dove	dived
draw	drew	drawn
drink	drank	drunk
drive	drove	driven
eat	ate	eaten
feel	felt	felt
fly	flew	flown
forbid	forbade	forbidden
forgive	forgave	forgiven
forsake	forsook	forsaken
get	got	got *or* gotten
go	went	gone
grow	grew	grown
hang	hanged *or* hung	hanged *or* hung
keep	kept	kept
know	knew	known
lead	led	led
light	lighted *or* lit	lighted *or* lit
mean	meant	meant
prove	proved	proved *or* proven

Common Irregular Verbs

Present	Past	Past Participle
ride	rode	ridden
ring	rang	rung
rise	rose	risen
see	saw	seen
set	set	set
shake	shook	shaken
show	showed	showed *or* shown
sing	sang	sung
sink	sank	sunk
sleep	slept	slept
speak	spoke	spoken
spring	sprang *or* sprung	sprung
steal	stole	stolen
stink	stank *or* stunk	stunk
strike	struck	struck
swear	swore	sworn
swim	swam	swum
take	took	taken
teach	taught	taught
tear	tore	torn
think	thought	thought
throw	threw	thrown
understand	understood	understood
write	wrote	written

EXERCISE 29.1   Label as regular (*R*) or irregular (*I*) the verb forms in each of the following sentences.

1. The three soldiers *saluted* the flag.
2. I *pledge* allegiance to the flag.
3. The flag *flew* at half staff.
4. The special ceremonies *ended*.
5. The flag *danced* and *twisted* with the wind.
6. Most children like to *fly* the stars and stripes.
7. I *am* proud to display the flag on my front porch.
8. Several July 4 ceremonies are being *planned*.
9. One local business *promised* to purchase flags for every home in town.
10. The school children *stood* to salute the flag.

29b Understand the function of auxiliary verbs.

Auxiliary verbs join with regular and irregular verbs to indicate tense (chapter **30**), voice (chapter **31**), and mood (chapter **32**). Some common auxiliary verbs are below:

be, am, is, are, was, were, been
do, does, did
have, has, had
will, shall, would, should
can, could
may, must, might, ought to

I *did* finish the homework. [past tense]
The horse *is* stabled at the farm. [passive voice]
If he *were* faster, he *would* have won the race. [subjunctive mood]

EXERCISE 29.2 Circle and correct any misused verb forms in the following sentences. Mark any correct sentences with a *C*.

1. Midnight had just began to chime when a messenger bursted in.
2. "I've brung the pardon," he said breathlessly as he flung it on the warden's desk.
3. The prisoner was awoke by the guards.
4. As he arose, he was told that he would not be hung.
5. The prisoner thought back to the night he had been accused of murdering Coach Browning.
6. Browning encouraged his basketball team to foul, so the referee throwed the coach out of the game.
7. "I won't taken this," said Browning, "I'll see that you're fired, that you'll never set foot on a basketball court again."
8. Everyone hated the coach who drove his teams to win at all costs.
9. They never dreamt the referee would kill the coach.
10. Someone wrote to the governor, saving the referee's life.

EXERCISE 29.3 Identify any incorrect verb forms in the sentences below and supply the correct form. Mark any correct sentences with a *C*.

1. Chain letters be illegal, but many people send them anyway.
2. If you receive a chain letter, you are suppose to report it to the post office, but most people does not.

3. People who send chain letters say they sell something, but what they is selling is usually worthless.
4. To encourage you to mail money, the authors of chain letters imply that your earnings will have to be truck in.
5. If you are ask to join a chain letter, remember that most chains is broken.
6. Jack been spending all his time lately on the telephone.
7. He need to find a new job, because the company he work for has gone out of business.
8. The bosses was importing brass goods from overseas, but the quality was so poor no one buyed any.
9. It costed too much to return the goods, and the company had already spended all its money buying them.
10. The owner of the company end up with a garage full of thin, bended brass trays, candlesticks, and house numbers.

29c Do not confuse *sit* and *set, lie* and *lay, rise* and *raise.*

Sit, to occupy a seat, and *set*, to put or place something, are two different verbs.

Present	Present participle	Past	Past participle
sit	sitting	sat	sat
set	setting	set	set

Sit does not take an object, but it does change form:

Sit in that chair.
How long have you *sat* in the chair?

Set normally takes an object but does not change form.

Please *set* the chair in the corner.
We *set* two chairs there this morning.   [But: "The sun should *set* in about an hour." (no object)]

Lie, to recline, and *lay*, to put or place something, are also two different verbs.

	Present		*Past*
Present	*participle*	*Past*	*participle*
lie	lying	lay	lain
lay	laying	laid	laid

Lie does not take an object; *lay* does. Both sentences below require a form of *lie*, to recline.

> After working the sheep, the dogs *lay* down to rest.
> The dogs have been *lying* in the sun all afternoon.

The next two sentences require a form of *lay*, to put or place.

> The construction worker *laid* the dynamite carefully.
> The foreman had *laid* several dynamite caps on the hood of his truck.

Similarly, *rise*, to get up, and *raise*, to lift something, are two different verbs, although they cause fewer problems than *lie* and *lay*.

	Present		*Past*
Present	*participle*	*Past*	*participle*
rise	rising	rose	risen
raise	raising	raised	raised

Rise does not take an object; *raise* does.

> When the dough *rises*, put it in the oven.
> His party *raised* the roof, so the next day he *rose* before the group to apologize.

EXERCISE 29.4 Identify the correct verb in each of the following sentences.

1. After Sue (laid/lay) her books on the table, she decided to (lay/lie) down for a short nap.
2. After she had (laid/lain) in bed for an hour, she heard a noise and got up.
3. The sun had already (sat/set), but we (sat/set) outside for another hour.
4. After the bread has (raised/risen), (set/sit) it in the oven.
5. The balloon (raised/rose) over our heads and (laid/lay) against the clouds.

30

Verb Tense

Verbs change form to indicate the time of the action or a condition.

This paper *needs* more work.
This paper *needed* more work.

Such sentences in present tense and past tense cause few problems. Editing for tense and tense sequence, however, requires more than a knowledge of simple present and simple past.

Having announced
~~Announcing~~ his candidacy to the press at 2:00 p.m., Jesse Jackson walked to the podium at 6:00 p.m. to present a major address to the convention.

Careful editing can correct this type of error; because the *announcement* occurs well before the speech, it therefore requires the present perfect tense (see below).

30a   Know the basic verb tenses.

Simple tenses show one action in a finite time frame.

Present tense: what happens or can happen now

I *work* hard for a living. Jon *works* at the bank.

Past tense: what did happen at one time in the past

I *worked* until five o'clock.

Future tense: what will happen at a particular time in the future

I *will work* on my report until it is finished.

Perfect tenses denote an event that has already taken place. The present perfect tense uses the auxiliary verb *have* with the past participle; past perfect tense uses *had* with the past participle.

Present perfect: an action completed or continued in the present time

I *have worked* on my report for a week.

Past perfect: a past action completed before another past action

I *had worked* many months before I realized that the job stifled my creativity.

Future perfect: an action that will be completed in the future before a specific time in the future

I *will have worked* on this report for a month when I finally submit it.

Progressive tenses enable you to show a continuous action.

Present progressive: a continuous action occurring now

I *am working* frantically to finish my report.

Past progressive: a continuous action occurring at the time of another past action

I *was working* late at the office when I heard a scream.

Future progressive: a continuous action that will occur during another future action

I *will be working* while you are on vacation.

EXERCISE 30.1   Identify the tense forms in the sentences below.

1. Most automobiles *will be using* synthetic fuels or electricity in the not-distant future.
2. Gasoline *ranks* first as the chief product of petroleum.
3. Oil companies *have developed* stockpiles of oil to meet emergencies.
4. Some companies *are working* to improve synthetic fuels.

5. Petroleum *will be* scarce in the next century.
6. No one really *knows* exactly how petroleum develops.
7. The formation of oil *is going* on continuously even today.
8. The United States *had been* the world's largest producer of oil before the Middle East created its cartel.
9. Even after most oil supplies *have disappeared*, America's love affair with the automobile will continue.
10. Over the next few years, Americans *will be seeing* remarkable changes in transportation.

30b Keep tenses consistent.

> Lincoln *scribbled* the Gettysburg Address on the back of an envelope, but he *deliver~~s~~* ^ed it so movingly that it immediately ~~becomes~~ ^became famous.

In this case, the writer must edit the verbs to keep the past tense consistent. In the next example, editing maintains the consistency of present tense.

> As the inventory *decreases* during the Christmas buying season, retailers ~~were cutting~~ ^cut prices even deeper.

30c Edit for special uses of the present tense.

Of course, use the present tense for current actions and present conditions.

> This committee *accepts* your explanation. [present time]
> The group always *meets* at 12:00 every Tuesday. [habitual action]

But also use the present tense, not past tense, for universal truths and scientific principles, unless they are disproved. This form is known as the *historical* present tense.

On his historical journey Neil Armstrong saw in person that the moon *has* an earthrise.

Nobody is on the moon to see it now, but the earthrise continues to occur. The historical present tense can also substitute for past tense if you establish an exact date.

In 1944 Harry Truman reluctantly *decides* to drop the atomic bomb on mainland Japan, an action that *ends* the war but *initiates* the nuclear age.

The historical present tense is known also as the "literary present tense" when referring to works by a writer or artist, even one who is dead.

In his novel *Catch-22*, Joseph Heller *satirizes* the insanity of bureaucratic regulations.

The novel continues to satirize for today's readers, just as a painting continues to display meaning:

Picasso's *Guernica* displays the terror of peasants during the Spanish Civil War.

30d   Use the past tense appropriately.

Use the past tense to show simple past action or to relate information about the past:

Kafka *wrote* every night after he returned from work.

Use past tense for ideas now disproved.

Ptolemy believed that the sun *revolved* around the earth.

Compare this use of the past tense with the use of historical present tense in section **30c**.

Use the past tense for personal narratives, since the events have already occurred.

Judy and I *stop*~*ped*~ at a convenience store for supplies and *drive*~*o*~

toward the mountains for some hiking fun.

30e Use the perfect tenses appropriately.

Sentences sometimes need a perfect tense, which enables you to say that something happens before a certain time. In the sentence below, the present-perfect tense *have worked* shows that certain actions (the three jobs) preceded another (going to school).

> I *have worked* as a secretary, grocery checker, and waitress, but now I go to school full time.

The next example demonstrates the use of the past-perfect tense, which shows that one action (*used as a speakeasy*) preceded another past action (*opened a . . . restaurant*).

> The couple opened a family-style restaurant in an old building that *had been used* as a speakeasy in the roaring 20s.

30f Use verbals in the correct tense.

Verbals (see section **22c**), like verbs, can show tense. Use the infinitive form (*to show, to dance*) for an action occurring at the same time as or later than the main verb, no matter what the tense of the main verb.

> Judy Knight expected *to win* a scholarship.
>
> Jim Baker plans *to major* in engineering when he enrolls at Georgia Tech.

In these sentences, *to win* and *to major* both happen at the same time or immediately after the "expecting and the planning," so the present tense infinitive is appropriate.

Use the perfect participle for an action that precedes another.

> *Having joined* separate sororities, the sisters became fierce competitors for grades, social honors, and men.

EXERCISE 30.2 Edit the following sentences to correct errors in tense and tense sequence.

1. Since the beginning of recorded time, human beings *were* always *intrigued* by the heavens, often translating their lack of knowledge into superstitious beliefs and myths.

2. Although human beings have learned how to fly, the real beginning of space technology *had been* Germany's war-time development of long-range rocket launchers, which *were preparing* the way for launching satellites into the earth's atmosphere.

3. After the end of World War II, U.S. and Soviet scientists *would have liked to have found ways to have explored* conditions beyond the earth's atmosphere, especially the nature and intensity of solar radiation.

4. The actual history of space exploration is only about thirty years old, if we *are counting* from the launching of the first artificial earth satellite in 1957, the USSR's *Sputnik I*.

5. In 1957, *Sputnik II was carrying* a dog into orbit over 1000 miles above the earth.

6. The first man *to have orbited* the earth was the Soviet cosmonaut Yuri Gagarin, who *had spent* 90 minutes circling the earth in 1961.

7. In 1969 men *had landed* on the moon, taking the first step toward eventually establishing bases there.

8. Moon exploration *has faded* into the background by the late 1970s when space shuttles *have been found to represent* a more realistic program of scientific research and living in space.

9. Space shuttle launches *had been considered* almost commonplace when the shuttle *Challenger* exploded, killing all seven astronauts aboard, causing many people *to have called* for the end of the risky space program.

10. Even though the thrill and exhilaration of space exploration *has now been tempered* with caution, people *will be continuing to be risking* the dangers of space travel.

CHAPTER
31

Voice

Verbs that can take a direct object have two voices: active and passive (see section **20c**). In the **active voice** the subject *performs* the action; in the **passive voice** the subject *receives* the action. The active voice is more concise, vigorous, and emphatic than the passive voice.

> PASSIVE: *Safety is promoted by producers* of nuclear energy to alleviate public fears of a disaster.

> ACTIVE: *Producers* of nuclear energy *promote safety* to alleviate public fears of a disaster.

31a Use the active voice to emphasize the subject.

To rewrite sentences that have ineffective, passive verbs, find the most important actor and make it the subject.

> PASSIVE: *Political figures*, from the president to members of the local sewer district, *are pounced* on by newspaper columnists for the slightest mistake.

> ACTIVE: *Newspaper columnists pounce* on political figures, from the president to members of the local sewer district, for the slightest mistake.

The *columnists* are the actors and should appear as the subject.

> PASSIVE: *West Virginia is ranked* second only to Kentucky in coal production.

> ACTIVE: *West Virginia ranks* second only to Kentucky in coal production.

The passive voice above serves no purpose; the active voice makes the point more clearly and more emphatically.

> PASSIVE: The *rules* of campaign disclosures *have been ignored* by several council members.

> ACTIVE: Several *council members have ignored* the rules of campaign disclosures.

The active voice makes clear to the readers that the council members are the subject.

31b Use the passive voice only to emphasize the receiver and occasionally to add sentence variety.

> The missing film *was returned* to the lab by mail.   [The writer focuses on the film, not on the person who returned it.]

> Our new telephone system *will be installed* tomorrow.   [The passive voice emphasizes the telephone system, not who will install it, and avoids a wordy sentence: *Telephone company personnel will install the new telephone system tomorrow.*]

> All the files *were destroyed* in the fire.   [Active voice (*The fire destroyed all the files*) would shift the writer's focus from the files to the fire.]

Academic writing often uses the passive voice because the research, not the writer, is the focus of the paper.

> The data were collected from Class A, the primary control group.

EXERCISE 31.1 Edit the following sentences to the active voice. Write *C* by any sentence that uses the passive voice appropriately to emphasize the receiver.

1. One of the campaign promises made by Franklin D. Roosevelt in 1932 was that hydroelectric dams would be built on the Columbia River.

2. At the time, private power companies were controlled by large eastern holding companies.

3. Extremely high electrical rates for towns were charged by them, and farms were refused electricity altogether.

4. Roosevelt's promise was kept, and Bonneville and Grand Coulee dams were built, resulting in inexpensive power being brought to the surrounding valleys.

5. Even the social structure was changed by completion of the dams because news of the world was brought to people by radios, and homemakers were freed from time-consuming chores by electric appliances.

6. In 1941, folksinger Woody Guthrie was hired to write songs about the Northwest's hydroelectric power system.

7. Twenty-six songs were written and recorded in thirty days by Guthrie, including "Roll On, Columbia" and "Pastures of Plenty," but other songs were not released by the power administration.

8. Today, over 120 million kilowatt hours of electricity per year are generated by the system's fifty-five dams.

9. Over 200 million barrels of oil would be needed to generate the same number of kilowatt hours.

10. Not only is power provided by the dams, so that economic growth is encouraged by industrial development, but recreation and irrigation are also provided by the reservoirs.

CHAPTER
32

Mood

Verbs have three moods: indicative, imperative, and subjunctive. Use the **indicative mood** for most sentences to assert facts and ask questions.

> *Do* classes *begin* on Monday or Tuesday?
> I *have* a dentist appointment Monday morning.

Use the **imperative mood** to make entreaties or issue commands.

> *Be* on time for the classes that begin on Tuesday.

Use the **subjunctive mood** to make a wish or make statements contrary to fact.

> I wish I *were* still in bed.

> The college stipulates that each student *attend* every class session, including the first one.

The subjunctive mood uses only *were* (the plural past tense form of *be*) or the infinitive form of the verb (in this case, the verb *attend*). Use subjunctive mood in certain subordinate clauses beginning with *if* (see **32a**) and a few that begin with *that* (see **32b**).

32a   Use the subjunctive mood in *if* clauses that express conditions contrary to fact.

were
If Jack ~~was~~ captain of the team, he would rotate the forwards.
∧

Our chance to win the debate would be improved if Meredith
were
~~was~~ better prepared.
∧

The clauses express conditions contrary to fact: Jack is not the captain and Meredith is not well prepared. *Were* is the only past-tense form of *be* in subjunctive voice.

Do not substitute *would have* for *had* in subjunctive *if* clauses; the word *if* expresses the contrast.

had
If the concrete ~~would have~~ been reinforced, the building would not have collapsed.
∧

EXCEPTIONS: You must distinguish between *if* clauses that express ideas contrary to fact, like the above sentences, and *if* clauses that represent alternatives or possibilities:

s
If it *rain* tomorrow, the marshall will probably cancel the parade
∧
again.   [It could rain.]

32b   Use the subjunctive mood in *that* clauses following words such as *ask, request, desire, insist, recommend, wish.*

We insist that George ~~goes~~ to the concert with us.

be
I move that the meeting ~~is~~ adjourned.
∧

I desire that José *signs* the contract.

Professor Higgins asked that everyone *submits* the report on time.

The corrections above show that subjunctive mood requires the infinitive form of the verbs: *go, be, sign, submit.*

EXERCISE 32.1   Edit the following sentences for correct use of the subjunctive mood. If a sentence is correct, mark it with a *C*.

1. I wish that I *were* rich.
2. If John *was* alive, he would help us now.
3. The general's orders were that the troops *are* camped in the woods, not by the river.
4. She requested that the carpet *be* relaid because the seams were not straight.
5. If you *would have* complained, they would have turned down their stereo.
6. Ms. Hatchett insisted that everyone *is* at work tomorrow or else!
7. The rule requires that each employee *reports* all overtime.
8. Some psychologists think that all people *are* addicted to something, if not drugs or cigarettes, then work, chocolate, or certain kinds of relationships.
9. Even if she *do* only the minimum amount of work, Janis will pass biology.
10. John likes surfing so much, he wishes it *was* summer all year long.

Adjectives modify nouns and pronouns (see section **20d**). Adverbs — which tell how, when, where, why, or to what degree and affirm or deny — modify other adverbs, adjectives, verbs, and whole clauses (see section **20e**). Adjectives and adverbs can take the form of words, phrases (see chapter **22**), or clauses (see chapter **23**).

> The *weary* technician announced the test results.   [adjective modifying the noun *technician*]

> The technician *wearily* announced the test results.   [adverb modifying the verb *announced*]

> *When the game ended*, the players *on the losing team* started a fight. [adverb clause modifying the main clause *the players . . . a fight* and adjective phrase modifying *players*]

33a Understand the differences between adjectives and adverbs.

Everyday speech does not always maintain the differences between adjectives and adverbs, but in your writing, make sure to distinguish between such words as *sure* and *surely*, *real* and *really*, *easy* and *easily*, and *certain* and *certainly*. The key is to identify the function of the word that the adjective or adverb modifies. (Remember that the *-ly* ending can function on adjectives as well as on adverbs: "the *cowardly* man"; "the man behaved *cowardly*.")

> *Surely* and *easily* the burros walk down the trails in the Grand Canyon.   [adverbs modifying the verb *walk*]

> The footsteps of the burros are *sure* and *easy*.   [adjectives modifying the noun *footsteps*]

The adjectives *good, bad,* and *well* and the adverbs *well* and *badly* have confused many writers. In general, use the adjectives after linking verbs (see section **33c**) to modify the subject:

> They felt *good* about what they had done.   [meaning *happy* or *positive*]

> The dog was pleased that she smelled *bad*.   [meaning *unpleasant*]

> He appeared *well* after the long recovery.   [meaning *healthy*]

Use the adverbs, which tell *how*, to modify action verbs:

> She played *well* in the tournament.   [meaning *successfully*]

> He wants that scholarship *badly*.   [meaning *intensely*]

Some other words that can function as both adjectives and adverbs are *hard, little, slow, straight, early, fast, thus.*

> Professor Lesley gives *hard* exams.   [adjective]

> It rained *hard* all weekend.   [adverb]

Some adverbs have two forms, such as *slow* and *slowly, hard* and *hardly.*

> The city hall's clock runs *slow*.

> The clouds moved *slowly* across the sky.

In a sentence such as *Keep your money safe*, you must decide whether to modify the verb *keep* with the adverb *safely* or modify the direct object *money* with the word *safe*.

Do you consider this person *faithful*?   [adjective]

Do you attend this church *faithfully*?   [adverb]

EXERCISE 33.1   Label the adjectives and adverbs in the following sentences.

1. Two blimps *noisily* circled the golf course.
2. *Two different* crews were televising the game.
3. *One* golfer *angrily* shook his fist at the *noisy* blimp.
4. It is *good* that golfers play so *well* under the circumstances.
5. One golfer looked *coldly* at a *boisterous* spectator.

33b Use adverbs to modify verbs, adjectives, and other adverbs.

The bolt *easily* slid into place.   [adverb modifying verb]

Members of the class were *terribly* sorry that the fire had destroyed all of the experiments.   [adverb modifying adjective]

The committee considered your proposal *very* seriously.   [adverb modifying adverb]

Avoid **double negatives** that often occur with negative adverbs such as *not, never, hardly,* and *scarcely* (see section **34f**).

FAULTY: We could *not* scarcely identify the artist's signature.

BETTER: We could scarcely identify the artist's signature.

33c Use an adjective as a subject complement.

Adjectives that help the verb describe or modify the noun are called predicate adjectives or **subject complements** (see section **21d**). Subject complements usually take linking verbs (see section

20c), the most common of which are *be, appear, taste, look, seem, become, smell,* and *sound.*

The body felt *cold.*

He is *angry.*

33d   Use an adjective as an object complement.

An adjective that functions as an **object complement** modifies a direct object and often immediately follows it (see section **21c**).

The dean thought the program *foolish.*

The adjective *foolish* describes the program, the direct object.

33e   Use comparative and superlative forms of adjectives and adverbs appropriately.

Adjectives and adverbs have three forms: the positive form, the comparative, and the superlative. Use the **positive** form to describe one item (*a soft pillow*), the **comparative** form to compare two items (*yours is* softer *than mine*), and the **superlative** form to distinguish one item from two or more other items (*Tammy's is the* softest *of all*).

Most one- and two-syllable **adjectives**—often those ending in a vowel sound—add *-er* for the comparative and *-est* for the superlative: *happier, happiest; nicer, nicest.* Check your dictionary if you are unsure about the correct spelling.

> This exam is *easier* than the last one.   [comparative]
> This exam is the *easiest* of all we have taken this year. [superlative]

Longer adjectives require *more* and *most* or *less* and *least: most delightful, least fulfilling.*

> The lab technician is *more helpful* (or *less helpful*) than the lab assistant.   [comparative]
> The lab supervisor is the *most helpful* (or *least helpful*) person in the lab.   [superlative]

Most **adverbs** of one syllable require the *-er* and *-est* endings (*hard, harder, hardest*), but adverbs of two syllables, including those ending in *-ly*, require *more* and *most* or *less* and *least* (*sensibly, more sensibly, most sensibly*).

A few adjectives and adverbs have irregular forms: *good, better, best; well, better, best; little, less, least; bad, worse, worst; badly, worse, worst.*

> This month's test results are *good*.   [positive]
> This month's test results are *better* than last month's. [comparative]
> This month's test results are the *best* of the last three months' scores.   [superlative]

The table below gives examples of the regular and irregular forms.

Positive	Comparative	Superlative
sweet	sweeter	sweetest
fast	faster	fastest
good	better	best
bad	worse	worst
little	less	least
beautiful	more beautiful	most beautiful
quickly	more quickly	most quickly

Use comparatives and superlatives carefully; it is often easy to use mistakenly the superlative form for only two items or the comparative form for three or more items.

> Taste tests between aspartame and saccharine show that aspartame is the *sweetest*. ~~er~~

The sentence compares only two sweeteners.

> Although Honda and Suzuki motorcycles have captured a large share of the market, Harley Davidson remains the ~~more~~ *most* popular.

The sentence identifies one of three motorcycles.

Do not use **double comparatives** or **double superlatives**, which usually combine *-er* or *-est* with *more* or *most*: *more deeper, most deadliest, more funnier*. Use one form or the other (*most deadly* or *deadliest*), not both.

Lake Titicaca is the ~~most~~ highest navigable lake in the world.

Absolute modifiers cannot have comparatives or superlatives. *Unique, perfect, dead, square, circular,* and *singular* describe absolute concepts: something is either unique (which means *the only one*) or it is not. If it is not dead, it is alive. Although you will hear phrases like *most unique*, a phrase such as *most unusual* or *most special* is more precise.

John's dive is *more* ~~perfect~~ *precise* than Anne's.
                            ∧

EXERCISE 33.2   Edit the following sentences to correct any misused adjectives and adverbs. Mark correct sentences with a *C*.

1. Spying and espionage have become most sophisticated than in the past.
2. For example, satellites and airplanes can take accurately and sharply pictures of areas as small as one meter.
3. Governments watch more worriedly any private companies that launch their own satellites.
4. Governments cannot scarcely control who buys satellite photographs.
5. It is difficult to say which is most advanced, satellite spying or electronic espionage devices.
6. The United States razed some of its new built embassy in Moscow because the Soviets had planted miniature microphones deeply in the walls and even in the windows.
7. Yet despite the most perfect new gadgets, the foibles of human beings still play a large role in spying.
8. Trading sex for secrets is easy one of the most oldest spy practices.
9. Money — usually from selling photocopied documents to the higher bidder, whether Russian, Chinese, or Iranian — ranks as another motivation.
10. Spies will sure exist as long as nations keep secret information.

CHAPTER

34

Editing to Correct Nonstandard English

A **dialect** is a regional variety of a language, usually transmitted orally and differing in distinct ways from the standard language. Members of an occupational group, a family, and an entire social class may develop distinctive pronunciation, sentence structures, and vocabulary. In truth, everybody speaks a dialect.

At times, however, some writers have difficulty understanding the differences between dialect and standard English. (See chapter **16** for a discussion of formal and informal levels of English.) If your written prose is heavily influenced by a dialect or if English is your second language, this chapter provides techniques for solving specific problems.

34a Include all necessary verbs.

Standard written English requires a complete verb in each clause. (See section **20c**.) Most speakers of all dialects include action verbs instinctively, but they may omit a linking verb (such as *am, is, are* and other forms of *be*) because the meaning seems clear from the context.

Sanford *is* an excellent cook who gives demonstrations at the mall.

You cannot pass Dr. Flint's math course unless you *are* a genius.

You can form contractions with subjects and linking verbs (*Sanford's an excellent cook* or *you're* a genius), but you cannot omit the verb entirely.

The biology teacher ˄*has [or 's]* been focusing on the scientific content.

Also make sure to include helping verbs such as *has, have, can, will, should*, and *might*, where appropriate.

Do you know someone who ˄*would* benefit from such a course?

Add helping verbs (*is, have, does*) when they are required. Native French speakers use the present form of verbs (*il joue*) to mean several things (*he plays, he does play, he is playing*) and so are not familiar with using the helping verbs.

The soldier ˄*is* shooting into the crowd.

EXERCISE 34.1 Edit the following sentences to supply missing linking verbs and helping verbs.

1. When Dudley's career on the rise, he ignored his friends.
2. Instructors cannot tell whether he crazy or extremely intelligent.
3. Dudley be good at programming computers.
4. Did you know that he been given his own key to the computer lab?
5. With a little luck, he be named monitor of the lab.
6. Pisces a constellation and sign of the zodiac.
7. The grouping of stars located southeast of the great square of Pegasus.
8. The constellation named by early Romans.
9. It dominates the lives of those persons who born in March.
10. To see the constellation it help if you have a telescope because its stars do not shine brightly.

34b Add *-s* to form plurals of most nouns.

Although some dialects and languages suggest plural meaning only through such words as *three, four, all*, and *most*, in standard written English you must use the plural form of a noun as well. For example, Spanish and French both have singular collective nouns, but English does not.

> *s are*
> *Drug is* one of the major reasons why there is so much crime today.

> *es*
> He gave the children some *watch*.

> *s*
> All three *artist* are represented in the show.

Most nouns, as shown above, add *-s* or *-es* to form the plural. However, do not add *-s* to irregularly formed plural nouns such as *men*, *women*, *children*, and *mice*:

> All the *womens* gathered in a small group.

See **47f** for other plural forms.

EXERCISE 34.2   Add the appropriate word endings to the plural nouns.

1. Most book cost too much, such as this one about the history of Philadelphia.
2. Almost all first-time visitor are curious about the city's history.
3. Two famous politician, William Penn and Ben Franklin, helped build the city's reputation.
4. The newspaper said about 100 person per square mile live in this city.
5. Philadelphia covers 144-square mile, including 9 square mile of inland water.
6. Philadelphia has one of the largest city hall in the nation.
7. Three block west of City Hall are the city government buildings.
8. Every year visitors in the million visit Independence Hall and the Liberty Bell.

34c   Use *-s* or *-es* endings for verbs in the present tense that have a third-person singular subject.

> *s*   *s*
> Anne *play* the flute. She *practice* two hours every day.

Drug addiction affects the one who *use* the drugs and also the user's family and friends.

Spanish, in contrast, uses the *-s* ending with second person *tu*, not with third person.

Omit the *-s* or *-es* on all other singular and plural forms (*I play, you play, we play, they play*). (See chapters **26, 30**.)

I *plays* the violin, you *plays* the saxophone, and Anne *play* the

flute. Together, we *makes* a good combo.

REMEMBER: Do not add *-s* or *-es* to verbs used with plural nouns and pronouns.

Newspapers must *competes* with television and radio for customers and advertisers.

EXERCISE 34.3 Correct the verb endings in these sentences.

1. Poland cover an area about the same as the state of New Mexico.
2. Poland possess a long and interesting history.
3. The nation currently struggle to strengthen its economy after winning control from the Communist party.
4. The people speaks Polish as the standard language.
5. A legislature called the *Sejm* perform major legislative tasks.
6. The Solidarity party hold control of the *Sejm*.

34d   Use *'s* to form most possessives.

In editing for standard English, show the possessive by *'s* or other correct possessive form, not by noun position only:

Lance's transmission broke down just after the car warranty expired.

Some dialects allow speakers to drop both the apostrophe and the *s*, so edit carefully any words that show possession: *neighbor's car, cheerleaders' pompoms, the principal's office*. See also chapter **40**.

EXERCISE 34.4   Add the *'s* to mark possessive nouns in these sentences.

1. A radio station call letters sometimes stood for words, such as WGN, which meant "world greatest newspaper."
2. The archeologist story of opening the sealed tomb became a best-seller.
3. The children performance made the audience smile.
4. A writer journal may be her most valuable possession.
5. My friend stereo is on those shelves.

34e   Use personal and demonstrative pronouns carefully.

Some dialects use the personal pronoun as an appositive to emphasize or intensify the meaning of the noun (see also chapter **27**). Standard written English, however, deletes the pronoun when it immediately follows its antecedent.

> Florence Griffith-Joyner, ~~she~~ runs beautifully with long, powerful strides.

Spanish uses the nominative case after a preposition, but English uses the objective case:

We have seen many of ~~they~~ *m* take drugs for fun.

Demonstrative pronouns (*this, that, these, those*) identify nouns. Although some dialects use *them* to show "which ones," it is not a demonstrative pronoun. Therefore, use *those*, not *them*, as a demonstrative pronoun.

Those
~~Them~~ boxes will hold all our equipment.

EXERCISE 34.5   Correct the improper use of pronouns in the following sentences.

1. The supervisor instructed the crew to work overtime to install all them new stamping machines.
2. We uncovered them precious stones yesterday.
3. Now many bookstore chains, they buy books at discount prices so they can sell for less.

4. Some animals and birds, such as sparrows, deer, and Canada geese, they have adapted to human beings so well they have become pests.
5. Them books and them small statues go on the bookshelf.
6. If we pass them two tests, the rest of they will be easy.

34f Avoid double negatives.

Do not mix *no, not, never* with other negative words such as *not, never, hardly, scarcely,* and so on. Do not be influenced by Spanish, which *does* use double negatives.

We never had ~~no~~ problems with the experiment. *[any inserted above]*

We had hardly ~~never~~ seen such biology assignments.

They ~~didn't have~~ no way of telling the difference between the real and the counterfeit artifacts. *[had inserted above]*

EXERCISE 34.6 Correct any double negatives that you find in the following sentences.

1. The teamsters do not no longer have a powerful lobby in Washington.
2. Political action committees (PACs) can not give no higher donations to politicians than an individual can give.
3. The politician should not think the PAC doesn't want nothing in return for the donation.
4. Special interest groups never have no problem getting the attention of some senator or representative.
5. Members of Congress can't hardly avoid lobbyists of special interest groups.

34g Use the articles *a, an,* and *the* correctly.

Some dialects do not use the article *an*. Instead, they use the article *a* before all singular nouns, regardless of the sound that follows. Standard English uses *an* before all vowel sounds, even those words that begin with a silent consonant (*an hour*).

In some Florida neighborhoods residents are not surprised to

see *a*_∧alligator in the backyard. n

However, do not use the definite article *the* to specify a particular person, place, or thing. French speakers, accustomed to *le* and *la* (*le café*), may be tempted to add *the* unnecessarily:

> I prefer ~~the~~ coffee.
>
> In ~~the~~ Egypt our tour group spent four hours touring *a* Sphinx and the tombs.   *the*

There are many pyramids but only one Sphinx. Reserve the indefinite articles *a* and *an* for subjects being mentioned for the first time or a noun whose specific identity is unknown.

> *An* automobile, any kind, will serve always as a birthday gift, but
> ~~a~~ Thunderbird on Jenkin's used car lot is the one I want.   *the*

Omit articles before such proper nouns as names of persons, streets, cities, states, continents, countries, lakes, and mountains.

> We will vacation next year at ~~the~~ Lake Geneva.

Do use articles before buildings, departments, companies, and so forth.

> We vacationed last year at *the* Sands in Las Vegas.

Omit articles before mass nouns that refer to things in general or to abstractions (*hay, freedom, light*).

> Grandfather always raises ~~the~~ corn in the river valley and ~~the~~ hay in the west meadow.
>
> BUT
>
> We stored *the* burley tobacco on racks in the barn.

Most farmers raise corn or hay (things in general), but one crop of tobacco can be identified or limited by an article.

Omit articles before nouns that have been clearly identified by possessives or by pronouns such as *my, any, every, several* and so forth.

EXERCISE 34.7 Provide the correct articles *a, an,* and *the* to the following sentences.

1. Phoenix is fabled bird that Greeks made famous in their mythology.
2. It was the size of a eagle and represented sun.
3. According to myth, phoenix lived exactly 500 years.
4. At end of its life cycle phoenix burned itself on funeral pyre.
5. New phoenix, always male, rose from ashes of old phoenix.
6. Myth of phoenix is similar to Egyptian *benu*, sacred bird that is similar to stork.

34h Use the correct person, number, and tense for the verb *be*.

The verb *be* is fundamental to the English language, but it takes various forms. Make sure you know how to conjugate it and how to use its appropriate forms when writing.

Present tense	*Singular*	*Plural*
First person	I am	we are
Second person	you are	you are
Third person	he, she, it is	they are

He ~~be~~ *is* an outstanding research scientist.

I ~~be~~ *am* proud to study with him.

You ~~is~~ *are* the only student who got an A.

They ~~is~~ *are* going to the planetarium to study Mars.

Professor Hamilton says that we ~~is~~ *are* the hardest working committee.

Past tense	Singular	Plural
First person	I was	we were
Second person	you were	you were
Third person	he, she, it was	they were

He ~~were~~ *was* at school when the fire alarm went off.

I ~~were~~ *was* at work during that terrible snow storm.

You ~~was~~ *were* lucky to be at home.

Native French and Spanish speakers sometimes substitute *have* for the verb *be*:

I ~~have hunger.~~ *was hungry [or am hungry].*

EXERCISE 34.8   Correct errors in the use of *be* in the following sentences.

1. A caricature are an exaggerated drawing.
2. It be based on the peculiarities of persons, such as Winston Churchill's cigar or Adolf Hitler's little mustache.
3. Caricature were used by Greeks, Romans, Egyptians, and others down through the ages.
4. I have wrong to accuse you of stealing my purse.
5. Some caricatures is used by comic strips as well as political cartoons.
6. They was featured often in *Mad* magazine in the 1970s.
7. Some politicians be angry when they be caricatured.
8. I have anger with you.

34i   Use the correct person, number, and tense for the verb *do*.

Like *be*, the verb *do* is also fundamental to the English language. Learn how to conjugate it and how to use its appropriate forms when writing.

Present tense	Singular	Plural
First person	I do	we do
Second person	you do	you do
Third person	he, she, it does	they do

do
I ~~does~~ exercises every day.

does
Eddy ~~do~~ fifty sit-ups in five minutes.

doesn't
Duane ~~don't~~ exercise at all.

Past tense	Singular	Plural
First person	I did	we did
Second person	you did	you did
Third person	he, she, it did	they did

did
The doctors ~~done~~ everything possible to save him.

did
Bernard ~~done~~ all the talking and none of the listening.

If your sentence contains *did* as a helping verb, put the rest of the verb in the present tense:

did
We ~~done~~ *finished* the project on time, but it was a struggle.

NOTE: Use *done* only with a helping verb (*has done, were done*).

EXERCISE 34.9 Correct the present-tense errors of *do* in the following sentences.

1. Traditionally, a clown do his act for a circus.
2. Today many women does clown acts in various venues.
3. Sporting events use a clown dressed like a chicken who do all sorts of stunts.
4. Some rodeo events need clowns who does the dangerous job of protecting cowboys from bulls and wild stallions.
5. Some clowns does singing and dancing acts; others does silent pantomime.
6. A clown don't get star billing but nevertheless wins the greatest response from children and the young at heart.

EXERCISE 34.10 Correct the past-tense errors of *do* in the following sentences.

1. Although he faced many difficulties, James Cook done all he could to finish three voyages.

2. He done his best work by mapping the Pacific Ocean with scientific accuracy.
3. Great Britain recognized Cook for what he had did in claiming New South Wales as a colony.
4. His charts were did with care and patience despite the discomforts of the voyages.
5. The last of his work was did at the Sandwich Islands.

34j   Use the correct person, number, and tense for the verb *have*.

Like *be* and *do*, writers sometimes become confused with the conjugation of the verb *have*, which also is basic to the English language. Make sure you know how to use the appropriate forms of the verb.

Present tense	*Singular*	*Plural*
First person	I have	we have
Second person	you have	you have
Third person	he, she, it has	they have

These travelers ~~has~~ *have* lost their passports.

I ~~has~~ *have* seven projects to plan at work.

Laurie ~~have~~ *has* not seen her parents in three years.

~~Has~~ *Have* you visited the new administration building yet?

The past tense form is *had* for all three persons and for both numbers.

EXERCISE 34.11   Correct the uses of *have* in the following sentences.

1. Several football coaches has lost their jobs because a quarterback fumbled or was intercepted at the wrong time.
2. Most quarterbacks at some time has heard the jeering of the fans.
3. If you has attended many games, you know what I mean.
4. Some quarterbacks been called field generals and even assistant coaches.

5. A coach often have an intensely close relationship with the quarterback.
6. A coach usually have several set plays for the quarterback's first series of calls.

34k Select the correct form of irregular verbs.

Irregular verbs change form in no set pattern. See section **29a** for a list of the forms of many irregular verbs, or consult a dictionary if you are unsure about a particular verb.

We ~~seen~~ *saw* the space shuttle launch at Canaveral.   [the verb *see*]

She ~~begun~~ *began* working to help the family finances.   [the verb *begin*]

Use a helping verb (*have, has,* or *had*) with a verb in the past participle form:

She *has* begun working to help the family finances.   [the verb *begin*]

He had ~~drove~~ *driven* only fifty miles before the engine rods blew.   [the verb *drive*]

Do not force an irregular verb into the form of a regular verb:

That decision has *costed* the group several thousand dollars in pension benefits.   [the verb *cost*]

Similarly, do not change a regular verb into an irregular form:

Someone ~~drug~~ *dragged* a hose through the flower garden.   [the verb *drag*]

EXERCISE 34.12   Correct errors in the irregular verb forms in the following sentences.

1. With frontier justice the vigilantes hung the outlaw.
2. Several citizens seen the event but said nothing.
3. The victim was prove guilty only by flimsy evidence.

4. Someone digged the grave before the man was even hanged.
5. The whole affair hurted the reputation of the community.
6. Even though the outlaw sweared on a Bible, the vigilantes would not believe him.
7. Only after two other men had wrote a confession to the crime did anyone feel remorse.
8. The vigilantes finally knowed that they had slay the wrong man.
9. The episode teached a lesson to all the people.
10. Nobody in the town knowed the name of the vigilantes, at least that is what they said.

341 Add *-ed* when needed to form the past and past participle of regular verbs.

Sometimes in spoken English the *-ed* is not clearly enunciated: *smoothed, missed*.

The candidate *kiss*ₐ the babies' foreheads.

At other times the verb ends in a cluster of consonants like *sk, nk, ck* or *nt, rt, st: asked, trucked, stinted, pasted*.

The supervisor *ask*ₐ the foreman to inventory the warehouse.

In other cases the verb ending blends into the sound of the word that follows the verb: *used to, supposed to*.

We *us*ₐ to swim in the creek, but now we're not *suppose*ₐ to because of the pollution.

See section **30**.

EXERCISE 34.13 Correct the following sentences by adding *-ed* or *-d* to complete the verb forms.

1. We use to play doubles in tennis, but one person ask to drop out.
2. My backhand stroke was rough and jerky, but coach smooth it out.

3. The team was suppose to play in a tournament this weekend, but rain cancel it.
4. We ask coach to give us time off, but she ignore us.
5. We had play every weekend before this one.
6. One tournament post our scores in big letters for everyone to see.

EXERCISE 34.14 Replace any nonstandard word forms in these sentences.

1. Times has changed, and some poeple think we has lost self-discipline and strong morals.
2. A person don't always know how to make the right choice.
3. For example, one college want to change the rules for women living in dorms to the way they use to be in the 1960s.
4. Back then, women sign in and out at night and were suppose to be back in the dorms by ten or eleven on week nights.
5. Such practices, supposedly to protect young women, was called *in loco parentis*, which means "in the place of a parent."
6. The college women of the 1960s be the mothers of the college women of today.
7. When they was in college, they wasn't happy with the rules and fought to be treated the same as men students.
8. Today, they wondering if their daughters has too much freedom.
9. But if colleges treat men and women differently, they guilty of sex discrimination.
10. This situation show some of the old values in conflict with the new values of equal treatment for all.

EXERCISE 34.15 Replace any nonstandard verb forms with standard forms. Mark any correct sentences with a *C*.

1. Many television commercials more entertaining than the shows they sponsor.
2. The California Raisins has become as popular as many rock groups, and they has many spinoff products.
3. I seen dolls, tee shirts, and birthday cards with raisins on them.
4. Some people doesn't like the way commercials use classic rock tunes to sell products.
5. They think the original artist don't get enough credit and the song loses its original meaning.

6. One commercial even show a moon that look like Ray Charles singing an imitation of a famous Ray Charles song, but it does not give Ray Charles any credit.

7. The trend may have started with an airline commercial using the tune of "Up, Up, and Away," originally sung by the Fifth Dimension.

8. A product to unplug clogged drains shows a man dress only in a towel singing "Splish, Splash, I Was Taking a Bath," which be an old Bobby Darin song.

9. Even the *Wall Street Journal*, a newspaper that appeal to conservative business people, use to advertise with a song call "My Baby Takes the Morning Train."

10. A lot of these old songs has memories for people who hates to see them ruin by commercial use.

34m   Use prepositions correctly.

Prepositions in English are idiomatic (see section **17c**), which means they are peculiar grammatically and not easily translated. The French say, "Je vais à Nashville," which can be translated improperly:

I am going ~~at~~ *to* Nashville.

"To Nashville" is the correct idiom. Therefore, you must adjust the use of prepositions, especially those that follow verbs, such as *walk in, speak up, fall down*. The choice often depends on context (*disagree about, disagree with, disagree over*), so use a good dictionary for accuracy in phrasing.

EXERCISE 34.16   Correct improper idioms in the following sentences.

1. She disagree *upon* him.
2. She is independent *from* him and the marriage.
3. In truth, she considered her professional position superior *than* his.
4. She seemed unwilling to wait *on* the divorce papers.
5. At the courtroom she was consumed *of* anger.

34n Check spelling, capitalization, and use of accents.

A dialect may cause misspelling. For example, the Spanish *recibir* may cause reversal of the *ie* sound and even the use of the *b*.

The United States continues to ~~reciebe~~ *receive* major drug shipments from Colombia.

In addition, the word *major* is often misspelled as the word *mayor* because the *j* in Spanish is the sound of the English *y*.

Some dialects omit capitalization of nationality, but standard English requires it.

Many ~~a~~*A*merican officials hope to eradicate the drug supply from ~~s~~*S*outh ~~a~~*A*merica.

In like manner, Spanish does not capitalize the personal pronoun *yo* (*I*), days of the week, or months.

On ~~t~~*T*uesday, ~~i~~*I*f i come face to face with him, ~~i~~*I* will confront him about the insult to you.

Standard English does not, as a general rule, retain accent marks on foreign words translated into English.

Often drug shipments are routed through such countries as Panamá *e* the Bahamas, and Méxic*c*o.

EXERCISE 34.17 Correct errors in spelling, capitalization, and accents in the following sentences.

1. The problem of drugs is affecting everyone in latin america.
2. Usually, people believe the worst about columbia and its neighbors.

3. Even méxico and panamá are tarnished by drug traffic that flows through these countries.
4. In august of last year i witnessed personally a brutal beating on the streets of nogales.
5. The american attitude toward Latin America changes from monday to friday and from week to week.

PART

7

Punctuation

35
Periods, Question Marks, and Exclamation Points

36
Commas

37
Unnecessary Commas

38
Semicolons

39
Colons

40
Apostrophes and Quotation Marks

41
Dashes, Parentheses, Brackets, and Ellipses

Use end punctuation to clarify your meaning.

He really said that.
He really said that?
He really said that!

35a   Use a period to close statements.

Computers typeset the pages for many newspapers, magazines, and even books.   [declarative]

Submit your report to the laboratory supervisor by Friday. [command]

He asked if we had finished the experiment.   [indirect interrogative]

The vial exploded. The disaster ruined weeks of work. [exclamatory]

Statements that contain direct questions or strong exclamations take different end punctuation (see sections **35c–35d**).

35b   Use a period after most abbreviations.

Mr. syn. adj. assn. fig. tsp. p.

Some abbreviations of multiple words contain an internal period:

i.e. e.g. a.m. p.m.

Other multiple-word abbreviations, particularly of measurements, may contain no periods:

rpm mpg

Abbreviations consisting of all capital letters, such as those for states or academic titles, and acronyms of organizations usually do not use periods:

FL CA DC	BA BS RN
CBS NATO NAACP	AD BC

Check a dictionary or the *MLA Handbook for Writers of Research Papers*, Third Edition, for guidance with abbreviations.

If a sentence ends with an abbreviation, do not add another period.

The seminar begins at 8:00 p.m.

But *do* add a question mark or an exclamation point, if necessary.

Does the seminar begin at 8:00 p.m.?

See also chapter **43** for the use of abbreviations in a paper.

35c   End direct questions with a question mark.

Who first described the theory of black holes in space?

Do not use a question mark with an indirect question:

He wondered *if* Walt Whitman was really a homosexual.
She asked *if* sink holes can or should be filled.

Question marks may also serve an informal series of questions:

Did the Incas have the wheel? A monetary system? A written language?

35d Use exclamation points only to show strong exclamatory emphasis.

Use them as necessary in dialogue:

"Oh, no! I lost all my data," she cried.
"Leave me alone!" he screamed.

In formal writing avoid exclamation marks:

The computer somehow erased all the data. The committee must now begin from the start.

EXERCISE 35.1   Correct the use of periods, question marks, and exclamation marks in the following sentences.

1. Dr Science says the first reports of winged apes came from bird watchers, who thought they were seeing California condors!
2. Will you be ready to go at 9:00 a.m.?, or should we plan to leave later?
3. She asked me if I had ever seen a purple cow? and I answered, "a purple cow?! Never."
4. Our new fullback is half man, half gazelle!, and all American!!.
5. "*Raining cats and dogs* is a silly expression," Mark complained, asking if anyone had ever seen a cat out in the rain?

EXERCISE 35.2   Add appropriate punctuation to the following passage.

"Wow   " said Walter   "WGMV just announced that Dr Fishman resigned   Can you believe that   "

His mother came into the room   She watched silently as the broadcast continued   She wondered if the doctor had marital, financial, or business problems   She turned toward the kitchen, saying, "What a waste of talent   "

CHAPTER

36

Commas

The comma helps readers by signaling and separating units of thought.

36a Use a comma before a coordinating conjunction (*and, but, for, nor, or, so, yet*) that connects independent clauses.

You can use your acquaintances to form a job network, *but* you must have the necessary background and skills.

The roots of willow trees search a long way for nourishment, *and* life-sustaining water often becomes available in old sewer pipes.

The commas with the coordinating conjunctions *but* and *and* clearly separate two independent clauses. You will always be correct if you use commas in these situations.

Omit the comma only in short compound sentences where the meaning is absolutely clear:

The wind blew noisily out of the northwest and it pushed snow against the windows.

This sentence treats the wind in both clauses and the meaning is clear.

> The wind blew noisily out of the northwest, *so* George knew he faced a snowstorm.

This sentence treats two contrasting elements: the weather and George's reaction to it. It needs the comma.

To learn more about the contribution of compound sentences to your writing style, see chapter **8**.

36b   Use commas between items in a series of three or more words or word groups.

> A good architect understands the structural properties of wood, steel, concrete, and glass.

The commas clearly separate four items.

> The Internal Revenue Service requires self-employed people to keep records of all their expenses, to report all their income, and to pay estimated taxes quarterly.

The commas separate three distinct infinitive phrases.

> Make a file for each department: personnel, marketing and sales, accounts payable, and accounts receivable.

The final comma makes clear that accounts payable and accounts receivable are two separate departments.

36c   Use commas between coordinate adjectives.

Coordinate adjectives modify a noun equally and separately:

> Fashion designers favor *tall, slender, exotic-looking* models.

Each adjective modifies *models* separately and equally, so the word *and* could join them: tall *and* slender *and* exotic-looking. They also make sense if rearranged: slender, tall, exotic-looking models.

Some adjectives, however, are not coordinate, so do not separate them with commas:

> *Threatening black storm* clouds gathered in the west.

The adjectives build upon each other: *threatening* modifies the three-word noun phrase *black storm clouds; black* modifies the two-word noun phrase *storm clouds;* and *storm* modifies *clouds.* Use two tests: (1) Can the word *and* fit between the adjectives (threatening *and* black *and* storm clouds)? (2) Can you scramble the order and still make sense (storm black threatening clouds)?

EXERCISE 36.1   Insert commas correctly in the sentences below to separate *independent clauses, items in a series,* and *coordinate adjectives.* Mark any correct sentences with a *C.*

1. Your job search will involve writing dozens of letters and making hundreds of phone calls but all the effort will seem worthwhile later on.
2. Do not hesitate to carry copies of your résumé in a new polished leather briefcase.
3. Be wary of newspaper advertisements that require you to invest your own money to work on commission only or to pay for your own training.
4. Some excellent high-earning jobs may pay commission only but these appeal mostly to experienced self-confident salespersons.
5. Franchises to operate printing shops ice cream parlors fast-food restaurants and even gasoline stations can make good investments.
6. Independent consulting work demands that you work hard and take risks.
7. During the job search you must accept and overcome rejection yet never must you get discouraged and quit the hunt.
8. Most college graduates work for someone else before they gain enough skill and business experience and financial judgment to strike out on their own.

9. Liberal arts majors may become organization fundraisers they may edit medical or legal newsletters and they may even work as clerks or cooks.
10. Search out job leads through newspaper want ads trade magazines professional organizations acquaintances friends and relatives.

36d Use a comma to set off introductory phrases and clauses.

A comma signals the end of the introductory matter and the beginning of the main clause.

After his successful career as a spy for the British government , John Le Carré turned to writing novels.

Most introductory phrases and clauses function as adverbs to establish where, when, why, or how with regard to the action in the main clause.

When the champion seemed ready to fight , his wife stepped between him and the antagonist.

The comma avoids misreading by signaling the end of the introductory adverb clause and the beginning of the main clause.

Use a comma to set off short introductory units that describe a noun (see also section **22c**).

Flying too close to the sun , Icarus fell to his death when the wax in his wings melted.

To meet their deadlines , theater critics write their reviews as soon as they leave the performance.

NOTE: If no possibility of misreading exists, you may omit a comma after a short introductory phrase or clause.

During the Korean War some college students isolated themselves from foreign policy.

Generally, do not use a comma to set off adverb phrases and clauses that *follow* a main clause (see section **37e**).

36e Set off nonrestrictive units with commas.

Adjective phrases, adjective clauses, and appositives are word groups that may be restrictive or nonrestrictive. They are **restrictive** when they define and limit the meaning of a noun or pronoun, thereby being essential to the meaning of the sentence. Restrictive phrases and clauses do *not* require commas:

> The person *who left her purse on the jewelry counter* may claim it at the office.

If you remove the italicized clause, you change a reader's understanding drastically: *The person may claim it at the office.* Which person? Claim what?

Nonrestrictive units add meaning and information to a sentence but do not restrict, limit, or particularize meaning. Set them apart with commas:

> Nancy Johnson, *who left her purse on the jewelry counter,* will return in about an hour.

Units that describe a proper noun, like the example directly above, are usually nonrestrictive. However, word units that describe indefinite pronouns (*everyone* or *something*) are usually restrictive: "The president knew by first name everyone *who entered the room.*"

Set off nonrestrictive elements that interrupt and those that are at the beginning and end of a sentence.

> One Southern growth center, *known nationwide as the center for country music,* is Nashville, Tennessee.

> *Known nationwide as the center for country music,* one Southern growth center is Nashville, Tennessee.

> One Southern growth center is Nashville, Tennessee, *known nationwide as the center for country music.*

Use commas with nonrestrictive adjective phrases.

Verbal and prepositional phrases (see chapter **22**) require commas when they are not essential to the sentence.

> Horror movies, *usually portraying crazed killers,* are staples of teenage entertainment.

The participial phrase gives added information about all horror movies; the information is nonessential so it is set off. Compare a restrictive phrase: "Horror movies *featuring giant insects* are a subgenre."

Use commas with nonrestrictive adjective clauses.

Adjective clauses, which follow the noun or pronoun they modify, begin with *who, whom, whose, which, that, where,* and *when.*

> Your application and résumé, *which arrived last week,* will receive immediate review.

> The film editor cut the movie's original opening scene, *which depicted death, carnage, and merciless brutality.*

Although they add information about the modified nouns, the italicized clauses do not specify or limit. Compare restrictive elements: "The film editor cut the opening scene *that depicts the carnage of war* and retained the one *that introduces a quiet, eerie sunrise prior to the battle.*" These two restrictive clauses specify which scene was cut and which one remained.

NOTE: As a general rule, use *that* to introduce restrictive clauses and *which* to introduce nonrestrictive clauses.

> The test-tube *that* shattered contained a deadly virus.

> Hereafter, use these new laboratory vials, *which* are shatterproof, for all viruses and vaccines.

Use commas with nonrestrictive appositives.

Some appositives are nonrestrictive because they merely rename a noun or pronoun without limiting it.

> Emily Brontë's only novel, *Wuthering Heights,* ranks high on the list of great Gothic tales.

The phrase *only novel* limits the meaning to one novel, so the appositive *Wuthering Heights* is nonrestrictive and requires the commas. But the next sentence features a restrictive appositive.

> Jane Austen's novel *Pride and Prejudice* features the wit, intelligence, and independence of Elizabeth Bennett.

Here the writer uses the restrictive appositive *Pride and Prejudice* to specify one of several Austen novels.

My brother, *Ted,* has earned recognition for his musical talent.

The writer has one brother. Compare a sentence that uses restrictive appositives:

My brother *Ted* and my brother *John* have won scholarships to Ohio University.

This writer has more than one brother.

36f Use commas with titles, degrees, dates, and places.

James T. McKenzie, *Jr.*, is my uncle.
The "shot heard round the world" was fired in Concord, *Massachusetts.*
Mozart was born in Salzburg, *Austria,* but lived much of his life in Vienna.
June 15, *1990,* is graduation day.

Omit the commas if you invert the date (*The shipment is due 17 June 1991*) or if you give only the month and year (*The cold weather of April 1987 destroyed the peach crop*).

EXERCISE 36.2 Add or delete commas as necessary. Mark any correct sentences with a *C*.

1. Surprisingly, fast-food restaurants which usually pay only the minimum wage have little difficulty attracting employees.
2. Working long hours student employees find their school work often suffers.
3. Even though these workers may need it most the minimum-wage jobs offer little or no medical insurance.
4. Medicaid and Medicare tax-supported insurance plans for the elderly and poor take care of some pressing health-care needs.
5. Being comprehensive Britain's National Health Service guarantees medical care for everyone.
6. To meet the medical budget legislators must either raise taxes or cut spending.
7. With the taxpayers scrutinizing every increase politicians hesitate to propose new taxes for fear of being voted out of office.

8. Although unpopular but necessary the decreases in spending mean decreases in social services.
9. Voters who approve of new levies and bond issues are often in the minority.
10. Education which is essential to the future of the country suffers when the government cannot fund vital programs.

EXERCISE 36.3   Add or delete commas as necessary. Mark any correct sentences with a *C*.

1. Some small children, who are abused by parents or relatives, think abusive treatment is normal.
2. Children who are physically punished often grow up to treat their own children the same way.
3. Museum visitors often spend many minutes gazing at Leonardo Da Vinci's painting *Mona Lisa*.
4. The great jazz singer Ella Fitzgerald perfected scat singing which uses the voice like an instrument.
5. During dark winter days some people suffer a depression, known as "sunlight deprivation syndrome."
6. Smoke alarms which should be in every building save many lives each year.
7. The sciences, that examine human behavior, provide insights for advertising executives.
8. Flying too low the airplane hit the water tower.
9. During the battle some soldiers refused to fire on civilians.
10. One of my three brothers Ted received his orders this week.
11. August 22 1993 is the scheduled completion date.
12. Jason Douglas Jr. was born in Springfield Missouri.

36g   Use commas to separate units that interrupt the natural flow of the sentence.

Transitions connect ideas, but they often interrupt the sentence structure. Use commas to set off *for example, in fact, in my opinion, in the first place, unfortunately, certainly*, and other transitions.

Alexander Pope's poetry is, *in my opinion*, intellectually brilliant. John Keats's, *in contrast*, shows emotional fervor.

Unfortunately, my opinion had little influence on the discussion.

Conjunctive adverbs (*therefore, moreover, however, furthermore*, and others) often serve as transitions rather than as conjunctions (see section **20e**).

> Professional sports are big business today. The player-owner relationships, *consequently*, recall former labor-management conflicts.

NOTE: Commas are unnecessary when the meaning is clear or when the unit functions as an adverb modifying a nearby verb.

> His vote *no doubt* influenced the outcome.

> *However* he chooses to travel, Elkins always has interesting vacations.

Set off other expressions that are clearly parenthetical and transitional in nature:

> The initial voting, *as most of you know*, was illegal.

36h Use commas to set off sentence elements that are out of normal order.

Use commas to keep relationships clear if adjectives appear in unusual positions:

> The waves lapped at the shore, *monotonous but peaceful*.

> *Monotonous but peaceful*, the waves lapped at the shore.

Compare the wording in a normal position:

> The *monotonous, peaceful* waves lapped at the shore.
> The waves lapped *monotonously and peacefully* at the shore.

Use commas to separate an *absolute phrase* (see section **22c**) from the main clause, whether the phrase comes first or last:

> The two horses waited restlessly, *hooves pawing at the mud and tails swishing at noisy flies.*

> *The bank having forced a reorganization of his financing*, the rancher reluctantly sold his prize stallion.

36i Use commas to show contrast or emphasis.

He wanted fame, not fortune.
Unlike his conservative brother, he lived fast and died young.

36j Use commas to set off interjections, short questions, and the words *yes* and *no*.

Well, we tried to discover the lost mosaic, but we failed.
The committee decided, *no*, the expenditure is too great.
The committee will confirm the budget, *will it not*?

36k Use commas with direct address and interrupted quotations or dialogue.

"You now have the floor, Mr. Speaker, for ten minutes."
"It is remarkable," Mr. Nally said, "how much dogs resemble their owners."

See also chapter **40**.

36l Use commas to mark omissions.

To get a student loan is great but to win a tax-free grant, fantastic.

EXERCISE 36.4 Add or delete commas as necessary. Mark any correct sentences with a *C*.

1. People talk about the weather in truth when they have little else to say.
2. Fortunately the weather changes often enough to give variety to weather reports.
3. A bit flamboyant but effective Willard Scott is one of the wealthiest television personalities.
4. The weather as most people know can trick even the best prognosticators.

5. "I predict" said Scott "the storm will hit the gulf coast of Alabama."
6. A deceptive calm can descend in the middle of a hurricane, however, forceful the wind has been.
7. A hurricane will often decide no not that way and change its direction.
8. The weatherman was born and raised in Orlando Florida but broadcasts usually from Washington D.C.
9. Blizzards close communication networks interstate highways airports and yes even subway systems.
10. Unlike traditional weathermen Scott travels the country to report from a beach in South Carolina a ship in San Diego Bay or a corn field in Iowa.

Use commas for a purpose. Unnecessary or misused commas confuse readers, change meaning, and make writing choppy.

37a Do not use a comma to separate the subject from the verb or the verb from its object or its complement.

> This week swimmers in age groups 8–10 and 11–12⁄ will practice during the morning.

The comma must not separate the subject *swimmers* from its verb *will practice*.

> A Mexican businessman recontructed in every detail⁄ one of Christopher Columbus's three ships.

The comma must not separate the verb *reconstructed* from its object *one*.

> At age 40, Howard H. Baker, Jr., was⁄ the first popularly elected Republican senator from Tennessee.

The comma must not separate the verb *was* from the complement *senator*.

37b   Do not use a comma between compound elements unless they are independent clauses.

Always use a comma before coordinating conjunctions that join independent clauses (see section **36a**), but do not use commas indiscriminately with *and, or, nor, but, for, so, yet.*

> Watch bearings made of synthetic rubies,/and industrial cutting tools made of diamonds use precious jewels at an alarming rate.

The comma must not separate one part of the compound subject, *bearings*, from the other part, *tools*, and their verb, *use*.

> Miners first release underground minerals by explosives,/and then mechanically load them for shipment to the surface.

The comma above improperly separates the two parts of the compound verb, *release* and *load*.

> The basketball players soon realized that individual greed for glory would damage team morale,/ and that true teamwork could win championships.

The comma improperly separates a compound object. The players realized two things: that greed would damage morale and that teamwork could win championships (see also chapter **23**).

> We were more shocked by the vandalism at the site,/than surprised by the discovery of the urns.

The comma should not separate the two parts of the compound verb, *shocked* and *surprised*.

37c   Do not use commas with restrictive modifiers.

The ice caves formed by glaciers centuries ago/collapsed during the heat wave this year.

The comma above must not separate the subject *caves* from its verb *collapsed*. The word *formed* is not the verb of the sentence but part of an intervening restrictive phrase. In contrast, you should set off with two commas a *nonrestrictive phrase* (see section **36e**) that intervenes: "The Woolridge ice caves, *formed by glaciers centuries ago*, collapsed this year."

Swimmers/ who dive in shallow water/ risk their lives.

The commas improperly set off a restrictive clause that explains *which* swimmers.

Nathaniel Hawthorne's novel/ *The Scarlet Letter*/ explores the problem of repressed, secret guilt.

The commas improperly set off a restrictive appositive that identifies one of several Hawthorne novels.

37d   Do not use a comma before the first word or after the last word in a series.

Use commas to separate items within a series but not to separate the series from the main clause (see also section **36b**).

Several items that charities accept for resale are/ clothes, books, appliances, tools, and even antiques.

The comma must not separate the subject *items* from a series of complements.

Felix decided that majoring in law, business, or accounting/ would contribute to his political ambitions.

The comma must not separate the subject of a clause, *majoring*, from its verb, *would contribute*.

The U.S. National Weather Service warns people of dangerous

weather conditions like/ hurricanes, tornadoes, blizzards, and

thunderstorms.

A comma used after *like* or *such as* wrongly separates the connecting word from the series it tries to introduce.

EXCEPTION: *For example* does interrupt (see section **36h**) and may be set off by commas: "You have optional courses to fulfill your science requirements*, for example,* biology, botany, or organic chemistry."

The unnecessary comma below separates the adjective *rocky* from the word it modifies (see section **36c**).

Mountain climbing often means just hiking on steep, rocky/ trails.

37e   Do not use a comma before adverbial clauses that end sentences.

She spent a year traveling around the world/ after she graduated from college.

One graduate spent a year working as a deck hand on a freighter/

because he could not find a job in his specialty, medieval history.

The commas above must not separate essential, concluding adverbial clauses from the main clause. Such clauses begin with *after, as soon as, before, because, if, since, unless, until,* and *when*. In contrast, *introductory* adverb clauses require the comma (see section **36d**).

37f   Do not use a comma between adjectives that cannot be separated with the word *and*.

The dark/green water of the lake looked foreboding.

For a full discussion, see section **36c**.

37g   Do not use a comma before an opening parenthesis.

If words in parentheses immediately follow an introductory phrase or clause, place the comma after the parentheses, not before (see section **36d**).

To reboot the computer program/ (that is, to restart it)**,** simultaneously press the *ctrl, alt,* and *del* keys.

37h   Do not use a comma before or after a period, question mark, exclamation point, or a dash.

"That's it!"/ he thought.

During spawning season salmon begin to change/—finally, to spoil—even though they are still alive.

See also chapters **35**, **40**, and **41**.

EXCEPTION: Do insert a comma, as necessary, after an abbreviation that ends in a period (". . . at 5 p.m.**,** although . . .").

EXERCISE 37.1   Delete all unnecessary commas from the sentences below. Mark any correct sentences with a *C*.

1. Young women seem most susceptible to psychological eating disorders such as, anorexia and bulimia.

2. Anorexic people, who intentionally starve themselves, do not see their thinness realistically.
3. Bulimia sufferers gorge themselves, until they throw up.
4. These progressive, weakening, diseases are difficult to treat.
5. Many drug and alcohol abuse clinics compete for patients, because most of these clinics are operated for profit.
6. Tough, antismoking laws passed by many states, are driving smokers underground.
7. Smoke-free offices, classrooms, and public areas, leave few places for smokers to light up in peace.
8. As part of a healthful diet, eat yogurt to build bones, and bran muffins to lower cholesterol.
9. One fast food meal provides more than half the calories that most people need in one day, and is often too high in sodium and saturated fat.
10. "An apple a day keeps the doctor away" shows that some folk wisdom had a basis in fact, (although chemical spraying may now affect the apples and the wisdom).

38

Semicolons

A semicolon joins two or more closely related independent clauses and helps delineate items in a series that contain internal commas.

38a Use a semicolon between independent clauses not joined by a coordinating conjunction (*and, but, for, or, nor, so, yet*).

> One writer procrastinates until motivation disappears; another rushes into the project without prethought or preplanning.

The semicolon joins clauses that treat the same topic — the habits of certain writers.

> Each twin was brilliant in her own way; both became professionals, one a PhD in mathematics and the other a world-famous opera star.

Each was brilliant and each became a professional, so the relationship is strengthened by the semicolon.

> Student loans are difficult to get; applicants must show need and summer earnings.

The second clause explains the first, so a semicolon ties them together effectively.

38b Use a semicolon between independent clauses joined by a conjunctive adverb or a transitional phrase.

Conjunctive adverbs such as *moreover, therefore,* and *then* and transitional phrases such as *for example, in other words,* and *on the contrary* require the semicolon when they connect independent clauses. This next conjunctive adverb shows contrast:

> The Scottish poet Robert Burns wrote the words to "Auld Lang Syne," the traditional New Year's song; *however*, the music is an old folk melody.

A semicolon precedes the connecting adverb or phrase and a comma usually follows, but not always:

> Enter the museum through the main door; *then* turn left to the Chinese exhibit.

> Halloween goblins re-enact Celtic sacrifices made to the Lord of the Dead; *in contrast*, Santa Claus seems a wholly Christian figure.

38c Use a semicolon with a coordinating conjunction only if one or both independent clauses contain internal punctuation.

> She was greatly excited at first, and she kicked the stall door each time I approached; but after learning that I provided cracked corn, oats, and fresh hay she grew gentle.

The semicolon effectively signals a strong pause between the clauses.

38d Use a semicolon between items in a series when one or more items contain internal punctuation.

> One cruise line touted its ships as ocean-going luxury resorts, with a basket of fresh apples, pears, and cherries in every cabin; a turned-down bed with a mint on the pillow every evening;

table tennis, paddle tennis, and deck tennis; two large swimming pools; a five-star restaurant; and, of course, exciting ports of call.

Although some units in the series above have internal punctuation and some do not, the semicolon must separate each unit of the series. That is, if you must separate one item in a series with a semicolon, you must separate all other items with a semicolon.

38e Do not use a semicolon to connect a subordinate clause with an independent clause.

A subordinate clause cannot stand alone. Grammatically weak, it must attach itself to a main clause with no punctuation or, at most, a comma, *not* a semicolon (see chapter **23**).

> Although I felt I deserved a better grade, the instructor said my work was barely average.

The subordinate clause that begins with *although* must connect to the main clause with a comma.

> Because southern Louisiana became a refuge for French-speaking Canadians, called *Acadians*, the people descended from them, their language, food, and music are all called *Cajun*.

The opening word group that begins with *because* is an introductory subordinate clause, so it requires a comma, not a semicolon (see section **36d**).

EXERCISE 38.1   Find incorrect semicolons and commas in the sentences below and insert correct punctuation. Mark correct sentences with a *C*.

1. Many popular comic strips reflect the social and political view of their authors, at the same time, they want to amuse the readers.

2. Some readers think *Doonesbury*, by Garry Trudeau, belongs on the editorial page; especially when it makes fun of the president.

3. The strips *Cathy* and *Sylvia* gently mock the fears and foibles of liberated women, whereas others, such as *Born Loser, Tank McNamara*, and *Blondie* satirize the male ego.

4. *Calvin and Hobbes* appeals to college students, it is about an overimaginative little boy and his stuffed tiger.

5. *The Far Side*, which often presents animals and insects as they might view humans; appeals to intellectuals.

6. Animals that are smarter than their owners are popular, for example, Garfield always outsmarts his owner.

7. Garfield has gained commercial success; his image now appears on mugs and T-shirts and posters.

8. Comic strips that do not carry stories over from one day to the next are more popular with readers; although strips like *Mary Worth* substitute for soap operas in the minds of some readers.

9. *Peanuts*, probably the most popular strip of all time, seems like nothing more than amusing stories of precocious children, however, some people see it as a religious parable.

10. Comic strips have come a long way since they first appeared; when their main appeal was through slapstick violence and vaudeville-like jokes.

CHAPTER

39

Colons

The colon serves a distinctive role for the writer: it introduces elaboration on what the first clause said. When typing, use only one space after a colon.

39a Use a colon after an independent clause to introduce a series, a quotation, an appositive, a definition, or an amplification.

Introduce a series of words, phrases, or clauses.

> When you think about your future career, you must consider a number of questions: What work do I do best? Where will I live? Will my career allow me to grow intellectually? Does its future look promising?

Capitalize the first word of independent clauses following a colon *only* when they are questions or direct quotations. Do not capitalize words or phrases.

> When you think about your future career, you must consider all of the following: your interests, your skills, your education, even your location.

Use a colon before, not after, phrases such as *for example*, *that is*, or *namely*.

> In Great Books reading programs, participants read the classics: *for example*, Plato's *Republic* and Shakespeare's *Hamlet*.

Introduce a formal quotation.

> George Santayana's words ring truer than ever: "Those who cannot remember the past are condemned to repeat it."

Introduce an appositive.

> The president wrapped the mantle of the presidency around himself for one reason: protection from FBI investigators and Congressional committees.

A comma here would be correct but less formal (see section **36f**).

Introduce a definition or an amplification.

> Be wary of love that hypnotizes: it dominates both mind and body.

Colons and semicolons are not interchangeable even though both appear to link independent clauses. The semicolon means *stop*, whereas the colon means *go forward, there is more to come.*

> The engineer designed the perfect plan: a 10-foot concrete barrier would encircle the compound.

The amplification here explains the plan, so the colon is correct. If, however, the second clause does not explain the first, the semicolon is appropriate.

> The engineer designed the plan to encircle the compound; the contractor found it impossible to construct.

(See chapter **8** for further elaboration on the distinctions between the semicolon and the colon.)

39b Use a colon in salutations, in numbers to show time, and in ratios.

Dear Ms. Markle: Dear Editor:
9:58 a.m.   7:45 p.m.   *but* "Meet here at 1800 hours."
The new swim record is 3:38:17.
Always have a length-to-diameter ratio of 2:1.
Your chances of winning the lottery are 1,117,693:1.

NOTE: Many writers prefer to use a colon in references to books of the Bible: Genesis 7:1–4. MLA recommends periods: Genesis 7.1–4.

39c Do not use a colon after a linking verb, preposition, or relative pronoun.

The items you will need for camp are: a tent, a sleeping bag, a flashlight, and a stove.

The list of items above does not follow an independent clause.

The Mayor's commission on education consists of: civic leaders, educators, parents, and students.

The list above is the object of the preposition *of* and so should not be separated from the preposition.

We should remember that: "success is a journey, not a destination."

The quotation is part of the subordinate clause introduced by *that*.

EXERCISE 39.1   Add colons to punctuate correctly the following sentences.

1. Edmund Burke proclaimed "The only thing necessary for the triumph of evil is for good men to do nothing."
2. Citizens often fail to vote because they fail to consider a few benefits of citizenship to vote, to bear arms, to congregate, to protest, to speak freely.

3. In order of preference, I suggest that you visit these sites on your trip to Washington the space museum, the Capitol, the Lincoln Memorial, and Mount Vernon.
4. Teachers should learn to identify dyslexia it is a brain condition that causes abnormal difficulty in reading and spelling.
5. The coach explained the winning formula teamwork, teamwork, teamwork.

EXERCISE 39.2   Make the choice to use either a colon or semicolon between the main clauses of the following sentences.

1. We can do one of two things get a part-time job and remain in school or forget college and work full-time.
2. Most students today face a difficult decision remain in school with limited funding or drop out and work a full-time job.
3. The student who works full-time and also attends college has a special dedication the ones on athletic scholarships display the same spirit even though some people toss around the term "free ride."
4. Many students depend upon the services of the financial aid office they also turn to the banks in their hometown for help.
5. If you are a college student, you know the answer to this question Who needs tuition money?

Apostrophes signal possession, show omission in contractions, and form plurals of some letters, words, and abbreviations.

Quotation marks enclose direct quotations from printed sources and from direct speech. They enable a writer to reproduce another person's exact words. Quotation marks also enclose titles of short works. Like parentheses, quotation marks always open and close the featured element.

40a Use an apostrophe to create possessive nouns.

The possessive case shows or implies ownership:

Harold**'s** rock band	the Thunderbird**'s** design
Arkansas**'s** climate	several typists**'** ditto machines.

For all singular nouns, even if the last letter is an *s*, use an apostrophe before the *s*: 's.

boy**'s** toy, NASA**'s** catastrophe, heaven**'s** glory, ox**'s** yoke, actress**'s** role, Keats**'s** poems, Dickens**'s** novels

This issue marks *Saturday Review*'**s** golden anniversary.
This portrait of Karen**'s** is a work of art.   [Compare: *This portrait of Karen is a work of art.*]

For plural nouns not ending in _s_, use 's.

> child*ren*'s shoes   *mice*'s holes   deer's habitat
>
> The wom*en*'s tournament begins Saturday.

For plural nouns ending in _s_, use an apostrophe only.

> actress*es*' costumes
> The Jones*es*' house   [but Bob Jones's bicycle]
> The project will monitor the student*s*' study habits.

For compound nouns, use 's or s' after the last word, as appropriate.

> editor-in-chief's responsibilities   [one editor-in-chief]
> attorney general*s*' agreement   [two or more attorney generals
>   *or* attorneys general]

For indefinite pronouns (*everybody, nobody, each other*, and so on), use 's.

> anybody's guess   everybody's books   each other's eyes

To show *joint* possession, use 's after the last noun only.

> Adam and Eve's innocence
> Johnson and Hedrick's proposal   [one proposal]
> Joanne and James's books   [The books belong jointly to
>   Joanne and James.]

To show *separate* possession, use 's after each noun.

> Johnson's and Hedrick's proposals   [separate proposals]
> Joanne's and James's books   [Each owns separate books.]

40b   Use the apostrophe to form contractions or show omissions.

An apostrophe substitutes for one or more letters of a word.

> We aren't prepared for this type of contest.
> Butch replied, "Well, I'm not goin'."

NOTE: Avoid contractions in formal and academic writing.

40c To prevent misreading, use the apostrophe to form plurals of letters used as letters and words used as words.

Underline (italicize) the letters and words used as such.

Mind your *p*'s and *q*'s.
Dot your *i*'s and cross your *t*'s.
His grades were *B*'s and *C*'s.
The's, *and*'s, and *be*'s appear frequently in English prose.

In general, do not use 's to show the plural of numerals or abbreviations, though usage varies. (See chapter **44**.)

We were at 6*s* and 7*s*. OR We were at sixes and sevens.
The 1980*s* were the Reagan years.
All the ACT*s* were in the '20*s*.

40d Do not misuse the apostrophe.

Do not use an apostrophe with the possessive pronouns *its, whose, ours, yours, theirs, his*, and *hers*.

In particular, use *its* and *whose* to show possession and *it's* and *who's* to mean *it is* and *who is*.

The movie I recommend is in *its* last week at the Varsity.
It's the best movie now showing in town.
Whose review did you believe, Siskel's or Ebert's?
Who's the film critic for the school newspaper?

See also chapter **28** for a list of possessive forms.

Do not use an apostrophe with plural nouns that are not possessive.

Several of the dormitory resident/s have filed formal complaints against the head resident.

EXERCISE 40.1   Correct the misuse of apostrophes in the following sentences. Mark any correct sentence with a *C*.

1. The poet's lament was that her day's were lonely and her night's were weary.
2. Its been too long since we met.
3. Her's is the best paper on the topic.
4. The Thompsons' house is the two-story on the corner.
5. Adam's and Eve's sin was eating the fruit of the tree of knowledge.
6. Aspirin is truly a wonder drug, but physicians are cautious about it's side effects.
7. Does anyone know who's hat this is?
8. The bazaar made money for charity by auctioning my mother's-in-law quilt.
9. Reviewers say that Tom Robbins's new novel is his best.
10. The childrens' dream vacation is a visit to Disneyland.

40e   Use quotation marks around direct quotations in your text.

Quotation marks indicate the written or spoken words of another. Use them to enclose all quoted sentences, phrases, and words.

Everyone has thoughts on money. The Bible says, "The love of money is the root of all evil."

The president emphasized a "smaller deficit" than in previous years.

If you interrupt a quotation with your own words, enclose each quoted section in quotation marks:

Horace Greeley made famous the line, "Go West, young man," but many people overlook the rest of his sentence, "and grow up with the country."

Rewriting the words of another produces an *indirect quotation*, which does not take quotation marks:

One wit suggests doubling your money by folding each bill once and stuffing it into your purse or billfold.

To show one quotation within another, use double marks for the outer quotation and single marks for the inner quotation:

> Thomas Nelson observes, "Shakespeare often has less than kind words for family relationships, and this thought recalls his line: 'A little more than kin, and less than kind.'"

NOTE: If the quotation is four or more lines long, set it off by indenting ten spaces from the left margin. See chapter **50** on the research paper for examples and for ways to cite references in your text. See also chapter **45** on capitalizing quotations.

40f Use quotation marks to show dialogue and unspoken thoughts.

> "I'll not look for a job right away," Lola said to several friends over coffee. "First, I will write my novel and pray for success. If that doesn't score, then I'll job hunt.
> "I'm in no hurry," she added.
> "You must be joking," said Wanda. "I bet you don't have one page in manuscript."
> Later, Lola thought to herself, "All I need is a good opening, perhaps 'It was a dark and stormy night.' No," she realized, "readers might not recognize my ironic intent."

Every new speech begins a new paragraph, even when the same speaker continues to talk. If the same speech continues into the next paragraph (see paragraph 2 above), open it also with quotation marks but do not use the closing quotation marks until the end of the entire speech (at the end of paragraph 2). Unspoken thoughts (paragraph 4) also require the marks.

40g Use quotation marks around the titles of short works.

Journal, magazine, and newspaper articles: "The Salt Marsh"
Short stories and essays: "Young Goodman Brown"
Short poems: "Ode on a Grecian Urn"

First line of poem as title: "When, in disgrace with fortune and
    men's eyes"
Titles of sections and chapters of books: "The Years of Revolution"
Songs: "The Star-Spangled Banner"
Lectures and speeches: "The Gettysburg Address"

NOTE: Neither underline (italicize) nor put in quotation marks
              untitled parts of books (preface, chapter 2) or books of the
              Bible (Matthew 2:3).

Do not place in quotation marks or underline the title at the head
of your own paper. If you mention a short paper in the body of your
essay — your own or another writer's — place it within quotation marks:

> An unpublished essay by George Rushton, "Toward Another
> Ice Age," forecasts the cooling of the earth.

See also chapter **42** on using underlining with titles of books, magazines, newspapers, and other works.

40h   Use quotation marks correctly with other punctuation marks.

**Periods and commas always go *inside* both single and
double quotation marks.**

> "Conscience," H. L. Mencken said, "is the inner voice that
> warns us that someone may be looking."

**Semicolons and colons go *outside* the quotation
marks.**

> Lincoln echoed the past and spoke to the future when he talked
> about a government "of the people, by the people, for the peo-
> ple"; we still take these words very seriously.

**Question marks and exclamation points may go
inside if they are part of the actual quotation and
outside if they are not.**

> "Have you arranged your class schedule yet?" Tom asked.
> [Note that there is no comma after the question mark.]

The quotation above forms the question. Compare:

> Who wrote "A thing of beauty is a joy forever"?

In the next sentence, Sabina's remark is the exclamation.

> Sabina fumed, "What outrageous gall!"

Dashes go outside quotation marks if not part of the quotation.

> Thomas Paine said, "Give me liberty or give me death" — no, it was Patrick Henry.

If a line of dialogue ends with a dash, follow the dash with the close punctuation and quotation marks:

> "Who's there?" Horace whispered. "Answer me, or ———."

Use a colon, comma, or no punctuation at all after a word group that introduces a quotation.

The *colon* makes a formal introduction. Use it with a full-sentence introduction or to introduce a long, indented quotation.

> One hundred years ago John Seldon expressed words that apply more than ever: "'Tis not the drinking that is to be blamed, but the excess."

Use the less formal comma with *she said* or *he noted* to introduce or close a quotation.

> On family life, Leo Tolstoy says, "All happy families resemble one another, but each unhappy family is unhappy in its own way."

> "All happy families resemble one another, but each unhappy family is unhappy in its own way," says Leo Tolstoy.

Use no comma at all if the quotation fits smoothly into your sentence.

> Henry Thoreau wants us to "simplify, simplify." He argues that "life is frittered away by detail."

40i When you use words in a special or ironic sense, do not use quotation marks.

If human beings are so "civilized," why do we wage war?

If you're a so-called "writer," what have you published?

Some basketball players like to "hot dog" and "grandstand."

EXERCISE 40.2 Add or delete quotation marks and provide correct punctuation in the following sentences. Some sentences may require single quotation marks. Mark with a *C* any correct sentences.

1. "Never learn to do anything, Mark Twain said. If you don't learn you'll always find someone else to do it for you."
2. "Please read 'chapter 2' and Orwell's essay 'Politics and the English Language'," Professor Landon said as the bell rang.
3. I'm "embarrassed" to confess that my favorite author is Judith Krantz, whose books appear as television romances.
4. Dr. Ringler insisted that "all researchers found that omega-3 contributes to low serum cholesterol."
5. "The question is, 'Can we afford not to continue our exploration of outer space'?" said Senator Bludgins.
6. "What is originality?" asked William R. Inge. Although he answered his own question "—undetected plagiarism—" most people would assume he was being "ironic."
7. "There are only a handful of people that money won't spoil," Josh maintained. "But I'm one of them," I replied.
8. Three people will read from the Gettysburg Address during the Independence Day pageant.
9. What do you think Emerson meant when he said "Money often costs too much?"
10. Marcia had a sudden thought, What if some of the children cannot swim?

Dashes,
Parentheses,
Brackets, and
Ellipses

Stylistically, a dash indicates a sudden break in thought. It signals a stronger break than commas and is more emphatic than parentheses. Many writers tend to overuse the dash, which lessens its effect on the reader. Use it carefully.

Type dashes (alone or in pairs) on the typewriter as two unspaced hyphens with no space on either side:

```
Collectible coins--especially South African
Krugerrands--will increase in value.
```

```
Collectors hope the value of specially minted
coins will increase--or at least not
decrease.
```

41a   Use dashes to set off a summary, restatement, amplification, or explanation.

SUMMARY: The war on drugs — an embargo on supplies and drugs — may increase violence.

RESTATEMENT: The team's goal — to preserve the archaeology site — prevented expansion of the shopping mall, at least for now.

AMPLIFICATION: Manufacturers of dangerous toys are on the defensive from a powerful and sympathetic lobby — they are running from the parents of children injured by their toys.

EXPLANATION: Minorities and special interest groups frequently stage demonstrations to draw attention to their causes — everything from farm prices and better wages to nuclear dumping grounds and sexual liberty.

41b Use dashes for an interruption or an abrupt change of thought.

The stratosphere — or is it the ozone layer? — protects earth from ultraviolet radiation.

The supervisor bristled, "I should suspend you — no, I must dismiss you."

41c Use dashes with a list that contains commas.

Children driving dangerous vehicles — motorcycles, mopeds, and all-terrain vehicles, to name a few — often have serious accidents.

The pair of dashes identifies the appositives that rename *vehicles*.

Farmer, banker, mayor — in all three roles he enflamed the envy of more than one citizen of the small Ohio town.

41d Use parentheses for additional information or digressions.

Use parentheses to enclose supplemental information, such as digressions, afterthoughts, or nonessential remarks. They also have certain conventional uses. Stylistically, parentheses are quietly formal, unlike dashes, which splash boldly across the page. (See also section **37g** for use of commas with parenthetical materials.)

Anthropometrics, the study of human body measurements (not the kind used to judge beauty contests), contributes to comfortable office and furniture design.

The Nile (3,473 miles long) and the Amazon (3,300 miles long) are the longest rivers in the world.

41e Use double parentheses for numbered or lettered lists within sentences.

The information the banker must provide before you sign the contract includes three items: (1) a clearly stated interest rate, (2) the total monthly payment, and (3) the number of payments due.

41f Use parentheses for in-text citations.

Higgenbotham argues for the theory of diminished returns (147).

(See chapters **50** and **51** for discussions of in-text citations.)

41g Use parentheses correctly with other punctuation marks.

Do not precede an opening parenthesis with a comma or other mark of internal punctuation, except for in-text lists (see above).

No one has yet broken Smith's high-jump record, (set at the 1980 Olympic games).

Use appropriate punctuation following a closing parenthesis.

The residents prepared for the hurricane (the first of the season), *but* it swerved out to sea.   [The comma precedes the coordinate conjunction *but*.]

Use parentheses to enclose complete sentences.

Smith's high-jump technique has improved. (Compare his latest heights with his first jumps.)

Writers keep journals (do you keep one?) to record their thoughts and to note momentary inspirations.

NOTE: Only parenthetical sentences that are independent of a main clause (see above) require a capital letter.

Use normal punctuation within parentheses.

The science team kept journals for years (a daily log, a catalogue, a list of expenditures), but nobody can find them.

41h   Use brackets appropriately.

Brackets enable one writer to insert new matter into the quotation of another. Called an *interpolation*, it enables you to break into the words of somebody else with your own comment to clarify an otherwise ambiguous passage. If your keyboard does not have bracket keys, write them in by hand.

Use brackets to identify an unnamed person or title.

One reporter cautioned, "In the heat of a campaign the candidate [George Bush] has little patience with repetitive questions."

Use brackets to explain complex terms.

Joseph Alper explains that "nonlinear dynamics [a new type of mathematics] is built on the assumption that there's often order lurking within apparent disorder if one seeks systematically to find it."

Use brackets to clarify an ambiguous pronoun reference.

The mayor maintained that "allowing this [free bus service] will bankrupt the city."

Convention also allows you to replace the ambiguous word with the bracketed word or phrase.

The mayor maintained that "allowing [free bus service] will bankrupt the city."

The Latin word *sic* within brackets indicates that an error occurred in the original quotation:

The naturalist wrote that "the salmon swum [sic] upstream through the cold, rushing water."

Use *sic* only if an error otherwise could be attributed to you. Avoid declaring an error with *sic* when the matter is one of taste or disagreement, as when someone writes *"He reports on mankind's [sic] progress."* Most writers paraphrase to avoid all use of *sic*.

41i   Use ellipsis appropriately.

Ellipsis notes the omission of words, phrases, sentences, or paragraphs from a direct quotation. It enables you to edit the words of another person. You can concentrate on essential, relevant wording and omit the wording that is irrelevant to your point, *but you must be careful to maintain the integrity and the argument of the quotation*. (For a discussion of quoted material, see chapter **50**.)

To use ellipsis within a quoted sentence, type three equally spaced periods to mark the omission.

ORIGINAL: I like the silent church before the service begins, better than any preaching.   —RALPH WALDO EMERSON

QUOTED: Ralph Waldo Emerson says, "I like the silent church . . . better than any preaching."

To signal the omission of the end of a quoted sentence or the omission of one or more complete sentences, type a period before the three ellipses.

Not overly fond of bombastic preachers, Ralph Waldo Emerson says, "I like the silent church before the service begins. . . ."

In discussing writing, William Zinsser explains, "You learn to write by writing. . . . The only way to learn to write is to force yourself to produce a certain number of words on a regular basis."

In general, do not put ellipsis points at the beginning of a quotation because they serve no purpose. The reader knows from your introduction that you are citing only the relevant portion of a larger work.

EXERCISE 41.1   Use dashes, parentheses, brackets, or ellipsis points to replace less effective or incorrect punctuation. Mark any correct sentences with a *C*.

1. Pollutants from innocent-seeming sources, leaf fires and wood stoves, for example, release harmful cancer-causing substances.
2. Blue jeans, invented by Levi Strauss for gold miners, are the most popular articles of clothing in the world.
3. Many companies now publish their own documents (newsletters to annual reports to complete books) using desktop publishing software.
4. Desktop publishing systems require 1. consistent designs and formats 2. formatting codes, and 3. laser printers.
5. Hamlet's best-known line is probably ". . . To be or not to be, that is the question."
6. Television introduces more new words than any other industry: *sound bite, vee jay* [for "video jockey"], *couch potato*, and *televangelist* are just four recent examples.
7. Computer viruses another new term, by the way successfully attacked the health of major nationwide computer networks.
8. The Wright brothers were not the first ones to successfully fly an airplane a French engineer, Clement Ader, flew one earlier but the Wrights' plane was the first full-sized, motor-powered flying craft.
9. Who said "There are three things I always forget: names, faces . . . and I forget the third"?
10. Student government, a reflection of national government, begins with the same political process, petitions, caucuses, even deal-making.

PART

8

Mechanics

42
Underlining for Italics
43
Abbreviations and Acronyms
44
Numbers
45
Capital Letters
46
Hyphenation
47
Spelling

CHAPTER

42

Underlining for Italics

Italics is a slanting typeface used in printed material to emphasize or identify certain titles and words. Some computer printers can produce italics (see your manual for instructions); otherwise, indicate italics in your writing with one continuous underline:

> In <u>The Old Man and the Sea</u> Hemingway portrays the courageousness of Santiago, an aged Cuban fisherman.

> In Germany an author is called <u>der Schrift-steller</u>, <u>der Stifter</u>, <u>der Schöpfer</u>, <u>der Au-tor</u>, or <u>der Urheber</u>.

> Caught off guard during its Mideast mission, the USS <u>Stark</u> suffered major loss of life.

42a Underline (italicize) titles of major publications and other works.

Ballet: *Swan Lake*
Book: *Energy: Global Prospects*
Bulletin (in book form): *1988 Financial Report*
Cassette tape: *The Seven-Day Diet*
Drama: *Death of a Salesman*
Film: *High Noon*
Journal: *Psychological Abstracts*

Magazine: *Time, The Atlantic*
Newspaper: the Detroit *Free Press*   [but *New York Times*]
Opera: *Aida*
Painting: *American Gothic*
Poem (in book form) *The Faerie Queene*   [Look to the intro-
  ductions and notes to poems that you cite from anthologies
  (e.g., T. S. Eliot's poem, *The Waste Land*, is underlined, but
  his "Gerontion" is not).]
Radio series: *The Prairie Home Companion*
Record album: *The Broadway Album*
Symphony: *Eroica*
Sculpture: *Winged Victory*
Television series: *Family Ties*
Trials: *Marbury* v. *Massachusetts*   [Do not underline *v.* or
  versus.]
Yearbook: *The South Dakotan*
Videocassette tape: *Cartoon Cavalcade*

NOTE: Italicize articles (*a, an, the*) and names of cities only if they
    are part of the title.

Use **quotation marks**, not italics, for titles of shorter works and
unpublished pieces: articles, essays, chapters, sections, short poems,
stories, songs, lectures, sermons, reports, unpublished dissertations,
individual episodes of radio and television programs.

The song "Coal Miner's Daughter" is a country music classic,
just as the "Bakery" episode of *The Lucy Show* is a classic of television comedy.

Do not italicize or enclose within quotation marks these works:

Titles at the top of your own essays.
Titles of sacred writings: Bible, Koran, Old Testament, Gene-
  sis, I Corinthians 16, Mark 2.11
Government documents: Bill of Rights, Article 1 of the Con-
  stitution of the United States
Titles of editions or series: the Variorum Edition of Shake-
  speare's Comedies, third edition of *The Columbia
  Encyclopedia*
Parts of a book: chapter 2, appendix 3, preface, canto 4,
  Form, number, and key of musical works: Symphony No. 3
  in E-flat   [but *Eroica* symphony]

42b   Underline (italicize) the names of specific ships, aircraft, and other vehicles, not the name of the type of vehicle.

Aircraft: *Air Force One*   [*but* a Boeing 747]
Automobiles: the *Blue Flame*   [*but* a Ford Taurus]
Spacecraft: the *Challenger*   [*but* the space shuttle]
Trains: the *Zephyr*   [*but* the Burlington-Northern]
Ships: *Titanic*   [*but* not USS or HMS before a ship's name:
    USS *Enterprise*]

42c   Underline (italicize) words, phrases, letters, and numerals that serve as the subject of discussion.

Check again trial *Y* of the *16-b* test.
Sound the vowel as in the letter *a* of the word *play*.
Let *x* equal 17 and *y* equal 1, and *x* − *y* equal *c*.

But a definition that follows an italicized word is enclosed in quotation marks.

Many people object to the use of *hopefully* to mean "I hope."

42d   Underline (italicize) unusual foreign words used in English sentences.

Many foreign words have become common English: boutique, bourgeois, karate, amigo, gestalt. If you think a foreign term is clear and assimilated, and if you think your particular readers will understand it that way, do not italicize it.

no italics

The ⟨ambience⟩ of the restaurant suited our mood perfectly.

Otherwise, italicize any foreign words that you use.

The *nouveau riche* gradually clustered their mansions in the Watkins subdivision.

As a courtesy, translate any foreign term you think a reader may not understand. Set off the translation by commas, quotation marks, or parentheses.

> In World War II Paris escaped the *verbrannte Erde* (scorched earth) policy of the Nazi regime.

42e   Underline (italicize) names of genuses and species.

> Both the cashew and poison ivy are members of the *Anacardiaceae* family.

> Although bobcats and lynx are sometimes called cougars, scientists recognize only *Felis concolor* as the true cougar.

42f   Underline (italicize) for emphasis sparingly and only for good reason.

Italicizing calls attention to words and phrases, but it is often a lazy writer's technique and generally overused:

no italics

> The tone of Poe's "The Raven" suggests the narrator's *madness.*

In some cases italicizing a key word might be necessary to provide clear emphasis.

> The fundamental reasons for certain rules of the game often differ from the *application* of the rules during the heat of a game.

Generally, however, placing the key word at the beginning or end of the sentence will provide sufficient emphasis:

> A referee's application of a rule during the heat of a game may differ from original reasons for applying the rule.

EXERCISE 42.1   Edit the following sentences to correct any errors in the use of italics. Mark any correct sentences with a *C*.

1. When the band played *America*, the crowd stood and cheered.
2. Many Europeans write a 1 like a 7.

3. The class is required to read Hawthorne's novel *The Scarlet Letter* and Poe's poem *The Raven*.
4. The word "euthanasia," from the Greek, means "easy death."
5. The entire class rode the Santa Fe Chief from Emporia to Chicago.
6. When the space shuttle *Challenger* blew up, America sobered up from its euphoric high with earlier successful flights.
7. Professor Boswick read from George Bernard Shaw's preface to *The Apple Cart*.
8. Marya Mannes's essay "Park Avenue" appeared originally in her book "The New York I Know," but I read it in my textbook "Essays for Exposition."
9. The *TU Historical Society* discussed at length President Bush's nuclear arms policy.
10. The instructor *insisted* that I practice pronouncing "haben" and "heben" until I said them correctly.

43

Abbreviations
and Acronyms

Abbreviations are shortened forms of a word or words: *no., tsp., mpg, Ms., Esq.* The dictionary provides a list of standard abbreviations. **Acronyms**, formed from the initial letters of a group of words, create pronounceable words: *AIDS (Acquired Immune Deficiency Syndrome)* or *NASA (National Aeronautical and Space Administration).* In general, avoid abbreviations in your text, but use them in documentation and within parenthetical asides (see section **45g**).

43a Abbreviate titles before and after full proper names.

First use	*Thereafter use*
Sen. Albert Gore	Gore or Senator Gore [not *Sen.* Gore]
Prof. Sharon Miller	Miller or Professor Miller [not *Prof.* Miller]
Ralph M. Harper, MD	Doctor Harper
Roland W. Cunningham III	Cunningham
Ms. Nancy B. Matthews	Matthews [But use first and last names if two persons in the essay have the same last name.]

In academic writing, use a person's full name without *Mr., Ms., Mrs., Miss* at first mention:

Emily Dickinson   John Huston   William Shakespeare

Thereafter use the last name only: *Dickinson, Huston, Shakespeare.*
When you refer to persons by their initials only, use no periods:

Although he was assassinated more than 25 years ago, the legendary appeal of JFK (John Fitzgerald Kennedy) continues as strong as ever.

Usage varies, but MLA style prefers to abbreviate and delete the periods in academic degrees: *BA, MA, BS, JD, LLD, MEd, MS, PhD.*

Lorenzo Martinez earned his MD in 1985.

The university has named Sarah Johnson, MBA, University of Texas, to head its Business Communications Department.

43b Use acronyms and abbreviations for organizations and corporations as well as for geographic and technical terminology.

ORGANIZATIONS: NASA, NAACP, FBI, CIA, NEA, MLA, APA

COMPANIES: NBC, AT&T, IBM, ESPN

GEOGRAPHIC NAMES: USA or U.S.A., USSR or U.S.S.R., NY, AK, MI

Technical writing in particular frequently uses acronyms: DOS, LOCA, EEG, CAI, RFQ. No one will fault you for defining any technical acronym or abbreviation at its first use.

The Tennessee Valley Authority (TVA), like other electric utilities, adopted an ill-fated nuclear power program. TVA initiated nine such power plants in the 1970s.

43c   Abbreviate dates and numbers in your text.

Use abbreviations such as *a.m.* and *p.m., BC, AD, $,* and *no.* only with specific times, dates, or figures:

7:30 a.m. $7,659   no. 987

Flight no. 987 departs at 7:30 a.m., and the ticket price is $312.

NOTE: *BC* means "before Christ" and follows the number (*300 BC*); *AD* means "in the year of our Lord" and precedes the number (*AD 23*).

43d   Use abbreviations in parenthetical matter, addresses, and documentation.

In the words of Shakespeare, "What's done cannot be undone" (*Mac.* 5.1.74).

The following lists provide some examples of textual spelling and the use of abbreviations for parenthetical material and for documentation.

Text	*Abbreviation*
Charles J. Ardmore	C. J. Ardmore
Stevens and Son, Incorporated	Stevens and Son, Inc.
Harcourt Brace Jovanovich	Harcourt
Monday	Mon.
November	Nov.
California	CA
Germany, United States	Ger., US or U.S.
Avandale Boulevard	Avandale Blvd.
Independence Day	4 July 1989
English, history	Eng., hist.
chapter	ch. or chap.
section	sec.
page, pages	p., pp.
pint, pound, quart	pt., lb., qt.

EXERCISE 43.1 Edit the following sentences to correct errors in abbreviations. Mark any correct sentences with a *C*.

1. My new International Business Machines computer has improved my typing ability.
2. On Fri. the course in poli. sci. will meet in rm. no. 562.
3. Rev. Wm. Thompson and Mrs. Jennifer Smith are listed on the program, but Mrs. Smith is ill and Dr. Sam Johnson, PhD, will replace her.
4. The Dr. worked secretly for the CIA.
5. When NASA challenged the USSR for a role in the space race, Americans responded with special pride in USA astronauts.
6. The Columbia Broadcasting System has an annual battle for ratings with ABC and NBC, but now cable networks, such as CNN and ESPN, have entered the arena to fight for a share of the viewers.
7. The meeting adjourned at seven in the evening after the committee had allocated sixteen thousand dollars to the project.
8. The future of Christianity in the year BC 115 was indeed imperiled, for it was threatened by crushing blows of the Roman Empire.
9. Some books of the New Testament, e.g., Matthew, Luke, John, etc., disagree on minor details but express harmony on all major points in the life of Christ and his teachings.
10. The biography of Sen. Thompson is clouded by periods of obscurity about his life.

44a Spell out numbers that you can write in one or two words; use figures for other numbers.

Spell out numbers when they are used infrequently and when they can be written in one or two words: *thirteen, thirteen thousand*. When numbers appear frequently, such as in technical writing, spell out numbers one to ten and use numerals for the rest.

Seven hundred people preregistered.
The judge was surprised when 784 supporters honored him.
The committee must examine five hundred applications.

If the largest in a category of numbers is greater than ten, use figures for all:

We used 10 of the 52 subjects.

Although we made reservations for 300 guests, we registered only 215 swimmers and 9 coaches.

When one number immediately follows another, spell out the smaller number and use figures for the other:

The developer plans to build three 100-story buildings.   [or *100 three-story buildings*]
The loan on this automobile calls for twenty-four $255.05 payments.   [or *250 forty-dollar payments* or *250 payments of $41.95*]

Write out all numbers at the beginning of a sentence or recast the sentence.

> Three hundred and sixty-five people surprised us with generous donations to the fund.

> We were surprised that 365 people made generous donations to the fund.

44b Use figures in your text for specific places and exact figures.

1. *Addresses:* Mail it to 542 2nd Ave. N.W., Topeka, KS 66601.
2. *Average ages:* The subjects averaged 17.5 years of age.
3. *Exact dates:* The trial begins January 6, 1988.
   Even in AD 540 Christianity struggled to gain recognition.
4. *Decimals, percentages, and fractions:* The average weight is 3.5468.
   The control group scored 23.5 percent.
   The technician administered a 5-mg dose every two hours.
5. *Divisions of books:* Dramatic tension increases in act 2, scene 3.
   You will find the answer in volume 3, chapter 6, pages 231–42.
6. *Identification numbers:* My receipt numbered 5469000021 is enclosed.
   We traveled by Interstate 75 and state highway 41A.
7. *Exact amounts of money:* You owe parking fines of $43.65.
   His net worth is $5.2 billion.
8. *Statistics:* We recorded ACT scores of 11 to 27.
   Scores in the 11–27 range appeared frequently.
   Because of the storm, the game ended in a 7–7 tie.
   Seven 2-year-olds scored 6 on a 10-point scale.
9. *Time of day:* The sunrise will occur at 6:05 a.m.

NOTE: Use Arabic numbers regularly. Use Roman numbers only for titles of persons (Queen Elizabeth II), sections of an outline (I, II, III), prefatory pages (ii, iii, iv), or established terminology (Type II virus).

EXERCISE 44.1   Correct the following phrases to use appropriate figures.

1. in Table twelve
2. three o'clock in the morning
3. on the twelfth of November
4. on the fifteenth of May, 1988
5. a sum of two million dollars
6. in chapter six
7. a sum of thirty-four cents
8. three cows, six oxen, fourteen horses, and 329 sheep
9. about 400 years before the birth of Christ
10. three out of five people

EXERCISE 44.2   Edit the following sentences to correct any errors in the use of numbers.

1. Post the bulletin in a conspicuous place by January first, 1990.
2. His address is Twelve hundred Western Avenue.
3. The subjects have an average age of twenty-four and one-quarter years.
4. Johnny Westwood posted a three-hundred batting average.
5. Use interstate forty on your trip to Little Rock.
6. I searched volume six of *Encyclopaedia Brittanica*.
7. We noted scores of seven to six and nine to 16.
8. For Wednesday read *Hamlet*, act three, scene two.
9. Seven hundred and forty-five angry fans stormed the ticket office.
10. I will meet you at the airport at 9:20 a.m. on Tuesday, May six.
11. The subjects endured five, seven, and 10-minute trials.
12. The incorrect numbers were six, seventeen, twenty-eight, and ninety-one.

Capital Letters

45a   Capitalize words that begin sentences.

Necessity never made a good bargain.   —BENJAMIN FRANKLIN
Man is the only animal that blushes. Or needs to.
                                              —MARK TWAIN

Usage varies about capitalization of an independent clause after a colon. In general, capitalize the clause only if it is a quotation or a question.

> The committee finally reached a consensus: no further allocation of funds will be forthcoming.

> The committee finally reached a consensus: "No further allocation of funds will be forthcoming," the report said.   [quotation]

> The committee finally reached a consensus: Why should they allocate more funds to a wasteful cause?   [question]

Capitalize clauses within parentheses if they are not within another sentence.

> The candidate for president leaves today after a luncheon meeting with the council. (He has been here three days.)   [separate sentence]

> The candidate for president leaves today (he has been here three days) after a luncheon meeting with the council.   [clause within the sentence]

45b   Capitalize the first word of a direct quotation if it begins a complete sentence or is an exclamation.

Churchill said, "*N*ever have so many owed so much to so few."
Tom pointed and exclaimed, "*A* shooting star!"
Looking quickly, Laura murmured, "*W*ow."

If you interrupt a quoted sentence, do not capitalize the first word after your interruption.

"He is a self-made man," the cynic said, "and he worships his creator."

EXCEPTION: Because they are an integral part of the sentence, quotations introduced by *that, because, when,* and similar words do not require a capital even if they carried a capital in the original.

It was Churchill who said that "never have so many owed so much to so few."

45c   Capitalize poetry exactly as it appears in the original.

He likes a Boggy Acre
A Floor too cool for Corn —
Yet when a Boy, and Barefoot —
I more than once at Noon

— EMILY DICKINSON,
"A Narrow Fellow in the Grass" (9–12)

45d   Capitalize proper nouns and words derived from them.

In general, capitalize all proper nouns — the names of specific people, places, and things — and words that are derived from them. Do not capitalize common nouns. (See section **20a**.)

Proper nouns	Derivations of Proper nouns	Common nouns
President Reagan	Reaganomics	an economic plan
Democratic party	a Democrat	democracy
Apollo	Apollonian	a mythic god
Yale University	Yalies	students

Capitalize the names and nicknames of specific persons and the words of family members used as names.

When James, Butch, and *F*ather arrive, tell *G*randmother to light the candles.   [But: *The children and their father arrived late.*]

Capitalize titles preceding names.

*P*rincipal Ted Jones and *S*uperintendent Robert Boggs lectured all the county principals and assistant principals.   [But: *Ted Jones, principal of Valley High School, led the orientation program.*]

Capitalize articles or prepositions that are part of surnames only when they begin a sentence. If in doubt about proper spelling, check a standard biographical dictionary.

*D*e Gaulle's triumphant return to France hailed the beginning of a new era.   [But: *The people celebrated de Gaulle's triumph.*]

Capitalize personifications, which are the names of objects, animals, or ideas that you give human identity to.

I watched as Creeping Boredom smothered the audience.

Capitalize the names of countries, districts, regions, states, counties, cities, lakes, rivers, and so on.

Madison Avenue	the High Plains	the Midwest (US)
Brooklyn Bridge	the South (US)	Antarctica
Columbus, Ohio	Benton County	Gulf Coast
Flint Hills	Mississippi Delta	Lake Erie

The ocean-front condominiums along the *G*old *C*oast inflate in value every year.

The economy of the *S*outhwest rises and falls on the tide of oil prices.

The *A*llegheny *R*iver joins the *M*onongahela *R*iver to form the *O*hio *R*iver at *P*ittsburgh.   [But: *The Allegheny and Monongahela rivers join there.*]

But lowercase compass directions: *He drove south on Highway 101.*

Capitalize the names of nations, nationalities, races, tribes, languages, and persons identified by geographic locations.

European	Middle East rebels	Iranians
Shiite Moslems	Sunshine State	Floridians
Indians	Americanize	Latin

We need tutors for three *R*ussian language students.

In the *M*iddle *E*ast conflict, the *I*ranians play one *M*oslem sect against another.

Capitalize names of religions and their members, their deities, and sacred books.

Christianity	Methodist	Genesis
the Koran	a Moslem	Islam
Jehovah	Allah	the Bible

In the book of *G*enesis, *G*od warns Adam and Eve not to eat from the tree of knowledge of good and evil.

For clear reference, capitalize pronouns that refer to a deity.

The Lord advised Peter of *H*is higher mission.

But lowercase the word *god* used generically:

The ancient Greeks created anthropomorphic gods.

Capitalize the names of specific organizations, institutions, trademarks, departments, academic degrees, specific academic courses, documents, political parties, and fraternal clubs as well as historic periods, events, and movements.

President Bush invited the *Chi Omega* sorority at *Ohio State University* to a reception at the *White House*.

Students need both a *Polaroid* and a 35-millimeter camera for *Photography 2020*.

Capitalize the months, days of the week, and holidays but not the seasons.

The family gatherings were rituals for spring and summer, featuring an *Easter Sunday* dinner and a three-day weekend picnic for *Independence Day*.

45e Capitalize titles of books, articles, and works of art.

Capitalize the first and last word of a work's title and subtitle and all words in between *except* articles, coordinate conjunctions, prepositions, and the *to* of infinitives.

Gardening in the Tropics
"Between Pets and People: The Importance of Animal
   Companionship"
When a Stranger Calls
"A Lesson to Live By"
"An Obsession to Win"
"To Know Him Is to Love Him"

When the first line of a poem serves as the title or part of the title, reproduce the line exactly as it appears in the original:

"The Theme of Love in cummings's 'anyone lived in a pretty how town'"

Capitalize both parts of a compound word in a title.

"Grammar in an English-Speaking World"

But in the text, use "an English-speaking world."

45f   Capitalize the pronoun *I* and the interjection *O*.

Hamlet cries out, "*O* my prophetic soul! My uncle!"   [But: *The entire team seemed, oh, so weary.*]

45g   Capitalize abbreviations and acronyms formed from proper nouns.

MIT   CBS   NATO   Hond.   Cong.   Gov.

As a general rule, do not capitalize abbreviations of common words and most measurements: *bull., comp., geog., mm, tsp.* Consult a dictionary for correct usage. (See also chapter **43**.)

45h   Capitalize the names of genuses (but not species), geological periods, stars, and planets.

Tulipa
Liriodendron tulipifera
late *P*leistocene era
*S*irius, *R*igel, *U*ranus

EXERCISE 45.1   Edit the following sentences so that capitalization follows conventional rules. Mark any sentences that are correct with a *C*.

1. H. L. Mencken defined Politician as "Any citizen with influence enough to get his Mother a job as Charwoman in the City Hall."

2. To get a master of science degree in Scientific And Technical Communication at the University Of Washington, you have to take theoretical dimensions of technical communication, document design 510, and human/machine communication 515.

3. The Drama Critics praised *Going to Grand Rapids: a Musical Comedy* (Have you seen it?), even though one called the acting "hamming to the hilt."

4. Former President Jimmy Carter reached a Historic Accord at the Presidential Hideaway, Camp David, with Egyptian president Anwar Sadat and Israeli prime minister Menachem Begin.

5. Driving across the country from East to West we crossed the Appalachian and Rocky Mountains, the magnificent Mississippi and Missouri Rivers, the great plains, and even the desert at Death Valley.

6. Most states have nicknames (do you know the nickname for yours?); for example, Illinois is the Land of Lincoln, New Mexico is the Land of Enchantment, and Montana is the Big Sky country.

7. Ancient Gods gave us the names of some of the days of the Week: Tuesday is from Tiu, a germanic war God; Wednesday is from Woden, or Odin, the Supreme God and Creator in Norse mythology; Thursday is from Thor, God of Weather (The word *Thunder* is also from Thor); Friday, from Frigga, Odin's wife and the Goddess of Married Love; and Saturday is from Saturn for a day of feasting and revelry. Sunday, however, is not named after a mythic God and comes instead from *sunnan daeg*, "the day of the sun," and thus the first Day of the Week.

8. The Boss asked me to xerox this contract after I had printed copies from the ibm computer.

9. My paper in Modern Literature is "A Comparison of People as Automatons in Orwell's *1984* and Atwood's *the Handmaid's Tale*: What is Woman's Role?"

10. In Chapter 3, table 7 is a Comparison of Annual Revenue Requirements, listing the results from the formulas proved in appendix C.

Hyphenation

Hyphens join two or more words that have a single function to make the meaning clear for the reader. They may join multiple adjectives preceding a noun (*small-business office*; compare *the small business office*, which refers to the size, not the function, of the office), or they may combine words to create a new noun, adjective, or verb (a *forget-me-not; the drive-up window; I double-parked the car*). If you have a question about hyphenation, check a recent dictionary for common usage.

46a   Form compound words effectively.

Several guidelines will help you use hyphenated words effectively.

Hyphenate two or more words functioning as one adjective in front of a noun (but not if the words follow the noun).

> Now that is a well-placed punt.   [But: *a punt well placed*]
> She is a well-known television reporter.   [But: *She is a reporter well known on television.*]

EXCEPTION: Do not hyphenate the compound adjective if one part is an adverb ending in *-ly* (*a poorly pitched game* or *a frequently missed question*).

Show with hyphens that each adjective in a series modifies a noun.

> The encyclopedia comes in two-, three-, and four-volume sets.
> The subjects were four- and five-year-old females.

Form compound nouns with hyphens.

> She exemplifies the meaning of scholar-athlete.
> As actor-playwright, his attention was divided.

Hyphenate written fractions and compound numbers.

> The drum major is thirty-five years old.
> Two hundred thirty-eight dollars, which is one-fifth of my paycheck, went to pay the taxes.

Use the hyphen to create sound effects and unusual compound words.

> Ba-ram-ba-ram-ba-ram-ba-ram—"Yeah, Brudda! Give us your paycheck!
> —TOM WOLFE, *The Electric Kool Aid Acid Test*

> He prepared an I-don't-want-to-learn-how-to-cook cookbook for people who want special effects with frozen pizza or Hamburger Helper. Most of the recipes require only a minute to transform "how-awful-this-looks" to "not-bad-at-all."
> —MELANIE THOMPSON-SMITH, student

46b Use hyphens with prefixes and suffixes only in special cases.

Most words with prefixes and suffixes require no hyphen: *coed*ucation, *pre*fabricate, *post*test, *non*numerical, *multi*talented, *re*cast, or *un*defined. However, use a hyphen in the following instances:

Hyphenate prefixes and suffixes that appear with proper nouns, numbers, abbreviations, or a single capital letter.

> She suffers from post-Christmas blues.

The pre-1988 figures offer misleading statistics.

The X-rays are inconclusive.

Hyphenate all words with the prefixes *ex-*, *self-*, and *all-*.

Your ex-husband has enrolled in a self-help weight program.

Hyphenate all words with the suffix *-elect*.

The mayor-elect needs more contributions to pay campaign debts.

Hyphenate words that might be misunderstood.

Please re-pair the boots on this shelf.   [to pair again]

We need to re-cover the swivel chair.   [to cover again]

Hyphenate words that might be misread.

The diagnostic text included three word-exercises.   [compare *three-word exercises*]

46c   Follow conventions for end-of-line hyphenation.

Style guides for research papers now discourage breaking words at the end of lines, even to the point of leaving one line extremely short. One reason, of course, is to make the manuscript easy to read, edit, and typeset. Another reason is to avoid errors in hyphens and compounds.

However, if you must hyphenate at the end of a line, do so carefully. Follow the general guidelines for hyphenation given below, but always use a dictionary to check hyphenation of compound words.

Hyphenate between syllables only.

Do not hyphenate one-syllable words.

stu-dents   Amer-i-can   illus-tra-tion   doc-u-men-ta-tion

NOTE: In general, hyphenate between consonants or after a long or strongly pronounced vowel, as in *American*, above. If in doubt, check a dictionary.

Break compound words between full words only.

over-bearing   book-keeper   cross-breeding

EXERCISE 46.1 Underline the correct form for the words in parentheses. Use your dictionary as necessary.

1. The (heavily traveled, heavily-traveled) road is scheduled for resurfacing in July.
2. Many sections of the road have eroded into deep (potholes, pot-holes).
3. The road is a (rarely-used, rarely used) (bypass, by-pass).
4. The county cannot decide between making it a (two-, two) or four-lane highway.
5. Most (long distance, long-distance) truckers drive (1,500 mile, 1,500-mile) shifts.

EXERCISE 46.2 Edit the following sentences to correct errors in hyphenation. Mark any correct sentences with a *C*.

1. This end of the world novel is about an exgeneral of a small country.
2. She placed us in three-, four-, and five-student groups.
3. Each group practiced twenty five minutes every day on penmanship.
4. If one half of the groups scored well, she rewarded the entire class with chocolate chip cookies.
5. At the end of the year picnic, she gave me a T shirt for my performance as most improved student in penmanship.
6. As her exstudent, I nominated her for principal at a recent board meeting.
7. She was selected and now serves as principal elect.
8. With her co-operation, the schoolwork should improve rapidly at Wilson Elementary.
9. Some educational basics, such as penmanship and good writing, have been under-valued.
10. Her pre-tests and post-tests for students will quickly identify the academically-inclined students.

Correct spelling brings little praise, but misspelling only one word raises the reader's concern that the writer may not have been careful with other aspects of the paper as well.

To avoid misspellings in your work, keep a dictionary handy and use it often. Use an authoritative reference, such as *Webster's Ninth New Collegiate Dictionary* or the *American Heritage Dictionary*. The first spelling listed is the more common or the preferred usage: *among*, not *amongst*; and *ampoule*, not *ampule*. Also, use American spellings: *theater*, not *theatre*; *aging*, not *ageing*. Check spelling of plurals, especially words derived from foreign languages. For example, *thesauri* is giving way to *thesauruses*, and *formulae* has succumbed to *formulas*. See section **17a** on using the dictionary.

If you are writing on a word processor, use its spell checker function or software. However, be aware of the spell checker's limitations. It cannot correct improper usage of correctly spelled words (*except* for *accept* or *altar* for *alter*), and it does not contain a complete inventory of words.

47a Write word lists and practice speaking troublesome words.

With practice comes skill and confidence. Like a tennis player who practices a particular weakness, you must identify troublesome words and practice writing them and pronouncing them correctly. A personal spelling list should change constantly as you cross out words you have learned to spell and add new, difficult ones. Use the list of commonly misspelled words in section **47g** as your beginning list.

Pronouncing words correctly can contribute to correct spelling. Do not add syllables (umb-e-rella or ath-e-lete) or delete syllables (libary, probly, sophmore). However, pronunciation offers little help with some words; *site, cite,* and *sight* are all pronounced the same. In contrast, a written list gives you visual support. On this point consult the list of homophones in section **47c**.

47b   Proofread for spelling errors.

Anybody who has a history of poor spelling (and you know whether you do or not) should reserve time at the end of every writing assignment to proofread the paper for spelling errors. Do not proof it for everything at once; go through it one time, word by word, to check spelling. If you hesitate on any word, look it up, correct it, and then add it to your list of troublesome words.

Look especially for errors of homophones (see section **47c**), such as *they're* and *their, principal* and *principle.* Check pronouns; even the best spellers slip and use *it's* for *its* and *who's* for *whose.*

Check also words containing *ei* or *ie* and *-ant* or *-ent* (see section **47e**). Some words ending in *-ing,* such as *containing* or *beginning,* are easily misspelled as *containg* or *beging.*

Call upon mnemonics that you might have learned during grammar school to remind yourself of troublesome spellings:

don't choose booze	loose as a goose
sporty at forty	it's truly July
there's *a rat* in sep*arat*e	there are *lice* in *lice*nse
I have a *nice niece*	

If you write with a word processor, use the search or find and replace feature to track troublesome words. For example, if you have a history of misspellings—*alot* for *a lot* or *seperate* for *separate*—search for the words and correct the text accordingly.

47c   Distinguish between words that sound alike, and spell them correctly.

Pronunciation will not always serve your spelling needs, especially with pairs of words that sound alike —*passed, past; hole, whole.* Several troublesome areas are identified below.

Possessive pronouns and contractions

Pronouns do not have an apostrophe and *s*, but contractions do.

It's time to give the team *its* due credit.
You're required to buy *your* own uniforms.
There's a mistake in these uniforms: *theirs* are mixed with ours.

See also section **20b**.

Two-word phrases and single words

If you *allot* shares to *a lot* of people, nobody will have a dispro-portionate share.
Nobody noticed that the coffin contained *no body.*
Turn *in to* the right for the kitchen, reach *into* the cookie jar, and help yourself to a treat.
What you say *may be* true, but *maybe* I refused to accept it.
Everyday events, in truth, seldom occur *every day.*

Singular nouns that end in *-nce* and plural nouns that end in *-nts*

My two technical *assistants* will need *assistance* with this new case load.
For *instance*, one overworked assistant just *instants* ago failed to save some valuable programming.
The second assistant lost *patience* with three different *patients* during one shift.

Homophones

The list below shows pairs of words that sound alike but have dif-ferent meanings, different uses, and, especially, *different spellings.*

Some Common Homophones
accept (*verb*: to receive)
except (*preposition*: exclude or take out)

Some Common Homophones (cont.)

affect (*verb*: to influence)
effect (*noun*: result)

aisle (*noun*: a passage between seats)
isle (*noun*: an island)

allude (*verb*: to refer to something)
elude (*verb*: to escape)

all ready (*adverb* and *adjective*: completely prepared)
already (*adverb*: previously)

all together (*noun* and *adverb*: in one group and in agreement)
altogether (*adverb*: entirely)

ascent (*noun*: act of rising)
assent (*verb*: to agree)

bare (*adjective*: naked)
bear (*noun*: animal; *verb*: to carry)

berth (*noun*: place to anchor ship)
birth (*noun*: emergence of newborn)

born (*adjective*: brought forth as in a birth)
borne (*past tense verb*: to carry or endure)

brake (*noun*: device for stopping movement)
break (*verb*: to separate into parts)

capital (*adjective*: first in importance; *noun*: accumulated
    goods)
capitol (*noun*: building in which government meets)

censor (*verb*: to examine in order to suppress)
censure (*verb*: to condemn)

cite (*verb*: to quote)
sight (*noun*: a spectacle; *verb*: to see)
site (*noun*: a place or piece of ground)

coarse (*adjective*: of ordinary or inferior quality or appearance)
course (*noun*: path, a procedure, meal, curriculum of study)

complement (*noun*: something that completes or makes
    whole)
compliment (*noun*: praise)

Some Common Homophones (cont.)

council (*noun*: committee or advisory group)
counsel (*noun*: advice, the giver of advice; *verb*: to advise)

discreet (*adjective*: tactful and judicious)
discrete (*adjective*: distinct and separate)

die (*verb*: to stop living)
dye (*verb*: to fix coloring into fibers)

elicit (*verb*: to draw forth or bring out)
illicit (*adjective*: unlawful)

eminent (*adjective*: famous, standing above all others)
immanent (*adjective*: indwelling, existing only in the mind)
imminent (*adjective*: ready to take place)

fair (*noun*: exhibition; *adverb*: justly and completely)
fare (*noun*: money for travel; *verb*: succeed)

formally (*adverb*: in a conventional manner)
formerly (*adverb*: at an earlier time)

forth (*adverb*: forward)
fourth (*noun*: a number)

gorilla (*noun*: animal)
guerrilla (*noun*: independent soldier)

hear (*verb*: to perceive by the ear)
here (*noun*: this place; *adverb*: at this place)

heard (*past tense verb*: perceived by the ear)
herd (*noun*: group of animals; *verb*: to gather animals)

hole (*noun*: an opening into or through a thing)
whole (*adjective*: sound condition; *noun*: complete amount)

holy (*adjective*: sacred)
wholly (*adverb*: completely, totally)

its (*possessive pronoun*: of or relating to *it*)
it's (*contraction*: it is)

lead (*noun*: metal)
led (*past tense verb*: guided)

lessen (*verb*: to decrease)
lesson (*noun*: a reading or exercise of instruction)

Some Common Homophones *(cont.)*

loose (*adjective*: not fastened)
lose (*verb*: to misplace or be defeated)

manner (*noun*: habit, custom, style)
manor (*noun*: large landed estate)

maybe (*adverb*: perhaps)
may be (*verb*: to express purpose, contingency, or concession)

miner (*noun*: one who works in a mine)
minor (*noun*: one who is underage; *adjective*: inferior)

pair (*noun*: a set of two)
pare (*verb*: to cut or shave outside edges)
pear (*noun*: fruit)

passed (*past tense verb*: moved, proceeded, departed)
past (*noun*: a former time; *adjective*: elapsed; *preposition*: after)

patience (*noun*: the capacity to endure pain without
    complaint)
patients (*noun*: persons under medical care)

plain (*adjective*: lacking adornment; *noun*: level expanse of
    land)
plane (*verb*: to make smooth; *adjective*: flat and level; *noun*:
    airplane)

principal (*adjective*: chief or main; *noun*: leader)
principle (*noun*: rule, fundamental concept, basic truth)

rain (*noun*: water falling in drops; *verb*: to fall like rain)
reign (*noun*: authority of a sovereign; *verb*: to rule)
rein (*noun*: strap used for control; *verb*: to control)

raise (*verb*: to lift)
raze (*verb*: to destroy to the ground)

right (*adjective*: correct; *noun*: a just claim; *adverb*: exactly;
    verb: to vindicate)
rite (*noun*: a ceremony)
wright (*noun*: craftsman, usually in combination "playwright")
write (*verb*: to form letters)

scents (*plural noun*: fragrances)
sense (*noun*: awareness, consciousness; *verb*: to perceive)
since (*conjunction*: from past to present)

Some Common Homophones (cont.)

stationary (*adjective*: immobile and unchanging)
stationery (*noun*: material for writing or typing)

straight (*adjective*: free of curves, candid, virtuous, unmixed)
strait (*noun*: narrow passageway)

their (*adjective*: relating to *them* as possessors)
there (*adverb*: in or at that place)
they're (*contraction*: they are)

to (*preposition*: in the direction of)
too (*adverb*: also, besides, excessively)
two (*adjective* and *noun*: something that has two units)

who's (*contraction*: who is)
whose (*possessive adjective* and *pronoun*: possessor or agent)

your (*adjective*: possessor or agent)
you're (*contraction*: you are)

47d Understand and apply the rules for adding prefixes and suffixes to a root word.

Prefixes attach to the root without doubling or dropping letters.

*dis*agree	*dis*satisfied	*dis*union	*dis*appear
*un*usual	*un*appealing	*un*noticed	*un*seen
*mis*quoted	*mis*applied	*mis*spent	*mis*play
*re*play	*re*-establish	*re*-elect	*re*apply

Drop the final unpronounced *e* before suffixes beginning with vowels, but retain the *e* before suffixes beginning with consonants.

Root	*Suffix begins with vowel*	*Suffix begins with consonant*
age	ag*ing*	age*less*
care	car*ing*	care*ful*
desire	desir*ing*	desire*less*
improve	improv*able*	improve*ment*
manage	manag*ing*	manage*ment*

There are exceptions, such as *noticeable, changeable, mileage, argument, courageous, truly, ninth.*

Double the final consonant before a suffix beginning with a vowel if the final consonant is preceded by a single vowel and if it ends a one-syllable word or a stressed syllable.

One-syllable words		*Stressed syllables*	
bet	bet*ting*	abhor	abhor*rent*
drag	drag*ged*	begin	begin*ning*
shop	shop*pers*	commit	commit*ted*
tag	tag*ged*	occur	occur*rence*
sit	sit*ting*	prefer	prefer*red*
pen	pen*ning*	regret	regret*table*

Do not double the final consonant of most words (consult your dictionary as necessary).

adjust	adjust*ment*	appear	appear*ance*
acquire	acquir*ing*	creep	creep*ing*
sleep	sleep*ing*	ooze	ooz*ing*
stand	stand*ing*	board	board*ing*
truthful	truthful*ness*		
commit	commit*ment*	(*but* commit*ted*)	
wet	wet*ly*	(*but* wet*ting* and wet*table*)	

Change *y* to *i* before adding a suffix when the *y* is preceded by a consonant.

study	stud*ies*	stud*ied*
apply	appl*ies*	appl*ied*
comedy	comed*ies*	comed*ian*
dry	dr*ied*	

Do not change *y* to *i* when *y* is preceded by a vowel:

play	play*ed*	play*er*	play*ing*
pay	pay*s*		
attorney	attorney*s*		

Do not change *y* to *i* when adding *ing*:

dry	dry*ing*	study	study*ing*

Do not change *y* to *i* with any proper name ending in *y*:

the Murphy family the Murphy*s*

When adding *-ly*, do not drop a final *l* from a root word.

real real*ly* formal formal*ly*
cool cool*ly* usual usual*ly*

47e Use *ei* and *ie* correctly.

The old rhyme about *i* before *e* and its exceptions still works well:

I before *e*
Except after *c*,
Or when sounded like *a*
As in *neighbor* and *weigh*.

Words with *ie*: *chief, grief, pierce, field, niece, relieve, yield.*
Words with *ei* after *c*: *ceiling, conceit, deceive, perceive.*
Words with *ei*: *sleigh, freight, height, neighbor, stein, weigh.*

But memorize these important exceptions:

seize weird either sheik protein science financier
height foreign leisure

47f Spell plurals correctly.

Add *-s* to form the plural of most singular nouns.

three girl*s* several teacher*s* cat*s* six page*s*
three brother*s*-in-law the Thompson*s* six 10*s* the 1980*s*

For words ending in *o*, add *-s* when a vowel precedes the *o*, but add *-es* when a consonant precedes the *o*.

video*s* radio*s* Oreo*s*
tomato*es* hero*es* echo*es* potato*es* veto*es*

EXCEPTIONS: shortened words (*memos* [memorandums], *autos* [automobiles], *pros* [professionals]) and plural words that use either spelling (*zeros* and *zeroes*, *mottos* and *mottoes*, and *nos* and *noes*)

Add *-es* to form the plural of nouns ending in *s*, *ch*, *sh*, or *x*.

three losses in a row	two missing mailboxes
the Rosses moved today	three flight approaches
the window sashes	a choice of three waxes

For singular nouns ending in *y* preceded by a consonant, change the *y* to *i* and add *-es*.

strawberry	strawberries
sixty	sixties
company	companies
industry	industries

For some singular nouns ending in *f* or *fe*, change the ending to *-ves*.

thief, thieves   life, lives   leaf, leaves   shelf, shelves

Some nouns form plurals irregularly.

Do not use *-s* or *-es* with these nouns.

woman, women   goose, geese   child, children

Some foreign words retain their plural spelling.

Do not add *-s* or *-es* to these words.

medium, media   criterion, criteria
phenomenon, phenomena

47g Improve your spelling skills by focusing on your troublesome words.

Select from the following list to begin your personal list of troublesome spelling words.

absence	biscuit	disappearance
accidentally	boundaries	disappoint
accommodate	Britain	disastrous
accumulate	bureau	discipline
achievement	business	dissatisfied
acknowledge	calendar	economical
acquaintance	candidate	eighth
acquitted	category	eligible
advice	cemetery	eliminate
advise	changeable	embarrass
aggravate	changing	eminent
all right	choose	encouraging
altar	chose	environment
amateur	colonel	equipped
among	column	equivalent
analyze	coming	especially
annual	commission	exaggerate
answer	commitment	exhilarate
apartment	committee	existence
apparatus	comparative	experience
apparent	compelled	explanation
appearance	competitive	exquisite
appropriate	complexion	familiar
arctic	conceivable	fascinate
argument	conferred	February
arithmetic	conscience	foreign
ascend	conscientious	formerly
assassination	conscious	forty
athlete	criticize	fourth
attendance	deferred	frantically
bachelor	definite	fulfill
balance	descendant	generally
basically	description	government
beginning	desperate	grammar
believe	dictionary	grandeur
benefited	dilemma	grievous

guidance
height
heroes
hindrance
hoping
humorous
hypocrisy
intelligence
interesting
illiterate
immediately
incidentally
incredible
inevitable
ingenious
intellectual
irrelevant
irresistible
judgment
knowledge
laboratory
laid
led
license
lightning
maintenance
manageable
maneuver
manufacture
marriage
mathematics
maybe
mischievous
misspell
mortgage
ninety
noticeable
occasionally
occurred
omitted
opportunity
optimistic
pamphlet
parallel

paralyze
paralysis
pastime
performance
permissible
perseverance
personnel
perspiration
physical
picnicking
playwright
pneumonia
possibility
practically
precede
precedence
preference
preferred
prejudice
preparation
prevalent
privilege
probably
professor
prominent
pronunciation
prophecy
prophesy
quantity
quiet
quite
quizzes
recede
receive
recognize
recommend
reference
referred
repetition
restaurant
rhythm
ridiculous
roommate
sacrifice

satellite
schedule
scissors
seize
separate
sergeant
shining
siege
similar
sophomore
specifically
specimen
stationary
stationery
studying
subtly
succeed
successful
succession
supersede
suppose
surprise
temperamental
tendency
their
thorough
through
tragedy
unanimous
unnecessarily
until
vacuum
vengeance
villain
weather
weird
writing

47h Misspell only for a purpose.

Sometimes writers use a purposeful misspelling for effect:

The *univercity* exists in a world of its own.

This example combines two words into a new one. You might also stretch a word internally for effect, as with:

Laaazily, he crawled from the bed.

The popularity of "sniglets" demonstrates the human desire for renaming and respelling all sorts of things:

accordionated: being able to drive and refold a road map at the same time

percuburp: the final gasp a coffee percolator makes to alert you it is ready

The creation of sound effects may require creative spelling:

Ping. Kappppping. The bullets ricocheted off the metal banisters.

The creation of slang terms often involves spelling, especially in its application of new meanings such as *zod* for a person who is out of style or *rad* for "radical."

However, keep firmly in mind two principles before you experiment with unusual spellings: (1) know and use the fundamental conventions correctly before you experiment, and (2) use the technique with restraint and for a good reason.

EXERCISE 47.1 Add suffixes to words ending in an unpronounced *e*:

1. argue (add *-ment*):
   argue (add *-able*)
2. like (add *-ly*):
   like (add *-able*):
3. use (add *-ful*):
   use (add *-able*):
4. change (add *-able*):
   change (add *-ing*):

EXERCISE 47.2 Rewrite each word below in first the present participle form (-*ing*) and then the past tense form (-*ed*).

1. convert
2. run
3. omit
4. occur
5. halt
6. confess
7. borrow
8. buy
9. drop
10. insist

EXERCISE 47.3 Use either *ei* or *ie* to fill correctly the blanks in the following words:

1. n _____ ce
2. w _____ rd
3. pr _____ st
4. s _____ ze
5. bel _____ ve
6. rec _____ ve
7. th _____ r
8. _____ ght
9. rel _____ ve
10. dec _____ t

EXERCISE 47.4 Spell properly the plural forms of the following words

1. Haley
2. Doris
3. hero
4. memo
5. story
6. table
7. bench
8. cameo
9. potato
10 fifty

11. 20
12. 1980
13. gash
14. moss
15. life
16. datum
17. criterion
18. one
19. rodeo
20. money

EXERCISE 47.5   Correct spelling errors in the following words. Mark any correctly spelled words with a *C*. Try to apply the rules of this chapter to correct the words; use the dictionary when in doubt.

1. acheivement
2. wieght
3. alot
4. studing
5. assasination
6. funnyest
7. unusually
8. wooly
9. cupfulls
10. shriek
11. neice
12. humourous
13. fameous
14. irelevant
15. scarfs

Academic Writing

48
Logic
49
Writing an Essay Examination Answer
50
Writing the Research Paper
51
Writing Research Papers across the Curriculum

CHAPTER

48

Logic

Logic is the study of validity of arguments. Writers often argue a position or recommend a course of action after detailing and examining their facts. To argue is to defend a position (a conclusion) by sound, valid evidence.

An argument may be as short as a sentence or as long as a book. To be effective, however, it must exhibit not only correctness but also persuasiveness. In other words, it is possible to write logically but to leave the reader unconvinced. By using a few writing strategies, as explored in this chapter, the knowledgeable writer can do much to make an argument acceptable to the reader.

Of course, not all positions require support, or evidence. "It is hot" needs no support, for any casual observer can immediately see the truth of this conclusion. Positions that do require support are opinions or conclusions that some readers might disagree with, even though the writer strongly considers the conclusions to be correct. For example, "Colleges should require all students to study a foreign language for at least two years" will definitely require support because it is an opinion, and the reader will need to be convinced.

Illogical arguments harm the writer's cause because they diminish the writer's credibility. As a writer, you need to recognize and avoid incorrect arguments, called *fallacies*. Arguments are fallacious because their premises are invalid, irrelevant, or too weak to support the conclusion. Section **48f** introduces you to several common fallacies.

48a Learn to structure arguments.

An *argument* is a chain of reasoning that offers facts to support or refute a point. It has one conclusion and any number of premises. The premises provide the supporting evidence in the form of facts, observations, citation of authorities, and other data. Here is a paragraph that presents a conclusion and premises to support it.

> The Municipal Arts Council should receive no funding from taxes. First, art is a matter of individual taste in which governments should play no role. What one person considers to be valuable art, another person considers to be less than art. Second, the public should be taxed only to provide for the protection and well-being of citizens. Art is inessential to these concerns.

The first sentence states the writer's conclusion. Then the writer gives two premises, marked by the words *first* and *second*, why readers should accept this conclusion.

The conclusion may come after the premises:

> Young women consistently score below young men on college entrance examinations, yet once in college they earn better grades than young men. Therefore, colleges should not use entrance exams alone to determine who is accepted.

Here the premises that young men outscore young women on the tests and that young women make better grades in college build to the conclusion introduced by *therefore*.

In these examples you will note *indicator* words (*first, second, therefore*) that announce premises and conclusions. Other indicator words are *because, consequently, thus, so, hence, moreover, since, besides, furthermore,* and *for*. Although writers do not always use these words, you can use them to assert your conclusion and to introduce your evidence.

EXERCISE 48.1 In the following paragraphs, underline and label conclusions (*C*), premises (*P*), and indicator words (*I*).

> EXAMPLE: $\overset{C}{\underline{\text{The U.S. should not bargain with terrorists,}}}$ $\overset{I}{\underline{\text{for if}}}$
>
> $\overset{P}{\underline{\text{terrorists gain anything in the bargaining process they are}}}$

only encouraged to commit further acts of terrorism to gain further concessions.

1. The council encourages you to eat bread made of whole wheat flour because it contains rich nutrients and vitamins from the entire kernel of wheat.
2. Proposition 48 helps athletes. According to a survey by the *Atlanta Journal-Constitution*, the number of freshmen who did not qualify academically has dropped 42 percent in 24 Division I universities in the South. Of the 505 football players recruited, only 30 failed the standards of Proposition 48.
3. Quick and slow learners do not belong in the same classroom. Students need to learn at a comparable pace with their peers. Slow learners suffer undue pressure to perform, and quick learners gain a false sense of accomplishment by outperforming the slow learners. Slow learners also impede the pace of study, denying quick learners a wholesome academic experience.
4. The amount of funds in your checking account has dropped below the required minimum. For that reason the bank has assessed a service fee.
5. This questionnaire, which represents a good cross-section of the freshman class, shows that 48 percent of the college students know little about AIDS. Apparently, educational programs on AIDS are inadequate or nonexistent in the high schools.

EXERCISE 48.2   In the following paragraphs, underline and label conclusions (*C*), premises (*P*), and indicator words (*I*).

1. Because grasshoppers (or locusts) have plagued wheat farmers since Biblical days and because the government has placed limitations on the use of insecticides, the chances of eradicating the insect are infinitesimal.
2. Stem rust and leaf rust attack wheat with devastating results just after the head appears, while smut strikes the kernel itself. Insects, especially the Hessian fly and periodically the grasshopper, cause great damage to wheat. Therefore, farmers need an arsenal of weapons — fungicides, herbicides, and insecticides — to defend their crops.

3. The American public can forgive farmers who refuse to plant certain crops year after year. After all, inflation sprouts like weeds so that equipment, seed, and fertilizer costs spiral ever upward. Also, federal price supports are inadequate.
4. In some years of the 1970s Russia purchased as much as one-fourth of the wheat produced in the United States. These purchases inflated the demand for wheat, raised prices, and trapped the farmer into quick expansion on borrowed money. When President Jimmy Carter set embargoes on wheat shipments to Russia, the wheat farmer faced economic disaster.
5. Whole wheat flour contains rich nutrients and vitamins because millers grind the entire kernel of wheat.

48b Use inductive and deductive arguments.

Some arguments are stronger than others. We call an argument that absolutely proves its conclusion **deductive**.

> All men are mortal.
> Socrates is a man.
> Therefore, Socrates is mortal.

In the example above, the first premise makes a general statement about a group (men). The second premise names Socrates as a member of that group, and the conclusion applies the general statement to Socrates. As this example illustrates, the structure of a deductive argument guarantees that if the premises are true, then the conclusion must also be true.

Unfortunately, writers seldom have the luxury of presenting deductive arguments. In the real world, most of the arguments we encounter and create are **inductive** — that is, the premises do not absolutely prove the conclusion. They provide instead a *probable* or a *reasonable* confirmation.

> I will probably get an A on this test because I attended all the classes and did all the reading, I participated in class discussions, and the professor praised my insights. Furthermore, in the past, I have earned A's on his tests.

Here the premises strongly support the conclusion that this student will get an A on the test. However, the test could be the disaster of the semester for the student; the premises do not absolutely prove the conclusion.

If your argument is *deductive*, you can use such absolute indicator words as *all, every, certainly, without fail*, and *always* (or no indicator words at all) to signal your faith in a conclusion based on deductive reasoning:

> A molecule of water *always* contains hydrogen and oxygen.
>
> *All* AIDS victims carry the virus.
>
> Socrates is mortal.

If your argument is *inductive*, you can use such limited indicator words as *some, most, almost, probably, very likely*, and *almost certainly* to indicate the degree to which readers can trust your conclusion.

> The use of microchips in ever smaller sizes to create miniature electronic equipment means that wrist watches of the future will *probably* have numerous functions, such as time, date, alarm, television, intercom, telephone, and many more.

The argument above uses past evidence to affirm something about the future.

EXERCISE 48.3 Identify the following arguments as deductive or inductive reasoning. Be prepared to defend your answer.

1. An individual has certain inalienable rights. Within certain boundaries people are free to do what they like whenever they so desire. With the same twenty-dollar bill they can buy a Bible and a copy of *Penthouse*.

2. Regional experts on the rural plateau predict winter weather by counting woolly worms, the number of foggy mornings in August, the number of colors in the maple leaves, and other techniques. Their accuracy in recent years has been excellent, so I will consult their prognostications as well as that of the national weather service.

3. We know today that Ernest Hemingway, despite his personal bravado and his fictional code of the hero, was evidently insecure. His suicide serves as primary evidence.

4. The government should not enact laws that infringe on the rights of the individual within his or her own property. Laws that force the use of seatbelts infringe on individual privacy. Therefore, mandatory seat belt laws should be repealed.

5. Many people ignore the rights of the individual in deference to their prudish point of view and their own selfish interests.

6. The city of Ledbetter needs a farmer's market. The farmer's market in Fredonia, which allows farmers free space for selling directly to the public, has enabled many farm families to earn a good living and to remain on their land. The city commission of Ledbetter should institute a similar program to serve our area farmers and the general public.

7. There is a great need for more police officers. One senator reports that in 1951 the nation had three police officers for every violent crime committed but that now there are three violent crimes for every police officer.

8. Any high school graduate with an ACT score of 16 or better can enroll at this university. Marjorie Hill has a high school diploma and a score of 23 on the ACT. She can enroll at this university.

48c Use argument structure to organize an essay.

An argument may occupy a single sentence, several sentences, a paragraph, several paragraphs, an essay, or an entire book. In an essay or a short research paper, the presentation of a conclusion and premises can guide the organization of paragraphs. The thesis of the paper can be the argument's conclusion, and the topic sentences of the paragraphs can be the premises for the argument. These paragraphs will explain, justify, and illustrate the individual premises, preparing the reader to accept the argument.

Below is a draft of an essay that one writer built from his argument.

> *Voting in elections should be mandatory.* At each election our attention is drawn again and again to the declining number of Americans who go to the polls. In the last presidential election, less than half of all eligible voters went to the polls. Some

thesis (argument's conclusion)

argue that this decline signals resignation and disgust with the participating candidates of each party; others argue that eligible voters do not vote because they are generally happy with the way things are.

However, *low voter turnout*, most would agree, *is dangerous to the future of our democracy.* The fewer people who vote, the less likely the government is to represent the interest of all the people versus the interests of one or more special interest groups. For example, many Americans no longer bother to vote in local school board elections. As a result, teachers' unions have gotten out their members' vote in districts to elect their candidates to the school boards. Union-controlled school boards tend to give teachers what they want, most notably higher salaries. Whether or not you think such manipulation of school boards is a good idea depends on whether you favor the union's initiatives or see yourself as a beleaguered taxpayer.

Mandatory voting would increase voter turnout. Making voting mandatory should include some penalty for failure to vote, not just an exhortation to vote, so that no voter would fail to go to the polls without paying a price. Some possibilities for penalties include a higher tax rate, a fine, or revocation of the driver's license. With such a penalty in place, voters would have incentive to perform what most citizens consider a basic right as well as a civic responsibility.

Mandatory voting would increase the public's awareness of government activity and challenge our leaders to greater accountability. Not only would government represent the interests of all the people, but also the average person's knowledge of public affairs would improve because voters pay more attention to the issues than nonvoters. Consequently, the enlarged and better informed electorate would make more intelligent choices for the country, county, and city than the small, less informed electorate under an optional system. The quality of our leaders would be higher, and our country would become stronger and healthier faster.

—RYAN BREWER, student

premise 1

premise 2

premise 3

48d Carefully define key terms.

Many arguments leave the reader frustrated and questioning exactly what the writer intended to say because the writer failed to define his or her key terms.

> Affordable daycare should be made available to parents.

Here, the reader will want to know just what *affordable* means. What some parents can pay for, others cannot.

> The American tax system is unfair to our most productive and successful citizens.

How does this writer decide what is "fair" and what is "unfair"? On the one hand, the tax system takes more dollars from a wealthy citizen than it does from a poor one; on the other hand, wealthy citizens pay a smaller percentage of their income in taxes than do poor citizens.

EXERCISE 48.4 In the sentences below, underline vague words that need definition, then give at least two possible definitions for each underlined word.

1. The Showcase is the most comfortable coat you'll ever wear. One size fits all.
2. This thick spaghetti sauce is America's favorite.
3. Busy as things are today, you need a cereal that's hearty enough to help you go the distance.
4. A valuable coupon will arrive in your mail this week.
5. Today's Cellubright batteries last longer.
6. Win a premier Bahamas Cruise and Disney vacation with a "Cruise to Paradise."
7. Eating oatmeal is the wholesome way to start the school year.
8. In this contest you can win a BMW instantly.
9. This crunchy cereal gives you more for your morning.
10. There's only one spray that freshens the air while it destroys odors naturally.

48e   Recognize and address opposing arguments.

An effective, persuasive writer must address the objections that readers might raise about his or her conclusion. As the writer, you can accomplish this task by giving a brief, unslanted account of the opposing argument; to fail to do so is an admission of weakness. Then rebut the argument.

> I support continued funding for NASA for a number of reasons. Admittedly, others in this country feel that such spending takes too much money away from desperately needed social programs. However, I believe that space exploration has the potential to provide great social benefits, greater than those that could be produced by funneling NASA funds into today's social programs.

Here, with the tables turned, is another writer's argument:

> We should not be funding NASA at a time when people are hungry and without homes. Although the space administration argues that space exploration has the potential to provide great social benefits, it is only a potential, while money spent on today's social programs would have direct and immediate benefits.

Of course, research and talking over your ideas with friends will uncover opposing arguments that you may not be aware of. Impress your reader by treating fairly all objections that he or she might raise. Be careful to show respect for opposing viewpoints. Let the facts win your case.

48f   Avoid common fallacies.

A **fallacy** is a defective argument; it is an argument that is either reasoned incorrectly or based on invalid premises. Here are a few of the most common fallacies:

1. *Ad hominem* (argument directly against the person): This argument discredits not the opposing argument but the *person* holding the opposing viewpoint. The support of the argument, the attack against the person's character or circumstances, is irrelevant to the conclusion:

> People who argue for gun control have no respect for the Constitution. Therefore, there should be no gun control.

Whether or not these people respect the Constitution is irrelevant to the argument.

> Of course, Jones favors early parole for nonviolent criminals. He is a defense attorney. Early parole is a terrible idea.

The attempt to discredit Jones does not address the primary issues.

2. *Appeal to authority*: Writers often cite authorities who should be, but often are not, reputable, up-to-date, objective, or truly authorities in the area of discussion. Is an athlete really qualified to judge the best deodorant or shave cream? Is the *National Enquirer* a good source of information about the future of oil prices?

The example below provides authoritative evidence:

> Although an isolated expert here and there might assert that steroid use for short periods of time will cause no permanent damage to an athlete's body (Jones 33–35), most authorities argue that steroid use by athletes produces lasting, harmful effects (see esp. Barnes 16–29 and Lundlow 177–214). Coaches and administrators should enact strict rules to prohibit steroid use by athletes and should conduct frequent tests to enforce them.

Another question to ask is whether or not there *is* an authority in a particular area. Psychologists may know the workings of the mind, but they regularly disagree in courtrooms over whether defendants were or were not sane at the time of their alleged criminal activity. Do seasoned economic forecasters really *know* what will happen to the stock market next month?

The citing of common sense or of a consensus is one form of the appeal to authority. Watch out for "everybody knows (or agrees) that. . . ." Remember that at one time everyone believed that the earth was flat and also that the sun revolved around the earth.

3. *Post hoc ergo propter hoc* ("after this, therefore because of this"): This argument assumes that because one event occurred before another, the first caused the second.

> Just days after the engine was tuned it began to stall at intersections. Therefore, the mechanic did something wrong and caused the stalling.

The cause of the stalls might have been a broken part that had nothing to do with the tune-up.

4. *Begging the question*: This argument supports its conclusion with circular reasoning that simply restates the conclusion as a premise. That is, the premise would not be accepted by anyone who did not already accept the conclusion.

This next assertion assumes that every reader has a clear understanding of what constitutes a "master teacher."

> Master teachers deserve higher salaries.

The writer should find a common ground with the reader:

> If master teachers exist, and I believe we can identify them with clear criteria, they deserve higher salaries.

The next writer also begs the question by retreating into tradition, the very issue being questioned.

> Sororities are for women and fraternities are for men, so we must not consider any sort of merger.

Again, the writer should address the issue in a rational manner:

> Historically, sororities and fraternities have been segregated by sex, yet today's social climate suggests that we should re-evaluate their purposes and their membership requirements.

5. *Hasty generalization*: Drawing a conclusion from inadequate evidence creates a hasty generalization.

> Of ten women interviewed, seven preferred married life to being single. Therefore, it is safe to assume that most women prefer marriage.

This writer should not make a prediction about *all* women based on a sample of only ten. Yet some writers will make hasty generalizations based on a sample of only *one*, usually an eye-catching aberration that the writer knows of personally:

> Last Sunday Ted Jones, captain of the Lions football team, got in his car, buckled up, backed out of his driveway, and headed down Elm Street. Two blocks away he lost control of his car, ran off the road, turned over, and burned to death because he could not free himself from his seatbelt. I urge you to repeal the seatbelt law that brought about his ghastly death.

True, the writer can attribute *this* death to a seatbelt. Yet, has the writer established that seatbelts kill more people than they save? What are the survival rates for people using seatbelts compared to those not using them?

6. *False analogy*: Analogies are powerful at communicating similarities between objects and ideas. Unfortunately, analogies downplay differences, and when writers consciously or unconsciously downplay important differences, they create false analogies.

> Like a ship at sea, the ship of state needs a strong captain, the president, whose orders are not subject to question at every turn. Congress should keep its nose out of the president's conduct of foreign affairs.

The government is not a ship at sea. It is a complex organization with its own precise rules, set down by the Constitution, which give both Congress and the president roles to play.

7. *Either . . . or fallacy*: This error creates a false dilemma by arguing that a complicated issue has only two answers when, in truth, several options may be available. It reflects oversimplification by the writer.

> At this university a freshman either joins a sorority or a fraternity to enter the mainstream of social activity or the freshman will remain an outsider, isolated and lonely.

This dilemma—join or be lonely—ignores other levels of social support on the campus.

8. *False emotional appeal*: This fallacy comes in several well-disguised packages. **Flattery** uses insincere and excessive praise of the audience to disguise shallow reasoning. **Snob appeal** and the **bandwagon** encourage readers to join a cause or buy a product because the "best" people do it and because it will raise the self-esteem of readers. **Racial and sexist slurs** demean one class in a perverse appeal by one bigot to another.

> The enclosed bid offers you and a few other carefully screened freshmen an opportunity to join the most prestigious fraternity on campus, one that has produced more doctors, lawyers, and MBAs than all other local fraternities combined.

This sentence uses both flattery and snob appeal in its recruitment efforts.

9. *Non sequitur*: A conclusion may not follow from the premises, so the statement is illogical.

> The math team cannot win this next competition because the University of Arizona has three wizards on their team and our Mark James is ill with hepatitis.

Neither the absence of James nor the presence of three wizards can automatically defeat the math team; the conclusion does not follow from the premises.

10. *Red herring*: Some writers dodge the real issue by shifting the reader's attention to an unrelated issue. Sometimes called *straw man*, the fallacy derives from an old technique by which a straw man or a red herring is used to divert attention from the real target.

> Although one administrator seems eager to examine the status of fraternities on campus, his time could be spent on more serious matters, such as the pathetic condition of library holdings. Did you know that the library has canceled its subscription to such important periodicals as *JAMA*, *Southern Review*, and the *Browning Newsletter*?

This writer waves a flag on library problems to divert attention from the administration's examination of fraternities.

EXERCISE 48.5 Identify the type of fallacy that you find in each of the following sentences.

1. Railroad companies had to build their own roadways, so trucking companies should do the same and stop crowding our interstate system.
2. People who support a large defense budget are contractors who benefit from the funding. Cut the defense budget.
3. Everybody knows that Russia's economy is weak and unstable, so we need have no fear of war.
4. Early in his term of office, President Reagan held firm and refused to negotiate with the Russians. Sure enough, they soon capitulated and submitted to his terms.
5. George Bush became president in January 1989, and by late 1989 and early 1990 several European countries — Poland, East Germany, and others — had gained democratic reforms and had broken the iron grip of the Kremlin.
6. War is the only answer for countries that abuse Americans.
7. A poll of 20 students reveals that 80 percent of the student body thinks that Rob Longstreet has performed well as president of the Student Government Association.
8. One student, Jennifer Lockwood, worked as an aide to a congressman last year, and now she has a government loan to pay her fees.
9. One congressman died in a private plane crash in Arizona and another died under similar circumstances in Mississippi. Congressmen should fly only by commercial airline.
10. Higher salaries for teachers will improve education because you get what you pay for.

EXERCISE 48.6 Identify and be prepared to explain the strengths and weaknesses of the following arguments.

1. The streets of our city will soon become a dump site because of trash people can't fit into the allotted two cans. Some families have more trash than others.
2. We never had discipline problems with Robert until he began attending your nursery school. Therefore, we plan to cancel our contract with you and locate Robert in a new school.
3. Many students do not need a liberal arts core curriculum. After all, I'm going to be a businessman, not an artist or literary critic.

4. The government is like a benevolent parent and must protect the rights of the criminal as vigorously as it protects our right to vote.
5. Zip codes are an intrusion into the privacy of an individual. Begun as a device to serve mail carriers, zip codes now enable junk mail companies to target select audiences.
6. A knowledge of computers will serve you well in the business world.
7. An individual has rights and privileges because he or she is free and independent.
8. In the late 1970s President Carter imposed a grain embargo on shipments to Russia. Soon after, grain prices dropped rapidly and surpluses of grain overflowed storage bins. Consequently, farmers struggled to meet their mortgage payments and to get another crop planted. Many farm families across the nation lost their land.
9. Adding an upper-level deck to the football stadium will prove cost effective. The demand for season tickets exceeds available space by over 600 seats. The new section will seat 580. At a price of $240 per seat, the expansion, estimated at $1.1 million, will pay for itself within ten years.
10. The equator always crosses South America and never crosses North America.

Writing an Essay Examination Answer

Writing an essay for an examination question differs somewhat from other essay assignments in time constraints, purpose, and audience. In five minutes or more, your essay answer displays your knowledge about a specific issue for an instructor. Yet it remains an essay with a thesis that argues for a position and supports it with evidence (see section **48a**). It must address the problem, explore the issues, illuminate a solution, defend a supposition, or make a justification. It is not a plot summary, a list of quick answers, or a recitation of facts as called for in a short-answer quiz.

An essay examination has four important stages: reading the questions to get a quick overview, planning specific answers, writing the essay, and reviewing the paper as a whole. Prior to the test, of course, you will have formulated notes on major issues, learned the terminology, and pinpointed key issues.

49a Plan your answer.

Two activities are usually necessary prior to actual writing.

1. *Get an overview of the test as a whole, and proportion your time for the relative value of the questions.* Read each question quickly, note the value for each answer, and plan your time accordingly. Jot down notes to key ideas that might escape your mind when you begin writing individual answers.

2. *Plan your answer and make notes.* Consider important questions of your own:

>What does the question ask me to do?

>What does the instructor anticipate?

>Make a few preliminary notes. List ideas. Establish in your mind or on paper a thesis (answer). If time allows, sketch a quick outline to control your essay.

Determine the best form of your response from the question itself and from what you want to say. The wording of a question often dictates form and content. You may need to use comparison and contrast, cause and effect, or other rhetorical modes (see chapter **6** for a detailed discussion of all techniques for developing paragraphs). The following examples will provide some insight into methods of planning examination answers.

Question: *Identify the Wife of Bath.*

This answer should do more than say the Wife of Bath is a character in Chaucer's *Canterbury Tales*; it should provide details about Chaucer's characterization of her as an early feminist or a defender of marriage.

Question: *Describe Mark Twain's preoccupation with depicting Huckleberry Finn's raft as a sanctuary and haven from disorder.*

This answer must chart more than a physical description; it needs to explain the raft's peaceful safety in contrast with the chaos of life in villages along the river's banks.

Question: *Explain the significance of the Battle of Bunker Hill.*

This request demands ideas that build a case for this battle's contribution to the rebellion of the colonists and its consequences for the British Army. An answer cannot merely narrate historical events.

Question: *Compare caffeine in coffee and in soft drinks.*

This essay answer should show similarities as well as differences in the contents of the two drinks and should explore their effects on consumers.

Question: *Explain Carl Sagan's theory of nuclear winter.*

This essay answer should include an analysis of Sagan's premises and conclusion and provide observations about any weak points in the theory.

The point is this: every question deserves a moment or two of consideration that will organize a framework for the answer.

49b Address the point of the question.

Although individual answers must find their own path of development, most good answers conform to a fixed structure: *an early thesis statement precedes specific information.* Within that simple format, the writer must accomplish five tasks.

1. *Be direct.* You need no special opening devices to attract the reader. Just get to the point.
2. *Use key terminology.* The language of the course represents, in part, the heart of the study. If you know the correct words, their definitions, and how to apply them, you can discuss your topic precisely and economically.
3. *Cite specific facts and evidence.* Support your thesis with dates, figures, events, people and their titles, quotations, and any other matter of importance.
4. *Structure the essay according to a plan.* See section **49a** for details about planning your answers. If asked to trace the development of primates, keep your answer directed to the process. If asked to explain Ernest Hemingway's concept of the hero, cite specifics from the novels rather than merely generalize.
5. *Review your answers.* Quickly edit and proofread to be certain that you have clearly expressed an answer and have given supporting evidence. Where you have more than a one-paragraph answer, be certain that clear topic sentences set the direction for your discussion.

Do not leave any question unanswered. Write something! Start by rewording the question and by bringing into the paragraph whatever comes to mind. Make connections to ideas you do recall. Even if your answer is incomplete, you still give your instructor an option of granting you a few points instead of the zero he or she must record if you leave the space blank.

Sample Essay Examination Answer

Question: *Trace the development of Nick Carraway's character in* The Great Gatsby.

In *The Great Gatsby* Nick Carraway changes throughout the novel because of the moral questions he faces. Although he is not the main character, Carraway experiences both internal and external conflicts that force him to examine his values and to become a more compassionate person.

The thesis sentence answers the question.

In the beginning Carraway is a carefree midwesterner with the morals of an Easterner during the 1920s. His beliefs and desires —drinking heavily, smoking, using women, wasting money —are typical for the setting of the novel. The only compassion Carraway possesses is for himself. He wants to become wealthy and have fun at the same time. Social standings are more important than values. Not able to realize the severity of the crimes around him, he awakens too late to help anyone but himself.

The writer analyzes Carraway's character at the beginning of the novel.

Carraway buys his women everything they desire, yet he cannot maintain a happy life with women who also lack human compassion. Nevertheless, after numerous parties, uncaring affairs, and devastating debts, Carraway still has enough human compassion to change drastically. He realizes that love and money do not ensure happiness by observing Gatsby and Daisy and her husband, Tom. Daisy and Tom have affairs that lead to two deaths, one of them the death of an innocent woman. Carraway decides there is no justice in the world. Yet he does not become fully aware until an "innocent victim" is blamed for the woman's murder and, thus, Gatsby is murdered.

The writer defends her thesis by tracing the growth of Carraway and the changes in his character.

As Carraway gazes upon his murdered friend, his desire for wealth and material items ceases. Carraway buries his lack of values when he buries his buddy, and he sets off to find happiness with love not with money. Fitzgerald uses Nick Carraway to justify the lifestyle he, himself, led while writing the novel in the hope of making his own life change, just as Carraway's life changes.

The writer closes with the image of a new Nick Carraway and relates her thesis to the author, F. Scott Fitzgerald.

—AIMÉE CLAIRE BEAUDOIN, student

CHAPTER

50

Writing the
Research Paper

Research papers are major assignments in college classes. This chapter will help you select and narrow an appropriate topic, research it, take notes, arrange support of your thesis, and write the paper effectively with accurate citations to your sources.

Writing a research paper serves two general purposes. First, it exposes you to sustained intellectual challenges, for you must investigate, confront, and bring under control an elusive, sometimes unsolvable problem. Second, it provides practice in writing with precision.

Therefore, you need to approach the assignment with two attitudes, which on the surface appear contradictory. One part of your mind should respond openly and expansively to an issue or problem without reservations or control: What happens if? Suppose I approach the problem from this angle? Such questions have launched many experiments and pointed the way to the modern age. The other part of your mind must exercise control over form and style. Scholars have established standards for their written reports, and you need to follow the standards of the discipline.

50a Choose a subject and narrow it to a workable topic.

Almost any subject is worthy of research and careful study—floppy diskettes, fingernails, the use of Agent Orange in Vietnam, or the contributions of European immigrants to westward expansion of America. The writer's treatment of the subject will determine whether or not it merits research. What might appear trivial at first can become significant by the writer's approach. For example, the character Charlie Brown in the comic strip *Peanuts* might seem inappropriate for serious study, yet the subject lends itself to many psychological and sociological interpretations.

Therefore, you must select a topic that challenges your imagination and applies your point of view. Then you must address the issue seriously. Test a potential topic against two fairly simple questions: What is the problem? Who cares?

TOPIC: Chronic fatigue syndrome

PROBLEM: People do not comprehend its threat to physical or mental well-being.

AUDIENCE: Young professionals who seem most prone to be victims of the disease.

As you did in chapters **1** and **2** with your essay, narrow your research paper subject to a manageable topic. A broad, general subject such as "Political Commentary in Comic Strips" needs a focus on specifics, such as "Satire of the Presidency in *Doonesbury*."

In addition to the advice in section **1e** on choosing a topic, consider further techniques to find a subject for your research paper.

List issues that you wish to know more about.

You might want to pursue some issues that your other courses have raised, such as the following:

psychological reactions of people to fear
left brain–right brain theory
Civil War battles
the influence of Space Shuttle research
satire in newspapers and magazines

Select one subject and discuss it with your instructor for pointers on where to find interesting reading. Narrow it with another list to see if one idea dominates all others.

Satire in *Doonesbury*
    satire of the White House staff
    satire of individual presidents
    satire of political and party affiliations
    satire of domestic policies
    satire of foreign policies

Any one item from the list might serve as a worthy subject for a research paper. A combination of them might prove feasible, especially if you can subordinate issues under one main heading.

> Satire of domestic policies
> > focus on White House staff
> > focus on President Reagan
> > focus on public reaction to presidential policies

Consult library sources.

Widen your scope with an exploratory visit to the library. If you review a few books and articles on the subject, you can learn enough about the topic to be able to narrow it to a specific issue. Library resources are discussed fully in section **50c**. For now, however, skimming will supply a few ideas that you can respond and react to.

During your search for a topic, even before you begin taking notes (section **50e**), get to know the library, especially the *reference room*, which houses most of the bibliographies, indexes, and general reference works; the *reserve desk*, which maintains books and articles that instructors place on reserve; the *card catalog*, whether computerized or stored on cards, which alphabetically lists all books in the library and directs you by call number to proper locations; and the *stacks*, which house the books.

One writer, for instance, explored dictionaries and reference works to discover that her subject, chronic fatigue syndrome, was new and relatively undefined. Part of her purpose, then, was to frame a definition.

Consult with knowledgeable people.

A discussion with instructors can yield rich dividends, for they know topics that will produce good papers. Moreover, they can route you away from troublesome subjects that might be too narrow or too broad. Talk with fellow students and interview knowledgeable persons. Take notes on what they say.

Compare two subjects or combine them into one.

Exciting discoveries occur when researchers merge two subjects that may appear unrelated. For example, one student combined an interest in politics with his enjoyment of the *Doonesbury* comic strip. Later, he compared the political satire of *Doonesbury* with that of nineteenth-century cartoonists to discover that *Doonesbury* is mild in its sarcasm compared to an earlier age. Another student combined an interest in athletics with political science to produce a paper on the politics of coaching. Still another compared Abraham Lincoln's unfulfilled intentions for Reconstruction with those carried out by his successor, Andrew Johnson.

50b   Draft a preliminary thesis sentence.

After selecting a subject and narrowing it to a manageable topic, the next step before beginning your in-depth research is to frame a **thesis sentence** (see section **1g** for a full discussion with examples). It will limit the sources you must investigate.

> Chronic fatigue syndrome is a relatively new disease, or at least a new diagnosis, and both the medical community and the general public need to awaken to its perils.

This thesis sentence establishes a basis for the paper, which argues a position about an illness (see section **48a**). It will define and analyze the issues.

A working thesis may turn out to be false or unmanageable, but that is the point of research: to validate the working thesis. At any point you should modify or abandon a thesis that you cannot substantiate.

50c   Use all resources available to you for research.

As a researcher, you must conduct an orderly, progressive search that begins in the library and ultimately may lead you to other resources in the community. In the library, begin with general reference works to gain an understanding of the background of your topic. As you become familiar with your topic, you can use the library's card catalog to find specific books and various indexes to find specific articles.

NOTE: If you find that your sources are numerous, then your topic
is too broad; if your sources are scarce, then your topic is
too narrow.

You needn't limit yourself to the resources within your library.
Check the campus and community activity listings for any events
relevant to your topic.

General references

Early in your research, do some reading in general reference
guides, encyclopedias, dictionaries, yearbooks, almanacs, and the
like to develop a working knowledge of the topic. You might even
take a few general notes.

General reference guides

You can begin with a general guide to reference sources:

Where to Find What: A Handbook to Reference Service. 1984.
The New York Times Guide to Reference Materials. 1986.
Guide to Reference Books. 10th ed. 1986.

The librarian can also direct you to guidebooks for specific fields,
such as *Research Guide to American Historical Biography*, 3 vols., 1988;
Research Guide for Psychology, 1982; or *Where to Find Business Information*, 1982.

Encyclopedias

Begin with general encyclopedias that cover a wide range of topics:

Encyclopedia Americana. 30 vols. 1988.
Encyclopaedia Britannica. 15th ed. 32 vols. 1988. It contains
four parts: *Micropaedia*, vols. 1–12, brief essays; *Macro-
paedia*, vols. 13–29, essays in depth; *Propaedia*, vol. 30, an
outline of knowledge; and the *Index*, vols. 31–32.

Also search for encyclopedias on specific subjects, such as *Encyclopedia of Architecture*, 5 vols., 1989; the *Encyclopedia of the Biological Sciences*, 2nd. ed., 1981; or the *Encyclopedia of Business Information
Sources*, 1989, supplement. Specialized encyclopedias like these exist
for every field; your librarian will help you locate one for your topic.

Dictionaries and biographical references

The large unabridged dictionaries provide valuable insights into the origin and meaning of words. Use one to learn special terminology applicable to your research study.

> *The Oxford English Dictionary*. 2nd ed. 1989–.
> *The Random House Dictionary of the English Language*. 2nd ed. 1989.
> *Webster's Third New International Dictionary*. 1986.

Search also for specialized dictionaries in your field, such as *Dictionary of Biology*, 1986; *Dictionary of Computing*, 2nd ed., 1986; or *Dictionary of Banking and Financial Services*, 2nd ed., 1985.

To conduct research on a person, look at biographical dictionaries and encyclopedias, such as these:

> *Dictionary of American Biography*. 16 vols. and index. 1927–80. Supplements.
> *Dictionary of Literary Biography*. 87 vols. 1982–89.
> *McGraw-Hill Encyclopedia of World Biography*. 12 vols. 1975.
> *Webster's New Biographical Dictionary*. 1983.
> *Who's Who in America*. Annual.

Again, librarians can help you locate specialized biographies such as the *Dictionary of American Negro Biography*, 1983; *Contemporary Authors*, 127 vols., 1967–89; *Lives of the Saints*, 1990; *Who's Who of American Women*, 16th rev. ed., 1988; or *Who's Who in Philosophy*, 1969.

Almanacs and Yearbooks

Almanacs itemize the statistical data of any given year with charts, lists, and tables. Yearbooks provide brief essays that discuss the events and personalities of a specific year. Use almanacs and yearbooks if your topic centers on historical events.

> *Americana Annual*
> *Britannica Book of the Year*
> *Facts on File*
> *World Almanac and Book of Facts*

A yearbook in your special field may exist, such as *Yearbook of the United Nations* or *Annual Review of Nuclear Science*.

Bibliographies

A published **bibliography** is a list of books and related sources on a specific topic arranged by subject and/or by author. Early in your library research you might investigate one of these annual general bibliographies:

> *Books in Print.* An author, title, and subject index to all books currently in print.
>
> *Paperbound Books in Print.* Paperbound books currently in print that you might find in a local bookstore.

As you progress in your research, find a bibliography for your specific subject, such as *Bibliographic Guide to Music*. Consult your librarian and see also the list by discipline on pages 469–70.

The card catalog

Every library has a card catalog, which is an alphabetical list of all the books the library contains. Some libraries even have listings of the books available to students through interlibrary loan. The catalog cards are filed by the author's last name, by the title, and by the subject. Traditionally a large bank of printed cards, many libraries now store their catalogs on microfilm or in a computer.

The subject headings of the card catalog can help you find a subject, narrow it, and determine quickly the availability of books on the topic. For instance, a person researching chronic fatigue syndrome might look under the subject headings "Fatigue" and "Chronic diseases — Diagnosis." (If you cannot find a subject heading for your topic, consult the *Library of Congress Subject Headings*, explained below.) Write down the call numbers and search out the books that address your topic most closely. Create a working bibliography card (see section **50d**) for each book you use.

Catalog cards provide specific information about each book: the call number, publication data, the presence of bibliographies and special materials, and additional subject headings.

A catalog card

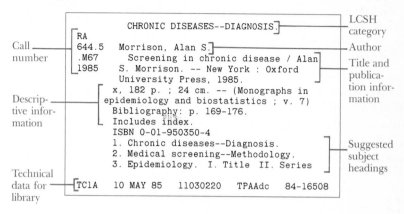

LCSH category

CHRONIC DISEASES--DIAGNOSIS.

Call number

RA
644.5 Morrison, Alan S. — Author
.M67   Screening in chronic disease / Alan
1985   S. Morrison. -- New York : Oxford
       University Press, 1985.

Title and publication information

Descriptive information

       x, 182 p. ; 24 cm. -- (Monographs in
epidemiology and biostatistics ; v. 7)
       Bibliography: p. 169-176.
       Includes index.
       ISBN 0-01-950350-4
       1. Chronic diseases--Diagnosis.
       2. Medical screening--Methodology.
       3. Epidemiology. I. Title II. Series

Suggested subject headings

Technical data for library

TC1A   10 MAY 85   11030220   TPAAdc   84-16508

Library of Congress Subject Headings

The *Library of Congress Subject Headings* (*LCSH*) lists subjects named and organized in the card catalog. Use the *LCSH* to locate quickly a subject heading for your topic. The brief passage below illustrates how a researcher looking for books on the diagnosis of chronic fatigue syndrome might locate pertinent subject headings.

Chronic diseases *(May Subd Geog)*
    [RA644.5-RA645 (Public health)]
    [RB156 (Pathology)]
    [RC108 (Internal medicine)]
    UF   Diseases, Chronic
    BT   Diseases
    NT   Chronic lymphocytic leukemia
           Chronic renal failure
           Fluorosis
  — **Diagnosis**
  — Patients
      USE Chronically ill
  — **Psychological aspects**
      BT Sick — Psychology

Indexes

While a bibliography lists books and other sources by author, title, and subject, an index goes one step further: it lists the specific pages in the books, periodicals, or newspapers where you can find an abstract, bibliography, article, or essay on your subject. The *Essay and*

General Literature Index, for example, lists hard-to-find essays and chapters of books that appear under titles that can be totally unrelated to your subject, and the *Biography Index* will send you to essays and entire books that provide biographical sketches on the lives of important persons.

In addition to using books as sources, make sure to check the published indexes for articles written on your topic in magazines, newspapers, and professional or scholarly journals. Articles often address more specific and more current issues than books. Indexes are compiled for general interest magazines, for newspapers, and for publications of scholarly disciplines. Ask the librarian which index to use for your topic.

Indexes to general magazines and to newspapers

> *Readers' Guide to Periodical Literature.* Lists articles in most major magazines, from weekly publications such as *Time* to monthly magazines such as *Psychology Today.*
>
> *Popular Periodical Index.* Lists articles in city and regional magazines such as *Texas Monthly.*
>
> *Magazine Index.* A microfiche index, updated monthly.
>
> *New York Times Index.* Contains highly condensed versions of each day's articles. Similar indexes exist for other major newspapers.
>
> *National Newspaper Index.* A microfilm compilation of selected articles from the *Christian Science Monitor, Los Angeles Times, New York Times, Wall Street Journal*, and the *Washington Post.*
>
> *Newsbank.* A microfilm compilation of selected articles from more than one hundred newspapers.

Indexes to scholarly works

You can increase the scholarly level of your work by consulting indexes to professional journals and books. You might start with these general indexes to broad fields of study:

> *Applied Science and Technology Index.* Articles in chemistry, computer science, electronics, engineering, geology, mathematics, photography, physics, and related fields.
>
> *Biological and Agricultural Index.* Articles in agriculture, biology, botany, zoology, and other related fields.

Education Index. Articles in education, physical education, health, and related fields.

Humanities Index. Articles in language, literature, history, performing arts, philosophy, religion, and related fields.

Social Sciences Index. Articles in economics, ecology, geography, law, political science, psychology, sociology, social work, and related fields.

You may also wish to investigate an index or bibliography for your specific discipline, as listed below. Your librarian can help you locate the right one and can show you how to use it.

ART:	*Art Index*
	Bibliographic Guide to Art and Architecture
BIOLOGY:	*Biological Abstracts*
BUSINESS:	*Business Periodicals Index*
	Bibliographic Guide to Business and Economics
CHEMISTRY:	*Chemical Abstracts*
COMPUTER SCIENCE:	*Computer Literature Index*
EDUCATION:	*Education Abstracts*
	Education Documents Abstracts
GEOLOGY:	*Bibliography and Index of Geology*
HISTORY:	*America: History and Life*
LANGUAGE AND LITERATURE:	*Abstracts of English Studies*
	McGill's Bibliography of Literary Criticism
	MLA International Bibliography
MEDICINE:	*Cumulated Index Medicus*
MUSIC:	*Bibliographic Guide to Music*
PHILOSOPHY:	*Philosophers Index*
PHYSICS:	*Current Papers in Physics*
	Current Physics Index
POLITICAL SCIENCE:	*ABA: Pol Sci*
	International Bibliography of Political Science

PSYCHOLOGY: *Psychological Abstracts*
RELIGION: *Religion: Index One*
SOCIOLOGY: *Sociological Abstracts*

Indexes stored in computers

A data base is a computer file. INFO TRAC, for example, will furnish you with a printout of magazine articles on a specific topic. NEWSEARCH and DIALOG, among others, are massive files to general publications. Specific data bases by discipline are also available. Ask your librarian for directions in using these files.

ART BIBLIOGRAPHIES MODERN (art)
BIOSIS PREVIEWS (biological sciences)
ABI/INFORM (business)
ERIC (education)
GEOARCHIVE (geology)
AMERICA: HISTORY AND LIFE (history)
MLA BIBLIOGRAPHY (languages and literature)
MATHFILE (mathematics)
RILM ABSTRACTS (music)
PHILOSOPHER'S INDEX
PAIS (political science)
SCISEARCH (physical and natural sciences)
SOCIAL SCISEARCH (social sciences)

Indexes to government publications

Government agencies and special committees produce articles and booklets on numerous subjects: pollution, water resources, highways, housing, outer space, and so on. To find government publications, begin with a search in INFO TRAC's index to government publications, if it is available. Next, examine the subject index of the *Monthly Catalog of United States Government Publications*. It will direct you by index number to a specific entry.

Your library will house some government documents, usually in a separate collection arranged by government agency or by index number, not by subject or author. If you need to order a document and time permits, write to the Government Printing Office in Washington, D.C., or to the U.S. Geological Survey in Denver, as applicable.

Sources outside the library

You need not depend entirely on materials in the library. Valuable information sources exist all around you; try some of the ideas listed here.

1. Broadcast media, such as a news documentary.
2. Audiovisual materials, such as a videotape lecture on your subject.
3. Bulletins and newsletters, such as a Chamber of Commerce newsletter.
4. Public addresses, such as a speech on campus or in a community organization.
5. Interviews, such as inquiries to your faculty and fellow students.
6. Questionnaires that you generate yourself, such as a five-part, yes-no survey on television viewing habits. (Submit the questionnaire to your instructor before releasing it to the public.)
7. Observation, experiments, and testing, such as counting a pattern of conduct (what choices of cold drinks do students make in the cafeteria line) or testing numerous samples of lake water for toxins. With guidance from your instructor, such experiments are well within the range of your ability.

50d   Prepare a set of working bibliography cards.

As you research your topic and find sources to support your thesis, make sure to record the complete bibliographic information of your sources so that you or your reader can locate the information at another time. The **working bibliography** consists of a list of all the books, articles, and other resources that you use for your topic. Recording the information on index cards is a convenient way both to keep track of your valuable sources and, later, to alphabetize the reference list that you will provide with your paper (see section **50j**).

Book

For books, record the card catalog's call number, the author's full name, the complete title and subtitle, the edition number (if any), the volume number and any multivolume information (if applicable), the place of publication, the publisher, and the date, as shown below.

Book bibliography cards

Goldberger, Leo, and Schlomo
Breznitz, eds. <u>Handbook of</u>
<u>Stress: Theoretical and</u>
<u>Clinical Aspects</u>. New York:
Free, 1982.

BF
575
.S75
H35
1982

Swenson, May. "Cat and the
Weather." <u>The Arbuthnot</u>
<u>Anthology of Children's</u>
<u>Literature</u>. Ed. Zena
Sutherland. 4th ed.
Glenview: Scott, 1976.
307-10.

R
808
ARB
1976

Journal or magazine article

For a journal article, record the author's full name, the title of the article, the title of the periodical, the volume and issue number (if applicable), the date, and the inclusive page numbers. Magazines, which are paged anew with each issue, do not need volume numbers recorded.

Journal and magazine bibliography cards

Holmes, Gary P., et al. "A Cluster of Patients with a Chronic Mononucleosis-Like Syndrome: Is Epstein-Barr Virus the Cause?" *JAMA* 257.17 (1987): 2297-2302.

Bazell, Robert. "Yuppie Plague." *New Republic* 27 Apr. 1987: 13-14.

Newspaper article

For a newspaper article, provide the author's name (if listed), the titles of the article and the newspaper, the date, and the section, page, and column numbers.

Newspaper bibliography card

Spear, Linda. "Local Chapter
Forms for Patients with
Epstein-Barr Virus." <u>New
York Times</u> 11 Jan. 1987:
V-31, col. 1.

For the types of information needed for other sources — pamphlets, interviews, videotapes, and so on — consult section **50j**.

50e   Take notes thoughtfully.

Remember that the research paper is a long work that cites sources; you cannot rely on your memory to retain research information. You need a supply of notes when you sit down at the typewriter or keyboard, preferably in a variety of personal thoughts, summaries, paraphrased ideas, and quotations — a reasonable mix. Collecting only photocopied sheets invites the use of one quotation after another. Remedy this problem early, while taking notes, not later during the drafting stage.

Personal Notes

From the start, write down your ideas so the essay will have your distinct input, in your own words. Save pieces of free-writing, jot down your ideas and reactions to readings, and build a storehouse of thoughts and ideas on cards or in a research log, a reading notebook, or a journal. Make a heading to remind you that the material is yours, not borrowed from a source. Personal notes preserve important private thoughts that might be forgotten.

Personal note card

My note on CFS

My aunt suffers from chronic fatigue syndrome, which seems to be an adult form of mononucleosis with the addition of mental distress and confusion because of memory loss.

Summary notes

A summary condenses material into a highly shortened version *in your own words*. For example, you might summarize the plot of a story to refresh your reader's memory.

Summary note card

My summary of YGB

In "Young Goodman Brown," Nathaniel Hawthorne narrates the story of a young man's midnight walk into the darkness of the woods and into the darkness of his own soul.

In like manner, you can summarize an article, a chapter, a pamphlet, or a book. (Make sure to record the pertinent page numbers, if appropriate; you will need to refer to them later.)

My summary of Salomon, Desperate Storytelling, 78-92
In his work on the mock-hero, Roger Salomon devotes an entire chapter to Don Quixote. He explores the work as adventure, exile and madness, parody, anticlimax, and ambivalence.

Quotation notes

As you read your sources, do not copy whole blocks of material, indiscriminately, just to fill a page. Summarize basic facts and general knowledge, and paraphrase relevant ideas. Reserve direct quotation of sources for words of a leading authority, for wording that is highly appropriate and distinctive in style and tone, and for evidence especially pertinent to your essay. Learn to be selective. Note below the size and length of the original material, the manner in which the researcher used only key parts of it, and how the researcher documented it. Note also that the researcher recorded the author's name and the page number of the quotation. As you will see in sections **50f** and **50i**, all sources must be completely documented in the paper.

Original statement

> Preliminary studies suggest fibromyalgia is extremely common and a major cause of lost work time and disability. Researchers say it may afflict as many as 10 percent of patients who visit general medical clinics, although its prevalence in the general population has not been studied.
>
> —JANE BRODY, "Personal Health"

Quotation note card

Fibromyalgia, Brody B18

A columnist for the New York Times says that fibromyalgia is "extremely common" and explains that "it may afflict as many as 10 percent of patients who visit general medical clinics . . . ."

Paraphrased notes

A paraphrase, like a summary, restates a passage in your words, but unlike a summary it does not condense the original. In about the same number of words, rewrite the information to avoid excessive use of direct quotation, to give your essay a consistency of style, and to demonstrate your ability to interpret the thoughts of others. Of course, if you retain phrases of the original, place them within quotation marks (see section **50h**).

Paraphrase note card

> Cause of CFS, Sakandelidze 112
>
> Although the actual cause of CFS is still unknown, researchers offer several theories. Recent Soviet research establishes a direct link between the central nervous system and the immune system. According to this research, certain emotional states, such as stress and depression, seem to inhibit the immune system of certain people and to cause "a predisposition to viral infection."

This paraphrase puts the material into the researcher's words with special emphasis on key words of the original. The writer wraps the critic's ideas into the discussion and thereby avoids inserting a long, formal quotation.

Take notes for a purpose.

As demonstrated above, a well-written note card is a building block of the research paper. It should defend and support the thesis sentence or a section of the outline. Therefore, as you encounter each article or book, carefully evaluate its contribution to your work. A single, small passage might well be the only portion of a book that you use. Check the book's table of contents and index or the article's abstract to see if the work contains what you are looking for.

Evaluate sources.

Be selective of whom you cite and of how you cite them in your research paper. Follow these guidelines.

Recent sources

You should search for up-to-date materials, especially for scientific and technical subjects. This rule is not as compelling in the humanities, where a biography of a person like Abraham Lincoln will remain pertinent for many years.

Reliable sources

Depend first on journal articles, which are timely and scholarly. Depend second on books, which are thorough, usually scholarly, but not necessarily timely. Depend third on magazine articles, which are seldom scholarly and sometimes biased in use of factual evidence.

Use *citation searching*, if necessary, to locate the most reliable experts on the subject. Find three or more bibliographies on your narrowed subject, compare names in these lists to find authors who appear more than once, and read the works by these writers. The fact that certain authors have been cited several times indicates their importance to the field and suggests that you, too, should read their works.

In addition, consult *Book Review Digest* for evaluations of books in the social sciences and humanities. Consult *Technical Book Review Index* for commentary on books in the physical and applied sciences. Consult *Magazines for Libraries* to check on a magazine's reputation for reliable reporting.

The author's purpose

If you understand what a writer has tried to accomplish with a work, you can determine more its relevance to your research. Read the abstract to a journal article. If none is available, look for clues to the writer's purpose by reading the first few paragraphs. With a book, consider carefully any subtitle, which often sets the direction of a work. Consult the writer's preface and/or the introduction. Look closely at the book's table of contents and index to determine how thoroughly the book treats your specific subject.

Use both primary and secondary sources.

A **primary source** is an original work, such as the following:

> novel, poem, play, short story, diary, or journal
> letter, speech, original essay, or autobiography
> interview or questionnaire
> original market research

A **secondary source** is another person's writing about a primary source. The following are secondary sources:

> history books and articles
> news reports
> critical reviews in magazines and newspapers
> critical biographies in books and journal articles
> interpretation of the writings and work of others
> evaluation of the scientific or artistic work of others

Thus, a speech by the president is a primary source; the analysis of the speech by a print or broadcast journalist is a secondary source.

Use primary sources frequently in your research paper. Use secondary sources cautiously and with restraint. Secondary sources are comments made after the fact. Experts as well as pseudo-experts appear to explain a presidential speech, analyze an economic plan by Congress, interpret a poem, or review a movie. Part of your work will require sifting through secondary sources to find valid statements by recognized authorities.

50f   Avoid plagiarism in your notes and text.

Plagiarism is the theft of another person's work. Some writers purposely borrow passages with no intention of crediting the source. Other writers are merely negligent, forgetting to cite the source or failing to paraphrase and quote it properly. The error often begins during note-taking when a researcher might fail to credit an author on a note card or forget to place quotation marks around borrowed passages. Plagiarism takes several forms:

1. The presentation of another person's essay or theme as your own, a form of stealing as well as deception

2. The wholesale copying of sentences and entire paragraphs without quotation marks and without credit to the sources
3. The paraphrasing of sources without credit to the original writers
4. Giving credit to the source but then copying parts of the original without use of quotation marks

Here is an original statement followed by samples that demonstrate two instances of plagiarism and two correct paraphrases:

ORIGINAL: Trudeau's getting away with it because his medium is the comic strip, and, ergo, not recognized as a serious form. Of course, Trudeau is quite serious. — "Satire Gap," *New Republic* (1 Dec. 1986: 42).

UNACCEPTABLE PARAPHRASE: G. B. Trudeau succeeds where others fail because of the medium, the comic strip, which people do not consider serious in form or content.

Readers will assume that this is the writer's own thought. It paraphrases the original but fails to credit the true author.

UNACCEPTABLE PARAPHRASE: The *New Republic* offers insight on this issue, saying that Trudeau gets away with bitter sarcasm because his medium is the comic strip, which is not recognized as a serious form (42).

This writer credits the source but has copied words of the original without placing them within quotation marks.

ACCEPTABLE PARAPHRASE AND QUOTATION: The *New Republic* adds the thought that Trudeau succeeds where others fail because of his medium, the comic strip, which is "not recognized as a serious form" ("Satire Gap" 42).

This combination of methods correctly introduces the source to show when borrowing begins, paraphrases a portion of the source, and encloses another portion within quotation marks. Parenthetical documentation (see section **50i**) signals the end of the citation.

ACCEPTABLE PARAPHRASE: The *New Republic* suggests that Trudeau succeeds where others fail because of the medium, the comic strip, which people do not consider serious in form or content ("Satire Gap" 42).

This paraphrase effectively restates the original and credits the source.

Avoiding plagiarism at the note-taking stage will serve your needs up to a point. During the writing stage, you must guard against unintentionally revising your notes back into the original wording. Generally, save all materials, including photocopies of original works, and double-check your draft for accuracy of direct quotation and for instances of plagiarism.

Common Knowledge Exceptions

You need not document information if it is common knowledge, even though you find it in sources. This includes major historic events, birth and death dates, accomplishments on record, familiar proverbs, well-known quotations, and so forth. General information is not the province of any one writer. The fact that General Lee surrendered to General Grant at Appomattox is common knowledge; you need not cite it even though a source mentions it. However, if one historian expresses an opinion about the event, such as that Lee capitulated too early without the advice and consent of the entire Confederacy, you must cite the source of the opinion.

50g Plan and write the paper.

After you have taken all of the notes you need, you are ready to organize your materials and begin drafting. The notes may initially appear disjointed, but if you researched a well-focused topic guided by a preliminary thesis sentence, your work will begin to take shape.

Focus on the thesis sentence and outline.

Because a research paper analyzes an issue in depth, the **thesis sentence** must be well focused, and the structure must clearly and logically support the thesis (see chapter **48**). If your evidence on the note cards does not match the argument, revise the preliminary thesis or return to the library for more research.

Develop an **outline** and arrange your notes to match (see section **1i** for a discussion of outlining forms). Your outline should be flexible to adapt to the information you have available. It should also be dynamic in its step-by-step progression through the issues, culminating with the best evidence for the strongest part of the paper — the last few pages.

Build the outline in stages. First, start with a list of the major categories and divide your note cards accordingly. Do you have supporting evidence for each category? If not, abandon a category or return to the library for more information. Second, subdivide each category into two or more parts (see section **6h** for tips about classifying for analysis). Third, adjust and subdivide further as you work through the draft.

NOTE: If you anticipate that readers will question your position, arm yourself with sufficient evidence and critical commentary. See chapter **48** for a detailed discussion about using inductive and deductive reasoning in defense of your thesis.

Develop the introduction, conclusion, and title.

The **introduction**, which some writers draft last, must identify and define your specific topic. Make certain that your thesis sentence has a prominent position. Have the thesis sentence begin the paper if you need to establish quickly the direction of the study; otherwise, delay the thesis until you have established the subject, narrowed to a key issue, defined key terminology, and explained traditional views and background information. For sample introductions, see section **2b**.

Write a **conclusion** that makes a judgment, endorses a position, defends an idea, or offers guidelines. Do not merely repeat your thesis and give a brief summary; rather, repeat it in modified form and reach beyond it to explain the significance of your findings. See section **2d** for a full discussion on writing effective conclusions.

The **title**, often written last, should describe clearly the subject and the specific issue or problem: "Creative Word Play in the Poetry of E. E. Cummings." Do not use abbreviated titles ("Word Play"), broad, unspecified titles ("The Poetry of Cummings"), or fancy literary titles ("Consuming Cummings").

Create the body of the research paper.

The **body** of a research paper, like that of an essay, must defend the thesis sentence with a careful classification and analysis of the issues and with sufficient factual data. See section **2c** for a full discussion of techniques for building the body of a paper.

The body of a research paper presents special problems not present in a regular essay, however. In a research paper, you must blend reference sources smoothly and correctly into your text. They must augment, not intrude upon, the flow of your presentation (see section **50h**). You should not insert isolated quotations without context or, worse, string together a series of sources without your commentary. Source materials reinforce your ideas and thoughts; they are not substitutes for them.

Revise and edit.

Revise the early drafts of your paper carefully. (See section **3a**.) When you are satisfied with the organization and argument and are ready to fine-tune the individual sentences, edit them for tone, consistency, and conciseness. (See section **3b** and chapters **16–18**.)

50h   Integrate quotations carefully.

As you add the words and ideas of source materials to your own ideas, remember that the research paper is *yours*, not a collection of other writers' voices. Do not insert isolated quotations without context or, worse, string together a series of quotations without your commentary. Integrate the quotations with your own thoughts, and, remember, you need not quote an entire sentence. (The documentation forms are addressed in section **50i**.)

```
One source argues that the design of college
facilities was made uncomfortable "lest the
students become distracted and fall asleep"
(Sommer 110).
```

Use a verb with your signaling phrases that specifies an authority's stance ("one source argues"); readers soon tire of "Jones says" and "Thompson says."

```
Thompson counters that . . .
Jones concludes her article with sage
    advice: " . . .
As one researcher discovered, " . . .
```

Use verbs appropriate to the circumstances, such as *admits, believes, claims, denies, illustrates, rejects, thinks,* and others.

Use the following techniques to incorporate quotations into your writing.

Capitalization

Use a comma or a colon after the signaling phrase and capitalize the quotation if it is a complete sentence.

```
Dennis Jones records a somewhat surprising fact:
"Approximately half of the immigrants who flocked
to Kansas in the decade following the Civil War
were women" (7).

As one historian notes, "Approximately half of
the immigrants who flocked to Kansas in the decade
following the Civil War were women" (Jones 7).
```

However, initial capital letters in quoted material can be changed to lowercase if the quotation is syntactically part of your sentence (see section **45b**):

```
Dennis Jones asserts that "approximately half of
the immigrants who flocked to Kansas in the decade
following the Civil War were women" (7).
```

The restrictive connector *that* (see sections **36e** and **37c**) makes a comma and capitalization unnecessary. See also section **36j** for punctuation guidelines.

Ellipsis

As shown in section **41i**, ellipsis points signal omissions within quotations. Use the ellipses to omit words that are unrelated to your argument and to keep your statements concise.

> Robert Sommer, in his discussion of
> hard architecture in schools, notes that
> "architects . . . were advised against making the
> furnishings too pleasant or comfortable lest the
> students become distracted or fall asleep" (110).

Brackets

Brackets enable you to insert your own wording within a quotation to clarify a point, to establish correct grammar, and to signal errors in the original (see section **41h**). If your typewriter or printer does not contain brackets, draw them in.

> One critic observes, "In this novel [<u>Sophie's
> Choice</u>] Styron hints autobiographically at his
> own passionate struggles to become a writer"
> (Webster 114).

> "What Ernest Hemmingway [sic] did for expatriots
> in Europe William Faulkner did for displaced whites
> and blacks of the South" (Thurman 34).

The word *sic*, which is Latin for "thus," indicates an error in the original.

Long quotations

Indent long quotations of four lines or more. Omit quotation marks, indent ten spaces from the left margin, and place the parenthetical reference outside the final period. Use a colon or a comma after the signaling phrase, whichever is appropriate.

```
At the end of "Winter Dreams" Dexter Green
confronts in bewilderment his frustrations:
                He wanted to care, and he could not
                care. For he had gone away and he could
                never go back any more. The gates were
                closed, the sun was gone down, and there
                was no beauty but the gray beauty of
                steel that withstands all time. Even the
                grief he could have borne was left behind
                in the country of illusion, of youth, of
                the richness of life, where his winter
                dreams had flourished. (Fitzgerald 338)
Not until The Great Gatsby would Fitzgerald explore
again this theme of anguished, lost love.
```

Poetry

Indent and space lines of poetry exactly as they appear in the text you are using.

```
In her poem "The Universe," May Swenson asks
questions that humanity has pondered from time
immemorial:
                        And what
                if the universe
                        is not about us?
                Then what?
                        What
                        is it about?
                And what
                        about us? (24-31)
```

If you are quoting two or three lines in your text, separate the lines with a slash (/) that has a space on either side of it:

```
In her poem "The Universe," May Swenson asks a
question that humanity has pondered from time
immemorial: "And what / if the universe / is not
about us?" (24-26).
```

50i   Use the MLA style of documentation for language and literature courses.

The form that you use to document source materials should be consistent and should conform to a recognized system. Each academic discipline has its own style. This chapter introduces the style of the Modern Language Association (MLA)—as detailed in the *MLA Handbook for Writers of Research Papers* (3rd ed., 1988)—which governs papers in language and literature. It sets guidelines for introducing, punctuating, and citing sources in the text and for listing all sources used in the paper. (See also Chapter **51**, which introduces the documentation style of the American Psychological Association [APA] for papers in the social sciences and other disciplines.)

Text references

When you are writing your paper, each time you paraphrase, quote, or summarize any borrowed material, you must provide the source of that material. State the source briefly in the text and in detail in the list of works cited at the end of the paper. It is also helpful to the reader if you introduce another person's work with a signaling phrase. The following subsections address the various treatments of borrowed material in the text.

General references

```
In his autobiography, A Time to Heal, Gerald Ford
explains that his attitudes about Congress changed
radically after he succeeded Nixon in the White
House.
```

The signaling phrase, indicated by italics, identifies the author, the title, and the context of the book. The general description gives no page reference because the writer refers to the book as a whole, not to a specific page or set of pages. Full citation to Ford's book will appear at the end of the paper (see the "List of Works Cited," section **50j**).

Source in parentheses

If the signaling phrase is nonspecific or is omitted, name the author and page number in parentheses after the quotation. Note that the period for the sentence follows the parentheses.

> After switching from Congress to the White
> House, one president recognized that "Congress
> was beginning to disintegrate as an organized
> legislative body" (Ford 150).

If the signaling phrase already provides it, the author's name does not need to be included in the parentheses.

> After becoming president, Gerald Ford recognized
> that "Congress was beginning to disintegrate as an
> organized legislative body" (150).

Multiple authors

For two or three authors, give the names in the text or in the parentheses:

> Borgman, Loveless, and Dimple, stressing the
> persuasive appeal of advertising slogans, argue
> that the witty, rhythmic phrasing causes a quick
> yes reaction (312).

For four or more authors, give the first author's name and then "et al." (Latin for "and others"):

> One group of doctors argues that the difference in
> the threshold is too small to distinguish between
> groups (Holmes et al. 2302).

No author

So readers will know where to look in the list of works cited, provide the title with the page number for works that have no author.

> One pamphlet labels the teenage drinking laws as the first step in a push for national prohibition (<u>The Ultimate Goal</u> 11).

Corporate author

> The Coalition of Southern States, which recently published <u>The Foreign Aid Burden</u>, warns that foreign aid programs have increased life expectancies in Third World countries, which might increase pressure for more aid from the United States (16).

This example uses the name of a corporate author in the signaling phrase. Use a shortened version (CSS) within the parentheses only after first mention of the full name.

Two or more works in the parenthetical citation

Cite each work in the normal fashion, but separate the sources by semicolons. If the citation gets too long, consider the use of an endnote (see pages 492 and 509).

> Independent investigations on three fronts produced similar findings about fraudulent political favors to campaign contributors (Booker 12; House Committee on Ethics 312; Tribble et al. 34–56).

Volume number, chapter number, and other details

A multivolume work may require citation to a specific volume and page number. Type the volume number, then a colon, a space, and the page number.

> "By mid-autumn of 1893," says Seale, "Cleveland had lost his political base, and his party was crumbling from dissension" (2: 607).

If a given page of a work contains more than one table or figure, name the page on which it appears and the specific illustration you are referring to.

> One authority advances the computer as one vital tool for assisting business executives "in any aspect of decision making" (Reid 13, Figure 1).

For classic literary works that may appear in several different editions, include chapter, act, scene, canto, and line as a service to those readers who may have a different edition in hand. As shown below, give the page number first, followed by a semicolon, and then abbreviated information about where precisely the event or quotation is located.

DRAMA

> In T. S. Eliot's drama, the four knights confront Thomas Becket and accuse him of breaking his oath and betraying the king (203; pt. 2, sc. 1).

POETRY

> Whitman is comfortable with his poetic role, saying "I do not trouble my spirit to vindicate itself or be understood" and also "I exist as I am, that is enough" (1052; st. 20, lines 410 and 414).

NOTE: Do not use the abbreviation *l.* or *ll.*, which readers might confuse with numbers.

PROSE

> Voltaire does not allow Candide to find satisfaction with life in any part of the world. Even in Eldorado Candide grows weary and complains to Cacambo that "we shall be no different from anybody else" (82; ch. 18). He wants to return to the old world where he can be richer than a king.

An indirect source

When a quotation appears in someone else's work, say so:

> Paul Klee describes a beholder's eye as a "grazing
> animal" that moves over the surface of a painting
> (qtd. in Colley 8).

The signaling phrase indicates the speaker, and the parenthetical citation names the source; the works cited entry will need to list Colley's work where the reader can find the information.

Nonprint sources

There can be no page citations for nonprint sources, so you should indicate in your text the special nature of the source and you must provide an identifying reference to your works cited page, usually the name of a person, either in the text or in parentheses.

> In a telephone interview on this subject, one
> professional defended the architectural design of
> the new building as a modern adaptation of gothic
> design (Pembroke).

> The lecture by Lewis Newhurst reminded everyone
> that "technological progress, while beneficial in
> many ways, may not be good for people in given
> instances."

Using notes with text references

Use footnotes or endnotes for three purposes only: (1) to provide bibliographic citations containing numerous sources, (2) to make evaluative comments on the sources, or (3) to offer an explanation or provide information that is not germane to your discussion. In the text refer to notes with raised numbers in consecutive order.

> Although numerous critics have examined Ishmael's
> role in <u>Moby Dick</u>,[1] Ishmael's sense of humor has
> not received its justified recognition.

Match that number with a footnote at the bottom of the page or, better, with an endnote on a separate "Notes" page that should precede the "Works Cited" page.

> [1] See, for example, the works of Weaver 90–154; Simon 314–56; Mumford 78–121; Auden 67; and Warren 208–23.

NOTE: List complete information on these sources in the list of works cited.

50j Create a list of works cited.

At the end of your research paper, on a separate sheet, prepare a page that lists all sources mentioned in the paper. The purpose of the Works Cited list is to name every source you refer to in the paper and to provide complete bibliographic information about each one. The list gives your argument credibility, and it provides all the information necessary for a reader to locate a given work and read further about the topic. (See page 510 for an example.)

Each entry on the list basically should include the author, the title of the work, the publisher, and the date of publication. Depending on the type of work it is, each entry may also contain information about the edition number, the editor's name, the volume or issue numbers, the page numbers, and any other data necessary to identify the given source. Consult the examples below and adapt your sources accordingly.

Format

Start each citation at the left margin and indent succeeding lines five spaces. Type two spaces after periods and one space after colons and commas. Double-space the lines throughout.

Begin your alphabetical list by inverting the first author's name or, if no author is listed, by the first important word of the title. Follow the guidelines for capitalization (chapter **45**) and italicization (chapter **42**) of titles.

If you have two or more works by the same author, list them alphabetically by title and provide the author's name only for the first entry. Thereafter, type three hyphens in place of the author's name (see the examples on pages 496, 497, and 511).

Books

For books, list the author's full name, the book's title and subtitle, and the edition, if applicable. Then type the city of publication, followed by a colon, the shortened name of the publisher, and finally the year.

One author

>   Kissinger, Henry. <u>White House Years</u>. Boston:
>   Little, 1979.

Two or three authors

>   Choy, Penelope, and James McCormick. <u>Basic Grammar
>   and Usage</u>. 3rd ed. San Diego: Harcourt,
>   1990.

>   Blacker, Roland F., Ralph Edwards, and Harold Y.
>   Richardson. <u>The Jet Stream</u>. New York: Bowan,
>   1990.

Four or more authors

Although you may write out all authors' names, it is generally easier to list the first author's name and then write "et al.," which is an abbreviation of *et alii* (Latin for "and others").

>   Kermode, Frank, et al. <u>The Oxford Anthology of
>   English Literature</u>. 2 vols. New York: Oxford
>   UP, 1973.

Editor as author

>   Goldberger, Leo, and Shlomo Breznitz, eds.
>   <u>Handbook of Stress: Theoretical and Clinical
>   Aspects</u>. New York: Free, 1982.

Corporate author

>   Chronic Fatigue Syndrome Society. <u>CEBU</u>. Portland:
>   CFSS, 1988.

Foreword, introduction, afterword

> Bailey, Elizabeth E. Foreword. <u>Contestable
> Markets and the Theory of Industry
> Structures</u>. By William J. Baumol, John C.
> Panzar, and Robert D. Willig. Rev. ed. San
> Diego: Harcourt, 1988. iv–xv.

Reprint of part of a book

> Huggins, Nathan Irvin. "The Rupture and the
> Ordeal." <u>Black Odyssey: The Afro-American
> Ordeal</u>. New York: Pantheon, 1977. Rpt. in
> <u>Short Essays: Models for Composition</u>. Ed.
> Gerald Levin. 5th ed. San Diego: Harcourt,
> 1989. 48–56.

A work in several volumes

> Nietzsche, Friedrich Wilhelm. <u>The Will to Power</u>.
> Trans. Anthony M. Ludovici. Vol. 14 of <u>The
> Complete Works of Friedrich Nietzsche</u>. Ed.
> Oscar Levy. 16 vols. New York: n.p., 1924.

NOTE: The *n.p.* refers to "no publisher." It can also mean "no place."

Part of an anthology or collection

The entry below cites a novel as reproduced in an anthology:

> Twain, Mark. <u>The Adventures of Huckleberry Finn</u>.
> <u>The American Tradition in Literature</u>. Ed.
> Sculley Bradley, Richmond C. Beatty, and E.
> Hudson Long. 3rd ed. 2 vols. New York:
> Norton, 1967. 2: 266–487.

The next entry cites an essay from a collection:

```
Golding, William.  "Thinking as a Hobby."  Readings
    for Writers.  Ed. Jo Ray McCuen and Anthony
    Winkler.  6th ed.  San Diego: Harcourt, 1989.
    573—80.
```

If you cite several sources from one anthology, simplify your entries by cross-referencing them to the primary source:

```
Bradley, Sculley, Richard C. Beatty, and E. Hudson
    Long, eds.  The American Tradition in
    Literature.  3rd ed.  2 vols.  New York:
    Norton, 1967.
Twain, Mark.  Huckleberry Finn.  Bradley, Beatty,
    and Long 2: 266—487.
---.  "The Man That Corrupted Hadleyburg."
    Bradley, Beatty, and Long 2: 226—65.
```

See the Twain entry above for a citation from one volume of a set. See also the Bradley entry above for a citation to an entire set.

Encyclopedias and other alphabetized works

```
Moldenke, Harold N.  "Flower."  World Book
    Encyclopedia.  1976 ed.
```

Periodicals

For articles, list the author (name inverted), the title, the publication name, the date followed by a colon, and the page numbers. Note, however, the slight differences in form among the magazine, journal, and newspaper citations.

Magazine article

```
Brothers, Hardin.  "Assembly in C Major."  PC
    Resource May 1987: 109+.
```

Journal article

```
Conners, Robert J.  "The Rhetoric of Explanation:
     Explanatory Rhetoric from Aristotle to
     1850."  Written Composition 1 (1984):
     189-210.
---.  "The Rhetoric of Explanation: Explanatory
     Rhetoric from 1850 to the Present."  Written
     Composition 2 (1985): 49-72.
```

Note that the volume number immediately follows the journal title. If a journal numbers its issues, type a period and the issue number directly after the volume number ("42.4").

Newspaper article

```
Bostick, Alan.  "Stereo Vibrations That Faded
     Fast."  Tennessean [Nashville] 9 Aug. 1989,
     Sunday ed.: 2-G.
Hershey, Robert D.  "Advances: Extracting Gold from
     the Desert."  New York Times 5 Aug. 1989: D6.
```

Most newspapers include the city's name in the title. If the newspaper you are referring to does not do so, add the city's name in brackets, as shown in the first entry above.

Miscellaneous works

Government document

Provide the government, the body, any subsidiary bodies, the title of the document, additional specifications, and publication facts.

```
United States.  Cong.  Senate.  Special Committee on
     Aging.  Living between the Cracks: America's
     Chronic Homeless.  98th Cong., 2nd sess.  S.
     Hrg. 98-1299.  Washington: GPO, 1987.
```

Computer software

> McVicar, Chris. <u>Image Print</u>. Computer software. Sunnyvale, CA: PC-SIG, 1987. C-basic diskette for IBM PC.

Data base source

> Nevin, John J. "Doorstop to Free Trade." <u>Harvard Business Review</u> 61 (1983): 88–95. DIALOG Information Services, 1983, record no. 83-N43.

Review

> Grevstad, Eric. "A Remarkable Writer." Rev. of <u>Textra 4.0</u> (computer software), by Ann Arbor Software. <u>PC Resource</u> May 1987: 127–28.
> Tozer, Eliot. Rev. of <u>Gardening for Love</u>, by Elizabeth Lawrence. <u>Horticulture</u> July 1987: 66+.

Interview

> Loven, Charles. Personal interview. 9 May 1987.

Lecture

> Sullivan, Margaret. "Mark Twain." Lecture on videotape. Durham: U of North Carolina, 1987.

Letter

> Warren, Robert Penn. Letter to the author. 15 Apr. 1987.

Painting

> Wood, Grant. <u>American Gothic</u>. The Art Institute, Chicago.

Unpublished manuscript

```
Cunningham, Susan Y. "The Incident at the Chinese
    Restaurant." Unpublished manuscript and
    notes. Heard Library, Vanderbilt U, 1987.
```

50k   Format and proofread the final version of the paper.

Type your paper on 8½- by 11-inch heavy stock, not onion skin or erasable paper. Set your margins at one inch on each side and on the bottom of the page. Type the running head, which consists of your last name followed by a space and the page number, one-half inch from the top of the page and ending on the right margin. Begin the first line of the page one inch from the top of the paper. Double-space all lines of type, and center all headings.

Indent paragraphs five spaces from the left margin, and indent quotations of four or more lines ten spaces from the left margin. The sample research paper below demonstrates the MLA format.

After you have typed your paper, make sure to proofread it carefully. Remember that typographical errors left in the work diminish your paper's credibility. Look for errors in spelling (use the spelling function if you are using a word-processing program), punctuation, capitalization, spacing, and so forth. Also read the final copy against the previous, edited draft to make sure that you did not inadvertently add or drop any words. If you can make the corrections neatly on your typewriter, do so. Otherwise draw a single line through the errors, place a caret (∧) directly underneath where your corrections should go, and print the corrections neatly above the typed line.

50 l   Sample research paper

The following research paper in MLA style demonstrates the format for papers in language and literature courses. Consult chapter **51** for the form and style of papers in the social sciences, in business, and in certain of the humanities.

Rogers 1

Melissa Rogers

Mrs. Rollins

Freshman Composition

May 7, 1990

For the format of an MLA paper, see pp. 493, 499.

Chronic Fatigue Syndrome

Chronic Fatigue Syndrome (CFS) is a disease that begins with conditions similar to the flu, but even with bed rest the victims sink into exhaustion and experience a variety of random, unrelated symptoms: exhaustion, fever, sore throat, headaches, dizziness, memory loss, confusion, and sensitivity to noise and extreme temperatures. Isolation of the patient also causes depression (<u>Decisions</u>). One sufferer describes her illness as ''chronic mono with a touch of Alzheimer's'' (qtd. in Johnson, ''Journey'' 56). Another victim describes herself as ''a Raggedy Ann with no stuffing'' (qtd. in Seligmann 105). The disease is more serious than mononucleosis, the so-called teenage kissing disease, and it attacks an older age group, especially aggressive young professionals. In truth, CFS is a relatively new disease, or at least a new diagnosis, and both the medical community and the general public need to awaken to its perils.

See pp. 43, 483 about writing a title.

Write a strong and effective introduction (pp. 32–34, 483).

Place the thesis carefully (pp. 21–23, 482).

Rogers 2

James F. Jones, a research
immunologist, argues that too many doctors
remain unaware of CFS (qtd. in "Elusive"
4). Such ignorance, if true, seems
inexcusable. USA Today reports that ninety
percent of Americans over thirty have been
exposed to the Epstein-Barr virus, although
it remains dormant in most people
("Elusive" 4). The Epstein-Barr virus is
what causes mononucleosis. Hillary Johnson
declares that some physicians "totally
ignore" the presence of the virus
("Journey" 57). One physician, Holly
Atkinson, takes CFS seriously and condemns
doctors who urge "there's nothing wrong"
or "it's all in your head" (flyleaf).

After all, the victims of CFS are
numerous. Kevin Scanlon reports that the
disease may cause exhaustion problems for
100,000 people in the United States (74).
He labels the syndrome "the yuppie plague"
because of the characteristics of the
victims--highly stressed overachievers
between the ages of thirty and forty
(Scanlon 74). Yuppies are identified in
part because they have the money and the
stamina to pursue a diagnosis. However,
Hillary Johnson warns that lower-class

Write a complete,
well-organized
body, and use a
variety of
sources.

Cite a title in the
text if the Works
Cited contains
more than one
work by the same
author.

Provide the au-
thor's name and
the page number
in an in-text cita-
tion (p. 489).

Rogers 3

victims often go undetected because of their "meager" financial situations ("Journey" 141). In addition, Johnson reports that "women are more susceptible to the illness because their overactive immune systems produce overwhelming responses to the virus" ("Growing" 55).

Although the actual cause of CFS is still unknown, researchers postulate many theories. Recent Soviet research establishes a direct link between the central nervous system and the immune system. According to this research, certain emotional states, such as stress and depression, seem to inhibit the immune system and result in a predisposition to viral infection (Sakandelidze 112). The evidence seems to indicate that there may indeed be certain psychological factors that may lead to CFS. Jane Brody says that many physicians link CFS with fibromyalgia, a debilitating fatigue. She cautions, however, that fibromyalgia may have similar symptoms but is most often the result of trauma and does not seem to have the characteristics of the disease associated with CFS (B-18).

Avoid plagiarism (pp. 480–82).

The primary cause of CFS seems to be

Rogers 4

viral. The leading candidate, according
to Dianne Hale, is the Epstein-Barr virus,
since it infects white blood cells and
defeats the immune system (56). The virus
is carried in saliva, so most Americans have
been exposed to it (Hale 56). Those persons
exposed may not acquire the syndrome, but
many of them could activate the virus in
their bodies by undue stress (Spear V-31).
Goldberger and Breznitz say the immune
systems will then work overtime to fight the
virus (26). These two writers use the term
"coping" as the psychological edge most
victims need in dealing with the disease
(Goldberger and Breznitz 24). Dean Edell
adds that the Epstein-Barr virus "could
be set off by another virus in the immune
system" (qtd. in Scanlon 75). And Allen D.
Allen, scientific director of the Center
for Viral Diseases, believes that CFS should
warn physicians that a disease exists in the
immune system (Scanlon 74).

 Unfortunately, the symptoms are similar
to those of other diseases, so the CFS
Society argues that the symptoms cannot be
the sole basis for a diagnosis. In its
pamphlet the CFS Society urges doctors to
examine symptoms and conduct a blood test to

To paraphrase a source, see pp. 478, 480–82.

Quote sources carefully (pp. 477, 480–82).

To summarize a source, see p. 476.

Rogers 5

measure for the Epstein-Barr virus antibody
titers.[1] One group of doctors argues
that the difference in the virus is often
too small to distinguish between patients
and nonpatients (Holmes et al. 2302);
nevertheless, CFS may be the proper
diagnosis if similar diseases are ruled
out and the symptoms persist ("Yuppie
Disease" 414).

    In brief, Chronic Fatigue Syndrome
results from the immune system working
overtime to fight the mysterious virus
(Eicher 34). According to research by
Spear, the symptoms begin as a flu-like
condition (V-31). For example, both Dianne
Hale and Robert Bazell in separate articles
report an "eternal flu" or a "yuppie
plague" (Bazell's terms) that afflicted two
hundred persons in Incline Village, Nevada
(Bazell 13; Hale 56). Both reports explain
that local doctors, Paul Cheney and Daniel
Peterson, knew the patients personally and
so rejected the idea that these incidents
were psychosomatic (Hale 57). The two
doctors diagnosed the outbreak as a virus
and advised the patients to rest; however,
the symptoms became worse. According to
Hale, the Center for Disease Control then

Use a superscript
no. to refer to a
content note (pp.
492–93, 509).

Separate two
sources by a
semicolon (p.
490).

Rogers 6

investigated the "exhaustion epidemic"
and diagnosed it as Chronic Fatigue
Syndrome (57).

Researchers suspect that the victims
have defective immune systems or that the
virus interacts with other viruses to weaken
immune systems, but why the Epstein-Barr
virus is active in some people and not
others is the subject of intense research
("Elusive Herpes" 4). In trying to
determine the exact cause, Robert Gallo, who
helped identify the AIDS virus, has examined
blood samples of some CFS victims and has
identified a new virus, HBLV, which is a
member of the herpes family that attacks
white blood cells (Bazell 13). Because HBLV
multiplies in a cell until it bursts, Gallo
has been unable to get a cell to live long
enough to conduct an investigation. Hillary
Johnson, reporting on Gallo's research,
suggests the possible source is the lowly
chicken ("Growing" 56). Gallo's statistics
are astonishing: ninety percent of chickens
tested were stricken with CFS-like symptoms
and, of this percentage, the majority were
middle-aged hens (Johnson, "Growing" 56).
Johnson warns that researchers should not
shun the idea of a virus being transmitted

Blend quotations,
summaries, and
paraphrases into
the text with
variety.

Rogers 7

from chickens to humans because the AIDS virus was passed on by African green monkeys ("Growing" 51).

Effects of CFS linger or disappear in part because of the victim's personality. Johnson finds that victims who accept the diagnosis and display positive attitudes will "lead more fulfilling lives" ("Growing" 46). However, Dianne Hale reports that most sufferers, because they are unproductive from the illness both at work and at home, consider their lives to be psychological or physical tragedies (58). Gidget Faubrion, president of the National Chronic Epstein-Barr Syndrome Association, claims that she receives six to seven suicide calls a day (qtd. in Marsa 160). The pamphlet The Thin Edge echoes this suicidal tendency, saying the depression sometimes becomes so powerful that sufferers have no reason to live.

Chronic suffers must learn to live with a physical disability of some sort, and a small percentage will experience mental disability and schizophrenia ("Elusive" 4). Johnson says that some victims may face "an enduring succession of heart attacks or strokes" ("Journey" 139). After the worst of the illness, the life of a chronic victim will consist of good and bad days. Scanlon reports that victims often abandon careers and even their families because of decreased energy levels and attention spans (74). Maria Mendez, who claims that "taking a shower is a major accomplishment," lost her job because of CFS (qtd. in Spear V-31). Darrell Anderson lost his job and his marriage yet blames himself "because I cannot get better" (qtd. in Eicher 34). The illness also affects the life savings of the victims. Eicher reports that victim Melanie Moore spent over twenty thousand dollars on doctor bills before she was properly diagnosed (34). Seligmann reports that a victim identified as Victoria spent money on twenty doctors before one finally diagnosed her Chronic Fatigue Syndrome (105). Now, even though Victoria's condition continues, Seligmann says Victoria "is enormously relieved to have a diagnosis at last" (105).

Better treatment, more precise drugs, and the growth of support groups will perhaps alleviate some distress for the thousands of victims. Treatments exist to reduce chronic symptoms, but Linda Marsa

Rogers 9

explains that medication cannot wholly
restore the patient's health (160).
Doxepin, an antidepressant and anti-
inflammatory drug, helps relieve patients if
it is coupled with proper diet and plenty of
rest (Marsa 160). Another source reports
that gamma globulin, the part of the blood
that contains antibodies, is one of the most
effective treatments ("Yuppie Disease"
414). Seligmann says that "some researchers
claim success with oral acyclovir, the drug
that was approved in 1985 for reducing the
symptoms of genital herpes" (106). The CFS
Society argues that the best advice is for
physicians to treat individual symptoms so
that victims can try to regain normal life-
styles.

Finally, support groups nationwide
must provide information and comfort to the
victims. Scanlon explains that uninformed
physicians and doubting doctors have forced
sufferers to fend for themselves (74).
After writing an article about the disease
in 1985, Martha Wolfe received letters from
victims who suspected that they too had CFS.
Working with Gidget Faubrion, Wolfe helped
form the first support group, the CFS
Society. Similar groups are now located in

Rogers 10

Canada, Australia, England, Israel, France,
New Zealand, and South America. Maria
Mendez, founder of another support group,
believes that "victims find comfort in
talking with people who understand this
illness" (qtd. in Spear V-31).

Chronic Fatigue Syndrome appears to be
the mystery illness of the 1990s, just as
AIDS started as the mystery illness of the
1980s. CFS changes life-styles and no exact
cure exists, so extensive research is vital
and public awareness is essential.

Write a strong
and effective con-
clusion (pp. 36–
38, 483).

Rogers 11

Note

[1] The article by Gary Holmes et al. in
JAMA provides a comprehensive explanation
of titers and the threshold levels. It
provides case studies, in-depth analysis,
two tables, and four figures that
graphically depict percentages and
distribution of titers in patients. It
also provides a thorough bibliography to
articles in medical journals.

For writing and
placing a content
note, see p. 492.

Rogers 12

See p. 493 to format a Works Cited list.

Works Cited

Atkinson, Holly. <u>Women and Fatigue</u>. New
    York: Putnam, 1985.

To cite a book, see p. 494.

Bazell, Robert. "Yuppie Plague." <u>New
    Republic</u> 27 Apr. 1987: 13–14.

Brody, Jane. "Personal Health." <u>New York
    Times</u> 7 Sept. 1989: B18.

To cite a newspaper article, see p. 497.

Chronic Fatigue Syndrome Society. <u>CEBU</u>.
    Portland: CFSS, 1988.

<u>Decisions: The Depressed Patient</u>. New York:
    Trainex, 1975.

Eicher, Diane. "Epstein-Barr: The Malaise
    of the '80s." <u>Denver Post</u> 21 Dec.
    1986: 24–25. Rpt. in <u>SIRS:
    Corrections</u>. Boca Raton: Social Issues
    Resources Series, 1987. 10 Art. 34.

To cite a reprinted work, see p. 495.

"Elusive Herpes Virus Often Misdiagnosed."
    <u>USA Today: The Magazine of the American
    Scene</u> 21 Feb. 1986: 4.

Begin the citation with a title when no author is listed.

Goldberger, Leo, and Shlomo Breznitz, eds.
    <u>Handbook of Stress: Theoretical and
    Clinical Aspects</u>. New York: Free,
    1982.

Hale, Dianne. "Why Are You So Tired?"
    <u>American Health</u> May 1987: 56–60.

Holmes, Gary P., et al. "A Cluster of
    Patients with a Chronic Mononucleosis-
    like Syndrome: Is Epstein-Barr Virus

To cite a journal article, see p. 497.

Rogers 13

the Cause?" <u>JAMA</u> 257.17 (1987): 2297–
2302.

Johnson, Hillary. "Journey into Fear."
Rolling Stone 30 July 1987: 56+.

---. "The Growing Nightmare of Epstein-Barr
Virus." <u>Rolling Stone</u> 13 Aug. 1987:
42+.

Marsa, Linda. "Chronic Fatigue Syndrome."
<u>Redbook</u> Apr. 1988: 120+.

Sakandelidze, O. "The Immune System: The
Sinews of Behavior." <u>Science in the
U.S.S.R.</u> Jan–Feb. 1990: 96–112.

Scanlon, Kevin. "Stress and a New
Plague." <u>Maclean's</u> 10 Nov. 1986:
74–75.

Seligmann, Jean. "Malaise of the '80s."
<u>Newsweek</u> 27 Oct. 1986: 105–06.

Spear, Linda. "Local Chapter Forms for
Patients with Epstein-Barr Virus." <u>New
York Times</u> 11 Jan. 1987: V-31, col. 1.

<u>The Thin Edge.</u> New York: Medcom, 1984. VTC
001.

United States. Dept. of Health and Human
Services. <u>Chronic Fatigue Syndrome</u>.
Atlanta: GPO, 1988.

"The Yuppie Disease: Epstein-Barr."
<u>Glamour</u> Sept. 1987: 414.

To cite two works
by the same au-
thor, see pp. 493,
496–97.

To cite a maga-
zine article, see p.
496.

To cite a govern-
ment document,
see p. 497.

51

Writing
Research Papers
across the
Curriculum

Different disciplines have different methods of documenting their scholarly papers. The MLA style, as detailed in chapter **50**, governs papers in languages and literature. Form and style in the sciences and in business differ from the MLA and from each other in several respects. Some of your instructors outside the English department will require a name-and-year system (usually the APA style) or a note system. Each of these systems is described below; your adjustment to them from the MLA style should be relatively easy. Consult chapter **50** for a full discussion of the major issues in the design and execution of research papers.

51a Use the APA system for most papers in business, social sciences, and education.

In-text citations

The American Psychological Association (APA) style of text citation, as set forth in its *Publication Manual* (3rd edition, 1984), is similar to the MLA style except that, in addition to naming the author and the page reference, the writer must also include the date of the source. (See the sample APA paper, section **51e**.)

For a *general reference*, include the year within parentheses immediately after the author's name.

> Vokey and Read (1985) attempt to disprove
> assertions that subliminal messages in popular
> music affect the behavior of listeners.

For a *direction quotation* or a *paraphrase* of specific, identifiable passages, cite the name (if not already given in the text), the year, and the page numbers in parentheses at the end of the quotation or at the end of the sentence, *before* the period, as shown below. Use the ampersand (&) in place of "and" for more than one author, insert a "p." to introduce the page number (or "pp." for inclusive numbers), and separate each element of the citation by commas.

> Jones asserts that subliminal messages in rock
> music especially have an effect upon the behavior
> of many adolescents (1984, p. 76).

> In response to assertions that subliminal messages
> in popular music affect the behavior of listeners,
> psychologists conclude that, "across a wide
> variety of tasks," they "were unable to find any
> evidence to support such a claim" (Vokey & Read,
> 1985, pp. 1231–1232).

Three or more authors

For *three to five* authors in a single text reference, name each author in the first occurrence (Barnwell, Bosley, & Finwick, 1987), but thereafter use the first author's name and "et al." (Barnwell et al., 1987). If two references shorten to the same form and year (e.g., Barnwell et al., 1987, for Barnwell, Bosley, & Finwick, 1987, as well as for Barnwell, Hodge, Edgeworth, & Peters, 1987), spell out all of the authors' names at each use. For *six* or more authors, list only the first author and "et al." in the first occurrence:

> Thompson et al. (1989) discovered two
> motivating factors.

Multiple citations

When you cite more than one work in parentheses, arrange them in *alphabetical order* according to the first name in each source, and separate the citations by semicolons. For multiple studies by the same author, arrange the dates in chronological order and separate them by a comma.

```
Much of this investigation has been influenced by
what researchers term the bilateral inversion
complex (Bergman, 1989; Koffworder, 1987, 1990;
Odel & Wellington, 1982a, 1982b).
```

Long quotations

Incorporate short quotations into the text, as shown in the examples above, but set apart a quotation of four or more lines. Indent the quotation five spaces, do not enclose it within quotation marks, and place the page number or numbers at the end of the quotation, *after* the closing punctuation.

```
Vokey and Read reach this conclusion:
        In summary, despite large effects in tasks
        requiring discrimination on the basis of
        physical parameters of backward speech, we
        could find no evidence that subjects are
        influenced either consciously or unconsciously
        by the semantic content of backward messages.
        (1985, p. 1237)
```

If you quote more than one paragraph, indent the first line of the subsequent paragraphs an additional five spaces.

Reference list entries

Arrange your list of references in alphabetical order. Start each entry at the left margin and indent succeeding lines three spaces. Double-space throughout.

APA style differs from MLA style in several ways in the reference list. For a paper in APA style, invert *all* authors' names, placing commas where necessary, and use the ampersand before the last author's name. Then type the date in parentheses and follow it with a period. For book and article titles, capitalize only the first word of the title and subtitle as well as any proper nouns. Also, type only one space after a period.

EXCEPTION: When you give a book or article title in the *text*, capitalize all major words and all minor words of four or more characters.

Book

```
Dixon, F. (1971). Subliminal perception: The
    nature of controversy. New York: McGraw-Hill.
```

Journal article

Note that the APA style does not enclose the article title in quotation marks, and it capitalizes only the first word of the article title and subtitle (as well as any proper nouns). The major words in the journal title, however, are all capitalized, and the entire title is underlined (italicized). If a journal numbers its pages consecutively throughout the year, place the underlined volume number after the journal title, separated from the title by a comma.

```
Vokey, John R., & Read, J. Don. (1985).
    Subliminal messages: Between the devil
    and the media. American Psychologist,
    40, 1231-1239.
```

If the journal numbers its pages anew in each issue, insert the issue number in parentheses directly after the volume number.

```
Garmezy, N. (1974). Children at risk:
    The search for the antecedents of
    schizophrenia. Schizophrenia Bulletin, 1(9),
    55-125.
```

Magazine or newspaper article

The date and page numbers for a magazine or newspaper reference differ from those for a journal article. Provide the full date, inverted, and insert "p." or "pp." after the publication title.

```
Sagan, C. (1987, September 13). Game: The
    prehistoric origin of sports. Parade,
    p. 10.
Sommer, J. (1984, February 28). Rockin' like the
    devil? Toronto Sun, pp. 26, 30.
```

For additional examples, see the reference list at the end of the sample APA research paper, page 528.

51b   Use the note system for papers in the humanities other than languages and literature.

Disciplines such as history, religion, music, dance, and art often use a note system to document sources. The writer inserts a raised number after a statement that requires documentation and then provides full source information in correspondingly numbered notes either at the bottom of the page (footnote style) or collected on a separate page at the end of the paper (endnote style). The endnote style is easier to use, and MLA prefers its use over the footnote style.

The note numbers in the text should follow all punctuation except a dash.

> We humans sleep in a celestial bed
> warmed by an electric blanket--the ozone
> layer. Unfortunately, this electric blanket
> has a short circuit and allows too much of
> the sun's radiation to enter the atmosphere.
> We humans, in truth, are responsible for both
> the depletion of the ozone layer and the
> creation of a greenhouse effect.[1] Pamela
> Zurer explains that ultraviolet radiation
> breaks down chemical elements in the
> chlorofluorocarbons that we pump into the
> atmosphere;[2] ultimately, the carbon atoms
> combine with the oxygen atoms to form carbon
> dioxide, which destroys ozone molecules.[3]
> Isaac Asimov notes that carbon dioxide
> molecules capture the infrared rays and
> keep them inside the earth's atmosphere,
> which causes the temperature to rise.[4]
> Consequently, one prominent scientist reminds
> us that "any technological solution to
> the looming greenhouse problem must be
> worldwide."[5] Many governments, indeed all
> nations, must begin regulating the production
> of chlorofluorocarbons.
>
> —CELESTE GOODWIN, student

Note style

Whether in footnote or endnote form, the sources should be arranged in an organized, consistent style. The examples provided below are in MLA style. If your instructor prefers another style, however, see the *Chicago Manual of Style* (13th ed., Chicago: U of Chicago P, 1982). (See also the list of discipline style manuals on page 518.)

If you are presenting your sources as endnotes, center the heading "Notes" one inch from the top of the separate page and double-space throughout. Indent the first line of an entry five spaces and begin all subsequent lines at the left margin. After a first full reference, use the last name and page number for all subsequent references to that source (see notes 3 and 5). Follow the numbering, punctuation, and spacing as shown below.

Notes

[1] Carl Sagan, "The Warming of the World," <u>Essay 2</u>, ed. Hans Guth and Renée H. Shea (Belmont: Wadsworth, 1987) 273.

[2] Pamela Zurer, "Producers, Users Grapple with Realities of CFC Phaseout," <u>Chemical & Engineering News</u> 24 (1989): 12.

[3] Zurer 13.

[4] Isaac Asimov, "For Mutual Survival We Must Bring Our World Together," <u>The Humanist</u> Sept.—Oct. 1989: 5.

[5] Sagan 273.

NOTE: A separate bibliography page is seldom necessary because the notes carry full documentation.

51c Use the appropriate styles of other disciplines.

Each discipline has its preferred style of documentation. This text has covered the prominent styles used in the humanities, the social sciences, and business (MLA, APA, and the note system — see sections **50i, 50 l, 51a**, and **51b**), but for your courses in the natural and applied sciences and in other technical fields, follow the procedures set forth in those disciplines' style manuals (see the list below). Your instructors will recommend which manuals to use.

Style manuals

American Chemical Society. *American Chemical Society Style Guide and Handbook*. Washington: American Chemical Soc., 1985.

American Institute of Physics. Publications Board. *Style Manual for Guidance in the Preparation of Papers*. 3rd ed. New York: American Inst. of Physics, 1978.

American Mathematical Society. *A Manual for Authors of Mathematical Papers*. 7th ed. Providence: American Mathematical Soc., 1980.

American Psychological Association. *Publication Manual of the American Psychological Association*. 3rd. ed. Washington: American Psychological Assn., 1983.

Associated Press. *The Associated Press Stylebook*. Dayton: Lorenz, 1980.

The Chicago Manual of Style. 13th ed. Chicago: U of Chicago P, 1982.

Council of Biology Editors. Style Manual Committee. *CBE Style Manual: A Guide for Authors, Editors, and Publishers in the Biological Sciences*. 5th ed. Bethesda: Council of Biology Editors, 1983.

Gibaldi, Joseph, and Walter S. Achtert, eds. *MLA Handbook for Writers of Research Papers*. 3rd ed. New York: Modern Language Assn., 1988.

Harvard Law Review. *A Uniform System of Citation*. 13th ed. Cambridge: Harvard Law Review Assn., 1981.

International Steering Committee of Medical Editors. "Uniform Requirements for Manuscripts Submitted to Biomedical Journals." *Annals of Internal Medicine* 90 (Jan. 1979): 95–99.

Linguistic Society of America. *LSA Bulletin*. Dec. issue, annual.

United States. Government Printing Office. *Style Manual*. Rev. ed. Washington: GPO, 1984.

United States. Geological Survey. *Suggestions to Authors of the Reports of the United States Geological Survey*. 6th ed. Washington: GPO, 1978.

51d Organize your paper according to the requirements of the discipline.

This text does not have enough room to elaborate on the variety of forms that instructors demand in various disciplines, yet a few guidelines may prove helpful.

Papers that review books and articles

Investigation of a topic often begins with a review and an evaluation of previous work as reported in the literature. You can develop your review in a number of forms. An **abstract** is a quick summary of the major ideas, accomplishments, or conclusions of one work. A **book review** surveys the content of a book and evaluates the contribution of the book to its field. An **annotated bibliography** is a list of publications on a topic that contains informative notes about each of the sources (pages 528–29 feature an annotated bibliography). A **review of the literature** is an essay that surveys the available articles on the topic, arranged chronologically or by classified topics (pages 522–29 feature a review of literature).

The review paper serves four purposes:

1. It tutors you in the state of current research.
2. It clearly defines the issue under investigation.
3. It summarizes previous investigations into the topic.
4. It searches out gaps in research and thereby opens windows to future work in the field.

Papers that analyze and advance a theory

The analytical paper examines a problem. It may clarify an abstraction, such as sexism, social biology, or genetic engineering, or it may analyze events and their causes and effects. In general, an analytical paper argues on the basis of published evidence, citing and analyzing the work of recent investigators. It is, in effect, a thesis or research paper, as discussed in chapter **50**.

Analysis of a problem serves three main purposes:

1. It examines an unresolved issue, such as subliminal techniques in advertising, to bring together in one paper the prevailing points of view.

2. It advances a theory in the form of a thesis sentence, which the writer can defend from the evidence gathered in books and articles.

3. It uses the original research studies of others but does *not* require first-hand research (see the next subsection).

Papers that report the results of an original study

On occasion you may conduct your own investigation of a problem. You will need a hypothesis, which is a statement that you advance as true for the purposes of investigation. In other words, you will offer a suppositional and conditional statement that you wish to prove with experimentation in the form of testing, observation, calculation, scoring, and other techniques. The results may prove you correct or they may invalidate your hypothesis; in either case, you should report the findings so that other researchers can build on your work.

Instructors in specific classes will direct your research to establish proper guidelines and procedures. Nevertheless, all papers of this type will conform in general to an established format, as follows.

1. Introduction

    Explain the problem under investigation. Include a brief survey of scholarly work in the field, especially to note any gaps or inconsistencies in previous studies. Advance your hypothesis and explain in some detail the purpose of the investigation.

2. Method

    Describe the design of the study. Generally, you must provide three subdivisions within this portion of the report: subjects, apparatus, and procedure.

    a. *Subjects.* Explain who participated in the study (two third grade classes at Miller Elementary school), how many participated (one control group of 25 third graders and one experimental group of 23 third graders), and how you selected them (a random choice from six third grade classes). Add other details as necessary, such as age, sex, and race. When you employ animals, give the genus, species, and strain number if such identification is available and important to the research.

b. *Apparatus*. Briefly explain the materials used in the study and their function. For example, describe any graphs, charts, drawings, or other stimuli that you presented to the experimental group of third grade students. Be specific so that subsequent research can duplicate your work.

c. *Procedure*. Explain each step in the execution of your research, such as your instructions to the third grade students, the arrangement of the students, and the nature of your testing.

3. Results

Summarize your findings and report the factual data without commentary. Include results that run counter to your hypothesis. Use tables, graphs, and charts to illustrate your results in a compact fashion. In cases where you have numerous scores or other raw data, summarize them in this section and put the data in an appendix at the end of the report.

4. Discussion

Analyze and interpret your results, especially to verify your hypothesis or refute it. In particular, explain what your research has contributed and how it confirms the hypothesis or resolves the initial problem.

51e Sample paper in APA style

The following paper illustrates one type of review article, demonstrates the APA style of documentation, and features an annotated bibliography.

Near-Death Experiences
1

Near-Death Experiences
A Selected Review of Literature
Aimee Beaudoin
Psychology 1030

Running Head: NEAR-DEATH EXPERIENCES

Near-Death Experiences

2

Near-Death Experiences

Selected Review of Literature

The literature on near-death experiences in recent years indicates that limited research has produced consistent findings. The near-death experiences contain transcendental or mystical elements that cannot be proven through scientific means since concrete evidence does not exist, yet the case studies and testimony of those who have had near-death experiences indicate an undeniable reality to these occurrences.

The writer introduces the topic and sets limits on the scope of the research.

After the publication of Raymond Moody's first book, Life After Life (1981), reports of near-death experiences occurred more frequently. New in-depth research now appears regularly, including Moody's latest, The Light Beyond (1988). He admits that "we are no closer to answering the basic question of the afterlife now than we were thousands of years ago" (Moody, 1988, p. 2), but more incidents occur monthly. "Other-world journeys," "near-death visions," or "near-death experiences" all contain the following similarities (Moody, 1988, p. 47):

a sense of being dead

peace and painlessness

The writer uses two pivotal books by Moody to establish the essential characteristics of the subject.

A page number is required with quotations.

Near-Death Experiences

3

    entering a dark region

    rising away from the body

    meeting deceased friends and relatives
      who are bathed in light

    encountering a supreme being also
      surrounded by light

    reviewing one's life

    a reluctance to return to earth

    In The Light Beyond, Moody pays
particular attention to the effects of near-
death experiences in children. The children
he interviews appear mature, sensitive,
and unafraid of death. They remain calm in
life-threatening situations. They are
understanding and pleasant toward others.
Even though society enforces the idea that
death is a terrible experience that must be
avoided at all cost, these children narrate
a different tale. Their "glimpse of the
beyond" enables them to view death as a
spiritual encounter (Moody, 1988, p. 154).

    Between Moody's two books, other works
have appeared. Robert Kastenbaum (1979) also
explores the borderline with Between Life
and Death. He describes his book as an
"effort to provide information, responsible
criticism, and sociohistorical context"

No page cita-
tion is required
for general ref-
erences to an
author's work.

Each paragraph
of the review
explores a spe-
cific work on
the subject.

Near-Death Experiences

4

(Kastenbaum, 1979, p. 1). He claims that a person's fear of death may trigger both physical and mental withdrawals which cause him or her, after recovery, to recall a "definite and mysterious link" between life and death (1979, p. 10).

Kenneth Ring (1985) in Heading Toward Omega also follows the guidelines established by Moody with one exception: his book attempts to describe the eventual "awakening." When a person returns from what Ring terms "Omega," he or she experiences a "higher spiritual reality." Ring believes the individual's new form of consciousness illustrates a "transcendental domain of preternatural peace and beauty" (1985, p. 6). Since the person discovers a new spiritual level, life changes completely after the return to life. Ring concludes that a fresh and fearless outlook allows those who experience near-death to live more productively with complete physical awareness that is accompanied by "an indescribable sense of understanding and compassion" (1985, p. 12).

William J. Serdahely's "The Near-Death Experience" (1987) interprets the

For book and article titles in the text, as shown throughout the paper, capitalize all major words and minor words of four letters or more.

525

Near-Death Experiences

5

"presence" felt or seen during near-death
experiences (p. 129). This presence allows
the experiencer to decide whether or not to
return to life by reviewing his or her past
and future while being surrounded by the
"brilliant golden light" (Serdahely, 1987,
p. 130). All three case studies in this
article recount experiences of "encounters
of the total self" (Serdahely, 1987,
p. 130). With a new sense of self-esteem,
the personalities of the individuals alter
drastically after their return to life.

      People who attempt suicide often
romanticize death. In his article in Suicide
and Life-Threatening Behavior, Bruce Greyson
(1986) concludes that suicide attempters
who have near-death experiences modify the
romantic notion because they undergo a
personality change. They no longer view
death as a way to punish those left behind;
accordingly, says Greyson, research in this
field may produce techniques for preventing
suicide (1986, p. 41). Statistics based on 61
suicide attempt cases support his hypothesis.
At least a quarter of his cases reported
similar descriptions of the near-death
phenomenon. Yet more research is needed to

Near-Death Experiences

6

relate the behavior changes more directly to
the dying experience.

Although investigation continues, the
absence of scientific proof suggests that
near-death experiences will remain an
intriguing phenomenon unless more in-depth
and scrutinizing research reveals facts
supporting this amazing theory. The thin line
between life and death remains invisible to
the naked eye.

The final paragraph reaches conclusions about the nature of the works discussed in the review.

Near-Death Experiences

7

References

Greyson, Bruce. (1986). Incidence of near-
    death experiences following attempted
    suicide. <u>Suicide and Life-Threatening</u>
    <u>Behavior</u>, <u>16</u>(1), 40—44. Greyson shows
    graphs and statistics supporting his
    hypothesis. Research is limited to 61
    cases. The text reveals no new
    discoveries.

Kastenbaum, Robert. (1979). <u>Between life and</u>
    <u>death</u>. New York: Springer. Kastenbaum
    uses various case studies to help prove
    that near-death experiencers no longer
    fear death. His research raises questions
    concerning when death actually occurs.

Moody, Raymond A. (1981). <u>Life after life</u>.
    St. Simon Island: Mockingbird Books. Moody
    examines the recovery and life-style of a
    person after a near-death experience.
    Compare it with his next book.

Moody, Raymond A. (1988). <u>The light beyond</u>.
    Toronto: Bantam Books. Moody fully
    describes all the stages a near-death
    experiencer passes through. He uses mainly
    case studies to support his ideas. He
    focuses on the religious aspect of
    returning to life.

Entry for a
journal article

Each entry is
annotated

Entry for a
book

Indent all sub-
sequent lines
three spaces.

For multiple
entries by the
same author, re-
peat the au-
thor's name for
each title.
(Compare MLA
style, pp. 493,
496, 497.)

Ring, Kenneth. (1985). <u>Heading toward Omega</u>.
    New York: Morrow, 1985. Ring concentrates
    on spiritual awakenings, describing the
    ''light'' as either Mary or God, but he
    never chooses one over the other.
Serdahely, William J. (1987). The near-death
    experience: Is the presence always the
    higher self? <u>Death and Dying</u>, <u>18</u>(1),
    129-134. Serdahely focuses around the
    ''light.'' He uses only three case studies
    to draw his hypothesis that an encounter
    occurs. Thus, his research appears limited
    and biased.

Business and Technical Writing

52
Business Correspondence
53
Résumés and Job Application Letters
54
Business and Technical Reports

52a Write succinct memos.

Memos (or memorandums) are brief forms of correspondence between members of an organization. They may circulate to one or more persons—a colleague, a committee, a department—and they communicate succinct and often immediate messages. As with all forms of writing, the audience and the purpose of the memo determine its level of formality.

The formality of memos is fairly standard. As shown below, always (1) address a specific audience; (2) give your name and title, if appropriate, and initial it (there is no signature on a memo); (3) give the date, with time of day if expediency is a factor; and (4) give a descriptive subject: "Nevin Avenue potholes," "Portable heaters for shipping department," or "Sales figures for August." Avoid a general subject like "For your information."

Make memos clear and accurate, for they sometimes serve as permanent records. Your first sentence should state the main point. The body, like the example below, gives only necessary information and instructions. It assumes the sales representatives know the product and will deal with the problem. The tone is appropriately informal, on a colleague-to-colleague basis. Referring by first name to someone known to all staff members is usual business practice.

Sample Memo

POND APPLE PHARMACEUTICALS

186 Bernard Avenue / Peterson, NJ 06987

TO: All sales representatives

FROM: Brad James,
National Sales Manager *B.J.*

DATE: October 14, 1989

SUBJECT: Dosage Change in Prinofin

Not all physicians are aware that we now offer
Prinofin in both 250 and 500 mg tablets. I
have sent you 100 copies of a brochure for you
to send to or leave with each of your clients
within the next two weeks. Doctors need to
hear about this change as soon as possible. We
will print soon an advertisement for the professional medical journals, but that will take
longer than your visit or direct mail.

If you need more copies of the brochure, call
the office and Jay will send them out.

52b   Write professional business letters.

Business letters place orders, sell products, inquire, complain, inform, discuss, acknowledge, congratulate — in short, they serve the
interests of commerce, industry, the government, and the general
public.

They should be courteous, respectful, and tactful, even if written
to complain, to refuse a request, or to demand a payment. They
should be formal or informal, never conversational.

Language and audience

Consider the reader's position, problem, or request, and write so that your understanding is apparent. This next sentence is too curt.

> ABRUPT: Our company is currently understaffed, so we do not have the time to conduct a tour for your group.

The self-absorbed sentence above focuses on the writer's problems and concerns and ignores the reader's.

> IMPROVED: Thank you for your interest in AZG's new robotics manufacturing operation. We would be proud to show it to your group, but our increased production schedules currently require the staff's full-time attention.

This reader-oriented sentence gives the same no answer, but less rudely, and it encourages a tour in the future.

Write in your natural voice, not old-fashioned stilted phrases like this: "In re yours of August 21, enclosed herewith please find, as per your request, one (1) gross Wizard firewarners."

Make your point clear. Know what you wish to accomplish and help your reader understand. If you complain about defective merchandise, what action do you want? A refund? A replacement? By what date? Even if angry, provide necessary facts to prove your point, be calm and reasonable, and be specific:

> Because you cannot repair the modem and because replacements are backordered, I want a refund of $176.89 by August 30. That amount includes the price of the modem, sales tax, and shipping and handling (copy of receipt enclosed).

Provide necessary background information. Say enough but avoid a redundant catalog of factual data.

> ABRUPT: Your request of November 16 will be filled whenever backorders arrive.

Which request? The writer may have written a number of requests that day.

TOO DETAILED: I have your letter of November 16, 1989, in which you request the following brochures: No. 71165, "Nutritional Content of Cold Cereals," No. 72344, "Meat Your Way to Health," and No. 72345, "Vegetables for Life." The request will be filled whenever backorders arrive.

BETTER: The nutritional brochures on cereals, meats, and vegetables that you ordered on November 16, 1989, will be sent to you as soon as possible.

This last example gives enough information to clarify the recipient's request without unnecessary detail.

Stop when you are finished. Do not repeat yourself in a conclusion or offer meaningless platitudes such as "I hope everything is well with you." If your letter already encourages a reply, do not say "I'm looking forward to hearing from you soon."

Format and organization

The block format is probably the most commonly used today. For stationery with a letterhead, begin all parts of the letter, including the date, paragraphs, and closing, at the left margin (see pages 537–38). For stationery that does not have a printed letterhead, type the return address, the closing, and the signature to the right of center on the page (see page 542).

Single-space the individual parts but double-space between the parts and between each paragraph. Quadruple-space between the complimentary closing and your name.

1. If your stationery does not have a letterhead, type your address and the date for the heading. Spell out the street name and so forth, but use the postal abbreviation for the state.
2. The inside address requires the name of the recipient, the person's title, the company name, and the address.
3. The salutation, followed by a colon, requires the conventional *Dear* with the name of the recipient. Use the recipient's first name only if you have already established a friendly relationship. If you do not know who will read your letter, choose one of these salutations:

Dear Sir or Madam:
Dear Signal Wrench Company: [name of company]
Dear Data Processing Manager: [title of an executive]

Use "Ms." unless the recipient has previously expressed a preference for "Miss" or "Mrs." If you know the name but not the sex of the recipient, find out or use the person's full name: "Dear Shelley Caulkins."

4. In the body, briefly express essential information. Keep paragraphs at a reasonable length, organized, and concise.

5. The complimentary closing requires a traditional expression such as "Yours truly" or "Sincerely yours." Capitalize only the first word. Use a warmer closing, such as "Cordially" or "Best wishes," if circumstances warrant. Type your name four lines below the closing expression. Sign the letter between the closing and your typed name. You may type a professional title below your name: "Sales Manager" or "Vice-President, Marketing."

6. Additional information below the closing may include (a) the initials of the writer in capital letters and the initials of the typist in lowercase letters (HLT/jc), (b) recipients of copies of the letter (cc: Donald Yeager), or (c) enclosures with explanation (Encl.: 100 brochures).

7. Address the envelope the same as the inside address, centered on the envelope. Type your own name and complete address in the upper left-hand corner unless you are using company stationery, in which case you may type your name above the letterhead.

Sample business letter

| **UNIVERSITY** **BROADCASTING** **CLUB** | 1419 Monticello Drive Charlottesville, VA 22901 | return address |

March 27, 1990 ⎤———————————————————— date

Mr. Patrick Sanderson ⎤
Station Manager, WUVR
2834 Industrial Line Road ⎬———————————————— inside address
Charlottesville, VA 22903 ⎦

Dear Mr. Sanderson: ⎤———————————————————— salutation

As students in the University Broadcasting
Club, we hope you will share your insights and
expertise with us. We invite you, Linda Sellers,
who hosts <u>Virginia</u> <u>Vantage</u> <u>Point</u>, and members of
the production and technical staffs to speak to ⎬———— body
the club about producing a daily live radio talk
show. Can you talk to us on Wednesday, May 20,
at 4:00 p.m. in the auditorium of Keene Hall?
Another afternoon more convenient to you could be
arranged.

All of us are preparing individually for
broadcasting careers, but we feel that a
perspective on the team effort required to
produce a show five times a week would be
valuable. We ask that your panel address not
only the duties of each individual on the team
but also how those duties--and people--depend on
one another.

We anticipate that the meeting, including the
discussion, a question-and-answer period, and a
reception, will take about two hours.

Mr. Patrick Sanderson   2   March 27, 1990

Thank you for your consideration. May we have
your response by Wednesday, April 15? In the
meantime, if you have any questions, please call
Jane Steiner, Speech Department secretary, or me
at 555-1234.

Sincerely yours,   — close

Stanley Tyson   — signature

Stanley Tyson
Chair, Program Committee

ST/js

cc: Dr. Yeary Synovon, Sponsor

The first paragraph of the letter explains who the writer is and the reason for writing; the second paragraph, while not essential, provides background and further detail; and the third and fourth paragraphs give practical information the recipient will need to make his decision. The tone of this letter is polite, neither stilted nor too informal. It is clear, considerate, and professional.

53

Résumés and Job Application Letters

53a   Design a well-aimed résumé.

Your résumé must be typed, accurate, and aimed at your target audience. Make sharp, clear photocopies or have it professionally printed. It should be short but thorough, on one page if possible. Include these elements:

1. Name, address, daytime telephone number.
2. *Objective.* Provide a sentence that states your short- and long-term job ambitions, as modified by the position you seek. Unless you have experience, anticipate and announce here an entry level management position in your field, such as retail manager trainee, computer programming trainee, and so forth.
3. *Qualifications.* Supply a sentence or two identifying your abilities that match the stipulations of the job description. Here you must quickly promote your experience and education.
4. *Positions held.* Provide an employment record listed chronologically from your current or most recent experience.
5. *Education.* Start with the most recently attended institutions. List inclusive dates and degrees earned. Do not include elementary schools.
6. Honors and awards.
7. *References.* Provide a statement that references are available on request. Before using their names, be sure that the people you list as references agree to recommend you.

Sample résumé

```
                    GRETA JACKSON
                    4319 86th Avenue SE
                    Mercer Island, WA 98040
                    (206) 234-5678

OBJECTIVE           Entry level sales position. Long-range goal:
                    Market research position involving both
                    public contact and statistical analysis.

QUALIFICATIONS      Degree in marketing with minor in
                    psychology, statistics emphasis. Summer
                    jobs in inventory analysis and retail sales.

POSITIONS HELD      Assistant Manager, Your 24 Store
May-Sept. 1988      2632 Rainier Avenue South
                    Seattle, WA 98156

                    Designed point-of-purchase rack displays
                    adopted by all stores. Increased sales of
                    sunscreens by 22 percent. Supervised three
                    part-time sales clerks.

Summers             Inventory Control Assistant, Your 24 Store
  1987, 1986        Regional Warehouse
                    Seattle, WA 98141

                    Monitored medical and cosmetic sales for
                    stores in Puget Sound area. Analyzed sales,
                    profiled stores with below-average sales.

May-Sept. 1985      Sales Clerk, Your 24 Store

EDUCATION           University of Washington, Seattle, WA:
                    BA, Marketing and psychology, 1989
                    Merit scholarship

                    Mercer Island High School: Diploma, 1985

AWARDS              Marketing Circle, Student Campaign Award,
                    "Marketing Elbow Grease," 1989

                    National Merit Scholar, 1985

REFERENCES          Available on request.
```

These next elements are optional:

8. Age, race, or marital status (Note: Companies cannot legally request this information.)
9. Salary earned or expected

53b   Write persuasive letters of application.

Send out the same résumé to several prospective employers, but write a separate, specifically targeted cover letter to each company. It must follow all the rules of good business letters (section **52b**) and feature these elements.

1. *Accuracy.* Research the company to learn the name of a person to address your letter and résumé to. Spell the person's name and title and company correctly.
2. *Conciseness.* Say that you are writing a general inquiry, answering an advertisement, or responding to a specific request by the company for your credentials. Do not be mysterious, funny, or long-winded.
3. *Qualifications.* Tell your reader what you can do for the company. Elaborate upon one specific accomplishment or skill in your résumé that should be of particular interest.
4. *Desires.* State specifically what you want: a job interview. Offer the best times at which you can be reached.

Sample letter of application

4319 86th Avenue SE
Mercer Island, WA 98040
June 16, 1990

Ms. Mary Turner
New Product Development
Glacier Home Products
1111 First Avenue
Seattle, WA 98190

Dear Ms. Turner:

I am responding to your advertisement in <u>Advertising
Age</u> recruiting market research trainees. My recent
marketing degree and my background in consumer sales
seem tailored to your needs.

As you can see from my résumé, I designed point-of-
purchase displays for suntan lotions at Your 24 Stores
during the summer of 1988. Before designing the
displays, I asked my friends why they bought suntan
products, and I also asked customers why they bought
particular brands. Although my research admittedly
was unscientific, I emphasized the selling points in
my displays. Sales in my store went up significantly,
and when my displays were adopted in other branches,
sales there also increased.

I think I could use my background and creativity to
help Glacier Home Products research the potential
market of new products, and hope I may talk to
you about it. I can be reached by telephone before
9:00 a.m. and after 3:30 p.m. at 234-5678. I will,
however, call you on the morning of Friday, June 30,
to see if we can make an appointment to meet.

Thank you very much for your consideration.

Sincerely yours,

Greta Jackson

Greta Jackson

54

Business and Technical Reports

Business and technical reports may convey the effect of a manufacturing plan, the history of yearly sales, or the results of a field survey. Reports have a definite purpose, a well-defined audience, and usually a standard format. Some reports are written regularly (weekly, monthly, annually) to inform key personnel about progress in a particular area such as sales, personnel, or finance. Others are one-time products, such as a scientific research project or a marketing analysis (see the sample report below).

54a Use objective language and a neutral tone.

The language of a report must suit its objective, factual purpose. In general, omit your role as performer and writer ("I found that . . .") and simply report your discovery: "The values of x and y varied with atmospheric pressure." A neutral tone maintains focus on the subject; personalities do not intervene to color the facts.

Remember, readers of reports are busy, seek particular information in a customary format, and want it clear, readable, and on time. They want no irrelevant facts, no extraneous information, and no personal feelings of the writer unless they bear directly on the information.

Be aware that technical and scientific reports sometimes use the passive voice to focus on an object under discussion: "New computer systems can be designed to solve problems simultaneously rather than sequentially." But most readers prefer the clarity and accuracy of the active voice (see chapter **31**).

54b   Follow a standard format and organization.

Reports usually follow established formats that include some if not most of the following parts, depending on length, purpose, and nature of the material. Follow your instructor's or your employer's preferences.

1. *Title.* The title should be brief, clear, and descriptive of the contents: "Marketing Survey of Fast-Food Lunch Menus." Omit "a study of," "report on," and other redundancies.
2. *Abstract.* Sometimes labeled *summary*, the abstract briefly describes purpose, method, and results in a highly condensed discussion. One way to write an abstract is to include a key sentence that summarizes each major section of the report.
3. *Introduction.* The introduction describes the problem or issue, explains the importance and purpose of the work, provides any necessary background information, offers the unique contribution of the report, and even specifies what the report does not do.
4. *Methods.* If needed, the methods section explains the design of the project and describes tools, procedures, subjects, and so forth. It demonstrates the validity and integrity of the work.
5. *Schedule.* A precise timetable usually accompanies preliminary proposals and reports on projects in process.
6. *Work in progress.* Some projects require periodic reports to update key personnel on the status of research and investigation.
7. *Results.* The results section reports the findings, often in tables and figures. Give results objectively without discussion: "Telephone solicitation produces 80 percent of Kentucky sales, 50 percent of Illinois sales, and 47 percent of Indiana sales." (Tables are lists of information, often in several columns; figures are drawings, graphs, photographs—that is, everything outside of the main text that is not a table.)

8. *Conclusion.* The conclusion discusses the importance or value of the results, offers recommendations, specifies directives, or suggests issues needing additional research: "Move the district manager of Kentucky to the home office to conduct a seminar for all district managers to explain motivation, method, and execution."

9. *Appendix.* This supplement at the end of the report includes useful material not properly part of the actual report. Some mathematical formulas or equations, copies of questionnaires or survey answers, financial figures, graphs, and similar data belong in appendixes.

10. *References.* The reference list cites the work of other researchers used in preparing the report (see sections **50i** and **51a**). Follow the form of your discipline for citing author, title, year of publication, and so on. Unless otherwise specified, use the APA style (see section **51a**) for business reports.

The following report summarizes an agreement and sets the stage for subsequent reports. The tone is professional but relatively informal. Because work toward the final goals has just started, the report cannot include results and recommendations. Subsequent reports will omit the summary information but will include more information about results, problems, and recommendations.

Sample report

WARD & ROSS ASSOCIATES
MARKETING CONSULTANTS

TO: Karen Ollsen, Director of Marketing
             Letter Perfect Software Corporation
FROM: Manuel Marga, Project Director
DATE: 1 September 1990
SUBJECT: Word Processor Marketing Strategy: Progress
             Report

Introduction
     In the two weeks since you asked this company to
develop a strategy to increase Letter Perfect's share
of the software market for word processors, Ward &
Ross has developed an initial plan. The preliminary
work will feature a survey to explore the market.
Shortly thereafter, we will analyze the data and
produce a final report with our recommendations.

Method
     The project will include these steps.
1. Survey individual users of Letter Perfect, retail
outlets, and purchasing agents for corporations.
2. Analyze the features and marketing strategies of
competitive word processing packages.
3. Analyze the three segments of the word processor
market and determine Letter Perfect's fit in each one.
4. Develop appropriate advertising campaigns designed
to appeal to the different segments.
5. Recommend new features for Letter Perfect and
also potential spinoff products to attract specific
segments of the market.

Schedule
     We will deliver the results of the surveys by
November 1. The December 1 report will include our
analysis of the surveys. In the meantime we will
work on the analyses of the market and especially
of competitors.

tion *away from* the speaker: "*Take* these lecture notes to the secretary to be typed."

bunch   Reserve *bunch* for things that grow together, such as "a *bunch* of bananas" (not a "bunch of people").

burst, bust, busted   The verb *burst* means "to explode" or "to fly into pieces." Its principal parts are *burst, burst, burst*: "We *burst* the four balloons, and the baby then *burst* into tears." There is no *bursted*. Avoid the use of *bust* and *busted* as variants of *burst*.

can, may   *Can* expresses the ability to accomplish something: ("I *can* fix the faucet." *May* expresses permission or chance: ("Yes, you *may* go. Fix the faucet because it *may* leak tomorrow during the formal reception."

capital, capitol   *Capitol* is a government building. Uppercase the word to refer to where the U.S. Congress meets (the U.S. Capitol building), and lowercase it to refer to where state legislatures sit (the state capitol building). Use *capital* in all other occasions (*capital* offense, *capital* city, *capital* letter, or *capital* assets).

censor, censure   *Censor* means "to examine and delete questionable material," or is the person who *censors*: "The Congressman *censored* several paragraphs from the *Congressional Record*." *Censure* means "to condemn, blame, or criticize." (Congress *censured* the guilty legislator.)

center around   Illogical; use *center* with *in*, *on*, *upon*, or *at*. Use *centered on* or *revolved about* because things revolve around a center, not the opposite: "The debate *centered on* the two late amendments."

climactic, climatic   *Climactic* is the adjective form of *climax*, referring to a culmination or moment of great intensity: "The *climactic* moment of the drama unfolded rapidly." *Climatic* is the adjective form of *climate*, referring to the weather: "The *climatic* extremes destroyed his love for Alaska."

compare, contrast   To *compare* means "to show similarities"; to *contrast* means "to show differences." However, *compare* is frequently used to mean both similarities and differences.

compare to, compare with   Use *compare to* to show that one thing is like another: "He *compared* the crowd *to* a swarm of bees." Use *compare with* when examining the similarities between items: "The article *compared* the arms ban negotiations *with* earlier SALT talks."

complement, compliment   A *complement* completes something, makes a whole, or brings to perfection: "A rose at each place complemented the delicate china." *Compliment* means "praise," "admiration," or "courtesy." (Sir George *complimented* his staff for their diplomacy.)

compose, comprise   The whole *comprises* the parts: "Strangely, the world *comprises* four hemispheres." The parts *compose* the whole: "The northern, southern, eastern, and western hemispheres *compose* the world."

conscious, conscience   *Conscious* is an adjective meaning "aware of" or "capable of thought." *Conscience* is a noun meaning "a sense of right and wrong." (My *conscious* feeling of guilt convinced the psychiatrist that I did indeed have a *conscience*.)

consensus of opinion   Redundant phrase because *consensus* means "general opinion." (The *consensus* was to initiate a recall vote.)

continual, continuous   Use *continual* for repeated events in a series (*continual* warfare, *continual* errors). Use *continuous* for an uninterrupted flow (*continuous* humming in my ear).

council, counsel   A *council* is a committee or advisory group: "The city *council* meets on Wednesday." *Counsel* is both a noun and a verb. The noun *counsel* means "advice" (I sought *counsel* from the department chairperson and the dean). It also names a giver of advice. As a verb, *counsel* means "advise." (The attorney *counseled* the jury to find the defendent guilty.)

criteria, criterion   *Criterion* is singular, meaning "*one* test or standard usable for making a judgment." The word *criteria* is always plural: "All the *criteria* for your decision *are* now before you."

data, datum   Use *data* as a plural in academic, scientific, and other formal writing: "The *data show* three areas of heat exchange." *Datum* is the singular form.

different from, different than   *Different from* is standard usage: "The agenda for this national conference is *different from* the one for the regional conference."

differ from, differ with   *Differ from* means "to be unlike." *Differ with* means "to disagree with." (You may *differ with* my view, but in truth my view does not *differ from* the one endorsed by the governor.)

discreet, discrete   *Discreet* means "tactful," "judicious," or "modest." (Tom's *discreet* behavior won him favor with the president.) *Discrete* means "distinct" or "separate." (The thesaurus, spelling checker, and help menu are *discrete* items on separate diskettes.)

disinterested, uninterested   *Disinterested* means "impartial" or "unbiased." (Labor and management need a *disinterested* arbitrator to solve their differences.) *Uninterested* means "having no interest" or "bored." (Several fans appeared totally *uninterested* in the game.)

doesn't, don't   *Doesn't* is the contraction for *does not*: "She *doesn't* enjoy Shakespeare." *Don't* is the contraction for *do not*, used with first-person and third-person plural: "We *don't*" and "*I don't*." But use "he *doesn't*," not "he *don't*."

due to, because of   Use *because of* as a preposition: "*Because of* the flood [not *due to*], he lost a manufacturing plant." Use *due to* with a predicate adjective following a linking verb (His success was *due to* his drive and persistence) and after a noun (The paralysis *due to* the stroke may be temporary).

each other, one another   Use *each other* to refer to two and *one another* for more than two: "My wife and I love *each other*. The members of our department exchanged gifts with *one another*."

economic, economical   *Economic* refers to economics or the economy (*economic* policy). *Economical* means "thrifty" (*economical* spending practices).

elicit, illicit   Do not confuse these words. *Elicit* means "to draw out"; *illicit* means "illegal" or "prohibited." (Reporters *elicited* the information that the candidate had used *illicit* drugs in his youth.)

enthused, enthusiastic   Use *enthusiastic*: "They were *enthusiastic* about the possibilities."

equally, equally as   Avoid *equally as*. Use *equally* alone: "The two courses are *equally* good for your program of study." Use *as* alone: "He seemed *as* bright, but less gregarious, as others in the group."

everyday, every day   *Everyday* is an adjective meaning "ordinary" or "commonplace." (The *everyday* dishes will be fine for this dinner.) *Every day* is a noun with modifier: "He needs access to the computer for 30 minutes *every day*."

everyone, every one, everybody   The single words *everyone* and *everybody* are relative pronouns meaning "every person." (*Everybody* helped clear the stage.) The phrase *every one* is a noun with modifier meaning "each single person or thing." (Did *every one* of the actors help clear the stage?)

expect, suspect   *Expect* means "to anticipate": "We *expect* opposition at the meeting tonight." *Suspect* means "to presume" or "to distrust." (We *suspect* the food was old.)

famed, famous   Use *famous* rather than the advertising and sports jargon *famed*: "The company's offices are headquartered in the *famous* [not *famed*] Jenney building."

farther, further   Use *farther* to refer to physical distance: "Atlanta is not much *farther* from Chicago than from Miami." Use *further* to refer to quantity, time, or degree: "We need *further* evidence. He will *further* his career by moving *farther* up the management ladder."

fewer, less   *Fewer* refers to a countable number (*fewer* people, *fewer* parts, *fewer* housing starts, *fewer* calories). *Less* refers to an amount or degree or something uncountable (*less* sunshine, *less* determination, *less* enrollment).

figuratively, literally   *Figuratively* means "metaphorically" or "in terms of another thing." (*Figuratively* this council is a lamb, not a lion.) *Literally* means "actually" or "not figuratively." (Your committee *literally* denied hearings on the legislation.)

finalize   Bureaucratic jargon. Substitute a precise term such as *complete*, *end*, *stop*, *cease*, *finish*, *conclude*.

first, firstly   *First* (*second*, *third*) is the preferred usage.

flout, flaunt   *Flout* means "to show scorn or contempt for, to defy." (Serious students of literature *flouted* U.S. Customs to smuggle James Joyce's *Ulysses* into the United States during the 1920s.) *Flaunt* means "to display conspicuously or ostentatiously." (She *flaunted* her diamonds.)

folk, folks   *Folk* is acceptable to refer to a people or ethnic group: "The indigenous *folk* of northern Canada." *Folks*, referring to either people in general or family members, is conversational: "Several people [not *folks*] arrived early for the conference."

former, latter; first, last   Use *former* and *latter* to refer to one of two antecedents: "President Page and Dean Butler will appear on the program. The *former* will discuss the budget and the *latter*, new academic policies." Use *first* and *last* with more than two: "President

Page, Dr. Jones, Dr. Smith, and Dean Butler will attend the program. The *first* will talk about the budget and the *last* about academic policy."

funny   Overused and vague, except when it means "amusing." Use more precise words: *curious*, *unusual*, *strange*, *odd*, *humorous*.

get   Avoid conversational uses in writing: (He *got* sick); Screeching chalk *gets* to me). Use more precise words: *became*, *irritate*.

good, well   *Good* is an adjective; *well* is an adverb: "This committee functions *well* together because it's composed of *good* people." Always use *good* to complete the linking verb: "It smells *good.*"

great   Overworked when used in place of precise words such as *enthusiastic*, *skillful*, *clever*, *brilliant*, *artistic*, *excellent*.

hanged, hung   *Hung* is the past tense and past participle form of the verb *hang*, meaning "to suspend." (The posters are *hung* on most bulletin boards.) Reserve *hanged* for an execution: "The posse *hanged* the outlaw without a trial."

hardly, scarcely   These words are negatives, so do not add *not*, *can't*, or another negative: "We could *hardly* hear the announcement [not *couldn't hardly*]."

hopefully   Used frequently as a sentence modifier meaning *it is hoped* or [*someone*] *hopes* (*Hopefully*, the river will not flood), it is more effective to name who hopes: "*Residents* along the river bank *hope* the river will not flood."

imply, infer   *Imply* means "to suggest by word or actions." (The dean *implied* that he would reconsider the resolution.) *Infer* means "to draw conclusions." (After listening to the dean, we could easily *infer* that he would not fund the proposal under any circumstances.)

in, into   Use *in* to refer to location or condition: "Your jacket is *in* the hall closet." Use *into* to refer to movement or a change in condition (from outside to inside): "Three strangers dressed in black suddenly walked *into* the courtroom."

incredible, incredulous   *Incredible* means "unbelievable." (Your naiveté in these matters is *incredible*.) *Incredulous* means "skeptical, doubting, unbelieving." (Your *incredible* proposal has left the entire committee *incredulous* and shocked.)

individual, person, party   Use the word *person* in most instances. Reserve *individual* for designating a single human being as unique from others: "Will this resolution protect the rights of the *individual*?" The word *party* as a reference to a person appears in legal documents only: "the *party* of the first part."

inferior to, worse than   Avoid using *inferior than*. Something is *worse than* or it's *inferior to*: "The wording of this resolution is *worse than* I thought. This resolution is *inferior to* [not *more inferior than*] the Thomas resolution."

ingenious, ingenuous   *Ingenious* means "inventive" and "clever." (Your *ingenious* methods enabled the committee to salvage the resolution.) *Ingenuous* means "naive, straightforward, frank." (Your *ingenuous* smile does not fool anyone, Thomas.)

in regards to   Avoid. Use "with regard to," "in regard to," or "as regards."

irregardless   A double negative because both *ir-* and *-less* mean "not." Always use *regardless*: "We plan to pass this resolution *regardless* of its cost."

is when, is where   Avoid this ungrammatical use of an adverb after a linking verb, especially in definitions: "The drop-add period *allows* you [not *is when*] to change your class schedule." *Is when* and *is where* are acceptable to suggest time or place: "It *is* only *where* freedom of the press is stifled that freedom of the people ends."

its, it's   *Its* is a possessive pronoun: "The committee finished *its* work and left for the night." *It's* is the contraction for *it is*: *It's* typical of this committee to finish *its* work early."

-ize   Avoid adding this suffix to create awkward or questionable verbs such as *fraternalize, finalize, budgetize, racialize*. Most such words have more precise synonyms.

kind(s), sort(s)   *Kind* and *sort* are singular: "That *kind* of tea *grows* only in Ceylon." *Kinds* and *sorts* are plural: "Those *kinds* of teas *are* blended for English breakfast tea." Do not add *a*: "This kind of committee," not "this *kind of a* committee."

Follow *kind of* and *sort of* with nouns: "Dr. Turner is the *sort of* professor that students trust." Avoid using them as adverbs meaning *rather, somewhat*, or *more or less* or to show indecision: "F. Scott Fitzgerald *more or less* [not *sort of*] self-destructed."

latter See **former, latter; first, last.**

lay, lie *Lay* is a transitive verb, taking a direct object meaning "to put" or "to place." Its principal parts are *lay, laid, laid*: "Please *lay* the report on my desk." *Lie* is intransitive, meaning "to rest in a reclining position." Its principal parts are *lie, lay, lain*: "The report *lay* on the table, where it had *lain* since Tuesday."

learn, teach *To learn* is to gain knowledge; *to teach* is to give or convey knowledge: "I want to *learn* that new graphics program. Maybe John can *teach* me."

leave, let Use *leave* to mean "depart" or "remain stationary"; use *let* to mean "permit" or "allow." (The supervisor will not *let* anyone *leave* until 3:00.)

liable, likely *Liable* means "responsible" or "legally obligated." (You are *liable* for damages to the ballroom.) *Likely* shows probability or credibility: "The resolution will *likely* pass on second reading."

loose, lose *Loose* (pronounced *luce*) is an adjective meaning "not fastened" or "not tight," or a verb meaning "to untighten" or "let go"; *lose* is a verb meaning "to misplace" or "be defeated." (The *loose* sand blowing in our eyes caused us to *lose* our way.)

lot, lot of, lots of Conversational usage for *many, much, a lot, a great deal.* See also *alot.*

mankind Use nonsexist terms such as *human beings, humankind,* or *people* instead.

may be, maybe The two words *may be* serve as a verb phrase meaning "having the likelihood of" or "permitted to be." (Your sources *may be* truthful.) *Maybe* is an adverb meaning "perhaps." (*Maybe* your sources are truthful.)

may of, might of, must of Nonstandard for *may have, might have, must have,* formed from the pronunciation of the contractions *may've, might've,* and *must've.*

media, medium *Media* is the plural form of *medium,* referring to the forms of mass communication. It takes a plural verb: "When choosing from all advertising *media,* two *are* available: local newspapers seem to be the best *medium* for print ads and television the best *medium* for broadcast."

mighty   Avoid using this word as an intensifier in your writing, as with "*mighty* tough" or "*mighty* good." It means "powerful" and "strong" and should be used that way: "a *mighty* blow."

most   Avoid substituting *most* for *almost*: "*Almost* [not *most*] all professors give mid-term examinations."

myself   *Myself* and other *-self* words are intensive or reflexive pronouns. They require an antecedent: "I *myself* will serve as chairperson." Do not use *myself* as a substitute for *I* or *me*: "The dean and *I* [not *myself*] will co-chair the committee." See also section **20b**.

nauseated, nauseous   Standard English requires "nauseated" to mean "ill, affected with nausea." (Three people became *nauseated* after inhaling the fumes.) Restrict *nauseous* to causing nausea: "The *nauseous* fumes swept across the parking lot."

notable, noticeable   Use *notable* to mean "remarkable" or "prominent" (a *notable* event or a *notable* speech). Use *noticeable* to mean "perceptible" or "observable" (a *noticeable* limp or her *noticeable* resemblance to her mother).

nowhere, nowheres   *Nowhere* is correct. *Nowheres* is nonstandard.

off of   *Off* alone is sufficient.

OK, O.K., okay   Conversational. In writing use *all right, correct, approval,* or other appropriate terms: "The chairman gave the plan his *approval*."

ought not   Use *ought not to* followed by a verb, or replace with *should not*: "You *ought not to* [or *should not*] leave your money on your desk."

people, persons   Use *people* to refer to a large group of individuals collectively: "*People* slowly gathered for the hearing." Use *persons* to refer to a relatively small and specific group: "*Persons* needing forms must go to window 2." However, *people* is acceptable with any plural number: "820 people."

percent, percentage   Always use *percent* with numbers: "Only twenty *percent* of the registered voters cast ballots in the last election." Some disciplines' styles use figures in technical papers (82%). *Percent* can take a singular or a plural verb depending on the number of the noun it refers to: "Twenty *percent* of the lumber is warped. Eighty *percent of the bricks are* laid."

Use *percentage* without numbers: "A large *percentage* [not *percent*] voted." When *percentage* is preceded by *the*, it takes a singular verb: "*The percentage* of lawyers who pass the bar exam on the first attempt *is* small." If *percentage* is preceded by *a*, the verb may be singular or plural, depending on the number of the noun referred to: "A small percentage of *lawyers are* incompetent; a large percentage of the *population is* honest." Do not use *percentage* loosely for *part*: "A large *part* [not *percentage*] of the work has been done."

phenomena, phenomenon   A *phenomenon* (singular) is one occurrence; several such occurrences are *phenomena* or *phenomenons*, but not *phenomenas*: "The man dancing on the roof was the latest *phenomenon* in a day filled with strange *phenomena*."

plus   Avoid using *plus* as a conjunction or conjunctive adverb. Use *and* or *also*, *moreover*, *besides*: "I flunked biology, and [not *plus*] I may fail algebra. Moreover, [not *plus*] my tuition check bounced." When *plus* is used to show addition, the verb is singular: "Persistance *plus* skill *gets* the job done. Two *plus* two *equals* four."

precede, proceed   *Precede* means "to come before another" in time, order, or rank: "Security officers *precede* the president into press conferences." *Proceed* means "to go forward" or "to carry on." (Reporters may *proceed* with their questions.)

pretense, pretext   *Pretext* is an excuse, usually one that conceals the truth: "She was dismissed for absenteeism, but that was only a pretext." A *pretense* is a false claim, reason, or appearance: "His high praise was surely *pretense*."

principal, principle   *Principal* is an adjective meaning "chief" or "leading." (The *principal* language of the region is German. The *principal* of our school teaches German.) *Principle* is a noun meaning "rule," "fundamental concept," or "basic truth." (The general *principles* that should govern this body have been ignored.) *Principle* is never an adjective.

proved, proven   Both *proved* and *proven* are acceptable forms of the past participle: "She *has proved* [or *has proven*] her value several times in the past."

quote, quotation   *Quote* is a verb; *quotation* is a noun. Avoid using *quote* as a short form of *quotation* in formal writing: "Each chapter opens with a *quotation* [not *quote*] from Shakespeare."

raise, rise   *Raise* means "to lift," "to increase," or "to move upward"; it requires a direct object: "Will the college *raise* tuition again next year?" *Rise* means "to get up," "to ascend," or "to extend upward"; it does *not* take an object: "Tuition *rises* every year by about 10 percent." (See section **20c** and chapters **29**, **30**.)

real, really   *Real* is an adjective that means "actual" or "genuine" (*real* diamonds, *real* gentlemen). *Really* is an adverb (*really* difficult). Avoid the conversational use of *real* for *really*: "We were *really* [not *real*] pleased with the results." However, another adverb (or none at all) might be more precise and effective than *really*: "The exam was *extremely* difficult."

reason . . . is because   Use "that" rather than "because" or delete "the reason is." (The *reason* this project failed *is that* funding never materialized. This project failed *because* funding never materialized.)

relevant   Something must be relevant (or irrelevant) *to* something else: "Although Shakespeare wrote centuries ago, his portrayal of human nature is *relevant to* people's actions in these modern times."

reluctant, reticent   A *reluctant* person does not want to act; a *reticent* person is reserved or hesitates to speak.

respectively, respectfully   Respectively means "singly in the order given." (We submit plans for funding the child care center, the indoor tennis complex, and the cafeteria annex, *respectively*.) *Respectfully* means "marked by respect." (The board considered our proposals *respectfully*.)

sensual, sensuous   *Sensuous* means "appealing to the senses." (Enjoy the *sensuous* pleasure of our tropical beach.) *Sensual* means "gratifying the physical senses, especially sexually." (The dancers' movements grew more *sensual* as the tempo increased.)

set, sit   *Set* is a transitive verb, meaning "put." It requires a direct object: I *set* the booklet on his desk." *Sit* means "to be seated." It does *not* take an object: "The book now *sits* on the desk."

shall, will   In formal grammar, *shall* is the auxiliary verb in the first person (*I*, we) to show future action; today, however, *will* is used in all persons to show the future tense. *Shall* is generally used only to ask polite questions (*Shall* we leave now?) or for emphasis (You *shall* do as I say).

since, because   Use *since* to signal time: "The committee has waited *since* Tuesday for your resolution." Use *because* in most other contexts: "We need help from several people *because* the box is huge and heavy."

sometime, some time, sometimes   *Sometime* is an adverb meaning "at some indefinite time." (Let's have lunch *sometime*.) *Some time*, two words, consists of an adjective modifying a noun; together they mean "a period of time." (We haven't met for *some time*.) *Sometimes* is an adverb meaning "occasionally." (We see each other *sometimes*.)

stationary, stationery   The adjective *stationary* means "not moving" or "unchanging in condition or value." (The stock market remained *stationary*.) *Stationery* is the noun for "writing materials." (I sent her a box of embossed *stationery*.)

sure, surely   Use *sure* as an adjective (a *sure* method) but not as an adverb in place of *surely* or *certainly*: "He is *certainly* [not *sure*] bewildered by this computer program." Use *sure to* not *sure and*: "Be *sure to* vote today."

than, then   *Than* serves as a conjunction for comparisons; *then* is an adverb showing time: "*Then* the coach knew that Jones was stronger *than* Edwards."

that, this   Avoid use of *that* or *this* as subjects: "The council is overspending its budget, and *this deficit* [not *this* by itself] really bothers the president."

their, there, they're   *Their* is the possessive form of the pronoun *they*: "*Their* candidate received only three endorsements." *There* is an adverb of place or expletive: "Your book is over *there*." *They're* is a contraction of the pronoun and verb *they are*: "*They're* the candidates with little hope of winning."

thusly   Pretentious. Use *thus*, the correct adverb form.

to, too, two   Distinguish the adverb *too* (meaning "also," "very," "excessively") from the preposition *to* (as in "to town") and the numeral *two* (as in "two towns"): "We *too* have been *to* the dean with our *two* suggestions."

toward, towards   *Toward* is the preferred form.

try and, try to.   *Try and* is nonstandard; use *try to*: "Joan Benoit will *try to* win the Boston Marathon."

unique   *Unique* means "the only one of its kind" or "unequaled," so it cannot sensibly be modified by *more* or *most*: "This plan is *unique* [not *most unique*]."

up   Avoid the use of *up* as a verb meaning "increase" or "raise." (The manager will *raise* [not *up*] the price tomorrow.)

usage, use, utilize   Avoid substituting *usage* for *use*, meaning "the employment of." (The *use* [not *usage*] of the computer will speed your work.) Reserve *usage* for established convention or social custom, particularly referring to language: "The correct *usage* of *imply* and *infer* is often confused." *Utilize* means "to put to use for a specific purpose," but the less pretentious *use* is often preferable: "Can we *use* [not *utilize*] the newspaper staff to help write copy?"

use to, used to   *Use to* is nonstandard; *used to* is always past tense, so do not drop the hard-to-hear *-d*: "The library *used to* subscribe to *Playboy* magazine."

wait for, wait on   Use *wait for* in the sense of "remain until something occurs." (We are *waiting for* the eight o'clock bus.) Use *wait on* only in reference to service: "We need a flight attendant to *wait on* us."

way, ways   Use *way*, not *ways*, to indicate distance: "We live a long *way* [not *ways*] from the factory."

where, that   Do not use *where* for *that* to show that a fact or idea follows: "I heard *that* [not *where*] the vice-president has resigned."

which, who   Use *who* to refer to people and *which* or *that* to refer to things: "One of the candidates *who* spoke last evening left his briefcase, *which* I found beside the podium."

while   Because *while* can either suggest a period of time or mean "although," be sure your meaning is clear: "*While* [*Although?*] most of the stage crew wanted to work on the flats, we painted the floor, instead."

who's, whose   *Who's* is the contraction of *who is*: "*Who's* scheduled next?" *Whose* is the possessive form of *who*: "*Whose* schedule will we follow?" They are never interchangeable.

-wise   Avoid adding this suffix meaning "manner" or "in regard to" to coin new words such as *campuswise, weatherwise, jobwise*, or *computerwise*. Some *-wise* words are standard: *clockwise, likewise, otherwise*. See also **-ize**.

you, one   Avoid *you* as an indefinite synonym for "anyone." Not: "*You* can see seven states from Lookout Mountain in Tennessee." Better: "*Visitors* to Lookout Mountain can see seven states." *You* is acceptable for instructions: "First *you* must release the emergency brake; then shift into gear."

your, you're   *You're* is the contraction of *you are*: "You're the winner." *Your* is the possessive form of *you*: "*Your* ticket was drawn by Johnny."

Copyrights and Acknowledgments

Index

Numbers in **boldface** refer to rules; other numbers refer to pages.

a, an, **34g**: 343–45; 548. See also *article.*
abbreviations, **35b**: 358, **43**: 406–08
  academic titles and degrees, 358, 407
  in academic writing, 407
  acronyms, 358
  of addresses, **43d**: 408
  capitalization of, 358; **45g**: 418
  dates, **43c**: 408
  of documentation, **43d**: 408
  of geographic and technical terminology, **43b**: 407
  l., ll., 491
  multiple-word, 358
  numbers, **43c**: 408
  organizations and corporations, **43b**: 407
  of parenthetical matter, **43d**: 408
  plural of, 387
  prefixes with, 421
  states, 358
  suffixes with, 421
  titles with proper names, **43a**: 406–07
  units of measurement, 358
absolute modifiers, 337
absolute phrase, 161, 269; **22d**: 273
  commas with, 273, 368
abstract, 519, 544
abstract noun, 245
abstract words, 217–18, 344
academic courses, 417
academic titles or degrees, 358, 407, **36f**: 366, 417
academic writing, 327, 387, 407, **48**: 441–53; **49**: 456–59; **50**: 460–511; **51**: 512–29
accent marks, **34n**: 353
accept, except, 548
acronyms, 358, **43b**: 407
  capitalization of, **45g**: 418
active voice. See *voice.*
AD, BC, 408
ad hominem fallacy, 450
adapt, adopt, 548

addresses
  abbreviations in, **43d**: 408
  figures in, **44b**: 411
adjective clause, 131, 159
  nonrestrictive, **36e**: 364–65
  placement, 275
  restrictive, 364
adjective phrase, 160–61, 269
  nonrestrictive, **36e**: 364–65
  restrictive, 364
  and subordination, 135
adjective(s), **20d**: 250–51; **33**: 332–37
  absolute modifiers as, 337
  clauses as, 251
  commas with, **37f**: 375
  comparative form, **33e**: 335–37
  compound, 420
  coordinate, 361–62
  demonstrative, 251
  distinguished from adverb, **33a**: 332–34
  double comparative form, 336–37
  double superlative form, 336–37
  ending with *-er* or *-est,* 335, 336
  ending with *-ly,* 333
  good, bad, and *well,* 333
  indefinite, 251
  irregular forms, 336
  less and *least,* 335
  and linking verbs, 333
  more and *most,* 335
  nominalized, 154
  as object complement, **33d**: 335
  phrases as, 251
  positive form, 335, 336
  possessive, 251
  predicate, 251, 261, 263
  in a series, 421
  as subject complement, **33c**: 334
  superlative form, **33e**: 335–37
adverb clause, 131, 275
  commas with, **37e**: 374
  introductory, 274, 275, 363, 374
  for variety, 159
adverb phrase, 162, 269, 363
adverbs, **20e**: 251–52; **33**: 332–37
  vs. adjectives, **33a**: 332–34
  clauses as, 251
  comparative form, **33e**: 335–37

adverbs *(continued)*
  conjunctive, 124, 255, 368
  derived from adjectives, 251
  ending with *-er* and *-est*, 336
  ending with *-ly*, 251, 333
  hard and *hardly*, 333
  irregular forms, 336
  modifying adjectives, 251, **33b**: 334
  modifying other adverbs, 251, **33b**: 334
  modifying verbs, 251, 333, **33b**: 334
  negative, 334
  phrases as, 251
  positive form, 335, 336
  slow and *slowly*, 333
  superlative form, **33e**: 335–37
  with two forms, 333
  well and *badly*, 333
advice, advise, 548
affect, effect, 548
afterword, 495
ages, average, 411
aggravate, irritate, 548
agree to, agree with, 548
agreement, pronoun-antecedent, **27**: 299–304
  antecedents joined by *and*, **27d**: 302
  antecedents joined by *or*, etc., **27e**: 303
  collective nouns, **27f**: 303
  relative pronouns, **27g**: 303–04
agreement, subject-verb, **26**: 292–97
  collective nouns, **26h**: 296
  compound subjects, **26d**: 294; **26e**: 294
  and expletives, 293
  intervening words, **26a**: 292–93
  subjects joined by *and*, **26d**: 294
  subjects joined by *or, nor*, **26e**: 294
  nouns ending in *-ics*, 297
  with plural-noun form, **26i**: 296–97
  with predicate nominative, **26b**: 293
  title of work, **26j**: 297
  who, which, that, **26g**: 295
  word used as word, **26j**: 297
ain't, 548
aircraft, names of, **42b**: 403
all-, 422
all ready, already, 548
all together, altogether, 549
alliteration, 110–11, 144–45
allusion, illusion, 549
almanacs, 465
almost, most, 549
a lot, alot, 549

alphabetical order, in citations, 513
alright, 549
although, 379
a.m., p.m., 408
American Heritage Dictionary, 424
among, between, 549
amount, number, 549
ampersand, 513
amplification, **39a**: 382, 394
analogy, false, 452
analysis, in paragraph development, **6h**: 93–95
analytical paper, 519–20
and
  antecedents joined by, **27d**: 302
  and comma, 360
  in-text citation, 513
and etc., 549
anecdote, 33–34
annotated bibliography, 519, 528–29
ante-, anti-, 549
antecedents
  ambiguous reference to, **27b**: 300–02
  collective noun as, **27f**: 303
  compound, **27d**: 302; **27e**: 303
  joined by *or, nor*, **27e**: 303
  and relative pronouns, **27g**: 303–04
anthology, 495, 496
anybody, any body, 549
anyone, any one, 549
anyway, any way, anyways, 550
anywhere, anywheres, 550
APA documentation style, 488, **51a**: 512–15
  in-text citations, 512–14
  list of references, 514–15
  sample research paper, **51e**: 521–29
APA Publication Manual, 512
apology, 38
apostrophe, **40**: 385–87
  to form possessive, **34d**: 341; **40a**: 385–86
  to indicate plurals, **40c**: 387
  misuse of, **40d**: 387
  to show omissions, **40b**: 386–87
appeal to authority, 450–51
appendix, 545
application letter, **53b**: 541–42
appositive phrase, 268, 273
appositives
  colon with, **39a**: 382
  nonrestrictive, **36e**: 365–66
  pronoun case in, **28d**: 310
  and subordination, 134

Arabic numbers, 411
archaic words, 204–05
argument, 441, 442
    conclusion, 446
    deductive, **48b**: 444–45
    in essay, **48c**: 446–47
    facts in, 442
    fallacies in, 441, **48**: 449–53
    indicator words in, 442
    inductive, **48b**: 444–45
    key terms, **48d**: 448
    opposing, **48e**: 449
    points, 442
    premises, 446–47
    structure, **48a**: 442
article (*a, an, the*)
    as adjective, 251
    capitalization of, 415
    definite, 251
    in nonstandard English, **34g**:
        343–45
    omission of, **13e**: 183
articles. See *periodicals*.
as, 550, **28e**: 311
as, like, 550
ask, 330
audience
    of business memo or letter, 532–35
    of business or technical report, 543
    of essay, **1c**: 8–10
    general, 9
    of letter of application, 541
    of research paper, 461
    of résumé, 539
    specialized, 9
    and style, **7c**: 108–10
audiovisual material, as resource, 471
author names
    in APA style citations, 512–14
    in MLA style citations, 488–90,
        493, 494–96
automobiles, names of, **42b**: 403
auxiliary verbs, 250, **29b**: 317
    list of, 317
awful, awfully, 550
awhile, a while, 550

bad, badly, 550
ballet, name of, 401
bandwagon, 453
be
    as auxiliary, 317
    forms of, 314–15, **34h**: 345–46
    with subjunctive mood, 329
    unemphatic use of, 150

because, 379
begging the question, 451
being as, being that, 550
beside, besides, 550
biased or sexist language, **17f**:
    220–22, 453
Bible, 402
    colon in references to, 383
    italics in reference to, 390
    period in references to, 383
    quotation marks in references to,
        390
bibliographies, 466
bibliography cards, working, **50d**:
    471–74; **50e**: 474–82. See also
    note cards.
    book, 472
    journal or magazine article, 473
    newspaper article, 474
biographical dictionary, 415, 465
biographies, 465
Biography Index, 468
block format of letter, 535
body
    of business letter, 535
    of essay, **2c**: 34–36
    of research paper, 484
    revision of, 44–45
book
    APA documentation forms for, 515,
        528
    anthology or collection, MLA form,
        495
    bibliography card, 472
    capitalizing title of, **45e**: 417–18
    in citations, 490–91
    divisions, 411
    italicizing title of, **42a**: 401
    MLA documentation forms for,
        494–96
    multivolume, 490–91, 495
    parts of, 402
    prefatory pages, numbering of, 411
    reprint, 495
    section and chapter title, 390
    unpublished manuscript, 499
    untitled parts, 390
    use, in research, 479
    in Works Cited list, 494–96
book review, 519
Book Review Digest, 479
Books in Print, 466
brackets, **41h**: 396–97, 486
bring, take, 550–51
broadcast media, as resource, 471

bulletin
  in book form, 401
  as resource, 471
bunch, 551
burst, bust, busted, 551
business reports, **54**: 543–47
  format and organization, **54b**:
    544–45
  language and tone, **54a**: 543–44,
    545
  sample, 546–47
business correspondence, **52**: 532–38
business letter, **52b**: 533–38
  format and organization, 535–36
  job application, **53b**: 541–42
  language and audience, 534–35
  samples, 537–38, 542
  tone, 538
business stationery, 535, 536
but, **26e**: 294. See also *conjunctions*.

cadence, 111
can, may, 317, 551
capital, capitol, 551
capitalization, **45**: 413–18
  of abbreviations, **45g**: 418
  of academic courses, 417
  of academic degrees and titles, 358,
    417
  of acronyms, 358, **45g**: 418
  of article titles, **45e**: 417–18
  of book titles, **45e**: 417–18
  in business letter, 536
  following a colon, 381
  of days of the week, 417
  of departments, 417
  in direct quotation, **45b**: 414
  of documents, 417
  of fraternal clubs, 417
  of genuses, **45h**: 418
  of geological periods, **45h**: 418
  of historic periods, 417
  of holidays, 417
  of *I* and *O*, **45f**: 418
  of institutions, 417
  of months, 417
  of names and nicknames, 415
  in nonstandard English, **34n**: 353
  of organizations, 417
  of parenthetical sentence, 396
  of personifications, 415
  of planets, **45h**: 418
  in poetry, **45d**: 414
  of political parties, 417
  with prefixes, 421–22

  of proper nouns, **45d**: 414–17
  of quotation, 485
  of religions, deities, 416
  of stars, **45h**: 418
  of states, 358
  with suffixes, 421–22
  of titles preceding names, 415
  of trademarks, 417
  of words that begin sentences, **45a**:
    413, 415
  of works of art, **45e**: 417–18
card catalog, 462, 463, 466–67. See
    also *library resources*.
case, **28**: 307–13
  of appositives, **28d**: 310
  in compound constructions, **28a**:
    308; **28b**: 309
  in elliptical expressions, **28e**: 311
  with gerunds, **28f**: 311
  with infinitives, **28e**: 309–10
  nominative, 307, **28a**: 308
  objective, 307, **28b**: 309; **28c**:
    309–10
  possessive, 307
  subjective, 307
  who or *whom*, **28g**: 312–13
  whoever or *whomever*, **28g**: 312–13
  after *than, as*, **28e**: 311
cassette tape, title of, 401
catalog cards, 466–67
cause and effect, **6g**: 92–93
censor, censure, 551
center around, 551
chapter number, in citations, 490–91
checklists
  editing, 52
  fragment trouble-shooting, 282–84
  revision of body, 45
  revision of conclusion, 45
  revision of introduction, 43–44
Chicago Manual of Style, 517
chronological order, 74–75, 514. See
    also *paragraph(s)*.
citation searching, 479
citations, in-text
  APA style, **51a**: 512–14
  MLA style, **50i**: 488–92
  parenthetical, **41f**: 395; **50i**:
    488–92; **51a**: 512–14
classification, **6h**: 93–95
clause(s), **23**: 274–75
  adjective, 275
  adverb, 275
  independent, 274
  introductory, 363

noun, 275
in parentheses, 413
subordinate, 174, 225, 274, 379
clichés, 236
climactic, climatic, 551
climactic order, 76–77, 146–47. See
also *paragraph(s)*.
closing, 535, 536
clustering, 14–15
coherence
in paragraphs, **5**: 73–85; **8c**: 127
revisions for, **3a**: 42–45
collective nouns
pronoun agreement with, **27f**: 303
verb agreement with, **26h**: 296
colloquialisms, **16c**: 202–03
colon, **39**: 381–83
without conjunction, 125
before explanation or summary,
25d: 288
in numbers to show time, **39b**: 383
and quotation, 485
and quotation marks, 390, 391
in ratios, **39b**: 383
in salutations, **39b**: 383, 535
in scriptural references, 383
to introduce appositive, **39a**: 382
to introduce definition or
amplification, **39a**: 382
to introduce quotation, **39a**: 382, 413
to introduce series, **39a**: 381–82
unnecessary, **39c**: 383
commas, **36**: 360–69
and absolute phrase, 272, 368
and appositive phrase, 272
between coordinate adjectives, **36c**:
361–62
and coordinating conjunction,
123–24, **25b**: 287; **36a**: 360–61,
372
and dashes, **41c**: 394
with dates, **36f**: 366
with degrees, **36f**: 366
with dialogue, **36k**: 369
with direct address, **36i**: 369
for emphasis, **36i**: 369
with interjections, **36j**: 369
with interrupted quotations, **36k**:
369
after introductory phrase and
clause, 271, **36d**: 363
between items in a series, **36b**: 361
for omissions, **361**: 369
with nonrestrictive appositives, **36e**:
365–66

with nonrestrictive adjective clauses,
36e: 365
with nonrestrictive adjective
phrases, **36e**: 364–65
with parentheses, 395
with places, **36f**: 366
and quotation, 485
and quotation marks, 390, 391
with short questions, **36j**: 369
to clarify meaning, **36h**: 368
to show contrast, **36i**: 369
with titles, **36f**: 366
and transitions, **36g**: 367–68
in translation, 404
unnecessary, 368, **37**: 371–75
after *yes* or *no*, **36j**: 369
comma splice, **25**: 286–89
common noun, 245
comparative form, **33e**: 335–37
compare, contrast, 551
compare to, compare with, 551
comparison
incomplete, 181–82
parallel elements in, 181–82
comparison and contrast
comma in, 369
as figurative language, 235–36
in paragraph development, 95–97
compass directions, 416
complement, compliment, 552
complete subject, 259
complex sentence, 132, 164, 265
complimentary closing, 535, 536
compose, comprise, 552
composition. See *essay; research paper*.
complete predicate, 260
compound numbers, 421
compound structures, completing
using articles, **13e**: 183
using comparisons, **13c**: 181–82
using intensifiers, **13d**: 182–83
with *that*, **13b**: 181
with verbs and prepositions, **13a**:
179–80
compound words, **46a**: 420–21, 423
compound-complex sentence, 164,
265
computer software, in citations, 498
computers, research using, 470
conclusion
of argument, 442
business report, 545
essay, **2d**: 36–38
research paper, 483
revision of, 45

concrete noun, 245
concrete words, **17e**: 217–18
conjunctions, **8a–8b**: 123–26; **20g**:
    254–55
  without colon, 125
  coordinate, 125, 254
  correlative, 126, 255
  and semicolon, 125, 255
  subordinating, **9b**: 131–33, 255,
    274, 281, 289
conjunctive adverbs, 124, 255
  list of, 255
  and semicolon, 124–25, 255; **25e**:
    288; **38b**: 378
  as transitions, 368
connotation, **17d**: 215–16
conscious, conscience, 552
consensus of opinion, 552
consistency
  in point of view, 48–50
  in tone, 47
consonant cluster, 350
continual, continuous, 552
contractions
  and apostrophe, **40b**: 386–87
  in nonstandard English, 339
  and possessive pronouns, 426
contrast. See *comparison and contrast*.
conversational language, 199,
  200–201
coordinate adjectives, **36c**: 361–62
coordinating conjunction
  and comma, 123–24, **25b**: 287;
    36a: 260–61, 372
  linking main clauses, 254
  and semicolon, 125, **38c**: 378
coordination, 123
  to form compound sentence, **8a**:
    123–25
  parallel constructions, **8b**: 125–27
  repetition, **8c**: 127–28
corporations, names of, **43b**: 407
correlative conjunction, 126, 255
council, counsel, 552
criteria, criterion, 552
cross-referencing, 496

dangling modifier, **12a**: 170–71
dash, **41**: 393–94
  for amplification or explanation,
    41a: 393–94
  without commas, **37h**: 375
  for interruptions, **41b**: 394
  with list containing commas, **41c**:
    394

with question marks, 391
  to summarize or restate, **41a**: 393
data, datum, 552
data base source, in citations, 498
dates
  abbreviated, **43c**: 408
  in citations, 512, 514
  commas with, **36f**: 366
  exact, 411
days of the week, capitalization of, 417
deadwood, 51, 266
decimals, 411
deductive argument, **48b**: 444–45
definition
  colon with, **39a**: 382
  in dictionary, **17a**: 208–10
  following italicized word, 403
  of terminology, **6e**: 91–92
degrees, academic, **36f**: 366, 407
deities, capitalization of, 416
denotation, **17d**: 215–16
dependent clause. See *subordinate*
  clauses.
description
  fragments as, 282
  to illustrate thesis, **6c**: 89–90
desire, 330
dialect, 338
dialogue, 113–14
  commas in, **36k**: 369
  fragments in, 282
  and quotation marks, **40f**: 389
dictionary, **17a**: 208–14, 465
  all-purpose, 210
  biographical, 415, 465
  definitions, **17a**: 208–10
  information, 208–09
  sample entries, 200, 211, 214, 244
  specialized, 465
  spelling, 424
  standard abbreviations, 406, 418
  synonyms, **17b**: 211
  use in revisions, 51
  word classification, 243–44
different from, different than, 552
differ from, differ with, 552
direct address, **36k**: 369
direct discourse, **15d**: 193–94
direct object, **21c**: 262, 309
direct questions, 358
direct quotations, **40e**: 388–89
  capitalization in, **45b**: 414
  in-text citations, 513
  in note-taking, 477
discourse, shift in, **15d**: 193–94

discreet, discrete, 552–53
discriminatory language, **17f**: 220–22
disinterested, uninterested, 553
do
  as auxiliary, 317
  forms of, **34i**: 346–47
documentation
  abbreviations in, **43d**: 408
  APA style of, **51a**: 512–15; **51e**: 521–29
  capitalization of, 417
  MLA style of, **50i**: 488–92; **50j**: 493–99, 510–11; **50 l**: 499–511
  note style of, **51b**: 516–17
  styles of other disciplines, **51c**: 517–18
doesn't, don't, 553
double comparatives, 336
double negatives, 334, **34f**: 343
double parentheses, **41e**: 395
double superlatives, 336–37
draft, 32
  sample, 39–41, 59–63
  thesis sentence, **50b**: 463
drama, 401, 491
due to, because of, 553

each other, one another, 553
economic, economical, 553
-ed ending, in nonstandard English, **34 l**: 350. See also *verb forms; verb tense*.
editing
  checklist, 52
  for consistency in present tense, **30c**: 322–23
  of nonstandard English, **34**: 338–53
  for point of view, **3b**: 46–48
  research paper, 484
  sentence, 50–51
  for tone, **3b**: 44–45
  of words, 51–52
either . . . or
  fallacy, 452
  linking antecedents, **27e**: 303
  and subject-verb agreement, **26e**: 294
-elect, 422
elicit, illicit, 553
ellipsis, **41i**: 397–98, 486
elliptical expressions, after *than, as*, **28e**: 311
emphasis
  alliteration for, 144–45

climactic order for, 146–47
and comma use, **36i**: 369
expletives in, 145–46
fragments for, 282
inverted word order for, 144
italicizing for, **42f**: 404
metaphor for, 145
punctuation for, 143–44
repetition for, 111–13, 144
simile for, 145
underlining for, **42f**: 404
and voice, 326–27
word placement for, **10a**: 142–43
encyclopedias, 464, 496
English, nonstandard. See *nonstandard English*.
enthused, enthusiastic, 553
envelope, 536
equally, equally as, 553
-er, -est ending, 336
essay
  audience of, **1c**: 8–10
  body, **2c**: 34–36
  conclusion, **2d**: 36–38
  defining, **1d**: 11–12
  drafting, **2**: 31–41
  editing, **3b**: 46–52
  explanatory, **1b**: 6–7
  expressive, **1b**: 6
  focusing the topic, **1g**: 21–24
  introduction, **2b**: 32–34
  outline, **1i**: 28–29
  peer review, **3d**: 56–57
  persuasive, **1b**: 7, 36
  planning, **1**: 3–28
  prewriting, **1e**: 12–19
  proofreading, **3c**: 56
  purpose of, **1b**: 5–8
  revising for coherence, **3a**: 42–45
  structure of, **1h**: 24–25
  subject selection, **1a**: 4–5
  thesis statement, **1g**: 21–24; **1h**: 24–25
  title of, 389, 402
  topic selection, **1f**: 20–21
Essay and General Literature Index, 467–68
essay examination, **49**: 456–59
  answering strategies, **49a**: 456–58; **49b**: 458
  sample answer, 459
  sample questions, 457–58
et al., 489, 494, 513
etc., 549
euphemisms, 205

everyday, every day, 553
everyone, every one, everybody, 553–54
ex-, 422
examination, essay, **49**: 456–59
examples, to clarify concept, **6d**: 90–91
exclamation point, **35d**: 359, 375
  avoiding, in formal writing, 359
  in dialogue, 359
  and quotation marks, 390–91
expect, suspect, 554
experiments, as resource, 471
explanation, 394
explanatory writing, 6–7, 50, 106–07
expletives, 145–46, 293
expository writing, 6–7, 49–50
expressive writing, 6, 48
extended modifier, 176

facts, to support argument, 442
fallacies, 441, **48f**: 449–53
  ad hominem, 450
  appeal to authority, 450
  begging the question, 451
  either . . . or, 452
  false analogy, 452
  false emotional appeal, 453
  hasty generalization, 451
  non sequitur, 453
  post hoc ergo propter hoc, 451
  red herring, 453
false analogy, 452
false emotional appeal, 453
famed, famous, 554
farther, further, 554
fewer, less, 554
figurative language, **19**: 233–37
  creating new, **19c**: 235–37
  metaphor and simile, **19a**: 233–34
  mixed metaphor, **19d**: 237
  to sway opinion, **19b**: 234–35
figuratively, literally, 554
figures
  abbreviated, 408
  in citations, 491
film, name of, 401
finalize, 554
first, firstly, 554
flattery, 453
flout, flaunt, 554
folk, folks, 554
footnotes. See *notes*.
foreign words
  italicized, **42d**: 403–04
  plural spelling of, 433
  translated, 404

foreword, 495
formal writing, 47, **16a**: 199–201, 387
format
  block, 535
  business report, **54b**: 544–45
  research paper, **50k**: 499
former, latter; first, last, 554–55
fractions, 411, 421
fragments, **24**: 278–84
  attaching to sentence, **24a**: 280–81
  in description, 282
  in dialogue, 282
  for emphasis, 282
  stylistic use of, **24c**: 282
  trouble-shooting checklist, **24d**: 282–84
  turning into sentences, **24b**: 281
frame of reference, 90
fraternal clubs, 417
free-writing, as prewriting technique, 15–17, 475
funny, 555
furthermore, 368
fused sentence, **25**: 286–89

general reference guides, 464
general references, 464–66, 488–89, 512–15
generalization, 217–19, **18a**: 224–25
general-to-specific order, 77. See also *paragraph(s)*.
genuses, names of, **42e**: 404; **45h**: 418
geographic terminology, **43b**: 407
geological periods, capitalization of, **45h**: 418
gerund
  phrase, 28, 268, 271
  and possessive case, **28f**: 311
get, 555
good, bad, well, 333, 555
government documents or publications, 402, 470–71, 497
grammar, 243
great, 555
guidebooks, 464

hanged, hung, 555
hardly, scarcely, 555
hasty generalization fallacy, 451–52
have
  as auxiliary, 317
  forms of, 346, **34j**: 348–49
  unemphatic use of, 150
he, she. See *person*.
helping verbs, 339

historical documents, periods, events, movements, 190, 417
holidays, capitalization of, 417
homophones, 209, 525, 426–30
hopefully, 403, 555
however, 368
hyperbole, 237
hyphen
    in citations, 493
    as dash, 393
hyphenation, **46**: 420–23
    in adjective series, 421
    to avoid misreading, 422
    between syllables, 422
    of compound numbers, 421
    end-of-the-line, **46c**: 422–23
    with prefixes and suffixes, **46b**: 421–22
    of written fractions, 421
    to clarify meaning, 422
    to create sound effects, 421
    to form compound words, **46a**: 420–21

I, 106, 192–93, **45f**: 418. See also *person*.
identification numbers, 411
idioms, 214, 352
if clauses, 329, **32a**: 330
illustrations, in citations, 491
imperative mood, 191, 329
imperative sentence form, 258
imply, *infer*, 555
in, *into*, 555
in regards to, 556
incredible, *incredulous*, 555
indefinite adjective, 251
indefinite pronoun, 248, **26f**: 295
indention
    APA reference list, form of, 514
    MLA reference list, form of, 493
    Note style, form of, 517
    of paragraphs, 499, 523
    of long quotation in APA paper, 514
    of long quotation in MLA paper, 389, 486–87
independent or main clause, **8a–8b**: 123–26; **9a–9d**: 130–33; **23**: 274
    commas with, **37b**: 372
    semicolon with, **38**: 377–79
index cards, 471
indexes, 467–71
    computer, 470
    general magazine, 468

government publication, 470
    newspaper, 468
    scholarly works, 468–69
    for a specific discipline, 469–70
indicative mood, 191, 329
indicator words, in arguments, 442, 445
indirect discourse, **15d**: 193–94
indirect object, **21c**: 263, 309
indirect questions, 358
indirect quotation, 388
individual, *person*, *party*, 556
inductive argument, **48b**: 444–45
inferior to, *worse than*, 556
infinitives
    objective case with, **28c**: 309–10
    and verbals, 324
infinitive phrase
    as modifier, 272
    as noun, 271
    in topic outline, 28
informal language, **15e**: 194–95; **16a**: 199–201
informative writing, 6–7, 49–50
ingenious, *ingenuous*, 556
initials, 407
in regards to, 556
inside address, 535, 536
insist, ⌐30
institutions, names of, 417
intensifiers (*so*, *such*, *too*), 182–83, 228
intensive pronoun, 247
interjections, **20h**: 256
    commas with, **36j**: 369
interrogative pronoun, 247
interview
    in citations, 498
    of individual, 18
    in researching topic, 18, 462, 471
in-text citations
    APA, **51a**: 512–14
    MLA, **41f**: 395; **50f**: 480–82; **50h**: 484–88; **50i**: 488–92
intransitive verb, 261
introduction
    in book citation, 495
    business report, 544
    of essay, **2b**: 32–34
    revision of, 43–44
    of research paper, 483
introductory phrases
    avoiding unnecessary, 228
    punctuation of, 271, **36d**: 363
    verbal, 171
inverted word order, 144
investigative paper, 520–21

irregardless, 556
irregular verbs, 249, 314–15
    in nonstandard English, **34k**: 349
    list of, 315–16
is when, is where, is because, **14b**:
        186–87, 556
it. See *person.*
it is construction, avoiding, 229
italics (underlining)
    for emphasis, **42f**: 404
    for foreign words, **42d**: 403–04
    for letters used as letters, 387
    for major publications, **42a**: 401–02
    for names of genuses and species,
        42e: 404
    for names of vehicles, **42b**: 403
    in reference list entry, 515
    signaling phrase, 488
    for subject of discussion, **42c**: 403
    for words used as words, 387
    for works of art, **42a**: 401–02
its, it's, 387, 425, 428, 556
-ize, 556

jargon, 51, **16b**: 202
joint possession, 386
journal, personal, as prewriting
        technique, 17–18, 475
journals, 401, 515. See also *periodicals.*

key idea, in topic sentence, **4a**: 67–68
key terms, in argument, **48d**: 448
key words and phrases, **5d**: 84–85,
        404
kind(s), sort(s), 556
Koran, 402

language
    appropriate, **16**: 199–206
    archaic or obsolete, 204–05
    avoiding shifts in, **15e**: 194–95
    biased, **17f**: 220–22
    bombastic, **16d**: 203–04
    of business letter, 534–35
    in business report, **54a**: 543–44,
        545
    concise, **17**: 208–22; **18**: 224–30
    conversational, 199, 200–01
    discriminatory, **17f**: 220–22
    figurative, **19**: 233–37
    formal, **15e**: 194–95, 199
    informal, 199
    new or invented, 205–06
    nonstandard use of, **34**: 338–53

pretentious, **16d**: 203–04
    sexist, **17f**: 220–22; **27a**: 299–300
latter, 554–55, 557
lay, lie, **29c**: 318–19, 557
learn, teach, 557
leave, let, 557
lectures, 390, 498
less and *least*, 335
letter, in citations, 498
letterhead stationery, 535, 536
letters, business. See *business letter.*
letters of alphabet
    plural form of, **40c**: 387
    as subject of discussion, **42c**: 403
    used as letters, **40c**: 387
liable, likely, 557
Library of Congress Subject Headings
        (LCSH), 467
library resources, 462, **50c**: 463–71.
        See also *research.*
    card catalog, 462, 463, 466–67
    general references, 464–66
    indexes, 467–71
    reference room, 462
    reserve desk, 462
    stacks, 462
lie, lay, **29c**: 318–19
like, 374
limiting words, 173
linking verbs, 249–50
    in nonstandard English, 338–39
    punctuation with, **39c**: 383
    with subject complements, 334–35
list. See *series.*
list-making, 12–13
literary criticism, 190–91
literary present tense, 323
literary work(s)
    MLA documentation for reports
        about, **50i**: 488–93
    tense, shift in, 190–91, 323
    title punctuation of, **40g**: 389–90
    writing about, 459
literature, review of the, 519, 522–29
logic, **48**: 441–53. See also *arguments.*
loose, lose, 557
loose sentence, 142, **11a**: 156–58
lot, lot of, lots of, 557
-ly, 432

magazine, 402. See also *periodicals.*
Magazines for Libraries, 479
mankind, 557
may be, maybe, 557
may of, might of, must of, 557

mechanics, editing for, **3b**: 46–52. See also *abbreviations*; *acronyms*; *capitalization*; *hyphenation*; *italics*; *numbers*; *spelling*.
media, *medium*, 557
memos, **52a**: 532–33
  formality of, 532
  sample, 533
  tone of, 532
metaphors
  creating new, **19c**: 235–37
  defined, 234
  effective use of, **19a**: 233–34
  for emphasis, 145
  mixed, **19d**: 237
methods section, of business report, 544
mighty, 558
miscellaneous works, MLA documentation for, 497–99
misplaced modifier, 170
misplaced parts
  extended modifiers, 176
  limiting words, 173
  modifying phrases, 173–74
  single-word modifiers, 175
  split infinitives, 177
  squinting modifiers, 174
  verb phrases, 173–74
misspelling. See also *spelling*.
  avoiding, 424
  proofreading for, **47b**: 425
  to create slang terms, **47h**: 436
  to create sound effects, **47h**: 436
mixed constructions, **14**: 185–87
mixed metaphors, **19d**: 237
MLA documentation style, **50i**: 488–92
  endnotes, footnotes, 492–93
  in sample research paper, **50l**: 400–511
  text references, 488–93
  works cited, **50j**: 493–99
MLA Handbook for Writers of Research Papers, 358, 488
mnemonics, 425
modifiers, **12**: 170–77
  adverbs as, 175
  clauses as, 174
  dangling, **12a**: 170–71
  extended, 176
  misplaced, 170, **12b**: 172–74
  phrases as, 173–74
  placement of, **12b**: 172–75
  single-word, 175

squinting, 174
and subordination, **9e**: 134–35
money, exact amounts of, 411
Monthly Catalog of United States Government Publications, 470
months, capitalization of, 417
mood, **32**: 329–30
  imperative, 329
  indicative, 329
  shift in, **15a**: 191–92
  subjunctive, 329, **32a**: 330; **32b**: 330
more and *most*, 335
moreover, 368
most, 558
Mr., *Ms.*, *Mrs.*, *Miss*, 407, 535
multiple authors, documentation forms for, 489, 494, 573, 515
myself, 558

names
  capitalization of, 415
  personal, 190
  proper, 406–07
  titles preceding, 406–07, 415
narration, 88–89
nauseated, *nauseous*, 558
negative constructions, 231
neither
  linking antecedents, **27e**: 303
  and subject-verb agreement, **26e**: 294
neologisms, **16e**: 205–06
newsletters, as resource, 471
newspaper. See also *periodicals*.
  article title, **40g**: 389
  bibliography card, 474
  indexes, 468
  name, 402
  in MLA documentation, 497
  in reference list, 5
nicknames, capitalization of, 415
nominalizations, **10c**: 153–54
non sequitur, 453
nonrestrictive units, **36e**: 364–66
nonprint sources, 492
nonstandard English, **34**: 338–53
  accents, **34n**: 353
  action verbs, 338
  articles, **34g**: 343–45
  capitalization, **34n**: 353
  be conjugation, **34h**: 345
  contractions, 339
  and dialect, 338
  demonstrative pronouns, **34e**: 342

nonstandard English *(continued)*
  do conjugation, **34i**: 346–47
  double negatives, **34f**: 343
  -ed endings, **34 l**: 350
  have conjugation, **34j**: 348
  helping verbs, 339
  irregular verbs, **34k**: 349
  linking verbs, 338–39
  personal pronouns, **34e**: 342
  plurals, **34b**: 339–40
  possessives, **34d**: 341
  prepositions, **34m**: 352
  spelling, **34n**: 353
  verb endings, **34c**: 340–41
nor
  linking antecedents, **27e**: 303
  and subject-verb agreement, **26e**:
    294
not only . . . but also, **27e**: 303
notable, noticeable, 558
notes
  in MLA paper, 492–93, 509
  system of documentation, **51b**:
    516–17
note cards. See also *bibliography cards,
    working*.
  paraphrase, 478
  personal, 475
  quotation, 477
  summary, 476
note-taking
  avoiding plagiarism in, **50f**: 480–82
  for a purpose, 478
  in research, 18–19, **50e**: 474–80
noun clause, 275
noun phrase, 28, 260, 268–69
noun(s), **20a**: 244–45
  abstract, 245, 344
  and articles, 343–45
  collective, **26h**: 296; **27f**: 303
  common, 245
  compound, 386
  concrete, 245
  ending with *-ics*, 297
  mass, 344
  plural forms of, **26i**: 296–97, 386
  possessive, 345, **40a**: 385–86
  predicate, 261, 263
  proper, 245, 344, **45d**: 414–15,
    421–22
  singular form of, 385
nowhere, nowheres, 558
n.p., 495
number
  abbreviated, **43c**: 408
  Arabic, 411

at beginning of sentence, 411
  compound, 421
  consistency in, **15c**: 193
  identification, 411
  as plural noun, 549
  plural of, 387
  Roman, 411
  series of, 410
  shift in, **15c**: 193
  as subject of discussion, **42c**: 403
  in words or figures, **44a**: 410; **44b**:
    411

O, **45f**: 418
object complements, **21c**: 263; **33d**:
    335
objective case, 307
  in compound constructions, **28b**:
    309
  with infinitives, **28c**: 309–10
object
  direct, **21c**: 262, 309
  of prepositions, 309
  pronouns as, 309
  retained, **21c**: 262
observation, as resource, 471
obsolete words, 204–05
off of, 558
OK, O.K., okay, 558
one, avoiding use of, 50
opera, title of, 402
or
  antecedents joined by, **27e**: 303
  and compound subject, 294
organizations, names of, **43b**: 407, 417
order of sentences in paragraph. See
    paragraph(s).
ought not, 558
outlines, **1i**: 26–29
  formal, 27–29
  research paper, 483
  Roman numerals in, 411
  scratch, 26–27
  sentence, 29
  topic, 28
Oxford English Dictionary, 465

paintings. See *works of art*.
page number
  in APA documentation, 514–15
  in in-text citations, **50h**: 484–88,
    489–92; **51a**: 512–14
  in MLA documentation, 495–98
  in note style of documentation, 517
  in note-taking, 473, 474, 476, 477,
    478, 493

Paperbound Books in Print, 466
papers, other forms of academic, **51d**:
519–21
that analyze and advance a theory,
519–20
that report results of original study,
520–21
that review books and articles, 519
paragraph(s)
analysis, **6h**: 93–95
chronological order in, 74–75
classification, **6h**: 93–95
climactic order in, 74–77, 146–47
closing, 69
coherence in, **5**: 73–85
defining terminology in, **6e**: 91–92
describing a process, **6f**: 92
description in, **6c**: 89–90
development strategies of, **6**: 86–98
discussing cause and effect, **6g**:
92–93
general-to-specific order in, 77
introductory, 69
irrelevant statements in, **4c**: 70–71
narration in, **6b**: 88–89
organizing principle of, **5a**: 74–79
parallelism in, **5b**: 81–82
pattern combination in, **6j**: 97–98
process, **6f**: 92
repetition in, **5d**: 84–85
rhetorical devices in, **7d**: 110–15
question-and-answer order in,
78–79
short, **6a**: 86–88
spatial order in, 75–76
specific-to-general order in, 77–78
style of, **7**: 102–14
topic sentence, **4a**: 67–68; **4b**:
69–70
transitions, **5c**: 82–83
unity, **4**: 67–71
using examples, **6d**: 90–91
parallelism
in coherent paragraphs, **5b**: 81–82
in coordination, **8b**: 125–26
with correlative conjunctions, 126
paraphrasing, 478, 481–82, 503, 505,
513. See also *note cards*.
parentheses, **41d**: 394–96
for additional information, **41d**:
394–95
citations in, 484–88, **50i**: 488–92;
51a: 512–14
for digressions, **41d**: 394–95
with internal punctuation, **41g**:
395, 396
for in-text citations, **41f**: 395
for numbered or lettered lists, **41e**:
395
punctuation following, 395
punctuation preceding, **37g**: 375,
395
for translation, 404
participial phrase, 134, 269
introductory, 271
placement of, 271
parts of speech, **20**: 243–56
passive voice. See *voice*.
peer review, **3d**: 56–58
sample, 57–58
people, persons, 558
percent, percentage, 411, 558–59
perfect tenses, 321
period
with abbreviations, **35b**: 358
in academic degrees, 407
to close statements, **35a**: 357, 375
with ellipsis, 397
with initials, 407
with quotation marks, 376
in scriptural references, 383
periodic sentence, 142, **11a**: 156–58
periodicals
in APA documentation, 515
bibliography card for, 473, 474
capitalizing titles of, **45e**: 417–18
indexes to, 468
italicizing titles of, **42a**: 401–02
in MLA documentation, 496–97
punctuating article titles in, **40g**:
389, 390, 402
person (first, second, third)
point of view, 48–50
-*s* or -*es* endings, **34c**: 340–41
in nonstandard English, **34h**:
345–46; **34i**: 346–47; **34j**: 348
shift in, **15b**: 192–93
and style, 106–07
personal narration, 190
personal pronoun. See *pronouns*.
personification, 236, 415
persuasive writing, 7, 36, 107–08
phenomena, phenomenon, 559
phrasal prepositions, 253
phrase(s), **22**: 268–73
absolute, 161, 269, **22d**: 273
adjective, 135, 160–61, 269
adverb, 162, 269
appositive, 268, 273
gerund, 28, 268, 271
infinitive, 28, 271, 272
introductory, 171, 271, 228, 363

phrase(s) *(continued)*
  noun, 28, 260, 268–69
  redundant, 51
  as subject of discussion, **42c**: 403
  subordinated, 133
  for variety, **22a**: 268–69
plagiarism, avoiding, 480–82
planets, names of, **45h**: 418
plurals
  of abbreviations, 387
  of foreign words, 433
  of nouns, **34b**: 339–40, 385–86,
    432–33
  of numerals, 387
  spelling of, **47f**: 432–33
plus, 559
poetry
  capitalization in, **45c**: 414; **45e**:
    417–18
  in book form, 402
  first line as title, 390, 417
  indention of, 487–88
  in-text citation of, 491
  quoting, 487–88
  spacing of, 487–88
  title of long work, **42a**: 402
  title of short work, **40g**: 389–90
point of view, 5, **3b**: 48–50
  first-person (*I*, *we*), 48–49
  second-person (*you*), 49–50
  third-person (*he*, *she*, *it*, *they*, *one*),
    50
political parties, 417
positive constructions, **18b**: 231
positive form, 335, 336
possessive adjectives. See *adjective(s)*.
possessive case. See *case*.
possessives, 307, **34d**: 341
  and apostrophe, **40a**: 385–86; **40d**:
    387
  and articles, 345
  and contractions, 426
post hoc ergo propter hoc fallacy, 451
precede, *proceed*, 559
predicate, **21b**: 260–61
  complete, 260
  compound, 261
  with intransitive verb, 261
  with linking verb, 261
  simple, 260
  with transitive verb, 261
predicate adjective, 251, 261, **21d**:
    263
predicate nominative, 293
predicate noun, 261, **21d**: 263

prefixes, **46b**: 421–22. See also
  suffixes.
  with abbreviations, 421
  all-, 422
  ex-, 422
  with numbers, 421
  with proper nouns, 421
  and root word, **47d**: 430
  self-, 422
  with capital letter, 421
premise, in argument, 446–47
prepositional phrase, 161, **22b**:
    269–70
  for variety, 269
  wordy, 225–26
prepositions, **20f**: 252–53; **34m**: 352
  in compound structures, **13a**:
    179–80
  as part of surname, 415
  phrasal, 253
  punctuation of, **39c**: 383
  at sentence end, 253
  as single words or phrases, 253
present tense, **29a**: 314–16; **29c**:
    318–19, 320; **30c**: 322–23
  historical, 322–23
  literary, 323
pretense, *pretext*, 559
prewriting, **1e**: 12–19
  brainstorming, 18
  clustering, 14–15
  free-writing, 15–17, 475
  journal, 17–18
  note-taking, 18–19
  questions, 13
  reading about subject, 18
  words and phrases, 12–13
primary source, 480
principal, *principle*, 559
pronoun(s), **20b**: 246–48
  agreement, **27**: 299–304
  and antecedent, 246, **27**: 299–304
  case of, **28**: 307–13
  demonstrative, 248, **34e**: 342
  gender, 221
  indefinite, 248, **26f**: 295, 302, 386
  intensive, 247, 304
  interrogative, 247
  personal, 246–47, **34e**: 342
  possessive, 426
  punctuation with, **39c**: 383
  reciprocal, 248
  reflexive, 247, 304
  relative, 132, 134, 247, 275, **27g**:
    303–04

self, **27h**: 304
and sexist or biased language, **17f**:
220–22; **27a**: 299–300
spelling of, 425
pronunciation, 424, 425
proofreading, **47b**: 425
of essay, **3c**: 56
of research paper, **50k**: 499
proper noun, 245. See also *noun(s)*.
and articles, 344
capitalization, **45d**: 414–15
derivations, 414–15
with prefixes and suffixes, 421–22
prose, in-text citation of, 491
proved, proven, 559
public addresses, as resource, 471
punctuation. See also the specific
types of punctuation.
for emphasis, 143–44
internal, **38c**: 378; **38d**: 378–79
purpose
of essay, **1b**: 5–8
of note-taking, 478
of research paper, 460
of a resource's author, 479

question-and-answer order, 78–79.
See also *paragraph(s)*.
question mark, **35c**: 344–45
with comma, **37h**: 375
with direct question, **35c**: 358–59
in question series, 359
and quotation marks, **40h**: 390–91
questionnaire, as resource, 471
questions
capitalization of, 413
commas with, **36j**: 369
direct, **35c**: 358–59
in essay conclusion, 37–38
in essay examination, 457–58, **49b**:
458
indirect, **35c**: 358–59
listing, 13
series of, 359
quotation
capitalization in, 413, **45b**: 414
colon with, **39a**: 381, 382
commas with, **36k**: 369
ellipsis in, **41i**: 397–98
exclamation point in, 390–91, 414
formal, 382
indention of long, APA, 514
indention of long, MLA, 389,
486–87
indirect, 388

integrating into research paper,
50h: 484–88
long, 486–87, 514
note card, 477
of poetry, 487–88
question mark in, 390–91
within a quotation, 389
quotation marks, 385, **40**: 388–92
with dash, **40h**: 391
for definition following italicized
word, 403
with dialogue and unspoken
thoughts, **40f**: 389
with direct quotation, **40e**: 388–89
double, 389
with exclamation point, **40h**:
390–91
and paraphrasing, 478, 480–81
with period or comma, **40h**:
390–91
with question mark, **40h**: 390–91
in reference list entry, 515
with colon and semicolon, **40h**:
390–91
single, 389
and title of short work, **40g**:
389–90, 402
for translation, 404
quote, quotation, 559

racial slurs. See *biased or sexist
language*.
radio series, title of, 402
raise, rise, **29c**: 319, 560
*Random House Dictionary of the English
Language*, 465
reading, as prewriting technique,
18–19, 475
reading notebook, 475
real, really, 560
reason . . . is because, 560
reciprocal pronouns, 248
recommend, 330
record album, title of, 402
red herring fallacy, 453
redundancy, 226–28
reference list (APA), 514–15, 528–29.
See also *documentation*; *works cited
(MLA)*.
reference sources. See *sources*.
references, personal
in business report, 545
in résumé, 539
reflexive pronoun, 247. See also
pronoun(s).

regionalisms, 203
regular verb. See *verb(s)*.
relative clause, 139–40, 159
relative pronoun, 132, 134. See also
    pronoun(s).
    and adjective clause, 275
    list of, 247
    pronoun-antecedent agreement,
        27g: 303–04
relevant, 560
religions, capitalization of, 416
reluctant, reticent, 560
repetition
    avoiding, 85, 226–28
    for emphasis, 111–13
    of form, 112
    to aid coherence, **5d**: 84–85; **8c**:
        127
    to reinforce ideas, 111–13
reports, business, **54**: 543–47
request, 330
research, 18–19
    library resources, **50c**: 463–71
    log, 475
    note-taking, **50e**: 474–80
    recording information in, **50d**:
        471–74
    resources outside library, 471
research paper
    analytical, 519–20
    APA documentation style, **51a**:
        512–15; **51e**: 521–29
    body of, 484
    choosing subject of, **50a**: 460–63
    conclusion of, 483
    consulting sources for, 462
    drafting thesis sentence for, **50b**:
        463
    editing, 484
    formatting, APA, **51a**: 512–15; **51e**:
        521–29
    formatting, MLA, **50h**: 484–88;
        50i: 488–93; **50j**: 493–99; **50k**:
        499
    introduction of, 483
    listing issues for, 461–62
    MLA documentation style, **50i**:
        488–92; **50j**: 493–99
    note style, **51b**: 516–17
    for other disciplines, **51c**: 517–18;
        51d: 519
    outline for, 483
    planning and writing, **50g**: 482–84
    proofreading, **50k**: 499
    quotations in, **50h**: 484–88; **51a**:
        512–14

reporting study results, 520–21
researching, **50c**: 463–71
revising, 484
samples, **50 l**: 499–511; **51e**:
    521–29
text references, APA, **51a**: 512–514
text references, MLA, **50i**: 488–93
thesis sentence of, 482–83
title of, 483
to review books and articles, 519
working bibliography cards, **50d**:
    471–74; **50e**: 474–82
Works Cited list for (MLA), **50j**:
    493–99
writing, **50**: 460–99
respectively, respectfully, 560
restatement, 393
restrictive units, 364, **37c**: 373
results, in business report, 544
résumé, **53a**: 539–41
    cover letter for, **53b**: 541–42
    elements of, 539–41
    sample, 540
return address, 535, 536
review of the literature, 519, 522–29
review, in MLA documentation, 498
revision, 42
    of body, 44–45
    checklist for, 43–44
    for coherence, **3a**: 42–45
    of introduction, 43–44
    of research paper, 484
    of title, 43
rhetorical devices, **7d**: 110–15
rhythm, 111
rise, raise, **29c**: 319, 560
Roman numerals, 411. See also
    outlines.

-*s* and -*es* endings, **34c**: 340–41
salutations
    in business letter, 535–36
    colon in, **39b**: 383, 535
schedule, in business report, 544
scholarly works, indexes to, 468–70
scientific principles, 322
scratch outline. See *outlines*.
sculpture. See *work of art*.
seasons, 417
secondary source, 480
self, 422
self pronouns, **27h**: 304
semicolon, **38**: 377–79
    in citations, 490, 491, 514
    and conjunctive adverb, 124, 255,
        25e: 288; **38b**: 378

and coordinate conjunction, 125,
    38c: 378
without conjunction, 125, **38a**: 377
between independent clauses, **25c**: 288
between items in a series, **38d**:
    378–79
with quotation marks, 390
and subordinate clause, **38e**: 379
and transitional phrase, **38b**: 378
sensual, sensuous, 560
sentence(s)
    basic patterns, **21f**: 266
    beginning, 143
    choppy, 132–33
    comma in, **36h**: 368
    complex, 132, 164, 265
    compound, **8a**: 123–25; **9d**:
        133–34, 164, 265
    compound-complex, 164, 265
    coordination, **8**: 123–29
    defined, 258–59
    development methods, **11d**: 167–68
    of differing structures, **11c**: 164–66
    editing, 50–51
    emphasis, **10**: 142–54
    emphatic placement, **10a**: 142–47
    end, 142–43
    fragments, **24**: 279–84
    fused, **25**: 286–90
    general, 218
    imperative, 258
    incomplete structure in, **13**: 179–83
    inverted word order in, 144
    loose, 142, **11a**: 156–58
    mixed construction in, **14**: 185–87
    outline, 29
    parts, **21**: 258–66
    periodic, 142, **11a**: 156–58
    punctuation, 143–44
    simple, 164, 259, 264
    sprawling, 138–40
    style, **10**: 142–54; **11**: 156–68
    variety, **11**: 156–58
separate possession, 386
series
    and colon, **39a**: 381
    and comma, 361, **37d**: 373–74; **41c**:
        394
    and dash, **41c**: 394
    for emphasis, 114
    numbered or lettered, **41e**: 395
    and semicolon, **38b**: 378–79
sermons, 402
set, sit, **29c**: 318–19, 560
sexist or biased language, **17f**:
    220–22; **27a**: 453

shall, will, 317, 560
shifts, **15**: 189–95
    in form of discourse, **15d**: 193–94
    in mood, **15a**: 191–92
    in number, **15c**: 193
    in person, **15b**: 192–93
    in tense, **15a**: 189–91
    in tone or style, **15e**: 194–95
    in voice, **15a**: 191
ships, names of, **42b**: 403
short story. See *literary works.*
sic, 397, 486
signaling phrase, 488, 489, 490, 492
simile
    creating new, **19c**: 235–36
    defined, 233
    to provide emphasis, 145
    to sway opinion, **19b**: 234
since, because, 561
sit, set, **29c**: 318–19
slang, 47, 49, 51, 201, 436, **16c**: 202–03
slash (solidus), 488
snob appeal, 453
sometime, some time, sometimes, 561
songs, 390, 402
sound effects, 421, 436
sources. See also *documentation.*
    classic literary work, 491
    common knowledge, 482
    corporate author, 490
    data base, 498
    determining writer's purpose in,
        479
    evaluating, 479
    general references, 488–89
    indirect, 492
    in-text citations, APA, 512–14
    in-text citations, MLA, 488–92
    outside of library, 471
    multiple-author, 489
    multi-volume work, 490–91
    no author, 490
    nonlibrary, 471
    nonprint, 492
    primary, 480
    recent, 479
    reliable, 479
    secondary, 480
    text references, MLA, 488–92
spacecraft, names of, **42b**: 403
spatial order, 75–76. See also
    paragraph(s).
species, names of, **42e**: 404
specific words, **17e**: 217–18
specific-to-general order, 77–78. See
    also *paragraph(s).*

speeches, 390, 471
spell checker, 425, 499
spelling, **47**: 424–36. See also
    dictionary.
  adding *-ly*, 432
  American, 424
  -ant, -ent, 425
  changing *y* to *i*, 431–32
  and pronunciation, **47a**: 424–25
  and dialect, **34n**: 353
  dropping final *e*, 430–31
  doubling final consonant, 421
  ei, ie, 432
  of homophones, **47c**: 426–30
  and mnemonics, 425
  -nce, -nts, 426
  in nonstandard English, **34n**: 353
  of plurals, **47f**: 432–33
  possessive pronouns and
      contractions, 426
  practice, 424–25
  prefix and root, **47d**: 430
  preferred or common, 424
  and proofreading, **3c**: 56; **47b**: 425
  retaining final *l*, 432
  as skill, 424–25
  suffix and root, **47d**: 430–32
  troublesome words, list of, **47g**:
      434–35
  two-word phrases and single words,
      426
  writing word lists, **47a**: 424–25
split infinitive, 177
squinting modifier, 174
stars, names of, **45h**: 418
stationary, stationery, 561
stationery, business, 535, 536
statistics, 411
stereotypes, avoiding, **17f**: 220–22
straw man. See *fallacy*.
structure
  of argument, **48c**: 446–47
  of essay (outlines), **1i**: 26–29
structured series, for paragraph style,
    113
style
  defined, 102–03
  determined by audience, **7c**:
      108–10
  determined by purpose, **7b**:
      106–08
  emphasis and, **10**: 142–55
  in paragraphs, **7a**: 103–05
  rhetorical schemes and, **7d**: 110–19
  variety and, **11**: 156–69
style manuals, list of, 518

subject, grammatical, **21a**: 259–60
  ambiguous, 171
  complete, 259
  compound, 259
  simple, 259
subject complements, 263, **33c**:
    334–35
subject of essay
  narrowing to topic, **1f**: 20–21
  reading to research, 18–19
  selection of, **1a**: 4–5
subject of research paper
  comparing or combining, 462–63
  selection, **50a**: 460–63
subjunctive mood, 191–92, 329. See
    also *mood*.
  in *if* clauses, **32a**: 330
  in *that* clauses, **32a**: 330
subordinate clause, 274. See also
    clause(s).
  introductory, 379
  as modifier, 174
  punctuation in, **38e**: 379
  wordy, 225
subordinated phrase, 133. See also
    phrase(s).
subordinating conjunctions, **9b**:
    131–32, 133, 255, 274
  and comma splices, **25f**: 289
  and editing of fragments, 281
subordination, 123
  of compound clauses, **9d**: 133–34
  excessive, **9g**: 138–40
  inverted, **9f**: 137–38
  of less important dates, **9a**: 130–31
  reducing clauses, **9e**: 134–35
  using conjunctions, **9b**: 131–32
such, 374
suffixes, **46b**: 421–22
  with abbreviations, 421
  adding to root, **47d**: 430–32
  -elect, 422
  with numbers, 421
  with proper nouns, 421
  with single capital letter, 421
summary, of writing, 393, 544
supposed to, 350
superlative form, **33e**: 335–37
sure, surely, 561
syllables, stressed, 431
symphony, title of, 402
synonyms, in dictionary or thesaurus,
    17b: 211–14

table, in citations, 491
Technical Book Review Index, 479

technical language, 9
  acronyms in, **43b**: 407
technical reports. See *business reports*.
television series, title of, 402
tense. See *verb tense*.
term paper. See *research paper*.
terminology, defining, **6e**: 91–92
testing, as resource, 471
text references. See *in-text citations*;
  documentation.
than, pronoun case after, **28e**: 311
than, then, 561
that. See also *which*.
  and antecedent, **26g**: 295
  as restrictive connector, 364, **37c**:
    373, 485
  beginning clause, 139, 181, 330
  to refer to animals or things, 304
that, this, 561
the, **34g**: 343–45
their, there, they're, 561
them, 342
there is construction, avoiding, 229
therefore, 368
thesaurus, 51, **17b**: 211–13
thesis sentence
  in argument, 446
  in essay, **1g**: 21–24; **1h**: 24–25,
    32–33
  in essay exam answer, 457, 458, 459
  in research paper, **50b**: 463,
    482–83
they. See *person*.
thusly, 561
time, 408, 411
title. See also *documentation*.
  of article, **45e**: 417–18
  of book, **45e**: 417–18
  of business report, 544
  edition or series, 402
  of essay, 402
  italicized, **42a**: 401–02
  of persons, **43a**: 406–07, 411, 415
  quotation marks around, **40g**:
    389–90, 402
  of research paper, 483
  of sacred writings, 402
  short works, **40g**: 389–90
  verb agreement with, **26j**: 297
  of works of art, **45e**: 417–18
  writing and revising, 43
to, too, two, 561
tone
  of business report, **54a**: 543–44,
    545
  defined, 46–47

editing for, 46–47, 49–50
  shift in, **15e**: 194–95
topic
  focus of, for essay, **1g**: 21–24
  narrowing subject to, for essay, **1f**:
    20–21
  of research paper, **50a**: 460–63
topic sentence for paragraphs, 44
  and key idea, **4a**: 67–68
  placement of, **4b**: 69–70
topic outline. See *outlines*.
toward, towards, 561
trademarks, 417
trains, names of, **42b**: 403
transcription errors, 56
transitional expressions
  commas with, **36g**: 367–68
  conjunctive adverbs as, 368
  in paragraph cohesion, **5c**: 82–83
  and semicolon, **38b**: 378
transitive verb, 261
translation of foreign term, 404
trials, names of, 402
troublesome words, list of, **47g**:
    434–35
try and, try to, 561
typographical errors. See *proofreading*.

underlining. See *italics*.
unemphatic use
  of *be*, 150
  of *have*, 150
unique, 561
unity, in essay, 44
universal truths, 322
up, 561
usage, use, utilize, 561
use to, used to, 350

v or *versus*, 402
variety
  from loose and periodic sentences,
    11a: 156–59
  mixing sentence structures, **11c**:
    164–67
  and passive voice, 327
  in sentence content, **11d**: 167–68
  varying phrases and clauses, **11b**:
    159–63
vehicles, names of, **42b**: 403
verb(s), **20c**: 249–50
  active and passive, **10b**: 150–51
  agreement with subject, **26**: 292–97
  auxiliary, 250, 317
  in compound structure, **13a**:
    179–80

verb(s) *(continued)*
  helping, 339
  intransitive, 261
  irregular, 249, 314–16, **34k**: 349
  linking, 249–50, 334–35, 338–40,
    383
  nominalized, 154
  plural, **26d**: 294
  regular, 249, 314
  singular, **26f**: 295; **26h**: 296; **26i**:
    296–97; **26j**: 297
  transitive, 261
  voice of, 191
verbals
  and infinitive form, **30f**: 324
  as phrases, **22c**: 270–71
  and subject-verb agreement, **26g**: 295
verb forms, **29**: 314–19
  auxiliary, **29b**: 317
  basic, **29a**: 314–16
  of *be*, 314–15, **34h**: 345–46
  of *do*, **34i**: 346–47
  of *have*, 346, **34j**: 348
  irregular, **34k**: 349
  lie, lay, **29c**: 318–19
  rise, raise, **29c**: 319
  sit, set, **29c**: 318–19
verb phrase, 160, 176, 268, 270–71
verb tense, **30**: 320–24
  consistency, **30b**: 322
  consistent with voice and mood,
    15a: 189–91
  in historical events, 190
  in literature, 184–85, 323
  in nonstandard English, **34h**:
    345–46; **34i**: 346–47; **34j**: 348;
    34 l: 350
  past, **30d**: 323
  past-perfect, 324
  perfect, **30e**: 321–24
  in personal narration, 190
  present, **30c**: 322–23
  present-perfect, 324
  progressive, 321
  simple, 320–21
  of verbals, **30f**: 324
videocassette tape
  as resource, 471
  title of, 402
voice, **31**: 326–37
  active, **31a**: 314–15
  and emphasis, **10b**: 150–51
  passive, 326, **31b**: 327
  shift in, **15a**: 191
volume number, in citations, 490, 497

wait for, wait on, 561
way, ways, 561
we. See *person*.
*Webster's Ninth New Collegiate
  Dictionary*, 424
*Webster's Third New International
  Dictionary*, 465
what, to refer to animals and things,
  304
where, that, 561
which. See also *that*.
  and antecedent, **26g**: 295
  as nonrestrictive connector, **36e**:
    364–66
  to refer to animals and things, 304
which clause, 139–40
which, who, 561
while, 562
who, whom
  and pronoun case, **28g**: 312–13
  and subject-verb agreement, **26g**:
    295
who clause, 139
whose, who's, 387, 425, 430, 561
-wise, 561
wish, 330
word(s)
  abstract or general, 217–18
  archaic or obsolete, 204–05
  choice of, **17**: 208–23
  colloquial, **16c**: 202–03
  concrete and specific, **17e**: 217–18
  connotations, **17d**: 215–16
  with correct meaning, **17c**: 213–14
  denotations, **17d**: 215–16
  foreign, 403–04
  idiomatic, 214
  informal or conversational, **16a**:
    199–201
  ironic, 392
  jargon, 51, 202
  limiting, 173
  new and invented, **16e**: 205–06
  pretentious or flowery, **16d**: 203–04
  redundant or repetitive, 226–28
  regional, 203
  slang, 51, 201
  special, 114–15, 392
  as subject of discussion, **42c**: 403
  technical, 9
  trite or worn out, 51
  unnecessary, **18a**: 224–29
  used as words, **40c**: 387
  vulgar, 51
word order, inverted, 144

word processor
  find and replace feature, 425
  search feature, 425
  spell checker, 424
  thesaurus, 212
wordiness, **18a**: 224–31
work in progress, status of, for
  business report, 544
working bibliography cards. See
  bibliography cards, working.
works cited (MLA), **50j**: 493–99. See
  also *documentation; reference list (APA).*

work of art
  capitalizing title of, **45e**: 417–18
  in citation, 498
  italicizing title of, **42a**: 401–02
  present tense in, 323
writing process. See *essay.*

yearbook, 402, 465–66
yes and *no*, commas with, **36j**: 369
you, one, 563. See also *person.*
your, you're, 563

A 0
B 1
C 2
D 3
E 4
F 5
G 6
H 7
I 8
J 9

INDEX OF COMMON ERRORS

The examples listed here display common writing errors. Find the sentence that resembles the problem you are concerned with, and refer to the section or chapter given in parentheses for a discussion of the issue.

Sentence Structure, Placement, Punctuation

Comma Splice: The actor who allows his ego full rein will become arrogant and obnoxious, *he* will impress only himself. (**25**)

Dangling Modifier: *By studying extra hard*, the final exam should be easy. (**12a**)

Fragment: In mathematics, universal sets consist of all members being considered at the same time. *Called a universe and represented by the letter U.* (**24**)

Fused Sentence: The actor who allows his ego full rein will become arrogant and obnoxious *he* will impress only himself. (**25**)

Misplaced Modifier: During the ceremony, the colonel awarded medals to honored soldiers *of gold and bronze.* (**12b**)

Mixed Construction: *When children are punished without cause* can damage their self-images. (**14**)

No Comma after Introductory Element: *When the champion seemed ready to fight* his wife stepped between him and the antagonist. (**36d**)

No Comma in Nonrestrictive Element: *Known nationally as the center for country music* one Southern growth center is Nashville, Tennessee. (**36e**)

No Punctuation in Compound Sentence: Mark Twain wrote *Huckleberry Finn* and he based it on his own childhood so the novel was part autobiographical and part fictional. (**8a**)

Word Form, Agreement, Word Choice, Usage

Misuse of Apostrophe: *Its* the best movie showing in town. Several of the dormitory *resident's* have caught the flu.

Pronoun Agreement and Reference: No *doctor* wants *their* patients to suffer needlessly. (**27a**)

Shift in Person: *We* struggled to the top of the rocky ridge, and *you* could not believe how beautiful *our* valley looked. (**15b**)

Shift in Tense: The river *rises* and *falls* at least a foot whenever the tugboat *pushed* loaded barges past the pier. (**15a**, **30b**)

Subject-Verb Agreement: The unruly *behavior* of the players *are* being investigated. (**26**)

Vague Pronoun Reference: The Camaro approached the red van. *It* suddenly veered to the right and crashed. (**27b**)

Wrong or Missing Preposition: I am going *at* Chicago. (**17c**, **20f**, **34m**)

Wrong Verb Form: Nancy and Michael *droved* to the concert. (**29**)

Wrong Word: I *suspicioned* him and reported my findings to the supervisor. (**17**)